D0768885

RENEWALS 458-4574

DATE DUE

GAYLORD			PRINTED IN U.S.A.

Tchaikovsky not only composed, he also wrote about music. This substantial anthology of Russian writing on Russian music also features the most influential critics of nineteenth-century Russia. They wrote on the first two generations of Russian composers from Glinka to Musorgsky, Tchaikovsky and Rimsky-Korsakov. The volume reveals through contemporary Russian eyes how the foundations of the hugely popular Russian classical repertory were laid, providing a vivid picture of the musical life of the opera house and the concert hall from which this repertory sprang.

Featuring most extensively the critical writing of Odoyevshy, Serov, Cui and Laroche, the volume contains the first authoritative reviews of key works, such as Musorgsky's *Boris Godunov*, Tchaikovsky's *Romeo and Juliet* and Rimsky-Korsakov's First Symphony.

This is the first anthology of its kind. With editorial commentary provided for each extract, it shows how Russian music criticism developed in step with the growth of Russian musical life, from initial dilettantism to well-informed professionalism.

Russians on Russian music, 1830–1880

Russians on Russian music, 1830–1880

An anthology

Edited and translated by Stuart Campbell

WITHDRAWN
UTSA LIBRARIES

CAMBRIDGE
UNIVERSITY PRESS

Published by the Press Syndicate of the University of Cambridge
The Pitt Building, Trumpington Street, Cambridge CB2 1RP
40 West 20th Street, New York, NY 10011–4211, USA
10 Stamford Road, Oakleigh, Melbourne 3166, Australia

© Cambridge University Press 1994

First published 1994
Reprinted 1996

A catalogue record for this book is available from the British Library

Library of Congress cataloguing in publication data

Russians on Russian music, 1830–1880: an anthology / selected,
translated and annotated by Stuart Campbell.
  p. cm.
Translated from Russian
Includes index.
ISBN 0 521 40267 0 (hardback)
1. Music–Russia–19th century–History and criticism.
2. Opera–Russia–19th century. I. Campbell, Stuart.
ML300.4.R87 1994
780'.947' 09034–dc20   93–17690 CIP MN

ISBN 0 521 40267 0 hardback

Transferred to digital printing 2004

WITHDRAWN
UTSA LIBRARIES

SN
Library
University of Texas
at San Antonio

Contents

Preface

A small number of technical points, and a longer catalogue of indebtedness, must be recorded.

The term *narodnost'*, which occurs with great frequency, requires some explanation. I have usually translated it as 'national identity', though 'nationality' and 'people's quality' are also conceivable; 'nationness' or 'peopleness' are starting-points for the translator. The words *narod* and *narodnïy* have sometimes been rendered 'nation' and 'national', and at other times as 'people' and 'popular'; during the Soviet period they were much used as 'People's'. This dual interpretation ('national', and 'popular' or 'folk') should be kept in mind. The word *narodnost'* had a further usage, however. It was part of the slogan put forward in 1833 by the Minister of Education (actually, 'Popular Enlightenment'!) which acted as a summary of the state's official creed: Orthodoxy, Autocracy and Nationality (often rendered into English as 'Official Nationality' – the Russian word is again *narodnost'*). This highly charged political element is relevant in considering *A Life for the Tsar*, which Nicholas I was right to perceive as a work useful for his purposes, whatever may have been Glinka's intentions.

Two other terms in particular may occasion difficulty. *Romans* is the word usually employed in Russian when the equivalent of an art-song, a *Lied* or a *mélodie*, is meant. I have generally retained 'romance' as its translation. *Deklamatsiya* was an important component of the ideas developed by Dargomïzhsky, Cui and Musorgsky in relation to how words should be set to music. I have normally used 'word-setting' as the English equivalent, though I have tried to indicate those places where a wider meaning may be denoted.

All dates are given in Old Style, which means that they are twelve days behind the European calendar. The transliteration is based on that used in *The New Grove Dictionary of Music and Musicians*, with slight modifications.

Completion of this book was advanced by study leave allowed by the University of Glasgow and by a Visiting Scholarship granted by St John's

College, Oxford. Glasgow University Library (especially the Inter-Library Loan Department), the Slavonic Division of Helsinki University Library, the British Library, the Bodleian Library and the Library of the School of Slavonic and East European Studies provided help.

In annotating articles I have quarried liberally in the work of the Russian editors of sources listed elsewhere. Debts to David Brown (for *Mikhail Glinka* (London 1974) and *Tchaikovsky* (4 vols. London 1978-91)) and to Edward Garden for *Balakirev* (London 1967) must be acknowledged. *Kto pisal o muzïke* ('Who has written about music') compiled by G. B. Bernandt and I.M. Yampol'sky (4 vols. Moscow 1971–89) has been heavily used. *The New Grove Dictionary* is, of course, indispensable. The *Muzïkal'naya entsiklopediya* edited by Yu. V. Keldïsh (6 vols. Moscow 1973–82) and the same editor's *Muzïkal'nïy entsiklopedicheskiy slovar'* ('Encyclopaedic dictionary of music') (Moscow 1990) have also served handsomely. I wish to acknowledge the help of Anne Ramsay, who translated 1b, 3b, 3c and 8a, Gareth Rankin, who typed several of the articles, and Carolyn Ritchie, who obtained several texts and prepared the music examples. The project received a stimulus from an invitation to conduct a seminar in the University of Newcastle upon Tyne, for which I am indebted to Dr Isobel Preece. Penny Souster guided the project to completion, with an anonymous publisher's reader reshaping it substantially and for the better. Edward Garden, Hugh Macdonald and John Warrack, together with the late Peter le Huray, administered welcome encouragement. The shortcomings are, of course, mine alone.

Stuart Campbell
15 February 1993

Introduction

The aims of this book are, firstly, to record the progress of the art of
musical composition in Russia during the period of its most rapid development in the words of contemporary critics – that is, to provide a kind of
history through texts; secondly, to set this repertory in the context of the
distinctive ideas in which it burgeoned, or, in other words, to help to define
the elements from which what is widely known as Russian musical nationalism was formed; thirdly, to sketch something of the background of musical
life against which these new works were created.

Writing about music can scarcely exist without music, or criticism without
material to analyse and comment upon; by 'criticism' is meant here, naturally,
something more than a passage of a few hundred words lodged with an
editorial office before midnight on the day of a performance: published
Russian responses to new music usually involved lengthier discussion of
matters of principle than is possible in that format, and writing in which
such issues are raised is featured here. Material tending towards the 'music
theory' end of the spectrum has not found a place here. Russian music
criticism thus arose more or less in step with the growth of Russian music.
While certain factors in the rise of both music and criticism were common
to several European nations in the nineteenth century, others were peculiar
to one alone. Those relevant to Russia are set forth briefly here.

The Russian army's role in the defeat of Napoleon made the Russian
state a major actor on the European political stage. A new sense of Russian
national pride intensified a general Romantic interest in the history of
nations and peoples, their languages and folklore, with a consequent
increase in the production of dictionaries, collections of legends and
folksongs and sundry studies of the past; these materials in turn engendered
new works of art exploiting them in a variety of ways. One feature which
set the Russians apart from the western nations was their use of their own
Russian language, whose modern literature is largely of nineteenth-century
creation, albeit with roots in the second half of the eighteenth century. The

language had recently been forged into a homogeneous medium of expression capable of universal application: lyric poetry, drama, philosophy and all other forms of intelligent discourse were newly possible in the Russian language. Writers hastened to establish a wide-ranging literature which in turn furnished texts for use in songs and stage works by composers. The latter in turn aspired to create a repertory of music which would be as distinctly Russian as other music was peculiarly French, German or Italian; the potential of Russian music dawned on Glinka and Dargomïzhsky when they perceived the respective national qualities in Italian and French music while at large in western Europe. The struggle to formulate the principles of these new Russian compositions, to obtain regular performances and to win recognition is reflected in many of the passages in this book. Even by 1880, Russian music still had to be championed in its homeland against supporters of what was imported.

The half-century from 1830 to 1880 witnessed the creation of modern Russian music. Musical life became more active in reflection of increasing wealth and wider public interest. With technological advance came an expanding press issuing both sheet music and newspapers and journals, with some specialist periodicals supplementing the activities of the general periodical press. This process did not, of course, take place with relentless momentum, but we can identify the accession to the throne of Alexander II in 1855 as a crucial stage: the sense of liberation from previous rigidity and tight control, the encouragement of initiative and innovation, and the modernizing reforms of the 1860s brought new dynamism into Russian life, as we may observe in the setting-up of the Russian Musical Society with its conservatoires and the Free School of Music around the beginning of the 1860s.

Pushkin and Glinka played parallel and contemporary roles as the fathers of Russian literature and music respectively, though Pushkin is by far the more substantial figure. They are alike in being less familiar to the non-Russian world than their heirs; yet it will be clear from the contents of this volume that much later Russian music borrowed heavily – in principles and larger issues as well as in local ideas and fingerprints – from Glinka's work; moreover, these debts were universally recognized among both literary and musical artists. To the same generation belonged Gogol and Lermontov. During Glinka's lifetime, which ran from 1804 to 1857, further corner-stones of Russian literature were laid (in poetry, prose and drama) by Dostoyevsky, Ostrovsky, Tolstoy and Turgenev. The major works of Dostoyevsky and Tolstoy coincided, more or less, with those of Borodin, Musorgsky, Rimsky-Korsakov and Tchaikovsky.

These artists had contemporaries who wrote about music. Prince Odoyevsky was a member of the circle around Pushkin – indeed, they were fellow *littérateurs*, journalists and publishing entrepreneurs; Odoyevsky was typical of his time in that he wrote about music among many other subjects. The next generation, Serov and Stasov, emerged in 1847 almost simultaneously with Dostoyevsky (whose *Poor Folk* was published in 1846): their work is marked by a new polemical urgency, and in the case of Serov by a thorough command of musical technicalities which he did not refrain from parading: a parallel, perhaps, to the detailed, hard-headed approach of contemporary Realists in painting and literature, and to the down-to-earth practical work of the doctors and engineers held to typify the men of the 1860s (as against the aristocratic dreamers and visionaries of earlier decades). Cui and Laroche took their first bows in the mid-1860s, the period (roughly) of *War and Peace* and *Crime and Punishment*. While Cui, a fortifications engineer by profession, continued the tradition of the musician not professionally trained in that field – along with his colleagues in the early days of the Balakirev circle (or 'mighty handful',[1] or 'the Five') – Laroche (like Tchaikovsky) was among the first graduates of the new Conservatoire in St Petersburg, and brought not only a thorough knowledge of music but a penetrating mind and a sense of proportion. This anthology thus illustrates how, as in Russian society in general, influence shifted gradually away from the amateur gentleman-musician at home in the salons (such as Prince Odoyevsky) to the fully-trained technical specialist, albeit in the best cases (such as Laroche) with a wide cultural background; paradoxically, the bourgeois specialist required income, so that Laroche turned his fluent pen to the assessment of new French novels and other matters.

Close personal ties between composers and critics are not unusual. Characteristic of the nineteenth century is the composer articulate enough to find employment as a writer on his subject. In the case of Russia, Borodin, Cui, Serov and Tchaikovsky were composers active as critics, while Odoyevsky and Laroche, whom we rightly think of first and foremost as critics, also had some compositions to their credit. All of those just mentioned had considerable musical competence, which was not true of all the jobbing journalists who sometimes revealed their ignorance when tackling musical questions. Links with composers gave writers a clearer understanding of the composers' intentions and ideals, and this advantage is evident when Odoyevsky or Senkovsky is writing about Glinka's music, or Laroche about Tchaikovsky's. Stasov and Cui were the press heralds of the Balakirev circle, and Cui played an important part in formulating the group's principles in the field of opera through many articles discussing what he termed 'the New Russian Operatic School'. Strong factional loyalties did not preclude

---

[1] For discussion of this term's ramifications, see Richard Taruskin: *Musorgsky. Eight Essays and an Epilogue* (Princeton 1993), pp. xxxiii–xxxiv.

occasional unsympathetic notices, as we shall see. Serov usually spoke for himself alone, since he was a particularly quarrelsome character.

Some account of the structure of this book is desirable.

It begins, as in effect did Russian art music, in 1836 with the première of Glinka's first opera *A Life for the Tsar*. It is natural for that opera and its successor, *Ruslan and Lyudmila*, which reached the stage in 1842, to occupy the first chapter; these are the first masterpieces composed by a Russian, and since they pioneered principles and techniques exploited by most subsequent Russian composers, it is justifiable for them to take up a great deal of space, both on their first appearance and later on, when they were at the centre of the debate on Russian music which touched further, younger composers (see Chapter 4). Before the 1860s Russian musical life was a tender plant whose blooms could by no means be relied upon. The semblance of randomness in the contents of Chapter 2 testifies to this factor. Awareness of the fragmentary quality of musical life was the essential prerequisite for improvement, and this consciousness gave rise in the 1840s and 1850s to various new ventures in concert promotion and education. The decisive step was the establishment of the Russian Musical Society in 1859, when the combination of an eminent and strong-willed Russian musician (Anton Rubinstein) with appropriate contacts (in the worlds of music and high society) and a climate favourable to change proved irresistible. The Russian Musical Society and its conservatoires brought greater vitality and stability to concert life, and prepared the ground for a tradition of performance which is still alive. Their supporters encountered opposition from those fearful that Russian native musical qualities would be constrained by the rules set out in German textbooks, who sought a more strongly Russian art. The Free School of Music was opened in 1862 to give expression to a different understanding of musical progress. Musical conservatism and radicalism came into play, as did all the emotions provoked by disagreement and rivalry. A sense of the forces at work in this conflict is given, I hope, in Chapter 3. Some of the principal authors drawn out by that controversy extended their quarrel to the question of which of Glinka's operas was the better model in casting light on the way ahead for composers. At this point the great length (literally) to which Russian criticism went becomes clear; thorough discussion of the matter in hand from first principles comes into it; minute blow-by-blow accounts of music are common; intimate intellectual wrestling with the publications of opponents is also conspicuous. To give some flavour of this style of criticism, Serov's article on Glinka's operas has been retained in full in Chapter 4, even though the details of the dispute with Stasov are now even less relevant than they seemed in 1860.

The next chapter is largely concerned with the operas of Dargomïzhsky and Serov. The former had ploughed a lonely furrow, composing rather desultorily and with considerable changes of direction. He was taken up in the 1860s by a group of younger composers who shared the ideals which he was then espousing, especially in his *The Stone Guest*, and with their sympathetic encouragement he all but brought that opera to completion before he died. Through some of his romances, too, he showed the way ahead; he provided the only musical models for Musorgsky's songs of satire and social criticism. Serov's operas, on the other hand, were the most successful Russian operas composed in the 1860s. New streams thus joined the eventual flood of Russian opera at this point: 'musical truth' and speech-inflected melodies *via* Dargomïzhsky, and the grand operatic spectacle, now in Russian guise, though Serov. Modest further assistance came in the shape of *William Ratcliff*, the opera with a Scottish setting from a play by Heinrich Heine composed by the Franco-Lithuanian César Cui; the composer probably was more influential in formulating concepts in prose than embodying them in music. The ground was now prepared for *Boris Godunov*.

The younger generation who gave stimulus to Dargomïzhsky gathered at the feet of Balakirev. Inspired by Schumann, Berlioz and Liszt, and prodded to creative endeavour grossly disproportionate to their technical skills by their magnetic mentor, Borodin, Musorgsky and Rimsky-Korsakov embarked on compositions for orchestra; Tchaikovsky also fell under Balakirev's spell for a time. Balakirev himself was active as a composer in the 1860s – indeed his career as composer, conductor and *animateur* was then at its peak. Cui as critic, though not as composer, is represented in Chapter 6.

In the 1870s three major operas on Russian historical subjects were performed: while the space allotted in Chapter 7 to *Boris Godunov* will not occasion surprise, that given to Rimsky-Korsakov's *The Maid of Pskov* and Tchaikovsky's *The Oprichnik* may. It is in part a matter of setting Musorgsky's *chef d'œuvre* in context (since *The Maid of Pskov* is the product of thinking along lines parallel to Musorgsky's), and in part a matter of keeping pace with the still evolving ideas of the other two significant composers. Tchaikovsky's evolution is seen in the appearance in the same decade of *Eugene Onegin*.

This period also witnessed the flowering of Tchaikovsky's talent in non-operatic composition. This efflorescence is examined in detail by Laroche in the final chapter. Borodin continued to fit some composition in between periods devoted to professional commitments (he was a medical chemist); like Musorgsky, in proportion to his talent and creativity he is here perforce under-represented. The beginning of the next decade saw the death of Musorgsky, and thus provided Cui with the opportunity to review his work as a whole, though the critic concentrated on the works familiar through

performance and gave little sense of what treasures were still to emerge, and
showed only limited understanding of the works he knew.

Compiling an anthology such as this presents certain difficulties. It is hard
to include worthwhile material on every work one would wish to see
discussed by virtue of its familiarity, or influence, or both. In the early part
of the period especially, this is because coverage of musical activity was
either not systematic or was in the wrong hands. Later on, especially in the
case of Musorgsky, works of great significance were either not performed in
public or not commented on for some reason. Disappointment and surprise
at the absence of anything genuinely critical about *Kamarinskaya* ('the
acorn from which all Russian symphonic music grew', as Tchaikovsky put
it), and of anything at all on *Pictures from an Exhibition* or the *Songs and
Dances of Death* are legitimate but unavoidable; a just evaluation of
Musorgsky's work was not in any case arrived at in his lifetime (he died in
1881) or for a long time thereafter.

Another difficulty is that Russian musical life (by which is meant that of
the two capital cities of St Petersburg and Moscow) did not offer so very
many opportunities for the performance of music other than opera. Private
performances, of course, took place, but were not regularly commented on
in the press. Rezvoy's article in Chapter 2 gives an idea of the scale of
concert life in St Petersburg before the 1860s, when it expanded markedly,
thanks to the work of the Russian Musical Society and (in St Petersburg)
the Free School of Music, especially with orchestral concerts; in the longer
term, the conservatoires supplied talented and well-schooled executant
musicians who subsequently enriched the musical life of Russia and indeed
of other countries. Opera, on the other hand, was entirely under the control
of the Directorate of the Imperial Theatres in this period. This body consumed substantial resources, but was accused of being too much at the mercy
of the fashion-conscious aristocrats, their eyes fixed on western Europe,
who manned it, and who were moreover obliged to pay heed to the views
of members of the Imperial family (since the Directorate was subordinate
to the Ministry of the Imperial Court), and too preoccupied with bureaucratic
routine and intrigue. Musicians complained that too much money was
invested in Italian opera, while the Directorate's lack of faith in Russian opera
caused their neglect of it. A decisive change for the better occurred only
with the relaxation of the monopoly and the establishment of private companies from the mid-1880s. Without the latter step, Rimsky-Korsakov's
operas would hardly have been staged or the later ones, arguably, composed
at all. This is a simplified picture, but it holds good, I believe, for the St
Petersburg and Moscow stages throughout the period under consideration.

The material available for inclusion, in spite of some gaps, nevertheless is dauntingly extensive in quantity, and no one, I am sure, could reasonably claim familiarity with all of it. T. N. Livanova's *Muzïkal'naya bibliografiya russkoy periodicheskoy pechati XIX veka* ('A musical bibliography of the Russian periodical press in the nineteenth century') (Moscow 1960–76, 6 vols., some issued in several parts) indicates the enormous number of announcements, reviews, surveys, memoirs, letters, biographical accounts, etc. which were published. This quantity of material (together with the musical richness of the period) dictated the concentration on Russian compositions: Serov's view of Beethoven and Laroche's of Bizet or Brahms are, alas, absent; even western composers whose works exerted a decisive influence on those of their Russian colleagues (such as Berlioz and Liszt) find almost no place here. Comment on performance has had to be kept to a minimum. This is nowhere more regrettable than in concealing the part played in the emergence of Russian opera by a small group of singers without whose skills – musical and dramatic – and commitment Russian opera would hardly have come into existence: among them are O. A. Petrov (1807–78), the bass who created the roles of Susanin and Ruslan, the Miller and Leporello in Dargomïzhsky's *Rusalka* and *The Stone Guest* respectively, Ivan the Terrible in *The Maid of Pskov* and Varlaam; his wife A. Ya. Vorob'yova-Petrova (1817–1901), the contralto who created the role of Vanya and was an admired Ratmir, L. I. Leonov (1813 or 1815–c. 1872), the tenor who created the roles of Sobinin and Finn, and M. M. Stepanova (1815–1903), the soprano who was the first Antonida and Lyudmila; these exemplify the first generation: their successors showed like dedication. The skill and commitment of the conductor Eduard Napravnik (1839–1916) also deserve mention. The contribution of these artistes is underlined by their choosing to use their benefit performances to introduce works by their compatriots.

Excessive length often kept significant material out of the selection. A good instance is Laroche's *Glinka and his Significance in the History of Music* – a wide-ranging and fundamental discussion, but simply far too long for the present purpose.

The terminal date of around 1880 might be considered somewhat arbitrary, since it cuts off the careers of Rimsky-Korsakov and Tchaikovsky in full flight; on the other hand, it permits the completion of Musorgsky's work, and forestalls any temptation to move on to the next generation represented by the younger composers of the Belyayev circle. The work of the first two generations of Russian composers can be dealt with, from Glinka's extraordinary compositions of the 1830s and 1840s to such more familiar landmarks as *Boris Godunov* and *Eugene Onegin* in the 1870s. I hope that I may be allowed the licence of announcing the subject of the book as beginning in 1830 when the first event referred to did not occur until 1836: a half-century is neater than a period of forty-four years.

The most thoughtful and influential critics (Odoyevsky, Serov, Cui and Laroche) have been favoured at the expense of lesser men. Stasov is relatively neglected here, not on account of any underestimate of him or desire to minimize his role, but simply because some of his work is already available in English (see below).

Sources

Borodin = A. P. Borodin: *Kriticheskiye stat'i* ('Critical articles') (Moscow 1982)

Cui = Ts. A. Kyui: *Izbrannïye stat'i* ('Selected articles') (Leningrad 1952)

Cui 1918 = Ts. A. Kyui: *Muzïkal'no-kriticheskiye stat'i* ('Music-critical articles') (Petrograd 1918)

Laroche 2 = G. A. Larosh: *Izbrannïye stat'i* ('Selected articles'), vol. 2 (Leningrad 1975)

Laroche 3 = ditto, vol. 3 (Leningrad 1976)

Laroche 5 = ditto, vol. 5 (Leningrad 1978)

MLN = G. B. Bernandt (ed.): *V. F. Odoyevsky. Muzïkal'no-literaturnoye nslediye* ('V. F. Odoyevsky. Musical-literary heritage') (Moscow 1956)

NG = *The New Grove Dictionary of Music and Musicians*, 20 vols. (London 1980)

Serov 1895, 4 = A. N. Serov: *Kriticheskiye stat'i* ('Critical articles'), vol. 4 (St Petersburg 1895)

Serov 4 = A. N. Serov: *Stat'i o muzïke* ('Articles on music'), vol. 4 (Moscow 1988)

Serov 5 = ditto, vol. 5 (Moscow 1989)

Serov 6 = ditto, vol. 6 (Moscow 1990)

Stasov 2 = V. V. Stasov: *Stat'i o muzïke* ('Articles on music'), vol. 2 (Moscow 1976)

SO = G. Bernandt (comp.): *Slovar' oper, vervïye postavlennïkh ili izdannïkh v dorevolyutsionnoy Rossii i v SSSR* ('Dictionary of operas first produced or published in pre-Revolutionary Russia and the USSR') (Moscow 1962)

Tchaikovsky = P. I. Chaykovsky: *Muzïkal'no-kriticheskiye stat'i* ('Music-critical articles') (Leningrad 1986)

Russian writings on Russian music available elsewhere in translation

(1) in English

Herman Laroche: 'A Musical Letter from Petersburg. Apropos "The Sleeping Beauty", the ballet of M. Petipa, with Music by P. Tchaikovsky', in Roland John Wiley (sel. and tr.): *A Century of Russian Ballet. Documents and Accounts, 1810-1910* (Oxford 1990), pp. 377-84

Vladimir Stasov: the following are in Malcolm H. Brown (ed.): *Musorgsky in Memoriam 1881-1981* (Ann Arbor, Michigan, 1982), 'Occasional Writings on Musorgsky', tr. Richard Hoops:

'Cuts in Musorgsky's "Boris Godunov"' (1876), pp. 313-15
'Obituary for M. P. Musorgsky' (1881), pp. 315-18
'A Portrait of Musorgsky,' (1881), pp. 318-19
'A Concert in Memory of Musorgsky' (1881), pp. 320-1
'A Musical Outrage' (1883), pp. 321-4
'Concerning the Production of "Khovanshchina"' (1886), pp. 324-6
'Is this the end of "Khovanshchina"?' (1886), pp. 326-8

Vladimir Stasov: *Selected Essays on Music*, tr. Florence Jonas (London 1968)

Review of the Musical Events of the Year 1847, pp. 15–37
'Letters from abroad' (1869), pp. 38–51
'The Letters of Berlioz' (1879), pp. 52–61
'A Letter from Liszt' (1879), pp. 62–5
Twenty-five Years of Russian Art: Our Music (1883), pp. 66-116
'Liszt, Schumann and Berlioz in Russia' (1889, revised 1896), pp. 117–94
'A Friendly Commemoration' (1906), pp. 195–9

(2) in French

César Cui: *La Musique en Russie* (Paris 1880, repr. Leipzig 1974)

P.I. Tchaïkovski: *Ecrits, critiques, souvenirs* (Moscow 1985). This volume contains, among other material, the following:

'A propos de la *Fantaisie serbe* de M. Rimski-Korsakov' (1868), pp. 5–8
'Une voix du monde musical de Moscou' (1869), pp. 9–11
'*Don Juan* de Mozart sur la scène italienne. – *Freischütz* de Weber sur la scène de l'opéra russe' (1871), pp. 12–15
'La reprise de *Rouslan et Lioudmila*' (1872), pp. 16–20
'La deuxième réunion symphonique' (1872), pp. 21–3
'La troisième et la quatrième réunions symphoniques de la Société de musique russe' (1872), pp. 24–8
'Le commencement de la saison des concerts' (1873), 29–31
'Une explication avec le lecteur' (1873), pp. 32–5

'Chronique musicale. – *Don Juan* et *Zora* sur la scène italienne' (1874),
pp. 36–7
'La deuxième et la troisième semaines de la saison des concerts' (1874),
pp. 38–42
'La quatrième semaine des concerts' (1874), pp. 43–5
'L'opéra italien' (1874), pp. 46–8
'La deuxième réunion symphonique. – Le bénéfice de Mme Patti' (1874),
pp. 49–50
'La huitième réunion symphonique' (1875), pp. 51–2
'La deuxième semaine des concerts. – La neuvième réunion de la Société
de musique. – Quelques réflexions au sujet de la fécondité' (1875),
pp. 53–7
'Le Festival de Bayreuth' (1876), pp. 58–71

(3) in German

Alexander Serow: *Aufsätze zur Musikgeschichte* (Berlin 1955). This volume
includes:
'Das russische Volkslied als Gegenstand der Wissenschaft' (1869-71),
pp. 119-54
'Erinnerungen an Michail Iwanowitsch Glinka' (1860), pp. 155-202
'Das Schicksal der Oper in Russland' (publ. 1864), pp. 203-16
'Der Thematismus der Leonoren-Ouvertüre' (1861), pp. 217-34
'Die neunte Symphonie von Beethoven. Ihr Bau und ihre Idee' (1868),
pp. 235-47
'Spontini und seine Musik' (1852), pp. 248-90
'Hector Berlioz' (1869), pp. 291-326
'Richard Wagner in Petersburg' (1863), pp. 327-30
'Die Konzerte der Philharmonischen Gesellschaft unter Leitung von
Richard Wagner' (1863) pp. 331-7
'Briefe aus dem Auslande' (1858) pp. 338-86
'Autobiographische Skizze' (1870), pp. 101-15
Heinrich Stümcke (ed.): *Musikalische Erinnerungen und Feuilletons von
Peter Tschaikowsky* (Berlin, n.d., though Preface is dated 1899); this
volume contains a selection of the composer's critical writings.

CHAPTER ONE

Glinka's operas

The emergence of a Russian school of composition is usually traced with justification to the work of Mikhail Glinka. His operas *A Life for the Tsar* (also referred to by the name of its hero as *Ivan Susanin*), premièred in 1836, and *Ruslan and Lyudmila*, premièred in 1842, are corner-stones of the repertory and models for the composer's successors. It is logical to devote the first chapter to the contemporary view of these works, and worthwhile to devote a great part of Chapter 4 to them as well, since discussions of their relative merits in the 1860s had a role to play in shaping later Russian opera.

(a) V. F. Odoyevsky: Letter to a music lover on the subject of Glinka's opera *A Life for the Tsar*. *The Northern Bee*, 7 December 1836, no. 280. *MLN*, pp. 118–19

Prince Vladimir Fyodorovich Odoyevsky (1804–69) earns mention in many fields of activity. His life was divided between the two capitals: until 1826 he was in Moscow, from then until 1862 in St Petersburg, and thereafter in Moscow again. His career in the civil service took him to several ministries, the Public Library, the Rumyantsev Museum and the Senate, in all of which his interest in education, the natural sciences, technology and almost every other human endeavour was welcome, or at any rate potentially useful. He had a further career – the one for which he is most renowned – as a man of letters, writing short stories and the Utopian novel *The Year 4338. St Petersburg Letters (4338-y god. Peterburgskiye pis'ma)*, and being on friendly terms with Pushkin, Belinsky and other literary figures of the time. In the then small world of *belles lettres*, the same people were influential in the periodical press, where too Odoyevsky was active; much of his writing about music is in the context of a wider role in journalism and publishing. The literary circle overlapped with the philosophers (the young Odoyevsky was an enthusiast for German Idealism) and the social thinkers; noble birth gave him entrée to high society, so that he was in an uncommonly good position to observe his contemporaries and sometimes to bring his influence to bear. He was a pianist, an organ-lover and a good sight-reader. In his early years in Moscow he joined in the fashion for vaudevilles written collaboratively; his compositions are generally on a small scale (Balakirev thought well enough of a piano *Lullaby* to secure its republication in 1895) and sometimes of an experimental character, but also displaying his sound knowledge of the rules of conventional harmony and counterpoint. Russian folksong and old Russian church music absorbed a good deal of his energies, particularly in the 1860s. Odoyevsky's writing on music is unevenly distributed over his lifespan, with heavy concentrations in 1825 and from 1837 to 1839, and a regular flow between 1863 and his death. His work ranges from short items drawing attention to some imminent event of significance, to concert reviews of the kind normal in the periodical press, to more extended articles of a more learned character. Glinka was among his friends, and his reports rely on an understanding of the composer's intentions and the circumstances of performance. Odoyevsky was the first to claim that *A Life for the Tsar* marked the inauguration of a new era in music, a verdict which history has subsequently accepted.

You wanted me to pass on to you my first impressions of Glinka's new opera. I am carrying out my promise precisely, and am writing this immediately after the first performance [on 27 November 1836]. Consequently, do not expect what I write to be completely intelligible; I am aware that at the moment an abundance of emotions may well impede concise expression of thought. The charming, enthralling melodies of the opera are still ringing in my ears and at the present time I would rather sing about this work than write about it.

Glinka's opera appeared suddenly, as if from nowhere. There were no advance press tributes to the work. Neither *Le Journal des Débats*, nor *La Gazette musicale* nor *La Revue étrangère*[1] has prepared us over the course of an entire year for the delights awaiting us with stories about all the particulars of the rehearsals, the amazement of the experts, the magnificent performances of Pasta, Rubini and Lablache,[2] or about the admiration throughout Europe, and finally about any of the circumstances which often against our will force us to applaud with all our might so as not to appear uncivilized. Something was said in passing in *The Northern Bee* about a new opera, and it was rumoured that there would be Russian music in it.[3] Many music lovers expected to hear a few well-known if modified folk-songs in the opera, but nothing more.

Yet how can I convey the astonishment of true lovers of music when, from the first act onwards, it became clear that this opera was going to provide an answer to a question which is of vital importance to the arts in general and to the arts in Russia in particular – namely that of the very

1 The first two periodicals were published in Paris and the third in St Petersburg.
2 The most celebrated soprano, tenor and bass, respectively, of the time.
3 See the issue of 12 September 1836, no. 209.

existence of Russian opera, Russian music and, ultimately, the existence of national music.[4] As far as you, educated lovers of music, are concerned, this question has always been half-answered; you believed that just as there exist for the painter specific traits which determine the physiognomy of one race or another and allow him to draw, say, a Russian or an Italian face without actually having to paint someone's portrait, so too there exist for the musician specific forms of melody and harmony which determine the nature of the music of one race or another, and through which we distinguish German music from Italian, and even Italian from French. Even before Glinka's opera, moderately successful attempts had been made to seek out these general forms of Russian melody and harmony. We can find Russian melodies, which, however, are not imitations of any well-known folksongs, in the excellent works of Alyab'yev,[5] Count Wielhorski,[6] Verstovsky[7] and Genishta.[8] But never before has the use of these forms been carried out on such a large scale as in Glinka's opera. Initiated into all the secrets of Italian singing and Germany harmony, the composer has penetrated deep into the character of Russian melody! Rich in his own talent, he has demonstrated by this splendid attempt that Russian melody, naturally by turns melancholy, happy and daring, can also be elevated to the realms of tragedy. In the whole opera only the first two bars are taken from a well-known folk tune,[9] but after this there is not one phrase which is not highly original, and at the same time there is not one phrase which does not sound familiar to Russian ears.

Glinka's music has brought to light what people have long sought but not found in Europe – a new element in art. This is the dawn of a new age in the history of the arts – the age of Russian music. Such an exploit is, I can say in all honesty, a matter not of mere talent but of genius!

4 The last seven words were omitted in the original publication.
5 A. A. Alyab'yev (1787–1851). Composer of songs, chamber music, theatre music, etc. A promising career was interrupted by an unsatisfactory conviction for murder, which caused Alyab'yev to be exiled to provincial towns for over a decade following the Decembrist conspiracy of 1825.
6 Count Michał Wielhorski, or Mikhail Yu. Viyel'gorsky, (1788–1856). Composer and, like his brother the cellist Count Matvey (1794–1866), prominent patron. Social eminence (and sound musical education) gave the brothers considerable influence in the musical world of St Petersburg. The older brother met Beethoven and came into ownership of that composer's sketchbook now known by his name.
7 A. N. Verstovsky (1799–1862). Composer, chiefly for the theatre and of vocal music. He was employed in the administration of the imperial theatres in Moscow from 1825 until 1860. His background lay in vaudeville and works of the *Singspiel* type. His opera *Askol'dova mogila* ('Askol'd's Tomb', 1835) retained its popularity for some time after the appearance of Glinka's first opera.
8 I. I. Genishta (1795–1853). Russian composer and pianist of Czech ancestry. He played the solo part in some of the earliest performances in Russia of Beethoven piano concertos. Best known as a composer for his songs.
9 In fact, more extensive quotations from two Russian folksongs were used. See David Brown: *Mikhail Glinka* (London 1974), pp. 99, 106–7, 111–12.

**(b) Ya. M. Neverov: Mr Glinka's new opera *A Life for the Tsar* –
a letter from St Petersburg to the *Moscow Observer*. *Moscow
Observer*, 10 December 1836, book 1, pp. 374–84. T. Livanova and
V. Protopopov (edd.): Glinka, vol. 2 (Moscow 1955), pp. 209–14**

Yanuary Mikhaylovich Neverov (1810–93) made but a small contribution to music. His primary interest lay in the field of education where
most of his career was spent. Studies in Berlin came after the publication
of this article, and embraced music (among other subjects), pursued
with Rungenhagen and Otto Nicolai. Apart from over twenty entries
on composers for an *Encyclopaedic Lexicon* published in St Petersburg
between 1825 and 1841, this is his sole contribution to the literature
on music. It was written with the advantage of Glinka's friendship.

This autumn the people of St Petersburg have experienced many artistic
delights. The latest talk in local drawing rooms about the exhibition [at the
Academy of Arts] and its main heroes – A. A. Ivanov, M. N. Vorob'yov,
N. S. Pimenov junior, F. S. Zav'yalov and A. T. Markov[10] – had not even
begun to die down before everyone's attention was turned to the paintings by
Raphael, Guido Reni and Caracci[11] which has been brought to the Hermitage
from England. Rumours about the new opera by our own young maestro
Glinka, *A Life for the Tsar*, which was being prepared for production, were
mingled with talk of painting and sculpture. The first performance was
meant to mark the opening of the rebuilt Bol'shoy Theatre. The long-awaited
opening took place at last on 27 November, and the throngs of people there
were extraordinary. Everyone was in a hurry to see this new temple erected
to honour our national muses, and to hear the opera of a composer who has
won fame and respect through his charming romances, songs and instrumental compositions. 27 November [1613] is a memorable date in Russian
history: it is the day on which Ivan Susanin died. This year the day was
marked fittingly. More than 200 years have elapsed since that noble citizen,
a true son of Russia, gave his life to save his rightful sovereign – and now
his noble posterity in its gratitude mourns for him in a moving way. The
musician and the poet have brought Susanin back to life through the
creative power of their art, and, on the anniversary of his death, he makes
his appearance before a splendid company to convey his simple and sublime
feelings of love for his homeland and the throne. The first sounds we heard
from the new stage were Russian ones giving expression to the Russian
soul. It is as though Susanin has dedicated this new temple of the arts to all
that is Russian (*natsional'nomu*). God grant that this will be a good omen,

10 These artists exhibited paintings, except for Pimenov who showed the statue *Boy Playing
    Dibs* referred to later.
11 These are all artists of the sixteenth and seventeenth centuries.

and that we will in future hear more often on our stages works which show a national spirit (*v narodnom dukhe*). A start has been made – we have a Russian opera!

Before I go on to tell you about the music of *A Life for the Tsar*, I must first acquaint you with the content of the poem. An opera is a work where all the arts unite to charm the spectator and, although in this beautiful alliance it is music which is predominant, the composer, however original he may be, is nevertheless restricted somewhat by the poet, who indicates the points where his inspiration should be focussed. This is why in the case of dramatic music we should never forget the poem that serves as a base for the music.

The main preconditions for any theatrical work are life, movement, and a variety of feelings and desires. Our poet adhered unnecessarily to historical accuracy and did not allow himself a single episode, a single detail which would remind the audience that they were watching a work of art and not history. Of course, because of this, the opera has acquired a grand, sedate quality, but it would not have been disturbed by variety in the characters or a conflict of interests, in other words, by what we know as the plot of a drama. *A Life for the Tsar* is not a drama, but a picture. [There follows a summary of the plot.]

Although when one hears a poem one hears the idiomatic language of a nation, we must remember that in this case we are dealing with opera where it is very rare to find a single vivid stanza which the author has not had to rework several times to suit the composer. Knowing how difficult it is to adjust the poem of an opera to accommodate music, we should not reproach Baron Rozen for his verse. The musician is responsible for everything, and it is up to him alone to create and sustain the interest of the work as a whole. Our maestro has fulfilled this duty: he has given life and movement to the opera, and developed what the author only hinted at. For all that, many, hearing *A Life for the Tsar* for the first time, were left dissatisfied and did not try to understand the opera until they had heard it a second time. Attention was then fixed solely on the composer, and he captivated the audience completely. Mr Glinka did everything that was possible.

Simply read through the poem, and ask yourself who exactly Vanya is – you will not be able to give a clear answer. Yet listen to his music, and your mind will be filled with a very clear and beautiful picture of the orphan, mournful even in happiness, a bold, courageous person who loves his benefactor with reverent esteem, and who is devoted heart and soul to his tsar and country. In Vanya's final aria, his sadness seems so lofty and solemn; in truth, for the sake of this one aria alone, one would not be bored to be in the theatre twenty times.

But we have not yet reached the end of the good points in Mr Glinka's music. The important thing is that his opera is a purely Russian work, and as such embodies ideas of folk tradition, nationhood and homeland (*ego opera est' proizvedeniye chisto russkoye, narodnoye, rodnoye*). How do you communicate the rapture with which the maestro has filled the hearts of lovers of the arts and all those who appreciate what an important feat he has accomplished? Never before in Russia has a theatrical production aroused such lively, complete enthusiasm as *A Life for the Tsar*. The audience understood the composer, or, perhaps it is better to say that they were instinctively enthralled by his great talent. At the eight performances given so far there has not been an empty seat in the house, and each time the delighted audience has heartily applauded the famous maestro. Glinka richly deserved this attention: to create a national opera is a feat which will engrave his name forever in the annals of Russian art. We have long felt a need for national identity (*natsional'nost'*) in music. We were fully convinced that our folksongs represented a hitherto untapped, rich source of completely original melodies.

There have even been some attempts already to create a national opera. To look at only one of these attempts, we can see that Mr Verstovsky,[12] an intelligent composer with a genuine talent though not, however, a dramatic one, tried to transfer Russian song to the stage. He did not succeed in this, however, because he thought to create an opera by sometimes borrowing complete folk melodies and sometimes imitating them. Since there is nothing dramatic in the words or the music of our songs, the operas created from them had the same disjointed, lyrical character. Mr Verstovsky's best works, *Vadim* and *Askol'd's Tomb*, consist of nothing more than a collection of mainly charming Russian motives joined together by German choruses and quartets and Italian recitatives. If Mr Verstovsky had given up any claims to national character (*narodnost'*), and had written an opera as they are written in Germany and Italy, he could have presented us with charming works. As it was, there was no hint of national character (*natsional'nost'*) and, what is more, the work lost any proportion, and the opera appeared an arbitrary mixture of arias, duets and trios in all styles and from all countries, in which the listener sought in vain for some sort of unity or some dominant idea.

Mr Glinka adopted a different approach; he has delved deep into the character of our nation's folk music, observed all its characteristics, learned and mastered the music, and then has given complete freedom to his own fantasy, which has created images which are purely Russian and symbolize

12 For Verstovsky, see note 7 above. *Vadim* was first staged in 1832.

our homeland. As they listened to the opera, many people have noticed something familiar in it, and have tried to remember from which Russian song one motive or another has been taken, but they have not been able to find the original. This is a flattering compliment to the maestro; in actual fact there is not a single borrowed motive in his opera,[13] yet they are all perfectly understandable and familiar to us for the very reason that they exude a pure feeling of national character (*narodnost'*), that we hear our own Russian sounds in them. The main characteristic of the music of *A Life for the Tsar* is its grace, in which the national character is more accessible because Russian music has an extraordinary wealth of melodiousness and charm; but all of Susanin's part and some of Vanya's arias are in an elevated style with deep feeling, yet for all that, they are Russian through and through, which is a most important point! Until now we have never heard Russian music in this elevated vein – Mr Glinka is its creator. He has also created a thoroughly unique type of recitative and has thus enriched art with new ideas. His new recitatives are unlike either German or Italian ones; they combine the expressiveness and dramatic variation of the former with the melodiousness of the latter, and it would appear that you can even hear the intonation of Russian voices.

To those merits of this important work which I have noted we must also add the rich instrumentation which heightens the beauty of the composer's musical ideas; but he is stronger, however, in dealing with the vocal parts of the opera. Finally, I will say that in the score of *A Life for the Tsar* everything is new, fresh and original, from the basic idea through to the last details of its realization, and if anyone were to ask which numbers are the best, then I would find it difficult to choose and would say boldly that they are all beautiful, from beginning to end. The Mazurka, the Polish chorus accompanied by Susanin's recitative in Act II, Susanin's last scene in Act III, and the aria-terzet in the Epilogue (between Vanya, Antonida and Bogdan) made a particularly strong impression on the audience. The general movement in the theatre, the thunderous applause, and even the tears furtively wiped away show that in these pieces the composer penetrates right to the heart of the listener.

Scarcely three weeks have passed since the first staging of *A Life for the Tsar*, and already phrases from the opera can be heard not only in drawing rooms, where it is the main topic of conversation, but even in the street – new proof of the national spirit embodied in this opera. It is to be hoped that it will soon be famous not only in St Petersburg. At present only two arias and the Mazurka – the ballet – arranged for piano by the composer

13 See note 9 above.

have been published, but it is said that the opera as a whole, as well as a German translation of it, will be published before the end of January. By means of this translation *A Life for the Tsar* will be submitted to Europe's judgment.[14] I believe that a flattering reception awaits this work in other countries. Music, like all other forms of art, has rather exhausted those ideas around which it has so far moved this century. Something new and fresh was needed to rejuvenate these ideas, yet Europe has long since sought within itself for this without any success. Only in Russia is such a rich future to be found. Our fresh and youthful Russia, by its embodiment of national character (*natsional'nost'*), must renew the senescent artistic life of its mentor and introduce new elements. It seems that a new era is beginning when Russia will be obliged to offer Europe the fruits of her spiritual life, and Glinka's opera will be almost the first work to represent our national identity (*narodnost'*). Europe will be amazed by this new, unheard melody, and if they do not understand it immediately then they will be able to appreciate it later, and to take advantage of the new ideas developed by our maestro. Now we can say boldly that we have a national art; foreigners recognize the distinctiveness of our school of painting, but they do not yet know that we also have a national opera and a national school of sculpture. We will point out *A Life for the Tsar* and Mr Pimenov's statue *Boy Playing dibs*[15] to them. Yes indeed, a new era in Russia's genius for art begins with the names of Glinka, Bryullov[16] and Pimenov. For a long time this new era seemed to have got off to a shaky start, but now, apparently, it is well and truly on the right track indicated by the Russian nation.

[The final paragraph deals with the performance, singling out the 'superb' contributions of Petrov (Susanin)[17] and Vorob'yova Vanya'[18]]

---

14 Individual numbers were published for voice and piano between 1836 and 1838, the complete vocal score in 1856–7 and the full score in 1881.

15 See note 10 above.

16 K. P. Bryullov (1799–1852), the renowned painter, of among other things an enormous *Last Day of Pompei*.

17 O. A. Petrov (1807–78). Bass. After a varied career in drama, tragedy and operetta, he first appeared on the St Petersburg operatic stage in 1830, where he continued to work until 1878. One of the most important of all Russian performers, he was the first Susanin, Ruslan, the Miller (in *Rusalka*), Leporello (in *The Stone Guest*), Ivan the Terrible (in *The Maid of Pskov*) and Varlaam (in *Boris Godunov*).

18 A. Ya. Vorob'yova-Petrova (1817–1901). Contralto, married to O. A. Petrov. She sang on the St Petersburg operatic stage from 1835 to 1846, remaining with the company until 1850. The first Vanya.

(c) V. F. Odoyevsky: Second letter to a music lover on the subject of Glinka's opera *A Life for the Tsar* or *Ivan Susanin*. *The Northern Bee*, 15 December 1836, no. 287, and 16 December 1836, no. 288. *MLN*, pp. 119–26

The Northern Bee was a political and literary newspaper published in St Petersburg and widely read. Its editors were F. V. Bulgarin (1789–1859) from 1825 until his death and (from 1831–59) N. I. Grech (1787–1867). Both men had unsavoury reputations. The former had literary ambitions (see 1(e)). Were its large readership not attractive to a spokesman for a new and controversial development in the arts in Russia, this newspaper might not have been selected for Odoyevsky's articles.

My letters cannot keep pace with the performances of this opera. It has already been staged five times, and five times the composer has been called on to the stage not by the applause of friends but by the unanimous will of the audience. It does not follow, however, that Glinka's opera has been completely bereft of critics, often vociferous ones. This cannot be otherwise: music is unfortunately one sphere of the arts where everyone considers he is well placed to make judgements. The non-architect is wary of speaking about a building, the non-painter is cautious about discussing a picture, yet music, that most complicated art-form whose roots are buried deep in the inaccessible reaches of the human soul, is discussed by all and sundry, even those people who cannot tell a D from an F in music. I shall return later to say something more about the judgements of these people, which are extremely amusing. Any new, unusual phenomenon in art is the most marvellous way to highlight the level of understanding of certain amateurs. For well-known, celebrated pieces of music they have ready-prepared phrases taken from newspapers or conversations, and therefore giving the appearance of truth; but when a new advance in the arts renders this prepared knowledge redundant, then it is plain for all the world to see that these people's understanding of music is infantile.

I hasten to add, for the sake of the honour of the composer and the listener, that the number of these opponents is decreasing with every performance and the acclaim is intensifying. Anyone who has seen the opera twice will not say the same things after the second performance as after the first. This is a sign that the opera will have a sure and long success. Few people understood [Meyerbeer's] *Robert le diable* at the first performance, yet a *contredanse* is understandable at once. In addition, I must point out that the composer has scorned those prescribed phrases with which every Italian piece seems obliged to finish, in the same way that a letter finishes 'I beg to remain, respectfully yours . . .', from which the audience knows it is time to start applauding. In Glinka's opera the music continues without a break, and consequently at the first performance the applause of the audience drowned out the best parts of the opera, thus losing half of the work. At the next performances the audience was more careful, refraining from showing their enthusiasm during the best bits, but in return subsequently rewarding the composer a hundredfold for the pleasure he had given them.

But let us turn to the opera itself. I have neither time nor space to tell you about its content and its relationship with the music. In any case, anyone can get hold of the libretto.[19] The subject of the opera evolved in the composer's mind along with the music itself, and the whole development of the piece was conceived by him before he went to a writer to ask if he could put the opera into a theatrical form. Baron Rozen accomplished this task with unusual success despite some rather major difficulties which lay in store for him. Indeed, it must be said in passing that many passages of music had already been conceived in the composer's head before words were written for them, and as a result the poet was obliged to devise completely new metres for his verses. Those familiar with the intricacies of Russian versification will appreciate the magnitude of such a task. What is more, there are truly beautiful verses on each page which are strong enough to survive on their own outside the opera. Such a test calls for a toast to the talent, expertise and patience of the glorious poet![20]

The content of the opera is simple as, indeed, it should be for a subject familiar to every Russian where any imbroglio would be improper. In the first act there is a rural scene: imagine yourself in a field in summer; various sounds reach your ears – from one side the slow drawn-out[21] singing of the men, from the other the cheerful songs of the women. To these sounds are added the bold cries of rowers. In nature the union of heterogeneous melodies, as anyone can easily see, often sounds harshly on the ear, but there are times when by some chance these melodies blend together to form pure harmony. This blend of sound, so strange at first, takes on an unusual charm impossible to express in words. Everyone has experienced such a feeling. In music, as you know, there are means of capturing those moments when various melodies concur to form one harmony common to them all and, consequently, to preserve that animated feeling which is caused by this combination of melodies, without jarring on the ear. You must also be aware of the fact that these means can only be used by someone who has

19 This sentence is omitted in the published version.
20 An observer with no axe to grind would hardly share the author's enthusiasm on this count.
21 'Drawn-out' refers to a type of folk singing, *protyazhnoye*, which will be mentioned again; alternative translations are 'leisurely' and melismatic' (see Malcolm H. Brown: 'Native Song and National Consciousness in Nineteenth-Century Russian Music' in T. G. Stavrou (ed.): *Art and Culture in Nineteenth-Century Russia* (Bloomington, Indiana 1983), p. 83).

studied thoroughly the inner workings of harmony. Our musician has used the tools of his trade with extraordinary success; at first we hear the sedate drawn-out chorus of the men, this is joined by the lively female chorus, and then we hear the bold melodies of the rowers on the river. Finally all these choirs, by means of skilful counterpoint, blend into one choir[22] in which each group of singers maintains its distinctive character and in which one can hear each choir separately as well as all together without any obscurity or inconsistency. You need to listen to this chorus in order to understand the effect it produces. In the instrumentation the pizzicato is especially remarkable, separating itself completely from the singing: here the balalayka is elevated to art. The effect produced by this chorus is simply beyond description. The audience gave a rapturous response to Antonida's aria (sung by Mrs Stepanova)[23]. Although the beautiful fresh motive based on the words 'Tam v derevne za rekoyu' ('In the countryside beyond the river') keeps its Russian character entirely, it could equally obtain immortality in elegant drawing rooms for the best-known Italian operas. Such motives have been scattered throughout the whole opera by the composer with gay abandon. Meaner composers lucky enough to find even one such motive would not be afraid of repeating it at least twenty times in order to din it into the listeners' heads and to distinguish it from what the Italians call *arie di sorbetti* with which Italian operas are padded out. Our composer is not afraid of extravagance and has every right to be so. The audience were similarly enraptured by the charming trio of Antonida, the fiancé Sobinin (Mr Leonov)[24] and Susanin (Mr Petrov) singing 'Ne tomis' naprasno' ('Do not pine in vain') [no. 4, in Act I]. Incidentally, a word here about the fiancé: some of the audience, used to more traditional operas, certainly wanted to see some sort of hero in Sobinin, something along the lines of Tancredi or Orbazzano,[25] and they were disappointed that they did not see in Mr Leonov those formidable swings in temperament which are so characteristic of operatic lovers. Here is a fiancé of the sort we can always find in our own villages – in other words, a young man who is brave in a fight but open-hearted, bashful and, to some extent, carefree. These traits of

22 The score gives no indication that the rowers' music was added to that of the two choruses as described.

23 M. M. Stepanova (1815–1903). Soprano. She sang on the operatic stage in St Petersburg from 1833 to 1854. She was the first Antonida and Lyudmila.

24 L. I. Leonov (1813 or 1815 – c. 1872). Tenor. He sang in opera in St Petersburg from 1833 until 1864. He created the roles of Sobinin, Finn and Feb (Phoebus in Dargomïzhsky's *Esmeral'da*).

25 For Petrov, see note 17 above. Tancredi and Orbazzano appear in *Tancredi*, Rossini's *melodramma eroico* first staged in 1813, whose plot entwines rivalry in love with feuding families; set in eleventh-century Syracuse, this work is here made to stand for everything conventional, incredible and preposterous that may be conveyed by the adjective 'operatic'.

personality were created by the poet and the composer, and the young artist maintained them in the best possible way.

[The author highlights further items which made an impression on him.] In general, the composer has been successful in taking advantage of the individual characteristics of Russian and Polish music, as may be seen in all the exchanges between Susanin and the Poles; this change-over from one character to another with harmonious links between them is original in the highest degree. [. . .] the women's bridal chorus is based on the most original Russian motive in $\frac{5}{4}$ time and, you will notice, the Russian motive has not been borrowed from anyone else, something which applies to all the melodies in Glinka's opera.[26] This melody is one which, even if you heard it apart from the rest of the opera, you would still recognize as a wedding song. This underlines the thoroughness with which the composer has understood the rules governing the formation of Russian melodies. [. . .]

It must be said that the part of Susanin in the first two acts, without any departure from its Russian character, has a quality of weightiness which sets it apart from Antonida's mournful melodies and the carefree songs of the bridegroom Sobinin. [. . .] But in Act III when Susanin, having led the Poles deep into the impenetrable forest where they are having a rest and he, fearing torture, is, naturally enough, given to thoughts of his fate, while struggling inwardly between feelings of sacred duty, love for the tsar and his homeland and memories of his daughter, his adopted son and of a happy family, Susanin's song rises to a style of supreme tragedy (something which has hitherto not been heard), yet at the same time preserving its Russian character in all its purity. One simply must listen to this scene in order to convince oneself that it is possible to achieve this combination, a feat which up until recently had been considered merely a vain dream. Here, in my opinion, we can see the talent of the composer in all its glory. By his creation of this new quality the composer has earned himself a place of honour among European composers.

Skilful counterpoint and musical intricacies require a certain knowledge combined – it goes without saying – with talent. Successful motives, which are a question of successful organization, are not found in great numbers in opera. We know from Glinka's previous compositions that these motives do not have much significance for him; he writes them so easily that he does not even think that such an accomplishment deserves any gratitude. However, to create a new, hitherto unheard musical character, to raise folk melody to the level of tragedy, is a question of creative inspiration, which comes to

26 *Author's note:* This duet, arranged for piano and voices, has already been published and may be purchased from Snegiryov's Music Shop, Bryun House, 85 Nevsky Prospekt. All the other numbers in the opera, also in piano transcription, will be on sale there.

only a few people and then only occasionally. That is why I considered myself justified in the light of my initial impression of the opera and now of five subsequent performances, in repeating again that this opera signifies the beginning of a new era in art, the era of Russian music. Listening to Susanin, I could not help thinking of Pizzaro's musical quality in Beethoven's *Fidelio*, which was, of course, the direct starting-point for all of Weber's operas. It is to be hoped that the same thing might happen with the character of Susanin. [. . .]

(d) O. I. Senkovsky: Opera in St Petersburg. *Ruslan and Lyudmila,* music by M. I. Glinka. *Reading Library for 1842,* vol. 55, December, pp. 157–76. T. Livanova and V. Protopopov (edd.): *Glinka,* vol. 2 (Moscow 1955) pp. 237–49

Osip Ivanovich Senkovsky (1800–58) was a writer, journalist and orientalist. From 1822 until 1847 he was Professor of Arabic, Persian and Turkish Languages and Literatures at the University of St Petersburg, and he worked in the censorship from 1828 to 1833. He was the editor and publisher of the *Reading Library* from 1834; this was a publication with a large circulation aiming to keep its subscribers provided with the most diverse reading material until the following month's issue arrived. Senkovsky's pseudonym was Baron Brambeus. In the 1840s his St Petersburg home was something of a musical centre, and his considerable output of prose includes about eighteen items about music. The present article was written from a position sympathetic to Glinka.

The author provided page references to a libretto published with his article. I have replaced these with references to numbers in the score.

I have seen and heard *Ruslan and Lyudmila* in all its magnificence and charm three times now[27] and I am in a position to take stock both for myself and for readers of this journal of the virtues and shortcomings of this new work by the celebrated Russian composer.

With this opera M. I. Glinka has placed himself in the first rank of composers in the whole world and alongside the very foremost of them. *Ruslan and Lyudmila* is one of those supreme musical creations which will never perish and to which one may point with pride as representing the art of a great people. *Ruslan and Lyudmila* is a masterpiece in the full meaning of that word, from the first note to the last. It is splendid, majestic, incomparable. No one has or has ever had a better command of the orchestra than our Russian composer; no one has developed in a single composition so many bold, successful and original ideas; no one has confronted so many

27 The première took place on 27 November 1842.

harmonic difficulties and overcome them so well; no other opera contains such a variety of splendours emerging one from another in an endless chain, without clichés or conventional additions. But all this does not mean that I am entirely satisfied with Glinka's new opera.

My dissatisfaction stems from the fact that the opera is too splendid, too astonishing.

I shall state my opinion frankly. A first hearing of *Ruslan* in its entirety produces the wearying effect which we experience on reading very learned books in which every word is full of intricate and original meaning, every phrase is the summit of art and every period an ocean of pearls of genius. The attention has to pause over every word in order to grasp and exhaust all the intelligence and talent wrapped up in it. Reading it is hard. Blinded by the continuous firework display of multi-coloured lights, the reader is worn out by the third page. You have to read it through in peace four times in order to understand everything, to appreciate everything, to admire everything lit upon by chance sufficiently, before you can read the book from beginning to end with complete and free delight. In music, Beethoven's *Fidelio* in particular is like that; so is Weber's *Oberon*; so in general terms are many parts of the scores of Mozart and Meyerbeer: and this can be found conspicuously in celebrated magic operas[28] which are always based on great originality of form and details, since they express not feelings but ideas. Glinka's *Ruslan and Lyudmila* too is like this.

All the best musical compositions may be divided into two kinds: compositions which from the very first hearing send everyone into raptures and then gradually become less and less absorbing until at length they appear rather boring, and compositions to which we must listen carefully several times and which delight us the more the oftener we hear them.

Ruslan and Lyudmila belongs to the second kind of compositions in the company of *Fidelio*, *Oberon* and many other famous works of the harmonic school.[29] [. . .]

If the fate of all great artistic creations were decided by the first impressions of casual listeners and people of genius were obliged to give in to them, then Mozart, Beethoven and Weber would have had to consign the scores of *Don Giovanni*, *Fidelio* and *Oberon* to the flames the day after they were completed. These three immortal operas won renown precisely through

---

28 The term *Zauberoper* is used of operas which make great demands on stage machinery and for spectacular effects; it applies particularly to works in the Viennese *Singspiel* tradition. Works which exhibit some of its features include *Die Zauberflöte*, Kauer's *Das Donauweibchen* and Weber's *Oberon*. The title-page of *Ruslan and Lyudmila* describes it as a *volshebnaya opera* ('magic opera').

29 The 'harmonic school' is probably represented by works in which melodic beauty holds a lower priority than in, for example, Italian opera.

careful study of their treasures. The number of examples could be increased, but *Don Giovanni*, *Fidelio* and *Oberon* are more than enough.

The conclusion is that we, casual listeners, we, the bulk of the public, must give way before genius. But we find that hard! In music, we regard as geniuses those who are our slaves, our victims; and not without some justification: because music for us is a fleeting, momentary enjoyment.

This conflict will continue until the end of time. Meanwhile, Glinka has done well not to give in to us sooner. The more we study his new opera now the more treasures we discover in it, and the fuller does our enjoyment become.

I stated last month that our composer has written not a magic opera – that vein is exhausted – but an opera in the manner of a Russian fairy-tale, a fairy-tale opera (*opera-skazka*). This is a gigantic undertaking, because our fairy-tales, hyperborean in name, are derived from the same source as the Thousand-and-One Nights, and there is a combination in such a subject of the despondency of the northern snows with the wild massifs of the Caucasus, Asiatic languor, Moslem voluptuousness, Tatar coarseness, the brilliant and ungovernable fantasy of the East and the cheerful playfulness of the West, to which we belong as Slavs and Europeans. A man of genius is needed just to tackle and come to terms with all the aspects of a subject like this. To realize it in music, to realize it as subtly, intelligently and success-fully as is done in *Ruslan and Lyudmila*, almost surpasses what is possible at all. The person who gives due consideration to this matter must involun-tarily be struck by the scale of Glinka's achievement. But since this type of opera is new there are thus far no models to follow, so that in order to make an assessment of it one must have recourse in part to the elements of magic operas which most closely resemble fairy-tale operas.

A magic opera is a series of pictures or ideas, not a poetic development of certain feelings of the heart. It does not touch, but rather charms the imagination. Passion falls silent before the might of supernatural powers. *The Magic Flute* is just such a series of pictures as *Ruslan and Lyudmila*.

If we begin to recall and even give consideration to the music of the most celebrated magic operas, for example *The Magic Flute*, *Der Freischütz*, *Oberon* and so on and so forth, we shall observe that their composers did not portray the natural feelings of the heart. They expressed new ideas; and to express the newness of the ideas, the unusualness of the supernatural sit-uations, they always tried to be different from their predecessors by means of novelty particularly in instrumentation and in overcoming difficulties. Each composer was more or less successful in achieving his aim precisely by this method. Mozart, who was always simple and natural in combining sounds of various kinds, orchestrates with far more intricacy and complexity in *The Magic Flute* than in all the rest of his operas and introduces almost unperformable contours into the singing: for instance, the Queen of the Night's aria, which contains absolutely nothing but collections of sounds arranged in the most capricious way and at such high pitches that only the occasional good singer is able to perform them even moderately well. *Der Freischütz* and *Oberon*, more than all magic operas, are remarkable for the brilliance of their orchestration. Almost everything rests on the orchestra, as in Glinka's new opera. If the melodies in *Freischütz*, which are based on the Bohemian national character, were understood almost everywhere right from the start, that is because even before that they were spread throughout Europe like tooth-powders. The melodies in Glinka's first opera were immediately understood in Russia in exactly the same way. In *Oberon* Weber wished to rise higher. In *Freischütz* he told an old fairy-tale through contemporary tunes; but in *Oberon*, on the other hand, he tried to search for an ancient melodic expression and real ancient colourings for an old fairy-tale. In *Oberon* he is more truthful, loftier, more skilful, but on that account is not understood by casual listeners, and this immortal creation has not enjoyed positive success on the stage anywhere, while at the same time being the object of boundless astonishment to those who have studied and grasped its treasures.

Contours or melodies, instrumentation, and colourings for time and place – these, it follows, are the three important respects in which magic operas must be considered.

Let us consider and evaluate Glinka's fairy-tale opera from these points of view.

It is highly desirable that readers of this critique should first have read the text of *Ruslan and Lyudmila*, which is incorporated in the present number of this journal with that in mind. A knowledge of the text is absolutely essential if what I want to say is to be perfectly clear.

As regards [melodic] contour, there is no doubt at all that this fairy-tale opera is by no means inferior to any one of its magic rivals and probably surpasses many of the most famous.

The contour of Bayan's song (no. 1) is something truly Ossianic in an ancient Russian manner. It is impossible to divine the tones of remote, venerable antiquity with more profound instinctive genius. The living breath of Kievan antiquity is in the weighty movement of this fine melody; it is pure antiquity with all the solemnity of great age; your heart tells you that if the old bards sang, it was exactly thus: you cannot conceive any other representation of that time in sound. In a word, the *idea* of Normano-Russian antiquity is expressed superbly by the composer, and I would place Bayan's song in D major among the most successful of musical inspirations.

The contours of the choruses which accompany this song and the entire princely banquet of pagan times are immortal in the same respect. It is not like Napoleon's generals holding a party, but a genuine banquet of fabled heroes, colossal people inconceivable in Nature. There is nothing here of the present day, of the most modern times, nothing petty: everything is majestic, original, ancient – the very idea of the strength of the ancient warriors, their power, their *bogatïr'* courage is embodied in sound with inimitable art.

All of a sudden Lyudmila's cavatina (for soprano, no. 2) stands out wonderfully against this heroic background. How delicate is its outline! What an enchanting melody! How gently, from afar – from distant antiquity – it foreshadows present-day Russian melodies while, however, containing nothing of the present!

How much virgin sorrow, how much graceful feminine cheerfulness, how much happiness, hope, humour, irony reside in this cavatina, its every note filled with wit – so that it amounts to a whole poem in itself. The allegro 'Ne gnevis', znatnïy gost'' ('Do not be angry, exalted guest') and 'Pod roskoshnïm nebom yuga' ('Beneath the splendid sky of the south') is especially charming, lines which Lyudmila sings in G major to Farlaf and Ratmir.

Spurning all conventional forms, Glinka – I do not know why – avoids even repetitions of motives: it is very artistic, but very disadvantageous for him. Repetitions of motives, so common in Italian operas and indeed in Weber's *Freischütz*, have the advantages firstly of reducing the composer's labours and secondly of benefiting his reputation since the motives imprint themselves in the listeners' minds even at a single performance. Had Glinka decided to make use of this trick, every listener would have taken Lyudmila's charming *rondoletto* out of the theatre with him.

The design of the finale of Act I supports all these first-rate beauties superbly with new treasures of the same kind. Suddenly a clap of thunder is heard (no. 3) and Lyudmila is abducted by the magician Chernomor who envelops the banqueters in cold and gloom. This gloom, this horror, this freezing to the spot, and then the awakening of the father, the spouse, the heroes, their amazement, the summons to the chase, 'O vityazi, skorey vo chisto pole' ('O heroes, quickly into the open field') in E flat major (no. 3), the despair – all these things are portrayed in sound with such exceptional art, such powerful musical thought that one cannot fail to place these passages among the finest creations of recent music.

Act II opens with the ballad of Finn the wizard. A further new idea is expressed here too – that of the ancient Finnish North. In a foggy, distant way the motive recalls genuine Finnish melodies. To begin with, there is a cool narrative constantly accompanied by a single motive in A major. Then suddenly, in the course of the recollections, passions are aroused. This calm and these emotions are sketched in incomparably: how this movement is warmed by feeling! How agitated is the recounting of the recollections! How marvellously does passion flare up at the words 'Akh, i teper', odin, odin' ('Ah, now too, alone, alone', no. 5). The narrative is long: and at the same time how short it is thanks to the swiftness and variety of musical movement! Moreover, the instrumentation of this section deserves to be marvelled at. Another composer would have turned Finn's ballad into passionate song, and it would have turned out vulgar. With the steadfastness of a real artist, Glinka has kept within the boundaries of the heart of the matter without despising such a convenient opportunity to act with effect on unthinking listeners, and – we are most grateful to him. This is a model of epic music.

Farlaf's aria (a rondo, no. 7) strikes me as an addition. It is manifestly introduced to set off the precious strict design with an amusing grotesque buffo, to contrast the gloomy *idea* of the Finnish North with the jolly *idea* of the European South. In this respect Farlaf's rondo in F major is an extremely successful creation, and it would be a pity to leave it out. This jest boils over with life, *bravura*, bragging; it is swift, instantaneous, without preparation, and the Allegro of Farlaf's aria 'Pri mïsli obladat' knyazhnoy / Serdtse radost' oshchushchayet ('At the thought of enjoying the princess / My heart feels joyful'), where 'Presto' is written, has no rival in all of Rossini and is no whit inferior to the famous aria of the Negro in the same style in Mozart's *The Magic Flute*.

Then comes Ruslan's marvellous aria 'O pole, pole! kto tebya useyal myortvïmi kostyami?' ('O field, field! Who has strewn the bones of the dead across you?' no. 8), sung in masterly fashion by O. A. Petrov. This Andante in E major[30] is thoroughly novel in contour, feeling and movement. With inimitable faithfulness these sounds depict a *bogatïr*'s despair, the depression of a glorious hero who, wandering through a fearful wasteland, sees a heap of bones on the giants' battlefield of old and grieves at the thought that he will perish here unknown with no bards to sing of him. However fantastic this human situation may be, it nonetheless contains ideas of time, place and noble feeling which needed to be depicted in melody and which are depicted superlatively, such that even apart from its truthfulness and character this aria abounds in great beauties of strictly musical thought. Its incomparable Allegro portrays most skilfully *bogatïr' bravura* combined with tender reminiscence of Lyudmila, composed with the same power as Caspar's big aria in *Freischütz* but with the difference that no one carries away in his head any motive from Caspar's aria, whereas it is impossible to get the

30 Actually, a Largo in E minor.

delightful beginning 'O, Lyudmila! Lel' sulit mne radost'' ('O, Lyudmila! Lel' promises me joy', no. 8) out of your head once you have hear it twice.

Here the fog clears and amidst the bones the colossal Head of a dead giant can be seen; this is one of Roller's[31] miracles of scenery – he has scattered his miracles of brush and perspective throughout this whole opera. Inside the Head is the men's chorus who sing in a sepulchral tone in unison. The huge lips stir, the mouth opens, the eyes roll; the whole Head, detached from the giant's torso, follows Ruslan's movements. This scene creates a powerful effect of terror both pictorially and musically. Strict truth is maintained in the melody's contour. The successions and combinations of chords accompanying the deathly voice of the Head are so new that their like can be found nowhere else. These ten lines for the Head (nos. 9–10) can safely be ranked with the Commendatore's statue's answer in *Don Giovanni*. The Head's entire narrative is distinguished by the lofty qualities of truth, simplicity and art. But while giving full credit to the composer's genius I should declare here that I am not in favour of this Head. It is fine, but too long, far too long. By remaining too long on the stage the Head at length loses all the effectiveness which it achieved to begin with. It ought to have appeared for an instant, given answers in two or three short phrases and then disappeared, and not embarked on telling stories however musically wonderful. The idea is marvellous, the melody is a triumph, the orchestral playing is superb; but the impossibility of selecting many completely regular voices for the choir which sings inside the Head and the danger of continuing with such singing should have made the composer stop. At the point where the carrying-out of an idea becomes impossible a genius must be the first to desist. It is a pity, but this scene must be shortened. And since I have started to raise objections, I shall not stop with the Head. The composer has poured so many beautiful things, so many excellent things, into the first two acts that by diluting them a little with commonplaces and conventional forms to allow the listener's attention occasional relaxation there should be enough for a brilliant four-act opera. One must show mercy towards our span of attention and not tire it with a surfeit of intense pleasure which can quickly turn to boredom! In Nature all intense pleasures are of brief duration. However magnificent these two acts may be, however artistically created, some shortening of them would be greatly to the advantage of the work itself. Glinka significantly shortened Bayan's song in Act I before the performance; but the freezing scene still comes across in the theatre as too long: here at least the ritornello could be cut out. Nor would it be bad to shorten Finn's ballad and Ruslan's aria in Act II, even if only at the

---

31 A. A. Roller (1805–91). This artist was the principal set-designer of the imperial theatres in St Petersburg from 1834. He was an Academician from 1839.

beginning. I shall point later to the need for many abridgements in the last three acts. These things will not be lost: we shall wonder at them and be better able to appreciate them when we play the opera over at home after publication. On the stage one cannot afford to give expression to everything that is beautiful at the one time!

Act III is set in a magical country of the East where Persian and Arab character predominates. This act opens with one of the most captivating melodies in the Arab manner which I have ever come across. The wonderful scenery in a mixture of Arabic and Persepolis styles immediately defines this character for the eye, while the music enchantingly portrays it in sound for the ear. The maidens' chorus in E major, Gorislava's charming cavatina (no. 13), a kind of duet for soprano and bassoon – a pearl of the entire opera in feeling in the melody, in wit and delicacy of finish – Ratmir's fine aria in E-flat major with recitative (no.14) for contralto and cor anglais, are called forth from the East and brilliantly assimilated to European music. Every grace-note here, the fall of every phrase are decidedly new in the art of music. By virtue of the novelty of the motives the accompaniment is like a kind of commentary on the voice. At first these motives may seem incomprehensible but subsequently, on attentive examination of the beauty of their design, they will win over everyone by their allure. Here, then in the ballet in Act IV and finally in Ratmir's aria in Act V (contralto with muted orchestra), the composer has demonstrated the greatest boldness, originality and profound understanding both in the melody and the accompaniments imitating the voice and in the whole course of the harmony. In Ratmir's aria accompanied by an imitation of the human voice in the cor anglais the composer wished, it would appear, to represent the effect of hypnotic fascination. No one has ever succeeded in this, and neither has Glinka. It cannot be represented! He ought not to have tried to do something which is obviously impossible and which, being unsuccessful, is capable of spoiling movement and effect. One can represent the consequences of this enchantment – desire, voluptuousness, violent passion, and these are represented to perfection by the composer in the Allegro 'Chudnïy son lyubvi zhivoy' ('Magical dream of real love', no. 14). He should have begun with these words. They are a storm of passion in sound, something completely understood by every listener. In my opinion Act III demands the most significant cuts. Glinka will carry them out without fail to the patent benefit of his fine creation. He will probably shorten in just this way Ratmir's aria, and ask for Gorislava's cavatina to begin with the words in A minor 'Lyubvi roskoshnaya zvezda!' ('Love's sumptuous star!', no. 13) which blazing up in a wonderful musical phrase will constitute a splendid effect with the preceding contour and, most importantly, will shorten an excessively long scene. The ballet in this act is also open to substantial curtailment: the dances of the maidens who entice Ratmir are charming; the music for the dances is filled with incomparable grace, languor and voluptuousness. But all this is long, too long, far too long; it detracts from the impact of the most magnificent and original ballet in Act IV. This most interesting ballet, the most important one in the opera, appears to be too short by comparison with the ballet-scene casually allowed into Act III. Is there not a simple solution to the problem of the ballet of seductresses? In my view all magic occurrences should be brief: as soon as the dumbfounded spectator comes to his senses they cease to be magical. When Act III has been thus pruned and, after a momentary appearance by the seductresses, the action moves straight on to the incomparable transformation of the wonderful castle into the miraculous forest (no. 16), leaving out a large part of the finale which, for all its musical merits, does not in reality make the desired impression, then the effect of the third act, I am convinced, will be wholly charming.

We should not forget the forest. Roller who created it is truly an artist! Six or seven planes form one of the most beautiful forest perspectives. Nature is counterfeited to the point of complete deception. Many of the sets for the new opera are incomparably more magnificent; but art itself resides in this forest.

Let us go back to the music.

Act IV is a colossal creation, which will remain forever in music as a monument to what a great talent can accomplish with sounds, scales and instruments when all these elements are obedient to his powerful will. If this act is not understood, then probably it is not Glinka's fault, and the loss is not his but ours, I am ashamed to say, who do not always understand great things. There are such things here as the genius of Beethoven himself would have been proud to produce.

The castle of the evil magician Chernomor is suspended somewhere above the mountain-tops of the Caucasus. All is strange, wild, evil, capricious, caricatured, but at the same time marvellous, because magicians are the richest people to be found anywhere in Nature: they have a right to all the gold hidden in the bowels of the earth and like to enjoy it. The set designer and the composer were obliged to represent this impossible quality, one in colours for the eye, the other in sounds for the ear. Mr Roller showed his unusually ingenious imagination here. The fantastic and utterly improbable architecture of the many palaces covered in gold, surrounded by fountains and reflected in an enormous lake instantly gives one an idea of the extravagant taste, savage disposition and frightening power of Chernomor. Everything here is out of a fairy-tale, like Chernomor himself. Roses blossom in shells of pearl, boughs of long peacock feathers flutter on the palm-trees, and trees with silver trunks and golden leaves yield diamond and ruby fruit. All the wildness of the brigands' Caucasus and the ugliness of black Ethiopia submit to the power of Chernomor and make up his court. To depict this in sounds, to write this in the air with notes is a musical task such as would scare any composer. It is clear that our European music and our scale are not up to a feat like this. The music of devils has been imitated quite faithfully before now: but those devils were our own ones, they knew our scale, and in hell it is impossible that there should not be a great many of our composers and musicians. The music of the nether regions is of necessity a mixture of Italian and German features. It is not difficult, it's true, to imitate the wildness of hell's music, to compose *les valses infernales*. But it is difficult to cope with Chernomor! He does not recognize our devils: he has his own infidel ones; and they have their own scale made up of eighteen notes, instead of our twelve, which is quite incapable of adaptation to our instruments. Compose something, if you please, to suit the taste of this monster and for the strange festivities which he puts on for Lyudmila in his castle. Draw on your genius and use our instruments with their dozen notes and our harmonic resources to imitate this little scale, its vile works, its sharp and penetrating sounds, and to depict all the evil of Chernomor, all the wildness of his Caucasian court, all the infidel features of these unbelievers, and at the same time amuse us, the spectators of these unholy festivities, do not drive us away by disorder – on the contrary: compel us to find special charm in this grotesque music! Observe the important difference between the situation of those composers who have written devilish music successfully and the task presented to our Russian composer: the former imitated music as they imagined it which no one had heard, for which, moreover, they had a ready-made scale; our composer had to imitate music which really exists, he had in front of him a new, special musical nature which had to be transferred to our art and expressed by means of our resources. To judge the value of a musical creation one must carefully look into the essence of all parts of the subject treated in sound: but such an investigation will reveal that in the composer who did not take fright at such difficulties and indeed emerged from them victorious we have one of the very greatest talents ever to have existed in music, ever to have wielded the weapons of sound. It is terrifying to the imagination to delve into the artistic conditions for this act, into the courage of a man who undertakes to carry it out and into the astounding, unexampled manner in which he has done so. At every turn one must be new, original, unusual; one must encompass the whole science of sound, harmony and counterpoint with infinite knowledge; one must discover new resources within this science through sheer genius, and create everything out of nothing.

One may be wild, and only wild, without imparting anything elegant to one's wildness. But combining two such dissimilar elements is a triumph of art, and a triumph for Glinka.

Three different orchestras including a military band come into action all of a sudden during the festivities which Chernomor puts on along with the fantastic ballet of his own sorcerous devising: two orchestras above, on the stage, and the third below, underneath the stage. Each one, naturally, plays something different, yet they must together form a single harmonious whole. The imitation of the Asiatic scale and the colouring of Caucasian melodies is obtained exclusively by novel harmonic turns, incomplete chords, dissonances and by special exceptionally complex instrumentation. And at the same time everything merges into a single graceful whole, into the wittiest, most artistic grotesque which there has ever been in music. It is a masterpiece of counterpoint! It is the summit of harmonic thought! One can go no further or higher. The prankish rising chromatic scale in the military trumpets on the one hand separated from the splendid mass of wind sound and on the other blended with the nasal sounds of the bassoons, the pearly passage-work of the piano, the sonorous tinkling of two-and-a-half octaves of glockenspiel – this is a ploy worthy of Beethoven! At this point Mrs Andreyanova[32] dances the *lezginka*[33] with her especial deftness and grace.

It is already sufficiently clear that to form a correct judgement of Glinka's new opera it is absolutely essential to study it by attentive and repeated listening and to grasp the work in all its internal details. In this ocean of musical erudition every drop is a novel, ingenious or inspired feature. But then it is not easy to listen to an opera like this, I must confess! The constitution of the nerves is quickly worn out by the heavy labour of constantly straining all one's attention. Inattentiveness exposes one continually to the danger of pronouncing the most mistaken judgements. The composer himself will draw the logical conclusion that it is highly awkward to write too profoundly erudite operas for the great majority of unlearned listeners.

But I have broken away from the natural sequence of my review. Act IV does not begin with the festivities. After the raising of the curtain there comes the wonderful appearance in perspective of the mermaids bathing and hiding in the lake. It is mainly wind instruments in the orchestra which portray the lapping of the water disturbed by the mermaids. The instrumentation of this remarkable section is handled with inexpressible subtlety. Nothing better will be found in the whole of *Oberon*. Then, Lyudmila's

---

32 Ye. I. Andreyanova (1819–57) was the first Russian Gisèle in 1842 and the first Russian ballerina to appear abroad – in Hamburg, London, Paris and Milan from 1845.

33 This is a fast dance originally of the Lezgian people, in duple time, found throughout the Caucasus.

scene ('Vdali ot milogo v nevole' – 'Far from my loved one in captivity', in B minor, no. 18) with the invisible chorus of maidens: this is a scene of great musical effectiveness. Later on come Lyudmila's aria 'Akh, tï, dolya dolyushka' ('Ah, you, fate, fate'), the Adagio in D minor, including an incomparable motive, a kind of duet for contralto[34] and violin on the G string, and the golden trees play chimes. Then there is Chernomor's march in A minor with three orchestras, the grotesque ballet, and the finale 'Pobeda, pobeda!' ('Victory, victory!') in C minor, – 'Skoreye, skoreye v otchiznu' ('As fast as we can to our homeland') in A flat major, and so on. The whole cast of melody is new in the highest degree. Even among fantastic music there has scarcely been anything like it before. With an act such as this up his sleeve a composer can set off directly towards posterity without raising his hat to contemporary critics on the way.

But is this act without stain or reproach in all particulars? No! Some of its beauties are rather prolonged. For theatrical effectiveness one must shorten a little the beginning and the finale, especially the finale, and move more quickly straight to Kiev and the wonderful court of Prince Svetozar (no. 27), leaving out altogether the whole of the beginning of Act V, the whole scene in the *valley*, all of Ratmir's delightful, original, marvellously-scored aria [romance] in D flat major for contralto with muted strings in the orchestra, however dear it might be to the composer, however fascinating A. Ya. Petrova's[35] intelligent singing of it. This *morceau* is not for the stage, that is, it is too subtle for the stage, and it holds back the speed with which magnificent scenes must appear and disappear in a magic opera.

In the first three performances Act V began with precisely this scene in the valley, to whose musical merits I have given due acknowledgement; but I have heard that Glinka himself intends to omit it in subsequent performances. Thus we can go directly to the court with the luxurious brocade curtain concealing the pictorial view of ancient Kiev. The motive of the chorus in D minor, 'Radost', schast'ye yasnoye' ('Joy, serene happiness') in B flat major, and 'Slava velikim bogam' ('Glory to the great gods'), in D major (no. 27) – this is a lament from a heart in soul-rending distress, with plaints of grief in all their natural simplicity. The finale's design (no. 27) is very intricate, and it portrays vividly the feelings of triumphant joy with which the piece ends. There is nothing at all to shorten here. It is short and excellent!

If I were to go through the score of the new opera in this way, starting to count the excellent musical motives, I would have to agree that scarcely any opera, magic or not, offers so many musical contours of classic undying merit.

Let us look now at the work's scoring. The instrumentation of *Ruslan and Lyudmila* may be called an unbroken chain of exceedingly erudite ideas and

34 In fact, for soprano.   35 For Vorob'yova-Petrova, see note 18 above.

successful novelties in modulation and using the instruments themselves. Every connoisseur will recognize that among the most recent composers there is none to rival Glinka in instrumentation. His orchestration is the equivalent of a real picture by a great artist. It is a colour on Bryullov's[36] palette. The barely noticeable breath of the clarinet alters the whole amalgam of the sounds. The isolated sound of a string gives the ear an imperceptible sting and creates a new aural sensation. Lights and shades in sound are laid out over all the musical ideas in an exceptionally pictorial and perfectly natural way. Nowhere is there a crashing din, and there is not a single vulgarity. Pure, elegant, noble good taste reigns everywhere. The singing is kept wonderfully apart from the orchestral accompaniment, and neither harms the other anywhere, since they are separate; together, they constitute a masterly, harmonious picture: this is one of Glinka's triumphs which, I may say in passing, will scarcely be understood and appreciated by his ordinary judges. In the majority of well-known operas it seems as if the composer has grown tired by the third or fourth act, and the instrumentation is weaker. In *Ruslan and Lyudmila* there is not the slightest trace of this deficiency: on the contrary, the composer's art seems to grow stronger with each act, and goes on crescendo right up to the last one. But these nuances elude literary description: one would need to refer to numbered bars in the score. In this respect I have already indicated in passing at several points skilful and new uses of instruments, many passages in the violin parts, the contest or fusion of orchestras – I do not know what to call it – while retaining various contours (counterpoint); and other always successful characteristics of which there is an abundance, even a superabundance, in the new opera. Glinka has been a spendthrift, a prodigal in this area. Perhaps that will be his undoing. It is said that his instrumentation is too difficult. – But can it be performed? – Yes indeed! We have seen that a good orchestra can perform it excellently. Therefore, there is no question of difficulty. In fact, conductors and artists are in raptures over the instrumentation of *Ruslan and Lyudmila*, and all are unanimously astounded by it. Even those numbers which I have mercilessly condemned to banishment are irreproachable in respect of instrumentation.

It remains to say something about *couleur locale*. In surveying the work's design I pointed out in many numbers what places, what historical period, what morals and customs the composer had to represent. He had to sustain the most difficult battle. Our ears are nowadays under the yoke of European music, but *Ruslan and Lyudmila* is a Tatar fairy-tale in the purest Tatar tradition, a mixture of the East and the North. Glinka had to reconstruct the sound of the music which accompanied the joys and sorrows of people

36 For Bryullov, see note 16 above.

at the time when Rus' hobnobbed with Khazars[37] and Pechenegs,[38] and had no artistic contact with the nations whose people went about in top-boots. If Glinka, following Weber's example in *Der Freischütz*, had set underneath this ancient fairy-tale contemporary Russian national music, after filtering it as most recently through the Italian school, he would have enjoyed greater success but less deservedly. But he acted in the same way as Weber in *Oberon*, and his opera will probably share the fate of *Oberon*, towards which the public everywhere has remained more or less cold and which at the same time arouses enthusiasm among artists and experts.

In appraising *Ruslan and Lyudmila* even as a musical poem – if I could not get out of assigning it a place in accordance with its worth in the hierarchy of well-known operas – I should place it alongside *Oberon*, even though in my opinion the new Russian opera is in many respects superior to that work.

Our famous Russian composer should not be distressed either by decisive verdicts hastily uttered or by the analytical discussion to which I have subjected several sections of the opera after more leisurely investigation. For no talent on earth is it shameful for once in one's life to be in the position of the composer of *Fidelio* or *Oberon*. The example of *Fidelio* is a particularly striking one, and I believe that Glinka ought, indeed is obliged, to profit from it. This immortal opera which today along with *Don Giovanni* holds sway over all the most modern music did not stand up to its first performances. All of Vienna yawned. Without giving it much thought, the local critics declared Beethoven's opera boring, funereal, brief-case rubbish. At that time it had four acts. Beethoven trimmed it a bit. It was a failure again. He shortened it a little more. It failed again. Four times the unfortunate Beethoven shortened it, and four times it failed to achieve success. Finally he compressed it tightly into two acts, and only then was *Fidelio* successful. The fault did not lie with Beethoven, of course: his genius was unable to compose anything unworthy of the ears of his listeners and judges. The fault was with those who could not understand or appreciate him and who compelled him to eliminate half of the immortal treasures so that they could take away with them from the theatre a splendour of a quite different kind. The libretto was also to blame; it was more convoluted and in no wise better than *Ruslan and Lyudmila*, of whose merit readers may form their own judgement. I append the libretto here as a document. When the world

37 Rus': name used from the ninth century for the territory of the eastern Slavs. From at least the eighteenth century it was gradually supplanted by *Rossiya* ('Russia'). The Khazars were a people of the Turkic language group who from the fourth century roamed the west Caspian steppe.
38 The Pechenegs, a fusion of Turkic and other tribes in the Volga steppes in the eighth and ninth centuries, were to be found in the ninth century in the south Russian steppes.

of Russian letters produces such libretti for a composer, it must in conscience accept at least half of his responsibility.[39]

Mozart shortened and reworked many of his best operas several times. Weber cut *Oberon* very significantly after the first performance. Meyerbeer used to cut almost all his operas, particularly *Robert le diable*, although Meyerbeer has never risked a first performance without success being 'in the bag'.

The general conclusion is this: that *Ruslan and Lyudmila* must be cut; but cut broadly, generously, as Beethoven did it, if it is to be an opera for production in the theatre. Then its success will be complete: the treasures which remain will be understood better and more quickly.

I know that our celebrated composer intends to make cuts, and I say all this in order to rouse him to the necessary magnanimous sacrifice to the fundamental weakness of human nature. We really do not have the strength to listen to such learned music for over three hours! We can listen to trivialities with pleasure for as long as you like – even five hours! The proof is ... But that would take us into personalities. We don't need proofs.

I have had occasion to mention the services of Mr Roller as designer several times in the course of this article. It is no exaggeration to say that not a single magic opera has been offered to the public in a more brilliant or more artistic form. For his drawings for these poetic fantasies and for their erudite perspective the Imperial Academy of Fine Arts has honoured Mr Roller by electing him a Member of the Academy. That is the best evidence of the great merit of his work.

The *Reading Library* makes it a rule not to review the performance of artists who appear on the stage and I am very sorry that this unalterable rule denies me the opportunity of giving due praise also to the talented singers who took part in Glinka's new opera.

I cannot refrain from speaking with astonishment and gratitude about the generosity of the Directorate of the Imperial Theatres which has supported the work of a Russian composer with genuine patriotic zeal, with the solicitude of an enlightened patron of creative talent, and with the liberality of Harun-al-Rashid. The Directorate has spared nothing – effort, expense or its own love of art – to ensure that this work came before the public in the manner most advantageous to it. Fortunate is the composer who encounters along his thorny path such a theatre administration.

---

39 As the phrase 'the world of Russian letters' perhaps suggests, several writers had a hand in devising the libretto, a process even more chaotic than in the case of *A Life for the Tsar.*

(e) V. F. Odoyevsky: Notes for my great-great-grandson on the literature of our day and other things. *Fatherland Notes*, 1843, vol. 26, section 8, pp. 94–100. *MLN*, pp. 204–12

This item is credited to one Plakun Goryunov, retired titular counsellor ('Weeper Wretchling, retired clerical officer Grade 8' might give something of the flavour). The pseudonym is merely one aspect of a literary game played by an experienced practitioner. The other proper name mentioned, that of Mr Bichev, refers to a whip or, metaphorically, a scourge.

The author was deadly serious in his intention to counteract the widespread failure of sympathy and understanding which Glinka's operas encountered. In the *Literary Supplement to the Russian War Veteran* (30 January 1837, no. 5, pp. 43–5; *MLN*, pp. 126–30) he had castigated the champions in words only of Russian art who, faced with an example of it in reality, clung to their preference for what was familiar and estimable because foreign, who found Glinka's music barbarous, and who displayed poor (or no) musical taste; the highest aristocracy were included among his targets there. His aim here is similar, though the musical background is fuller.

It's a very long time since I wrote to you, my dear great-great-grandson – but what can one do! I've had no time! I ran into the shareholders of a magazine which has as many as three publishers, each one cleverer than the other.

On one occasion when I was trying to remember (my memory's already weakened by old age) what I might amuse you with, the bell rang. 'Who's that?'

'Mr Bichev would like to talk to you about a matter of his own.'

'I don't have the honour of knowing him; but ask him in.'

A young man came in, quite decently dressed, bowed politely and said: 'Are you the publisher of a magazine?'

'No, my dear sir; I know nothing at all about that, I've never been caught out in that business.'

'Could you not at least give me some help to get a short letter printed in some magazine or other . . . ?'

And with these words he took from his coat a rather thick notebook.

'The only thing I can do for you is to pass the letter on to my great-great-grandson . . .'

'To whoever you please – all I want is for my letter not to have been written fruitlessly; I took it to a journalist I know but he turned me down flat and said that my letter contains nothing that would amuse the public.'

I skimmed through the notebook and noticed at once that my new acquaintance was susceptible to an unfortunate weakness: he had faith in the existence of literature, art, music and other such things which are not spoken about in polite circles nowadays. What a shame, a real shame – such a fine young man!

Since I had given my word, I had to keep it. 'I am sending your manuscript to my great-great-grandson, my dear sir, and by the first post.'

'I'm extremely grateful. Would you permit me to impart to you in the future excerpts from my extensive correspondence?'

'Why not? There is plenty of space in my packets.'

'Here, for instance, is a letter to a friend of mine who owns a stocking factory about ways of protecting his purse against bad concerts, unscrupulous journals and speculations in book-selling . . . Will you allow me to bring them to you?'

'That would be very kind. It sounds like a sensible subject . . . I'll put it straight into a packet . . . but, the next time round . . .'

At that we parted. I liked that young man a great deal, so it was difficult to deny him anything. Oh, if it were not for his unfortunate weakness! What a shame, a real shame! A fine young man! You will say the same when you have read the letter which I'm sending with this one . . . I've torn the beginning off it – it dealt with his domestic relations with the journalist; but I think maybe something about that has been left in as well – forgive me: old age made me overlook it. Now read on.

Ruslan and Lyudmila, *the opera by the Russian musician Glinka (excerpt from a letter to a journalist)*

. . . and please be so kind as to tell the typesetter to be more careful and in general terms to read the proofs more meticulously: printing errors and omissions always give rise to misunderstandings. Just the other day I read somewhere, I don't recall where, one gentleman's declaration that 'at a performance of *Ruslan and Lyudmila* the public was cold and that neither the gentleman nor the public could understand this opera'.[40] There is obviously a slip there: the matter in hand is definitely not the St Petersburg public but apparently the public in Yekateringof, that is the public which acquired its musical education at Sunday festivities in Yekateringof or on Krestovsky Island[41] from the sound of the Tyrolean guitar or the barrel-organ. It is quite possible that the public of that sort did not understand the new opera; but I can assure you that I did not miss a single performance

---

40 Odoyevsky refers to Bulgarin's article 'Pervïye vpechatleniya, proizvedyonnïye operoyu "Ruslan i Lyudmila"' ('First impressions of the opera *Ruslan and Lyudmila*'), published in *The Northern Bee* of 1 December 1842, no. 269.
41 Both Yekateringof and Krestovsky Island were places of resort for the public of St Petersburg. The former was a suburban park with an old palace, while on the latter was the Krestovsky Garden, the capital's oldest suburban place of entertainment.

and saw and heard how the real St Petersburg public called four times in succession for the composer of the music; and how could it give any other reception to the new opera which, with *A Life for the Tsar*, has raised Russian music for the first time to the same level as the best works of the most recent music, to say the least? On the contrary, as I observed it, with each performance the public discovered new previously unnoticed treasures in the new opera, and is more and more able to comprehend all the charm, all the freshness of the melodies in which it is so rich; features which went unnoticed at the first performances are being accepted with genuine unfeigned delight at subsequent ones. It is precisely this gradual but long-lasting effect which is produced by strongly original music springing from the soul of a man of great talent; it is not an outburst of enthusiasm from friends gathered for the first performance which dies with the first performance, as happened with *Shnuka Nyukarlebi*[42] of blessed memory. All that is spurious will fail; the success of what is truly excellent becomes more and more firmly established with every day that passes. There is nothing new in this – it is quite natural; thus it has been with all works of true genius from Mozart's *Don Giovanni* up to and including *Ruslan and Lyudmila*. Appreciation of the beauties of brilliantly original music does not come easily at first hearing like a couplet from a vaudeville: it is essential to listen attentively; Meyerbeer's *Robert* at first seemed to be nonsense to ears unfamiliar with it, but the more we grew accustomed to it the more we liked it. This is all quite natural but, I repeat, the mistakes of a typesetter in a well-ordered printing-house are not natural. You will agree yourself – is it not strange? The public thinks one thing, feels one thing, then calmly goes to bed, wakes up in the morning and is brought an announcement that it thought and felt something completely different, and why? – all because of a printing error. The virtuous gentleman innocently intended to please the *dilettanti* of the barrel-organ and to give expression to their judgement in print, maybe for a joke within the family, but the typesetter left out a whole word and the private opinion of these *dilettanti* was converted into the general opinion and a most strange and even offensive absurdity was imputed to the whole public. Poor public! It is everywhere!

> Figaro quà,
> Figaro là,
> Figaro giù,
> Figaro su.

Tell them, if you please, I ask again, to be more careful about the proofs: misprints and slips always give rise to misunderstandings . . .

42 A drama written by Bulgarin and first performed in the circumstances alluded to on 1 September 1841.

And while we're on the subject of misunderstandings: please be so kind also as to explain my point of view to the readers also as clearly and in as much detail as possible; I consider this essential because I hope that with God's help this letter will not be the last. As you are aware, critics writing in the periodical press find themselves in a great difficulty; many gentlemen, no one knows who, no one knows why, take it unceremoniously upon themselves to be the representatives of public opinion and address the public rather, or as I would say, too, familiarly; they berate someone roundly, they mercilessly shower praise on someone else, and all the time quoting the public who have often never even heard of the person being praised or the person being criticized. Naturally then – who will dispute it? – one must salute the candour of these gentlemen: they issue their reproofs and their praises and then they give in and confess to their readers that 'I am guilty – I praised this one because we're related, out of nepotism, and in truth the thing I praised is quite worthless; and that one I censured sincerely, it's my fault; but now that I recognize the agreeable properties of what I condemned I see that I ought to have praised it, – which of us is without sin? Do not reproach or curse me.' This is all very well, and interesting in a way, and could provide a pleasant pastime for the family circle of a certain class of people – naturally, for those initiated into the secret. But put yourself in the public's position; they must guess whether these gentlemen write sincerely or in consequence of favouritism. It is very difficult for outsiders too: not everyone would wish to be viewed as someone belonging to this happy circle, or as someone who is angry without cause or as a permanent protector of his relatives. Therefore, dear sir, if on some occasion you wish to know my opinion about various matters of this world, please be so kind as to explain to the readers in more detail and if need be vouch for me as a man of even temper, generally of extremely good conduct who never gets angry, and should such a misfortune occur I never write in a fit of anger; add that I am a person of respectable behaviour who has not been found deceiving, faking or otherwise doing wrong, and has always conducted himself properly and decently; and do not forget to say that I have no relatives in the world of letters and I have no connection with anyone. I regard all these explanations as absolutely essential in the present state of literary affairs.

After thus cleansing my conscience I can now turn to the new opera and give you my opinion of it. I repeat, *my* opinion, for I lack the courage to pass off my opinion as that of the public in order to please my friends; to my mind, the public is hard to fathom; in this instance one can make a guess; but what the public actually thinks and why it thinks it God alone knows. For example: before considering what this one or that one thinks of the new music one should ask, for instance, whether he has heard it, and that too is a difficult and delicate matter. I am not speaking about the performance: that field has its own inveterate critics who will probably go over every note with a fine-tooth comb; my business is with the music as it actually is; fortunately it has been printed and put on sale, so that anyone may check my words against the notes themselves.

I reason thus in this regard: there are great musicians overseas – e.g. Meyerbeer, Halévy, Auber, perhaps even Bellini and Donizetti. Leaving aside all question of talent, these are all very experienced people. Libretti are written for them by Scribe or Romani; sometimes the initial idea lacks sense, but still it offers *dramatic scenes*, or situations, so that you find interest not only in the music but in the play itself; and the libretto is such an important thing that Spontini's famous *Olympia*, whose sets cost up to 300,000 roubles, and Cherubini's best operas *Lodoïska*, *Faniska* and *Anacréon* were killed stone dead by their libretti, whereas *The Watercarrier*, notwithstanding the fact that everyone learned the music off by heart and all the barrel-organs played it, held the stage for a long time thanks to the dramatic situations in the play itself. In addition, among musicians overseas there are such singers as Rubini, Tamburini, Lablache, García and Schröder-Devrient;[43] and if you give people like that even 'Pridi v chertog ko mne zlatoy' ('Come into my gilded hall')[44] to sing they will send you into raptures. The public overseas applauds the music in part, but principally they are applauding the singers; news of this applause eventually reaches us, and we, being educated and enlightened people, are ashamed to ask where exactly the applause was directed, or whether there might not be something banal, tasteless or second-hand about the music ... For heaven's sake, how could it be otherwise? Would they not then regard us in Europe as barbarians? And there is another matter: if a musician overseas has a single successful aria in his opera, and that aria passes through the vocal organs of someone such as Rubini, then the opera is saved; everybody wants to hear the splendid aria a thousand times, and thanks to it listens to the whole opera and becomes used to the music, and in the mind of everyone the opera acquires a charm similar to that which our national songs hold for us.

But all these are secondary matters which may apply or not in each country; but here is the most important thing: overseas people are extremely tired of those who imitate the imitators of Rossini, Bellini and Meyerbeer; everyone is looking for something new, and particularly for fresh melodies; it occurs to me that the sources of them have dried up in the West. You

43 Celebrated singers of the time – tenor, baritone, bass, bass-baritone and soprano respectively.
44 A popular aria from *Lesta, dneprovskaya rusalka* ('Lesta, Dnepr mermaid'), a Russian derivative of Ferdinand Kauer's *Das Donauweibchen*. The music for this version was the work of S. I. Davïdov (see Chapter 2, notes 19 and 21).

know the toy we call a musical kaleidoscope; it contains around 200 individual musical phrases on cut cards; put these cards together how you will, you will always have a new song or a new waltz, but, of course, it is always the same. Take any one of the newest melodies, analyse it carefully and you will find that in the main they are put together just as in the musical kaleidoscope: here is the beginning from *Semiramide*, the middle section from *Il Barbiere* and the end from *La Sonnambula*; hence the stamp of monotony which is on all the newest melodies. There are people who like this very monotony, whose thick skull can be pierced only by a familiar phrase; their head nods in a sign of pleasure only at a familiar phrase, and then usually out of time. What can be done with such people? There was one lover of painting – this is not a fairy story – who liked Wouwerman's pictures because he could find a white horse in every one; but such art-lovers are neither painters nor musicians; everything that is not a familiar phrase seems to them wild or tedious; art-lovers like these have existed in all ages, but fortunately a musician's fame does not depend on them, and here is the proof: thanks to them, Mozart, whose simplicity and graceful-ness are so striking to us, was referred to by these gentlemen almost up to our time as *wild Mozart*! It is funny and strange to speak about such things, to prove that music is only music when it breathes freshness and originality, and not when it is always repeating one and the same thing. What would poets say if someone assured them that the best poem would be a collection of the most successful lines from Pushkin, Zhukovsky and Prince Vyazemsky, and that any other method of composing verses was no good? But is that not the very thing that some people who pose as lovers and even connoisseurs of music are saying? – The best of foreign composers understand the full value of a new melody; they know that it does not come without some special inspiration; many are seeking a new path: some, especially instru-mental composers, have stopped caring about new melody and are content with arranging the melodies of others; as a result we have thousands of fantasias, études and such like – all on the same melodies from *Sonnambula*, *Semiramide*, etc.; others try to conceal the lack of melody by means of various musical wiles. Meyerbeer is a great and highly experienced musician; no one has more respect than I for his knowledge and inventiveness, but do you find many fresh new melodies in his works? On the contrary, he seems to take deliberately an old trivial motive and bring it forward by means of unexpected, original and brilliant treatment and instrumentation. Take just the first chorus in *Robert*, which is so effective on the stage: 'Versez à tasses pleines' – what could be more trivial than that figure? It stands up only by virtue of the artistic way it is treated. Or take Isabelle's famous aria 'Grâce!' – what Italian operetta is without that figure? In the whole of *Robert* new original melodies are to be found perhaps only in the cello solo in the Act III dances; in Meyerbeer's *Les Huguenots* there is still less that is fresh. All this does not in any way reduce the merit of that great artist; on the contrary – he amazes us by the artistry with which he hides the insufficiency of his ideas by means of brilliant, graceful arrangement; but it is a talent for colouring, not a talent for inventing – a matter of labour and erudition but not inspiration. Of all musicians alive today only Rossini is noted for a rare gift of melody inspired from on high: only in his music (especially *Guillaume Tell*) do you find a luxuriance of motives of striking freshness; this gift is not to be obtained either by effort or experience; the appearance of people who possess this gift is an epoch-making event in artistic history; they place the impress of their personality on all the works of their time and shape what we call the musical style of a given period.

Throw Glinka's musical works on to these scales. The growth of his talent is a most remarkable phenomenon: he started off where others finish. As early as his first opera *A Life for the Tsar* you will find no trace of imitation; after profound study of the works of western music, Glinka listened closely to the tunes of his own country and tried to unlock the secret of their conception, their primordial elements, and to base upon them a new species of melody, harmony and music for opera, a species unprecedented until then. I know that many people doubt the existence of national (*narodnoy*) music, though they admit to distinctively national poetry, national architecture and national painting. This doubt stems from the fact that we have no way of looking at all the things which surround us other than through western spectacles; whereas perhaps in order to judge various facets of our Russian world correctly we need to adopt a point of view directly opposed to the western one. It was not without reason that in previous centuries the powerful Slav race was at odds with the western race; this enmity is founded on the distinctive but opposed elements of each race; these elements were opposed to such an extent that from the same cause there arose in both races different effects, and on the other hand – the same phenomenon arose from foundations which were completely opposed to one another.

I am aware that this observation demands special evidence in support which would be out of place here; but in the matter of music the evidence is to hand: one race in the European world possesses *distinctive, characteristic, national melody based on a complete scale* – among the Slav race this characteristic melody has been preserved in the depths of the Slav spirit from time immemorial. Only the Neapolitans have an equally special characteristic melody, but that, it would seem, has been imported from Africa, since you cannot find it in the rest of Italy. Furthermore, neither the Germans, nor the French, nor the English have a distinctive national music.

The Swiss and the Scottish musical character arises only from an incomplete scale; but, I repeat, characteristic melody in conjunction with a complete scale exists only.among the Slav race. Therefore it would be contrary to the truth to conclude from the fact that there is no national music in the West that it does not exist at all. So! it does not exist in the West, but for that very reason it exists among the Slav race; without further evidence for this, inner feeling and the ear will convince everyone: it is hard to distinguish a German or Italian melody from a French one, but you can identify an ancient Russian folksong among thousands of melodies, for it stands out sharply even to a foreigner. This distinctive musical character in Russian melody was noticed by Glinka; he was not afraid to base an entire opera on it in which he elevated it to the style of tragedy, an idea which had not entered anyone's head until then. By this heroic feat he laid the basis for a new era in music: *A Life for the Tsar* is the kernel out of which, as at one time from *Don Giovanni*, a whole period in music must grow. – *Ruslan and Lyudmila* is the second branch pointing in this direction: the Slav character in its *fantastic* vein is predominant in it; it represents our fairy-tale, our legend – but in musical terms; its Russian character is in contact with the boundless world of fantasy and is made more general without losing its distinctiveness. To seek the usual drama here would be pointless; drama in the fantastic, fairy-tale world has its own terms, which belong exclusively to that world; the struggle with people which forms one of the elements of earthly drama is eliminated here; but there remains another element – conflicts with oneself and with non-human forces; and the latter struggle is here so fierce that while it is present no other conflict could be of any interest. I must confess that I am an enemy of fantastic productions on the stage; the forms of the theatre are too coarse to depict the passions, vices, virtues, sufferings and joys of the world of fantasy. A stage production requires completeness and specificity, whereas the character of a fantastic work lies in its lack of specificity or in its extraordinary nature; a fantastic writer must be concerned with those sensations which are hidden in the depths of the soul of man and cannot be expressed in words, sensations which can only be hinted at, not spelled out in letters. But this is not relevant to music; through its boundless, unspecific form music can endow a stage production precisely with that which it lacks in order to have the right to be called fantastic. But another condition must be met in that case: it is necessary for the spectator to be capable of being lost in his own inner, mysterious world and of forgetting for a time all the elements of reality which surround him; this condition is the most difficult, because everything diverts the spectator – even the beauty of the sets. Irrespective of this last condition, music for a fantastic opera can only be written by such a talent as is able to

rely on the freshness of his ideas; in dramatic situations the stage complements the music, just as music complements the stage; often a poor musical
phrase achieves an effect only because it is accompanied by a dramatic
situation on the stage. An opera which is fantastic from beginning to end is
a different matter; for a listener whose soul is in the normal everyday state
the interest in such an opera is concentrated either on the music alone or
on the stage alone: among theatre-goers, who has heard, for instance, the
music for the scene of the casting of the bullets in *Der Freischütz*? Extremely
few people; all the others have been too busy watching and criticizing the
way the birds fly. I can state firmly that among European musicians of the
present day there is not a single one with the freshness of fantasy to sustain
an entire fantastic opera which would be always new and always original.
Point out to me, on the other hand, a single phrase from *Ruslan and Lyudmila*
which could be described as banal or hackneyed. That is precisely why this
opera does not appeal to some listeners – because 'it was not written for
them'. I have in mind simply listeners and not certain gentlemen who have
been writing about this opera, one of whom – it may have been the same
one – was once speaking with the air of an expert about the *harmonics on
the piano*[45] and could in no wise distinguish melody from harmony . . . Is
there any point in discussing such nonsense?

If I had a voice, and if I could suppose that anyone's opinion was
influenced in the slightest by the ignorant clamouring of those knights of
the 'piano harmonics', I would deliver this simple speech: 'Sirs! *Ruslan and
Lyudmila* contains twenty-one numbers;[46] they include the following:
Bayan's song, Lyudmila's cavatina "Ne gnevis', znatnïy gost'" ("Do not be
angry, exalted guest"), Finn's ballad, Ruslan's aria "O pole, pole" ("O field,
field"), the chorus "Lozhitsya v pole mrak nochnoy" ("Night's darkness
settles on the field"), Gorislava's aria "Lyubvi roskoshnaya zvezda" ("Love's
sumptuous star"), Ratmir's "I zhar i znoy" ("Both warmth and ardour"),
"Ona mne zhizn'" ("She is my life"), Lyudmila's aria "Vdali ot milogo"
("Far from my loved one"), the march and dances in Chernomor's castle –
these numbers are of such freshness that if you told people whose music
you are afraid not to go into raptures over such as Meyerbeer, Halévy,
Auber – if you said to those people that if they were to go a hundred *versts*
on foot this music could be theirs, they would run all the way, and there
would be enough material for each to write a complete opera. I shall not
embark any further on a review of the opera: it would be interesting and
comprehensible only to musicians, because I would need to use technical

45 Odoyevsky had Bulgarin in mind.
46 The opera contains twenty-seven numbers. The author here refers to the first published
    vocal score in which some numbers were combined and instrumental entr'actes omitted.

terms to make things clear; I shall say only this: listen carefully to this music, try to get to know it, and you will come to be astounded by the thought that there could have been a single minute which you did not like.

Believe me! From Russia's musical soil has sprung a luxuriant flower – it is your delight, your glory. Should maggots try to climb its stalk and besmirch it, the maggots will fall to the ground and the flower will remain. Look after it: it is a tender flower and blossoms only once in a century.'

P. Bichev

CHAPTER TWO

The 1840s and 1850s

Important developments in Russian music took place at the end of the
1850s and the beginning of the 1860s. That was when the Russian
Musical Society with its first conservatoire and the Free School of
Music were founded. The Russian repertory was enlarged most significantly by Glinka's *Kamarinskaya* of 1848, and by his incidental music
for *Prince Kholmsky* (1840) and several orchestral pieces on Spanish
subjects from 1845 to 1851; the composer died in 1857. Dargomïzhsky
emerged as the composer of a grand opera, *Esmeral'da*, staged in 1847,
of an opera on a Russian subject, *Rusalka*, performed in 1856, and
during the 1840s and 1850s of many songs; his most influential opera
The Stone Guest lay in the future (see Chapter 5), and recognition of
him as 'the great teacher of musical truth', as Musorgsky called him,
occurred only in the 1860s. In the second half of the 1850s the dynamic
Balakirev began to attract the circle of young disciples whose compositions were to transform Russian music from the 1860s. This chapter,
then, may seem episodic as it illustrates the unsatisfactory pattern of
concert life and marks the appearance of some new works and some
new composers; its final item introduces the major critic Serov as he
comments in typically forthright and detailed fashion on new songs by
Balakirev.

(a) M. D. Rezvoy: Musical societies in St Petersburg. *Arts Gazette*, 1841, no. 10, pp. 1–4

Modest Dmitriyevich Rezvoy (1807–53) rose to the rank of colonel in
the Corps of Engineers in 1849 and was a talented miniaturist in por-
traiture. A cellist and composer, his most valuable service to music lay
through his translation of his teacher's work into Russian; J. L. Fuchs's
*Praktische Anleitung zur Komposition, sowohl zum Selbstunterricht,
wie auch als Handbuch für Lehrer, nebst einer besonderen Anweisung
für Komponisten des russischen Kirchengesanges* was first published in
the author's adopted city of St Petersburg in German in 1830, with the
Russian translation coming out there in the same year, and a second
edition in both languages issued there in 1841. With this translation
and subsequent similar publications, Rezvoy played a major role in

establishing the terminology of music in the Russian language. In 1843 he was elected a Corresponding Member of the Academy of Sciences in respect of that activity. The displacement of mainly German vocabulary by standard Russian equivalents was, of course, essential to the development of the study of music in Russia. He also contributed to Russian musical lexicography through his editorship of the musical entries in the *Encyclopaedic Lexicon* between 1835 and 1837, and by his authorship of many of them.

Whoever has been in Germany and loves music will, I suppose, recall with pleasure how the passion for that art is spread through almost all classes of society there.[1] There is no hamlet or village in which you would not find a very decent quartet, nor a town in which you could not form from among the amateurs a very fair orchestra capable of performing diligently and precisely works by both ancient and present-day masters. If one investigates the successes achieved over the last half-century by instrumental music, whose improvement belongs exclusively to German composers; if one enters the sphere of the symphony which has been elevated now to the highest level of genius and musical delight and has outstripped by its rapid development the other branches of the art of music, then one cannot fail to be envious of those places in which the great works in that field are accessible to music-lovers. When someone has savoured the delight of listening to a Beethoven symphony even once, a desire to repeat this delightful experience lodges within him, and each time it is repeated this desire, this thirst, increases in quick progression. All the arts have their own magical effect on us, but not a single one of them reaches into the innermost feelings of our soul so deeply as music, and especially music cleansed of any adulterations, music without verses, without dances, without spectacles, music powerful in itself, in the romantic sphere of the ideal, that is – music expressed in the symphony! The more we are convinced of the truth of this opinion through reading scores, the more, living in St Petersburg, we have commiserated with people about the impossibility, as for the residents of small towns in Germany (it goes without saying that there is no such problem in the large ones), of hearing and being enraptured by the performance of the great creations of the German symphonic school. What musical pleasures do the inhabitants of St Petersburg enjoy? The Russian and German opera companies, and concerts during Lent.

Our opera can be very satisfactory at times, but it condemns the music-lover to hearing too frequent repeats of the same works, and sometimes it does not meet the requirements or satisfy the taste of the various categories into which our music-lovers are divided. The person for instance who

1 This idea had taken firm root in Russia: cf. Chapter 3, item (a).

admires the works of Mozart, Beethoven and Meyerbeer finds little pleasure in hearing works by Bellini, Donizetti and their kindred, and vice versa. But these discomforts are unavoidable, and sectional interests must be sacrificed to the common cause.

Turning to public concerts, we find that in Russia they are given only over the course of five weeks, that is from the second week of Lent until Holy Week, which amounts to thirty-five days. On each of those days some two or three (or more) concerts are often given, but since one cannot expect even the most ultra-passionate music-lover to attend several concerts at the one time, and since daily concert attendance is almost impossible for someone living in the capital on account of the many other entertainments, activities or obligations, then it would appear that the very maximum number of concerts available to us is twenty. Throughout all the remainder of the year concerts are extremely rare or do not take place at all. But can these twenty concerts offer some compensation by their programmes for the year-long deprivation? We can reply without any difficulty at all: no! Concert programmes which are compiled here almost mechanically, to a uniform pattern, are made up mainly as follows: two overtures – it is all the same who composed them (since the public here seldom listens to them), two arias or an aria and a duet, by Rossini, Bellini, etc., sung by one male singer, by one female singer or by one of each from our opera company, then a concerto or variations for piano (which are mostly regarded as an inalienable part of our concerts), and finally a concerto for a familiar instrument and brilliant variations (sometimes of his own composition) performed by the artist who is giving the concert. Often a special item known as a 'finale' is added to this, during which *nothing* [of the slightest musical worth] is performed. The assemblage of these variegated musical elements is designated by the magnificent title 'Grand vocal and instrumental concert'. Is the aim of a concert like this to provide a few agreeable hours to people who have no other entertainment in the long evenings of Lent and who lack musical pretensions of their own; is it leading towards conferring approval on a local artist for the effort he has expended over the year to satisfy the public; or is it to satisfy curiosity at the appearance here of a virtuoso or male or female singer from abroad; or is it to enquire into how far the mechanical development of the art of musical performance on some instrument or other (including the human throat in the category of musical instruments) has progressed, or what state it has reached; or, finally, is it to provide an opportunity to show our favourable disposition towards the people taking part in the concert who for some reason interest us particularly? If any of these is the aim of our Lenten concerts then let us agree that it is frequently fully realized; but we must also agree that in all this, music, as a lofty art form, has become something secondary, while we are of the opinion that in a concert music must be the principal consideration.

Although we find that by means of such concerts the mechanical aspect is improved through the performance of music and the limits within which composers (who are sometimes compelled to put aside splendid ideas solely on account of the difficulty of performing them) are able to work are thereby pushed back, and though we do not deny that the playing of expert soloists such as Vieuxtemps, Knecht, Thalberg,[2] Henselt[3] and many others is able to furnish genuine enjoyment, yet in the purely musical respect our concerts give little satisfaction to genuine music-lovers. The concerts of the Philharmonic Society (of which there are not more than two per year), and of some solid musicians such as Messrs Keller[4] and Romberg,[5] represent an exception to the general uniformity of our musical pleasures during Lent; at those, and especially at the concerts of the Philharmonic Society, in the main, classical works are performed which are noteworthy for the selection and enthralling quality of their contents. To these four or five concerts in a whole year are our delights confined in the area of polyphonic music. In order to avoid this deficiency, societies for lovers of music have been formed repeatedly in St Petersburg. One of them, devoted exclusively to vocal (predominantly religious) music [the Singakademie],[6] under the direction of Mr Belling, has been in existence for about twenty years, and through the performance of classical works has given and continues to give sublime enjoyment to genuine lovers of music.

Societies formed hitherto to perform instrumental music have been less successful. The preponderance of the concerto style over the polyphonic idiom; the insufficiency among amateurs of wind-players, and the need to have recourse to the participation of professional musicians, and hence a significant increase in expenses; the slight acquaintance of our music-lovers with symphonic music and in many cases their coldness towards that species which demands a certain musical development; the dissimilarity and often even the opposition in tastes, from which discord about the choice of pieces has arisen; even the external brilliance itself of these societies, which

---

2 Henri Vieuxtemps (1820–81), Belgian violinist and composer, one of the leading performers of his day. He was first heard in Russia in 1838, and was engaged as solo violinist to the tsar in the second half of the 1840s. F. Knecht, cellist. Sigismond Thalberg (1812–71), Austrian pianist and composer of virtuoso music for his own use. His world tours from 1830 took in Russia in 1839.

3 Adolf Henselt (1814–89) was a German pianist and composer. He settled in Russia in 1838 where he was held in high esteem as a player and teacher.

4 J. F. Keller, *Kapellmeister* of the German opera company in St Petersburg from 1835.

5 Probably B. H. Romberg (1767–1841), cellist and composer who was a frequent visitor to Russia from 1807. It could be H. M. Romberg – see note 8 below.

6 A German choral society founded in St Petersburg in 1822 by A. A. Belling.

often diverged from their principal aim, was the cause of their short existence and downfall. In the last ten years several musical societies arose which had as their goal the performance of symphonic music. In the first of them the conductor of the orchestra was Mr Eisrich,[7] and for the second year Mr Heinrich Romberg;[8] after the lapse of a few years Mr Bernard[9] invited many amateurs who formed the orchestra, under Goedecke's[10] direction; finally last winter (1839–40) Mr Behr[11] formed a new society in which he himself conducted and which gathered weekly to play through overtures, symphonies and solos with orchestral accompaniment (not more than one each evening).

All of these societies were unable to become permanent because of organizational inadequacies. At the end of last year some amateurs with experience of previous unsuccessful enterprises, who have looked into the reasons for their failure, established a Symphonic Society on the most sure foundations. We wish and hope that it will, like the Singakademie, win permanent existence to console all the music-lovers who are athirst for artistic enjoyments.

All this winter this Society has assembled every week on Saturdays in the hall of the Peterschule.[12] The directing of the orchestra was entrusted to Mr Behr. A single glance at the programme for these musical evenings is sufficient to convince one of the sublime enjoyment which they provided: five *symphonies* by Haydn, four by Mozart, six by Beethoven (each of these latter was repeated), one by Bakhmetev[13] and one by Bommer;[14] *overtures*: five by Mozart, one by Gluck, two by Cherubini, two by Beethoven, one by Vogel,[15] two by Weber, two by Spohr, one by Himmel,[16] one by Steibelt, one by Boieldieu and one by Méhul; in addition, a grand fugue by Mozart, for orchestra (manuscript), and the classical concerto by K. M. Weber for piano: altogether, including the symphonies, thirty-eight pieces. What an immense mass of genius!

7 K. T. Eisrich (1770–1835), pianist, violinist and composer.
8 H. M. Romberg (1802–59), violinist and conductor. He conducted at the Italian opera in St Petersburg from 1827 or 1829 until 1843.
9 Probably M. I. Bernard (1794–1871), composer and from 1829 publisher of music. From 1840 he published the musical periodical *Nuvellist*.
10 Possibly H. G. Goedecke, *Musikdirektor* in Reval (Tallinn).
11 I. A. Beer (German spelling of the surname unknown), German violinist.
12 This school stood beside the Lutheran church likewise dedicated to St Peter, set back from the Nevsky Prospekt at nos. 22–4.
13 N. I. Bakhmetev (1807–91), composer and violinist, director of the Imperial Court Chapel Choir from 1861 to 1883.
14 Nothing is known of Bommer.
15 Probably J. C. Vogel (c. 1756–88), composer.
16 F. H. Himmel (1765–1814), composer and pianist whose opera *Alessandro* was premièred in St Petersburg in 1799.

Among the compositions mentioned are two works by amateurs: the symphonies of Bakhmetev and Bommer. The former was able to join the sword with the lyre and won impartial plaudits as virtuoso and as composer. His symphony is notable for its many beauties, the pleasing quality of its motives and its clever instrumentation. The latter (Mr Bommer), whose name had remained hidden from the musical world until now, suddenly appeared not as an amateur testing his powers but as a master refined by long experience and profound study. His symphony is full of originality and strength, so that you can listen to it with enjoyment even after Beethoven – and that is saying something!

To obtain the most successful possible performance of the pieces of music, the Society invited many professional musicians (among whom there were some who out of love for their art showed their readiness to take part without remuneration and were accepted into membership of the Society). At the head of the first violins was Mr Behr, the second violins Mr Al'brekht,[17] the cellos Society-Member Mr Knecht. Almost all the wind parts were furnished by the most expert professional musicians, amongst whom we should mention Society-Member Mr Tyumler,[18] the excellent bassoonist. The number of amateurs playing the violin extended up to 30, the viola 9, the cello 8, and the double bass 4, of whom two were amateurs and two professionals. One may conclude from these circumstances that the orchestra was complete and powerful and the performance of the music satisfactory.

On bringing these evenings to an end on 2 February, i.e. at the beginning of Lent or the St Petersburg concert season, the Society took all measures to secure its existence not only for next winter, we hope, but for all future winters. A few embarrassments found in the organization for this year have been eliminated for the future. We invite every true lover of the noble art to take part in these harmonic and melodic delights, and we hope that the musical society will have a favourable influence in spreading love for the fine arts and on the greater development of the art of music among our compatriots.

(b) D. Yu. Struysky: A few words about national identity (*narodnost'*) in music. *Literary Gazette*, 8 February 1842, no. 6, pp. 113–15

Dmitry Yur'yevich Struysky (1806–56) was a composer, music critic and prolific poet. He worked in the civil service, attaining the rank of court counsellor in 1844. From about that year his health progressively deteriorated. His most ambitious creative effort was probably the opera

17 K. F. Al'brekht (1807–63), violinist, conductor and composer. He conducted the première of *Ruslan and Lyudmila* in 1842.
18 Nothing is known of Tyumler.

Parasha Sibiryachka ('Parasha the Siberian Woman') whose music he wrote to his own libretto based on a play by Polevoy. Its première took place in 1840, but despite a star-studded cast it did not last beyond that season. His other works included both romances and large-scale symphonies. His contributions on musical subjects to the periodical press of St Petersburg and Moscow began in 1828 and ended in 1845; they number nearly forty. His most-used pseudonym was *Trilunnïy* ('Trilunar'), but the present article is signed as in the heading above.

The question of national identity in music was a central concern of musicians and critics at this time (cf. Preface and item (d) below).

Of what does national identity consist? Here is a question about which there are so many different opinions in our journals. If national identity in music lies in folksongs, then every successful counterfeiting of an ancient song gives its perpetrator the right to be called a national writer. How many Russian songs composed within living memory are already being sung by the whole nation (*narod*): for example, 'Vot mchitsya troyka udalaya' ('Here speeds the bold troika'), or 'Vo vsey derevni Katin'ka' ('Katin'ka in the whole village'), etc.! If you ask any artist where exactly the merit of such songs lies, or why they are so widely sung, no one will give you a satisfactory answer. These ephemeral creations are indeed incomprehensible phenomena! The crowd finds something graceful about them, based on some kind of sympathy for them, goes into raptures over them, repeats them for several years, then suddenly abandons them for ever – and great creations disappear like bubbles of soap. But meanwhile there are melodies which are eternally beautiful; they are not sung by the crowd, but then they invariably live on in the memories of people with a profound feeling for what is graceful. There are of course few such people; but truth is on their side.

If some musical antiquarian now conceived the notion of collecting obsolete romances, the stupidest among them would be those which have given most amusement to past generations of our dilettanti. There can be no doubting the truth of this because facts which are unfortunately utterly incontrovertible serve to prove it. For example: which has been more often performed on our stage – *Don Giovanni* or *Rusalka*?[19] *The Magic Flute* or *Knyaz' nevidimka* ('The invisible prince')?[20] The experts' voices were of course on the side of

19 This title refers not to Dargomïzhsky's later opera of the same name but to some part of the series of Russian derivatives of Kauer's *Das Donauweibchen* which went by the names *Rusalka* ('The mermaid'), *Dneprovskaya rusalka* ('The Dnepr mermaid') and *Lesta, dneprovskaya rusalka* ('Lesta, the Dnepr mermaid'). The Russian composers who supplemented and/or supplanted Kauer's music were S. I. Davïdov and K. A. Kavos. Cf. Chapter 1, note 44. The matter is elucidated in *SO*, pp. 250–1. The Russian premières took place between 1803 and 1807.
20 *Knyaz' nevidimka, ili Licharda volshebnik* ('The invisible prince, or Licharda the sorcerer'), opera by K. A. Kavos first performed in St Petersburg on 5 May 1805. Both this work and *Rusalka*, mentioned in the previous note, were described as 'comic-magic operas'.

the operas of Mozart, but the public judged in their own way – they yawned during *The Magic Flute* but were carried away by *Rusalka*. 'Pridi ko mne v chertog zlatoy!' ('Come into my golden mansion!')[21] – who could not whistle, sing or play that wonderful tune! But there were *stale pedants*, however, who even then preferred Sarastro's aria to it. Experienced people often advise a young artist to try to please the mass known as the public, but what would Mozart or Beethoven have been had they followed the advice of such people? Read Mozart's letter from Paris where he says that the *asses' ears* of French dilettanti could not listen attentively to his G-minor symphony,[22] – or read Beethoven's remarks, and then you will satisfy yourself that one cannot serve two opposing powers. Choose either of the two extremes: one road leads the writer into the temple of art, the other to money and tawdry success. Of course *Robert le diable* may be considered an exception to this rule; but to what does it owe its success – to its music, or to the sets and the novelty of the libretto, in which Bertram [i.e. the Devil] appears with all his entourage for the first time? That is a good question. *Robert* undoubtedly came before an educated public, and it was performed superlatively, but all the same it would not have run to so many performances without its mar-vellous ballet and enchanting sets. In the very same city of Paris *Don Giovanni* is put on, performed by the world's foremost singers – and it cannot sustain five performances a year. What is the meaning of this?

Our journals frequently refer to the judgement of the public as an irre-futable authority. But I should like to find out what they mean by the word 'public'. It would do no harm once and for all to define our understanding of this marvellous and mysterious being.

Let us take our musical public for an example. It is made up of several categories who can never agree among themselves. One – *the lowest class* – appears on Sundays at the Bol'shoy Theatre: these are dilettanti cut to a special pattern; to the measured cadences of favourite melodies they are quite prepared to nibble nuts and, enraptured by a favourite lady singer, they will shout out in delight: Probably none of our reviewers regards this public as an authority. The second public is *the middling sort* – they rarely glance at an opera of the Italian or German schools, take no active part in them, and just go along for want of anything better to do; and there is, finally, the third public – in my opinion, *the noblest*: they listen to a Beethoven symphony and to the Philharmonic Society's oratorios during Lent. This public amounts to no more than 200 persons, but the Russian writer should set store by their

21 Popular aria from *Lesta, the Dnepr Mermaid* by S. I. Davïdov; see note 19 above and Chapter 1, note 44.
22 Perhaps the composer's letter of 12 June 1778 to his father, though Mozart there writes in anticipation of Parisian reaction to the symphony K297, the 'Paris', which is in D major.

judgement. The question now arises: is it possible to join these varied publics into one? There is no doubt that it is not, and for the simplest of reasons: a person who admires the little pictures of cheap popular prints (*lubochnïye kartinki*) will probably not understand Raphael's frescoes. Nowhere else are there such subdivisions of the public as in Russia. In Germany the woman of the lower middle class sings Mozart on an equal footing with the countess; we do not have that, and thus it is still too early for us to have our own national (*narodnoy*) music. The melodies of the common people, for all that they have a certain merit, cannot fully satisfy an educated music-lover, and he demands something more; and the ear of the commonalty understands nothing of sublime music. These two diverse levels of understanding cannot and must not be combined. Is it not better to try to educate a little those who are backward, so as to bring them with the passage of time closer to the level of those who have outstripped them? An achievement of this kind would be more useful than that false national identity by which present-day Russian music now wishes to set itself apart. Take as instances the two main schools, the German and the Italian: they each bear a stamp which belongs particularly to them, but not a single German writer would think of posing as a German – they all write in a simple way, like a German, in the German manner. But in Russia everyone imitates the melody of the *zapevala* [the initial melody of a folksong, given out by a reduced number of voices] and thereby tries to demonstrate that he is writing in the Russian way! You see, it even enters a Russian's head to write an imitation of something Russian! But, if you will excuse me, the explanation is quite simple. Write a play on Tatar history, say, and everything in your work will show the Russian stamp; it is a law of nature. *Don Giovanni* is a German opera, and *William Tell* an Italian one, in spite of the fact that the action of the first takes place in Spain and that of the second in Switzerland. But what would have happened if Mozart had patterned his opera after the *bolero* and Rossini from a *ranz des vaches* melody? But Russian music has fallen in decisively with that system, and instead of genuine national identity (*narodnost'*) we now have the national identity of the common people (*prostonarodnost'*).

Even in literature there was such a time! All the writers started to speak the language of the ancient chronicles and to use peasant sayings, but fortunately, these attempts are becoming ever rarer and rarer nowadays. Our literary public is older than our musical one, and thus more experienced. It has the models of Derzhavin,[23] Karamzin,[24] Pushkin[25] and Marlinsky;[26] it

---

23 G. R. Derzhavin (1743–1816), leading Russian exponent of classicism in poetry.
24 N. M. Karamzin (1766–1826), leading historian of Russia and champion of literary sentimentalism.
25 A. S. Pushkin (1799–1837), the founder of modern Russian literature and creator of its language. The range of his art may be judged by the variety of musical works based on it,

will immediately cast off the pathetic excrescences of what is known as national (*narodnoy*) poetry, and young writers have again begun to speak in the language of educated people.

National literature is the fruit of the highest education of a nation; religion, philosophy, climate, the political importance of a state – these are the sources of national poetry. A truly national poet or artist never seeks national identity, but writes simply, giving expression to what is in his heart in an elegant form. That is how Raphael, Mozart, Goethe, Derzhavin and Byron created their works. But in Russia things are now going completely the other way: people seek to find national identity in personal names, songs, and the dilapidated literary style of the chronicles. Authors sometimes achieve success, but it is by extraneous means which are sometimes far from elegant. One could point to many works which aroused delight some six years ago but which people now just laugh at. Nowhere are there such rapid transformations as in Russia, because our public decides on the basis of a momentary impression, and not in accordance with the laws of criticism. Momentary impressions almost always depend on circumstances at the time; what might have held appeal yesterday becomes commonplace in a few days. Just imagine our lady dilettante singing 'Katin'ka, in the whole village' nowadays! And yet it was but a short time ago that it was one of their favourite romances. Why is it that Alyab'yev's 'Solovey' ('The Nightingale')[27] is attractive to educated music-lovers even up to the present time? Because it possesses intrinsic merit. A splendid idea represented in an attractive form has no pretensions and does not go out of fashion. Music has least need of national identity among all the arts since by its essence it is the common language of mankind and since it has *its own form* which is the least reliant upon the contemporary age.

(c) V. F. Odoyevsky: The Russian Concerts of the Society for Visiting the Poor from the musical point of view. *St Petersburg Bulletin*, 8 April 1850, no. 80

With the virtual ending of Odoyevsky's activities as a *littérateur* in 1844 (when his *Sochineniya* ('Works') were published), a new area of activity opened up with his commitment to the Society for Visiting the Poor of St Petersburg, a body giving help to the homeless and those in need of

which include *Ruslan and Lyudmila*, *The Stone Guest*, *Boris Godunov*, *Eugene Onegin*, *The Golden Cockerel* and *Mavra*.
26 A. A. Bestuzhev(–Marlinsky) (1797–1837), author of romantic poems and stories. Not nowadays accorded the classic status of his colleagues in this list.
27 This was one of the most popular romances, used by Liszt (Searle no. 250); for Alyab'yev, see Chapter 1, note 5.

money, medical aid, education and so on. Between 1846 and 1855 this Society, of which Odoyevsky became chairman, took up a great deal of time. The concert discussed here thus shows the champion of Russian music in partnership with the charity worker, the knowledgeable, encouraging friend of composers and the writer. In the light of Odoyevsky's several roles, it would be wrong to anticipate genuine critical comment which may include remarks deemed hostile by composers or performers; a critic's silence may, however, be eloquent. The article was signed *Prokhozhiy* ('Passer-by').

The significance of this concert, which took place on 15 March 1850, may be judged from its programme, which contained:

Kamarinskaya (première)	Glinka
Jota aragonesa (première)	Glinka
Recollection of Castile (première)	Glinka
Overture from the Anacreontic opera:	
The Triumph of Bacchus (première)	Dargomïzhsky
Tuchki nebèsnïye ('Clouds in the sky'),	
romance with orchestral accompaniment	Dargomïzhsky
Excerpt from the opera *The Gipsies*	Viyel'gorsky
Overture to the opera *Dmitry Donskoy*	Rubinstein
The Nightingale (romance)	Alyab'yev
Overture to the opera *Starosta*	
('The Headman')	L'vov
Russian Military Chorus	L'vov
Piano Concerto	Shchuplenikov
Prayer (romance, première)	F. M. Tolstoy
Song of the Children's Shelters	Anon.

(*MLN* p. 591)

Devising and performing such a programme displayed enormous enterprise well before St Petersburg's concert life received a charge of vitality in the 1860s. The educational value of music – singing in particular – was another of Odoyevsky's hobbyhorses; his support of choirs making music for the first time through the Chevé method was tireless.

The undertakings of our charitable societies are notable for the fact that, not satisfied with their good objectives alone, they spare no effort over the *artistic polish* of their occasions of celebration; in general they make use of their inventiveness and resources to arrange such enterprises as would be beyond the scope of anyone else and consequently in carrying out their job of mercy they in addition facilitate the development of enlightened artistic taste and acquaint the public with pleasures of such a kind as could never be realized for them otherwise.

The *Russian Concerts* of the Society for Visiting the Poor, and the Russian Bazaar of the Women's Patriotic Society, are phenomena which are new, unexpected, wholly national (*narodnïye*) and dear to the hearts of Russians. The peasant hut of the Russian Bazaar, the little shops with their appointments, their furniture and all the characteristic peculiarities of Russian life, are in themselves numbered among exemplary works of architecture; our everyday life is here raised to the level of poetry.

A *Russian* concert, comprising *exclusively works by Russian musicians*, has hitherto seemed something impossible. An artist who gives concerts would never decide to perform music which was *new*, about which there had been no fanfares in foreign journals, which did not reach us through the mail, with all the appurtenances of European celebrity and fame – if you like, creating a sensation and what is known as *furore*. An artist must rely on what is *certain*; doubtful experiments are frightening and unprofitable for him: what is more, every new piece requires many rehearsals, and each rehearsal requires nearly as much money as the performance itself. Thus the same overtures, the same arias by Verdi and Donizetti and other even less noteworthy talents move across from one concert to another as by command. It might not be new, but it's tried and tested! That is why with a few exceptions all concerts on the whole torment listeners by their uniformity. The public demands something that is new, but it is given what is old and threadbare from the fear that it will not get quickly into the way of the new. How many first-rate, fresh works are hiding in the briefcases of our musicians when these works could be adorning any concert in Europe! Remember the degree of respect with which the late Mendelssohn-Bartholdy spoke about the works of L'vov,[28] listen to what Berlioz says about Glinka: 'you are looking for something new and genuine in art; everything in Glinka is new: both the motives and the instrumentation; there is no imitation of anyone, but a talent which is fresh and original'.[29]

The Russian Concert of the Society for Visiting the Poor was a real musical feast for musicians and unexpectedly showed what a high level has been attained by music, an art so innate to the entire Slavonic tribe.

Pieces for singing by Count Viyel'gorsky,[30] Glinka, Dargomïzhsky and L'vov have become national (*narodnïye*) works in our country; these works

28 A. F. L'vov (1798–1870) was the most important Russian violinist of the first half of the nineteenth century. His high military rank precluded public performances in Russia, though he appeared abroad and in Russia at private gatherings. He enjoyed great influence as director of the Imperial Court Chapel Choir from 1837 to 1861. He was the composer of the Russian national anthem.

29 I have not found a written source for this statement, but its sentiment corresponds to that expressed in Berlioz's letter of 25 March 1845 to Glinka (no. 953 in the *Correspondance générale*) and in his article in the *Journal des débats* of 16 April 1845 (English translation in David Brown: *Mikhail Glinka* (London 1974), pp. 310–15).

30 For Viyel'gorsky, see Chapter 1, note 6.

of free capricious fantasy have their own sort of merit, but in the hierarchy of art they must cede their place to works which are more important, which demand more profound inspiration and more wide-ranging musical knowledge. But we would never have heard these works in normal concerts. The works both required an excellent and large orchestra which could only be gathered by a Society, and they had to be studied assiduously, conscientiously, in accordance with all the demands of art – and a private person would not have had sufficient resources or time for this. It is enough to say that the preparations for the *Russian Concert* lasted five weeks, and, as everyone knows, the orchestra alone cost the Society over 600 silver roubles. Were these efforts to acquaint the Russian public with Russian composers in vain? Time will answer this question: at least a beginning has been made, a path has been laid, the belief has been formed that Russian music is not only able to stand up to the competition with the music of all the nations of Europe but can often vanquish them.

Where in the music of recent years can you find anything worthy to stand beside the *Jota aragonesa* which Glinka wrote under the inspiration of Spanish melodies? How fresh are these melodies, what passionate colouring sets off their tints, what original, masterly instrumentation!

The miracle-worker carries you off against your will to a warm southern night, surrounds you with all its visions, you hear the strumming of a guitar, the gay tapping of castanets, a black-browed beauty dances before your eyes, and a melody full of character now gets lost in the distance, now appears again with full force . . . but something familiar has now been heard; it is a melody of the common people which you have heard a thousand times already – how can one rouse any interest in it? How does one, as the saying is, *idealize* it?

The *Russian fast-dance song*, or simply *Kamarinskaya*, is one of those whimsical but profound creations of our own genius of a musician which are accessible only to Berlioz and Glinka, with the difference that it would have been difficult for Berlioz to sustain constantly that Russian character which never betrays itself, despite the sumptuousness of its instrumentation, despite all the tasteful combinations of melodies, permeated by a deep knowledge of music. But it is not its technical finish which strikes you so much as the profundity of its contents. In it the Russian character is fully reflected with all its freedom, good nature, light-heartedness, cheerfulness . . . at first the motive is heard on its own, without any context, as a Russian person would sing it as he amused himself in a carefree way; the motive is repeated for a long, long time, and meanwhile various thoughts, various feelings which are reflected in this motive pass through the soul of the lover of singing; it becomes now cheerful, now doleful, now tempestuous – maybe the convivial fellow has remembered his distant sweetheart-beauty, and then after that some spirited squabble crossed his mind, and then he thought about being an ill-starred orphan in a foreign land; the musician has noticed these fleeting feelings as a painter notices the fleeting expression on a face or an effect of colour so that he can fix it on his canvas; they would have vanished had not the artist saved them from oblivion for us; they are in front of us, forever in our power, always obedient to our aesthetic demand. Glinka's *Kamarinskaya* is at one and the same time a marvellous musical work as well as a picture and a profound psychological observation.

In a journal article like this one cannot go into great detail about each of the pieces in this remarkable concert, each of which would deserve a special article. The overtures of Dargomïzhsky and L'vov and Shchuplenikov's[31] concerto are fit to stand beside the best works of European celebrities; L'vov's Russian Soldiers' Chorus in which a warlike character is united so felicitously with Russian melody will always be a favourite with the public. And how many more scores by our composers are not known to the St Petersburg public, in spite of the fact that several of them enjoy well-deserved success throughout the whole of Europe!

Among other things, in this concert the *Pesn' Detskikh Priyutov* ('Song of the children's refuges') attracted general notice; it was performed by the [female] pupils of the Women's Patriotic Society, the College for Mutual Instruction and the establishments of the Society for Visiting the Poor.

We rejoice heartily at this mutual assistance among the charitable institutions, an assistance which it seems has become normal for the Society for Visiting the Poor. It was impossible to look without emotion at this assembly of cheerful, healthy children while thinking that they were all orphans who without the aid of charity would have remained without shelter; the appearance of this cheerful crowd was greeted with unanimous applause by the public. Many people, seeing six- and seven-year-old little ones from the Juvenile School of the Society for Visiting the Poor were reluctant to believe that they too were taking part in the choir; but those nearer the orchestra satisfied themselves that these little children *were actually singing, and singing very reliably*. It is well known that the Society for Visiting the Poor takes great care of the musical element in its establishments in the conviction that nothing so much promotes the correct development of a child's chest as moderate singing, held within the natural limits of a child's voice; the children's healthy appearance demonstrates better than anything else could do the truth of this conviction. Of music's effect on the moral propensities and generally speaking on the ennoblement of the soul there is nothing to

31 M. P. Shchuplenikov (1824–1902), St Petersburg pianist active in the university concerts.

be said; this truth is now acknowledged by everyone in spite of Mr Fontenelle who asked, without the benefit of any conclusion reached from live experiment: 'Sonate, que me veux-tu?'[32] Observations made in corrective institutions and prisons of the penitentiary system have shown that of the most vicious criminals it is primarily those with an inclination towards music who reform; this result was an unexpected one, although it is perfectly explicable. But a whole book could be written about that; let us return to the concert, the more so since on Sunday 9 April the *Second Russian Concert of the Society for Visiting the Poor* awaits us,[33] the second and probably the *last* of the current year.

[All Russia's musical eminences aided the success of this concert.]

In this concert there are only two names which are not Russian – Rubinstein and Henselt, but Rubinstein is Russian by birth and upbringing; Henselt is Russian by long habit and out of love for Russia – like Field[34] and Maurer.[35]

Until now we have known Rubinstein as an excellent musician, primarily a pianist, and have grown used to finding respite in his music in the midst of the innumerable *études, arrangements of other people's music* and other rags and scraps paraded by the new piano school and the piano pugilists who come with a false sense of alarm to Russia from abroad. But we note with pleasure that our gifted artist is embarking on a new career and is at work on an opera whose title is *Dmitry Donskoy.*[36] The overture (which as everyone knows is written after all the other numbers) shows that this opera is already coming to an end; let us be sincerely glad that *our numbers* have grown.

Let me conclude with some general words about charitable celebrations. Some time ago a kind fellow remarked that there are many people in the

---

32 This remark was made by the French author, critic and forerunner of the *encyclopédistes*, who lived from 1657 to 1757, in disparagement of purely instrumental music.

33 At this second Russian Concert, conducted by Anton Rubinstein, the programme comprised:

First movement of Second Symphony	Viyel'gorsky
Excerpt from the opera *Tsïgane* ('The Gipsies')	Viyel'gorsky
Tarantella-Fantasia	Glinka
Aria from *Ruslan and Lyudmila*	Glinka
Russian Song with Chorus	Alyab'yev
Dmitry Donskoy Overture	Rubinstein
Chorus	Verstovsky
etc.	

The Society for Visiting the Poor benefited from an all-Dargomïzhsky concert held on 9 April 1853.

34 For Henselt see Chapter 2, note 3. John Field (1782–1837), Irish composer, pianist and teacher who settled in Russia in 1802.

35 L. W. Maurer (1789–1878). German violinist, conductor and composer who worked in Russia permanently from 1807.

36 This opera was first performed on 18 April 1852 in St Petersburg.

world who have the innocent habit of throwing money out of windows; charitable societies stand below, gather up the money throw out, distribute it sensibly to the truly needy, rescue orphans from cold and hunger, and what is most important of all from vice and its disastrous consequences. That is true, but it does not describe in full the *Russian Concerts* of the Society for Visiting the Poor; in this case the charitable idea, whose happy realization is obvious to everyone, is joined by *aesthetic* feeling, and together with it national feeling; the success of Russian concerts is the pledge of success for all Russian music, which, sooner or later, must take the first place in the history of European art. We would wish that our readers start to reflect on this idea.

(d) F. M. Tolstoy: Analysis of A. S. Dargomïzhsky's *Rusalka*. *The Northern Bee*, 1856, no. 118, 28 May, pp. 609–11; no. 125, 6 June, pp. 647–8; no. 131, 13 June, pp. 677–9; and no. 137, 20 June, pp. 702–3

Feofil Matveyevich Tolstoy (1810–81) is best known as the music critic Rostislav, though he also wrote short stories and novels and composed three operas and many songs. He studied music in St Petersburg, Moscow and Naples. His first article on music was published in 1851 and his last, some ninety items later, in 1880. Serov, Cui and Stasov wrote derisively of the critic's later efforts, and Musorgsky included him in *The Peepshow*.

Dargomïzhsky composed *Rusalka* between 1848 and 1853, and it was first staged on 4 May 1856 in St Petersburg. It was his second opera, following the 'grand romantic opera', *Esmeral'da*, based on Victor Hugo's novel, composed probably between 1838 and 1841 and premièred in Moscow in 1847.

First article

Should the striving towards original nationality (*natsional'nost'*) in our literature so urgently and doggedly advocated by the unforgettable Pushkin in the last years of his life be extended into the fine arts in general? This matter has not yet been sufficiently clarified and requires profound discussion. For instance, the existing subdivisions in painting – into Italian, Flemish and French schools – do not yet mark absolutely one nationality or another. In this case the distinction stems more from the variety of colouring and manner than from the choice of subject and the basic idea of the work. All schools of painting include pictures portraying historical subjects embracing all mankind, and what one might call local painting which depicts exclusively the types and costumes of some nation or other (like Teniers) is not necessarily a higher manifestation of art. A painter may belong to one school or other as regards colour and manner without being an Italian, a Frenchman or a Fleming, whereas in literature all truly great works bear the stamp of the author's nationality. In imitating the classics of Antiquity, Calderón remains a Spaniard; all the writers of the French neoclassical school remain true to their nationality (*natsional'nost'*), and the Romans, Greeks and Turks whom they portray are nothing but *Marquises* in disguise, as one of the French critics put it. Even universal geniuses such as Dante, Shakespeare and Goethe could not avoid the impress of nationality upon their works. Thus in literature the question of originality is one which was resolved long ago, and as far as our native literature is concerned it remains only to establish the frontiers beyond which national literature ceases to be *belles-lettres*. But in the other arts the case is different: there the very basis as regards nationality is open to doubt.

In music there are also various schools. In the Italian melody is predominant, in the French declamation, and in the German harmony.[37]

In music, as in painting, the diversity of schools arises not from the fundamental ideas (in symphonic music) or the choice of subject (in dramatic music), but from certain formulas and devices assimilated by one school or another. Composers, like painters, are not subject to the demands of an exclusive nationality. Until *Don Giovanni* Mozart wrote operas in a purely Italian style, whereas with *The Magic Flute* he accomplished the supreme manifestation of the German manner. Simone Mayr[38] vied with Paer;[39] without moving completely away from the French school, Gluck brought it to the highest degree of dramatic tension. Nonetheless, in music more than in the other arts one sometimes detects the stamp of nationality, namely in *folksongs*, among which the Russian and Spanish songs stand out by virtue of their particular, characteristic melodic quality. As a result of this, repeated attempts have been made to elevate national melodies to the status of dramatic music, treated in accordance with all the rules of art.

The most splendid of these attempts belongs to M. I. Glinka. In the opera *A Life for the Tsar* he made use of the national element in a masterly fashion and embellished musical ideas obtained from the wellspring of folk melodies with all the luxuriance of the art of counterpoint.

The question arises: did M. I. Glinka's classic work lay a firm foundation for national Russian dramatic music? It seems to me that the answer must be in the negative, because, firstly, Glinka himself turned aside from the path which he had chosen in his next work (*Ruslan and Lyudmila*) and, secondly, the actual reasons for this veering from his path, it appears, are fairly sound.

37 *Author's note*: This generally accepted view is not entirely accurate, since German symphonic music abounds in melodies.
38 S. Mayr (1763–1845). Italianized German composer prolific in opera and church music.
39 F. Paer (1771–1839). Italian composer most of whose career was spent abroad, notably in Paris.

In order to avoid recitatives with Italian formulas, which on the lips of a Russian person would seem highly inappropriate, Glinka thought to replace them with melodic phrases which were painstakingly perfected in both the vocal part and the orchestra.

Such a wealth of musical ideas ought to have served, one would have thought, as an ornament to the opera, but experience showed otherwise. The listeners' continual tense concentration gives rise to weariness and thus an opera brimming over with first-class virtues appears infinitely long. Another awkwardness (admitted, moreover, by the composer of *A Life for the Tsar* himself) resides in the monotony of the turns of phrase found in national melody, which in Russian melodies, as everyone knows, revolve mainly within minor keys. This produces inescapable monotony and a certain sombre quality endowing a dramatic work with an oratorio quality in spite of the element of Polish music which the composer contrasts with immense skill with the Russian element.

Consequently, firm foundations for Russian dramatic music meeting all the requirements for a wholly artistic and dramatic work have not yet been laid, but to turn aside completely from the manifestation of Russian musical speech indicated by Glinka in a drama based on a national subject is almost impossible.

There is no doubt that the talented composer of *Rusalka* kept all these considerations in mind. For the reasons set out above, he was not able to allow Russian peasants to bawl out Italian arias, but recognizing the need for greater variety or, so to speak, greater *universality* in the musical expression, he chose a subject with an admixture of the fantastic element.

The distinguishing features of A. S. Dargomïzhsky's new work, as I pointed out before (in no. 108 of *The Northern Bee*), are genuine, profound dramatic tension and the absence of any pretension to tawdry effects.

The plot of the opera is taken from an unfinished long poem (*poema*) by Pushkin. Here is a brief outline of its contents.

A young prince falls in love – whether through idleness or by attraction is uncertain – with a peasant girl Natasha, a miller's daughter. Intending to marry and take for himself a bride better befitting his rank, the prince himself announces his intention to the girl he has seduced and gives coldblooded answers to her tender reproaches:

> Chto zh delat' mne? sudi sama . . .
> Ved' mï ne vol'nï zhon
> Po serdtsu vïbirat'.
>
> ('What can I do? Judge for yourself . . .
> After all, we are not free
> To choose wives as our hearts dictate.')

Natasha, staggered by the terrible news, goes into despair, reproaches her father who encouraged her relations with the prince out of self-interest, announces her shame to the whole world, and throws herself into the Dnepr, changing into a *rusalka* ('mermaid'). The miller, her father, loses his reason. The prince, who has married calculatingly, cannot, naturally, ensure his wife's happiness. His memories trouble him. He becomes pensive and melancholy, paces up and down the bank of the Dnepr alone at night, despite the admonitions and jealousy of his young wife, and he finally perishes in the Dnepr, pushed off the bank by the insane miller at the *rusalka*'s request.

There is no doubt that the *rusalka*'s mystical significance is responsible for the introduction here of the pangs of conscience, repentance and the seducer's sad end – a just punishment. But I consider that the apotheosis concluding the opera in which the union of the prince and the *rusalka* is depicted in the underwater kingdom is utterly contrary to the poem's moral aim.

The grand overture preceding the opera is written in masterly fashion and carried on and developed with great skill, but in essence it does not provide, as it should, a general outline of the drama. The fantastic element in it is barely appreciable, and the graceful phrase (in A flat) given to clarinets and flutes represents a tender feeling rather than the dramatic, hopeless situation of the abandoned girl. This melodic phrase, if given greater development both in its structure and in sonority, would have made a more satisfactory impression. Let me repeat, however, that the overture to *Rusalka* as a separate symphonic piece earns complete approval; it is only in comparison with the opera's general character that it may appear insufficiently developed in respect of drama and fantasy.

Contrary to practices which have gained acceptance in recent times, the opera begins with an aria, and not with a brilliant introduction, with massed choruses, magnificent décor, double orchestra, with fuss and uproar and the other embellishments of the new school.

As I have already said, the composer of *Rusalka* was not thinking about applause or seeking means of winning over the public – he was imbued solely with the desire to achieve truth of dramatic expression.

[Tolstoy goes on to examine the remainder of the opera in comparable – indeed, probably greater – detail, singling out for praise the duet of the Prince and Natasha in Act I, the chorus of wedding congratulation in Act II, and the Miller's mad scene with the Prince; he notes 'the profound feeling for drama which 'is a distinguishing feature of the music of A. S. Dargomïzhsky'.]

I have analysed A. S. Dargomïzhsky's opera in detail, to the utmost of my understanding, and with heartfelt sympathy for the work of a compatriot. If the technical details to which I was on occasion compelled to resort seemed wearisome to some of my readers, then I ask them to take into consideration that criticism is not written for amusement. It is intended for a twofold purpose: to clarify for readers the composer's thoughts, and to indicate to the composer himself what is defective in his work. Criticism which does not achieve this dual aim is useless; it is impossible to achieve it without detailed analysis in both artistic and technical respects. In conclusion, let me repeat what I said in my first cursory assessment of A. S. Dargomïzhsky's opera. *Rusalka* can be boldly called a work which is serious, conscientious and highly important in many respects and it is notable in particular for its genuine, profound, dramatic quality. Talent, which is not open to the least doubt, and complete familiarity with the art of composition are clearly revealed in this new work by A. S. Dargomïzhsky. One may say correctly that the majority of the public, even if they did not appreciate *Rusalka* fully, at least expressed their sympathy with this capital work by our compatriot. May that sympathy serve as an encouragement to our respected and gifted composer to write further new works!

(e) A. N. Serov: Newly-published compositions. Balakirev's songs and romances (twelve pieces for a single voice with piano). *Theatre and Music Herald*, 1 November 1859, no. 43. Serov 4, pp. 172–6

Aleksandr Nikolayevich Serov (1820–71) was the most successful Russian opera composer of the 1860s (see Chapter 5). His three operas written in that decade show him as a competent but not inspired master of one of the prevailing styles of the day – that of Meyerbeer, in works full of stunning effects and scenes of local colour in pseudo-historical contexts. This practical reality contradicted his service as Wagner's leading Russian champion, his support expressed through many lengthy and acerbic articles. Indeed, vitriolic zest marks out most of Serov's prose, and with his certainties and absolutes (often self-contradictory) made him one of the most controversial figures in the Russian musical world of his day. He was to a substantial degree self-taught – in music as in other spheres. He studied alongside V. V. Stasov at the School of Jurisprudence, completing its course in 1840; youthful warm friendship with Stasov gave way to mature hotter enmity on both sides. Similarly good relations with the Balakirev circle in the late 1850s also turned sour subsequently. Serov's technical knowledge of music, familiarity with the repertory, the extent of his work and its literary verve made him one of the founders of Russian musicology. While his other compositions remained little known, musical echoes from his operas may be heard in the works of Musorgsky, Tchaikovsky and Rimsky-Korsakov, and their conceptions are also on occasion indebted to Serov's example. One might argue that in focussing on the relationship between music and drama the Russian operatic school of the 1860s and 1870s is developing a theme set by Wagner but forced upon it by Serov (see Richard Taruskin: *Opera and drama in*

Russia as preached and practiced in the 1860s (Ann Arbor, Michigan 1981)). Space precludes comprehensive representation of Serov's work as a critic – even though, at about sixty-eight items, the tally is relatively low.

These songs were among Balakirev's first compositions to be published. He had been in St Petersburg for only a few years but was making some headway. Serov here lets him off lightly: further examples show Serov relishing both pedantry and insults much more. In its ostentatious verbal virtuosity with Classical allusions and foreign tags, and in its frequent emphases, this article is typical of Serov's style.

'M. A. Balakirev's name must be very familiar to our readers. We have had occasion more than once to speak about this young talent's bright beams, for whom the most brilliant future lies in store.' Thus would some inveterate compliment-monger have begun, one with reasons of his own for such panegyrics lavished on each and every one 'out of love for his neighbour', who, naturally, is himself summoned to shower praises. The writer of these lines has had long enough to be regarded as a Zoilus[40] and has set himself in perpetually hostile relations with all our country's musical circles; probably, then, neither M. A. Balakirev nor my readers will doubt my truthfulness when from the bottom of my heart *I repeat the very same words* which I put forward here in the guise of a sworn compliment. In truth, for the severe profession of a critic struggling with dullness and ignorance, *poshlost'* [vulgarity, triviality and the commonplace] of taste and the obstinacy of producers, performers and assessors, fresh healthy blooms in the soil of Russian music are a great delight! I cannot find words of sufficient warmth to greet the twelve vocal pieces with which M. A. Balakirev opens his public activity as a composer.

Please do not think, however, that all these are model compositions. On the contrary, the greater part of these romances are quite immature and moreover in their actual character they are not at all *for the general taste*, whereas for the more refined and educated taste they contain little succulent nourishment.

But what is especially consoling about them is the noble musicality, which is a million *versts* removed from the vulgar trivialities and common-places (*poshlost'*) which flood our music shops; what is precious, nay, invaluable, in these first fruits is the *undoubted, genuine* talent which the composer possesses. Genuine musical blood related to that of Glinka and Schumann flows through this music's veins; the world's highest aristocratic principle – that is, an urgent vocation to art – flows here. Without forgetting also that this is the composer's début in the vocal field, that these are his *first*

40 Zoilus was a critic of the fourth century BC who dealt fastidiously and voluminously with the work of Homer.

songs, and comparing these twelve little pieces with the earliest romances of Glinka, that is with almost everything written up to the age of thirty ('Bedniy pevets' ('The poor singer'), 'Ne iskushay menya bez nuzhdï' ('Do not tempt me needlessly'), 'Utesheniye' ('Consolation'), 'Pamyat' serdtsa' ('The heart's memory'), 'Gor'ko, gor'ko mne' ('Bitter, bitter is it for me'), 'Gruzinskaya pesnya' ('Georgian Song'), 'Golos s togo sveta' ('A voice from the other world'), etc.), one may observe the extraordinary success of our nation's music of this kind. Glinka's romances (NB: from among *his very first* works) appear weak and dilettanteish in comparison with the melodic turn of phrase and harmonic treatment in M. A. Balakirev's experiments.

Besides, at the end of the twenties and the beginning of the thirties (the period of Glinka's first activities as a composer) *poshlost'* hung over Russian romances with all its force, the sickly sweetness of their melodic character – that Varlamovism[41] which even nowadays wins the affection of a very wide circle of 'music-lovers', but by those 'who are purer' it is assigned to its true home, to the social level of Izeler's[42] concerts and semi-servant parties held to the 'strumming' of the guitar.

M. A. Balakirev's works will never reach these strata, so that he need not count on popularity. However, it is time to acquaint our readers a little more closely with these twelve little pieces.

(1) 'Pesnya razboynika' ('Brigand's song'). Words by Kol'tsov. 'Ne strashna mne, dobru molodtsu, Volga-matushka shirokaya' ('You do not scare me, a bold warrior, broad mother Volga') – B major, $\frac{3}{4}$, Allegretto. A very simple melodic outline in the spirit of the sweeping songs of the Volga region. But the entire melody amounts to a mere eight bars (plus four bars of ritornello in unison). It has character, but is somewhat on the short side!

(2) 'Oboymi, potsaluy' ('Embrace me, kiss me'). Words by Kol'tsov. Allegro agitato, C minor, $\frac{3}{4}$. Music has been written to these words on very many occasions. Quite recently the romance by Baron Fitingof[43] was printed in which this very text served for a long vocal piece rather like a scena or an aria (*Durchcomponirtes Lied*). M. A. Balakirev has kept within the bounds of a short song where *one and the same* music serves for all three couplets. This is far better and more to the point. It

---

41 A. Ye. Varlamov (1801–48). He composed many Russian romances which enjoyed widespread popularity; they included *Krasnïy sarafan* ('The red sarafan'). Their musical character, however, was insufficiently strong for the taste of Odoyevsky, Serov and others – hence Serov's dismissive comment here.

42 I. I. Izeler (1811–77) was the proprietor of the 'Mineral Waters' Garden in St Petersburg.

43 Baron B. A. Fitingof-Shel' (1829–1901), composer of operas and ballets, etc. His recollections, entitled *Mirovïye znamenitosti* ('World celebrities'), were published in the Russian capital in 1899.

is a pity, though, that the rondo form in the text, that is the repetition of the opening words at the end of the song ('Oboymi zh, potsaluy . . . potsaluy goryachey!' ('Embrace me, kiss me . . . kiss me more ardently!') has not been preserved in the music. The passionate nature of the poem has on the whole been rather well captured by the composer, especially at the end of the melody. At the words 'eshcho raz, poskorey, potsaluy goryachey' ('once more, quickly, kiss me more ardently') (in the first couplet) the melodic outline is slightly flaccid and monotonous. (The words of the text contain annoying orthographical errors: [Serov gives three examples].)

(3) 'Barkarola' ('Barcarolle'). 'Prelestnaya rïbachka, prichal' na bereg moy' ('Charming fisherwoman, come and moor on my bank'). Words by A. Arsen'yev ('from Heine' should have been added, or otherwise this omission would have recalled that blessed time in Russian literature when Lyudmila-Leonora and Ibycus's cranes[44] were thought to have been invented by Zhukovsky). Andantino, B flat minor, $\frac{6}{8}$. A sweet melody, close to the Italian forms. In the second half of the romance (Agitato)' 'A serdtse to zhe more' ('But heart and sea are the same') the composer has been carried away a little inappropriately by the 'boiling' of sea and heart and has not given sufficient care to making the vocal melody interesting.

(4) 'Kolïbel'naya pesnya' ('Cradle song'). Words by A. Arsen'yev. Andantino, A major, $\frac{2}{4}$. Inasmuch as the words of the text lack both poetry and originality, the melody is not notable either for particular attractiveness or for freshness. Many turns of phrase recall either Glinka's 'Kolïbel'naya pesnya' ('Cradle song') (a *chef-d'œuvre* of its kind!) or the Cossack 'Kolïbel'naya pesenka' ('Little cradle song') by N. Bakhmetev[45] (rather plain but inspired) . . . Here too details of remarkable cleverness flash past in the harmonic treatment. (For instance, the harmony at 'Bayushki-bayu' ('Lulla-by') and the harmony in the penultimate bar of the concluding ritornello.)

(5) 'Vzoshol na nebo mesyats yasnïy' ('A fine moon has risen in the sky'). Words by M. Yatsevich. Andantino, D flat major, $\frac{4}{4}$ (the middle section Poco meno mosso, $\frac{6}{8}$). In form, melody and inner poetic fragrance, this work is incomparably superior to the first four. This

---

44 Zhukovsky recast Bürger's ballad *Leonore* in Russian as *Lyudmila* in 1808. Ibycus was a Greek poet of the sixth century BC who was murdered by brigands. His murderers were tracked down thanks to the help of a flock of cranes. This legend forms the subject of a poem by Schiller (*Die Kraniche des Ibykus*) which Zhukovsky translated into Russian as *Ivikovï zhuravli*. The Russian poet was responsible, as Serov implies, for many fine Russian translations of the classics of German poetry.

45 For Bakhmetev, see note 13 above.

romance is a complete work of art. Its sphere is not among the especially profound or the especially elevated; it is not an intimately tragic *scena* (like some of the immortal Lieder of Franz Schubert, or like some of the works of Glinka and A. S. Dargomïzhsky). It is a genuine *romance*, with all the charm and languorous colouring of a clear and peaceful moonlit night. From a technical point of view, a remarkable feature is the graceful counterpoint to the principal melody and the ritornello which when repeated at the end of the romance leads to the key of B flat minor, but immediately the repetition, of extraordinary aptness, of the cadence in D flat minor from the very opening bars rounds off the whole piece in its main key. A great deal of talent is shown in even a single such device!

(6)   'Kogda bezzabotno, ditya, tï rezvish'sya' ('When you play carefree games, child'). [Tempo di] Mazurka, A major, $\frac{3}{4}$. Words by K. V[il'de]. If someone who did not know M. A. Balakirev's other romances came across this mazurka with its pitiful text, its pretty insipid melody and containing great blunders in the matching of the music to the words (e.g. at the words 'mne grustno i bol'no' ('I am sad and sick') there is an extremely long trill!), such a person would probably say 'There is nothing here, apart from a poor imitation of Glinka's 'Kogda v chas vesyolïy' ('When in a cheerful hour') – an imitation which has almost turned into a parody'. (The text contains many misprints, which of course do not add to the beauty of this doggerel.)

(7)   'Rïtsar'' ('The Knight'). Words by K. V[il'de]. [Allegro marziale, C minor, $\frac{6}{8}$]. Once more, the choice of text is not entirely successful. The purport of the text is very tragic, but it is stated in rather coarse words, which provokes a smile rather than a serious reaction. In the sounds he has created M. A. Balakirev has corrected the shortcoming in the text; the song has a knightly character, and energy, and power, but the impression nevertheless remains unsatisfactory. The complaints of the knight's lady-friend and later of the knight himself 'O! Kak uzhasna!' ('O! How terrible!') are expressed in a not very dramatic way, yet the whole meaning of the ballad lies in these complaints. There is much that is remarkably good in the harmonic treatment. One can hear an orchestra in the piano accompaniment. That is always a sound guarantee of the originality of a musical idea.

(8)   'Mne li, molodtsu razudalomu' ('Was it to me, a fearless fine fellow'). Words by Kol'tsov. Allegretto, D major, $\frac{2}{4}$ [recte $\frac{3}{4}$]. A Russian song in pure folksong style. There is a great deal of life and *mastery* in the treatment. At the words 'Esli b molodtsu noch', da dobrïy kon', da bulatnïy nozh, da tyomnï lesa' ('If a fine fellow has the night, a good

horse and a trusty sword and *dark forests*') the composer modulates with extraordinary appropriateness very darkly (and fully in the spirit of *Slav* modulations) from B minor to D flat major. The bright D major after this 'gloomy forest' of chords sounds superb, and the oboe phrase with which the little piece opens is treated at the return of the ritornello in canonic imitation which is the equal of Glinka's. This song is a small thing, but not too short; it is developed dramatically as regards the accompaniment, but the melody is very simple; it lies in the most beautiful notes of the tenor register and should sound delightful on the lips of P. P. Bulakhov[46] to whom it is most aptly dedicated.

(9) 'Tak i rvyotsya dusha' ('Thus is the soul torn'). Words by Kol'tsov. D minor, Allegro agitato, [$\frac{9}{8}$]. His music for Kol'tsov's poetry enjoys particularly happy success for the young Russian composer. Generally speaking, this applies with special justification to the song which I have just discussed. The ninth romance shows animation and a *Russian* quality of passion, but it could be far better without leaving this form. The text is very rich!

(10) 'Pridi ko mne' ('Come to me'). Words again by Kol'tsov. G flat major, Andante, $\frac{3}{4}$. The Varlamov school will first be horrified by the *six* flats in the key signature, and then by the constant swaying of the accompaniment in triplets which with their rippling motion make the rhythm complicated. Non-Varlamovites will like this song perhaps more than all the others in the set of twelve. The accompaniment is graceful, the harmony is tender and interesting, and the melody eloquent.

(11) 'Pesnya Selima' ('Selim's song'). Words by Lermontov. 'Mesyats plïvyot i tikh i spokoyen, a yunosha-voin na bitvu idyot' ('The moon floats, calm and peaceful, but the youthful warrior goes on to battle'). Allegretto. D sharp minor, $\frac{2}{4}$. The music is in the oriental manner, as immutably demanded by the text. The harmonization contains innovations which at first sight are quite preposterous, but all are in character and incorporated in an organic fashion. The whole short piece shows a great deal of intellect, but one might wish for more inspiration.

(12) 'Vvedi menya, o noch', taykom' ('Lead me in, oh night, secretly'). Words by A. Maykov. F minor, Allegro agitato, [$\frac{3}{4}$]. The music is as original as the text is well chosen. In performance it will be rather difficult to observe the constant pianissimo, despite the *complexity* of the accompaniment. If pianissimo turns, as quite often happens, into a kind of neutral mezzo forte, the whole *meaning* of the romance will be violated and no one will understand a single one of the composer's subtle intentions.

---

46 P. P. Bulakhov (1824–75) was a tenor who made his début in St Petersburg in 1849. He was the first Prince in Dargomïzhsky's *Rusalka*. He also composed romances.

To conclude: after resolutely and fervently praising Nos. 5, 8, 10, 11 and 12, it remains to wish M. A. Balakirev all zeal and steadfastness of will in the difficult career of a writer of music! The Russian musician must constantly bear in mind that fame, honours and money are not for him. For all these things to appear as in a dream, what you need apart from talent (that goes without saying) is above all not to be *Russian*, not even merely to be born in Russia.[47]

47 *Author's note*: All the romances mentioned above are on sale in F. Stellovsky's music shop.

CHAPTER THREE

The Conservatoire controversy – a clash of ideals

The beginning of the reign of Alexander II (1855–81) was propitious for initiatives. After the stagnation of the previous period there was hope for reform and development in many spheres of Russian life. The musical world offered scope for the creation of new institutions for training musicians and raising performance standards. The prime mover in the most significant innovation, the establishment of conservatoires, was Anton Rubinstein. Education being a matter on which everyone has an opinion, and a body calling itself the Russian Musical Society presenting an obvious target when both national identity and music's past and future were topics of polarized debate, the controversy associated with Rubinstein's ideas drew in all the main commentators (Stasov, Serov, Cui and Laroche) and provided a focal point for the airing of their views about music in general and music in Russia in particular. It was at about this time that the dilettante *littérateur* lost the initiative in writing on music to the well-grounded specialist. From now on, musicography as an agreeable pastime lost its dominance.

(a) A. G. Rubinstein: The state of music in Russia. *The Age*, 1861, no. 1. A. G. Rubinshteyn: *Literaturnoye naslediye* ('Literary heritage'), vol. 1 (Moscow 1983), pp. 46–53.

Anton Grigor'yevich Rubinstein (1829–94) was a pianist of the highest distinction. Born in the Russian Empire, he completed his musical education in Berlin and returned to his homeland in 1848. The Russian Musical Society was founded in 1859 to promote concerts and run classes in music. The next step was to formalize this instruction through the opening of a conservatoire in St Petersburg, which took place on 8 September 1862. All this was achieved with the help of a member of the imperial family, the Grand Duchess Elena Pavlovna, and a small group of friends. Rubinstein had forfeited the good will of many Russian musicians by an injudicious article first published abroad several years earlier ('Die Componisten Russland's' appeared in *Blätter für Musik, Theater und Kunst* (Vienna, 1855), nos. 29 of 11 May, 33 of 25 May, and 37 of 8 June), where he expressed scepticism about the existence of national music and Russian national music in particular, and passed cutting judgements on several composers who enjoyed esteem among the musical community. Personal antagonism, distrust of a successful innovator's single-mindedness, differences in musical outlook, nationalism and specious arguments on Rubinstein's part combined to give rise to an especially sharp dispute.

> 'Who never ate his bread in sorrow
> Who never spent the darksome hours
> Weeping and watching for the morrow
> He knows ye not, you heavenly powers.'[1]

These words of Goethe, imbued with such deep truth for all those involved in the arts and hence also in music, do not hold the same meaning in Russia as elsewhere because in our country it is only amateurs who are involved in music – that is those who, because of their birth or social position, do not depend on music to earn their daily bread, but whose involvement in music is only for their own personal enjoyment. We could easily conclude from this state of affairs that the art of music in Russia is in a very healthy condition. We might even believe that music is developing quietly in its own way without the bane of those who would use it to satisfy their own material needs. However, such a conclusion would be completely unfounded: the art of music has until now not become well established in Russia, and its roots are in ground that is all too unfirm and uncultivated. Why should this be so? Precisely because the words of that great poet which I have just quoted cannot in any way be applied to Russia.

The art of music, like any other art, demands that whoever engages in it sacrifice all his own thoughts, all his feelings, all his time and his whole being to art. Only upon him who has devoted himself entirely to this art in this way will music occasionally smile, or permit him to discover her secrets. This chosen one will then have the right to call himself an artist and will have the privilege of proclaiming his art to the world – a frightening destiny, imposing on the artist a duty to provide those around him with constant pleasure and giving him as a reward only the status of a martyr.

By some strange concurrence of circumstances Russia has practically no artist-musicians in the usual sense of the word. This, of course, is a result of the fact that our government does not yet give music as an art the same privileges accorded to other arts such as painting, sculpture and the rest, in other words the government does not give those involved in music the *civic status of artist*.[2]

1 *Wer nie sein Brot mit Thränen ass*, from *Wilhelm Meister*.
2 The Academy of Fine Arts provided training in these fields, conferring professional status at various grades corresponding to ranks in the civil service. This institution, at least at certain periods after its foundation in 1757, had authority to regulate artistic life and distribute commissions.

The Theatre School and the Court Chapel Choir School are the only musical establishments run by the government in our country, but they train civil servants, not free artists.[3] Let us suppose that the son of a peasant or a merchant is endowed with a talent for music and wants to pursue his musical education outside one of these establishments. Once he has finished his education, he will be left without any official status and will be forced to choose another career; he will have to give up his art for good, an art for which he feels a calling, and which he might have been able to serve in an outstanding way.

Thus in Russia the only people who are engaged in music are amateurs.

As a result of the fact that the amateur is involved in music only for his own pleasure, he naturally avoids anything which might cause him dissatisfaction, and studies music only to the extent necessary to achieve his own ends. The serious, deep and idealistic side of art is beyond him, and he chooses only the light, superficial aspects. But surely this means that art will be deprived of its most beautiful sense? Surely leaving music in the hands of those people who see it only as a means of passing the time, and who do not allow those people who have devoted their whole life to the service of music to become involved, means that the country will lose one of the most vital driving forces of civilization?

It is understandable that a person who has responsibilities, whether they be civil or military, can only give himself up to his chosen art when he is free from his public responsibilities, and, as a result, he cannot master this art, nor become absorbed in it. I do not mean to imply by this that they should not take an interest in art at all, but everyone would doubtless agree with me that these people will never progress to the highest level of art because their official functions will not allow it.

Some people will object, saying that Petrarch, Rubens, Farinelli, Goethe and many others were envoys and ministers. This objection is easy to refute. The great people I have named were artists first and ministers second, and not the other way round. If they had been brought up to be envoys and ministers, they would never have become great artists, but having already become great artists it was then easy for them to be chosen as envoys and ministers.

Looking at their works, we cannot say that they were merely amateurs involved in the arts only for their own enjoyment; no, they must have been ready to submit themselves to the most stringent criticism; they had to account for their artistic inspiration and their dreams before the inexorable judgement of their fellow artists and of the whole of mankind and posterity.

The artist who demands recognition of his works, who turns art into his livelihood, thereby opens himself up to universal criticism – and without

3 Rubinstein means that the diplomates of these schools found permanent employment in several state-run artistic establishments, such as the imperial theatres.

that he will never produce anything of greatness. Disillusionment, beautiful dreams shattered by life's sad reality, the struggle of self-esteem with fate, artistic fanaticism unrecognized and ridiculed by the indifferent and uncomprehending public but respected and valued by a small number of people, a strict but fair criticism – these are the conditions without which it is impossible for the true artist to develop.

Let us now look to see whether these conditions exist for amateurs. Obviously they do not. The amateur whose interest in art is only for his own personal pleasure does not have to submit to the judgement of critics: on the contrary, his equals always praise him and even artists judge him leniently since art constitutes neither his main occupation nor his livelihood. This immunity of amateurs is fatal for art in a country where they alone hold the future of art in their hands and where there are no *responsible artists*.

In order to demonstrate the harmful influence of this state of affairs on music in Russia, let us examine just how far the abilities of our amateurs go. Let us start with the composers.

Who has ever been labelled witty because he made a witty comment once in his whole lifetime? Who has ever been called a philosopher because he expressed a single lofty thought?

For musical amateurs it seems that different rules apply. If an amateur manages to compose just one romance[4] whose content is more or less good, he then considers himself a composer. Woe betide anyone who tries to persuade him that his melody, although it is both effortless and pleasant, does not match the words of the romance, that in the accompaniment there are mistakes in the harmony, or that much study is required before one can compose even the smallest piece. The amateur will regard this *ill-intentioned critic* with scorn, will publish his romance, force some singer from the Italian opera to sing it, and begin to make judgements about art and artists as though he is in the best position to judge; he will then become a musical celebrity in his own town, will endlessly compose romances without noticing that they are all repetitions of the same melody, will not want to grasp the rules of harmony and composition, will start to contend that only melody has value in music, and that everything else is German pedantry; and he will end up composing an opera.

But suspecting, against his will, that composing an opera demands something more than just melody, he will take to reading Fétis,[5] Marx,[6] and

---

4 The author uses the term to denote a rudimentary composition for voice and piano.
5 F.-J. Fétis (1784–1871) was a prolific Belgian writer on the theory and history of music and the biographies of musicians. It is to his *Méthode élémentaire et abrégé d'harmonie et d'accompagnement* (Paris 1832) that Rubinstein refers.
6 A. B. Marx (?1795–1866) was a German composer, critic and author of textbooks. Rubinstein may have had his *Die Lehre von der musikalischen Komposition* (Leipzig 1837) in mind.

Berlioz's *Grand Traité d'instrumentation et d'orchestration moderne*.[7] With
the aid of these books and some work by a great composer, his opera will
soon be ready.

Composing an opera. This dream and ambition of the artist is also characteristic of most amateurs. Yet how much information, to say nothing of
talent, one must have in order to compose an opera. When those qualities are
present, how necessary is an all-round knowledge of all the arts, a feeling for
what is refined, which, if it is not instinctive, can be acquired by thoroughly
studying great works, experience in devising what is effective, familiarity
with the stage and creating characters, and many other conditions which
are the *sine qua non* of composing an opera. How necessary it is to know
the whole essence of your art, the different vocal registers, form (that logic
of art), all types of composition in their thousands and thousands of tiny
details, the art of accompanying singing, and so on. It is worth remembering
all these conditions in order to understand just how bold is the amateur as
he settles down to write his opera. The amateur, being involved in music
purely for his own pleasure, devotes only as much time to this interest as his
other commitments allow. Naturally, it is not appropriate to apply the well-
known saying 'honneur au courage malheureux' (all credit for trying) to
these attempts.

But without taking matters as far as opera, let us see what exactly these
romances of the amateur are like, this type of composition with which he
considers himself to be so familiar. Surely these romances match the words
which the amateur wanted to set to music? No, indeed not. It is already a
great achievement if the amateur avoids writing a bright melody to sad
words. But he will forget that sadness in music, as in life, has a multitude of
nuances such as melancholy, despair, bitterness, resigned submissiveness to
fate and so on. The amateur will be satisfied if he writes his melody in a
minor key, with arpeggios, most often choosing the generally used form of
couplets, not thinking that a completely different thought is often contained
in each stanza, and that this requires another melody – and suddenly the
romance is finished – and, having written it, he will savour the glory of being
a composer. If he does take it upon himself to write a romance which is not
in couplets, but is in what we call the artistic style, then a greater misfortune
awaits him. A single chord progression is a stumbling block for him.
Whether the composer starts with a pure triad or a seventh chord is neither
here nor there: he will lose himself in keys unrelated to that with which he
started. Supposing he wants to go back to the original key – but the words
have finished – what then? It is very simple: without worrying about com-
plying with the form of the composition or even the demands of the ear,

7 This book was first published in Paris in 1843.

relying on the commonplace paradox that nothing is easier than changing from one key to another by means of one chord, the composer imperturbably snatches at this easy way out of his difficulty, at the expense of both the music and the meaning of the words. Other dilettanti unceremoniously adhere despairingly to one and the same key from beginning to end, and pass off this tiresome monotony as a melancholy feeling.

Had I taken it into my head to go into all the shortcomings of a romance composed by an amateur, that would have been going too far. But an example of these shortcomings can be seen in the disregard for vocal registers shown by an amateur composing a romance. Such romances are never written for any specific voice but may be sung by everyone, that is by those with untrained voices, because the latter cannot leave their own register without being spoiled. Thus a romance of this kind is almost always written for the low register; it seems to have been written for a baritone or a contralto, when all of a sudden one comes across a phrase with A, B and C, in other words for a tenor and only a tenor, not even for a soprano, because these notes are sung by this voice at moments of the highest emotion in opera and not in romances. What must we conclude from all this about romances written by amateurs? That only sometimes do they have good melodies, yet surely enough of them to satisfy the demands of art? Of course not, and besides, the critic will say nothing, since criticism itself is dumb, and does not have the right to analyse the composition of an amateur who follows his art merely for his own pleasure, without any thought of fame or money; in any case, without such desires the arts have no chance. A person publishing his composition must try to make a name for himself in music, to win a right to glory, European fame and immortality. Only then will he work as people work when they want to become worthy of their art. For this, one must be a dedicated and complete artist and, most importantly, not do anything without ambition; the absence of this emotion is the distinctive characteristic of a mediocre nature, leading to the complete stagnation of intellectual abilities.

There are, it is true, amateurs who study musical theory, but here too they do not behave like true artists. They value not the rules but the exceptions; and having assimilated these exceptions they never give them up. Thus, in some work by a great composer we can, for example, come across a chord progression of an unusual kind. The amateur will take this and turn it into a rule for himself and will write only unusual harmonies, without taking into consideration the fact that where the great composer was concerned this harmony was a result of the overflowing of his inspiration, a cry of despair or ecstasy, and the logical consequence of the whole composition. The amateur, on the other hand, will do this only for his own amusement and will study in great detail what the theory of music considers a chance happening.

Amateurs are also characterized by the exclusiveness of their opinions, since they admire the work of some particular composer and can find nothing good in the works of other composers. They also carry along in their wake their own admirers who like what these amateurs praise and reject what they revile.

Amateurs who perform exert an even more disastrous influence on art for the very reason that in this case impressions are formed at the very moment of the performance. The musician who has done no more than give a good performance of the work of a composer will never be anything but mediocre. Only when he learns how to communicate the greatness of the work will he himself become great. In order to perform a piece of music well one must do long technical training. In order to communicate the greatness of a work, it is not sufficient to concern oneself with the technical mechanics; one needs in addition to understand and have great feeling for it, to go carefully into the piece, to lose oneself in it and to reproduce the idea of the work for the listener. This reproduction is in itself a second creative exercise. Anyone who has this ability can represent a mediocre work as beautiful, having lent it details of his own invention. Even in the work of a great composer one can find effects which the composer forgot to indicate or simply did not think about.

The amateur is afraid to appear distinctive, though he has taken upon himself the responsibility of original interpretation. Finally, speaking frankly, I do not believe that the amateur possesses the necessary gift of understanding, and because of this all that he can ever become is a good performer. But here, even more than in the theory of art, he has turned an exception into a rule. An example of this is the fact that Chopin sometimes played *tempo rubato*. But the reason for this lay in his sickly condition[8], in the turbulent state of his ideas and emotions, in his melancholy and poetic nature; his whole performance gave the impression of enmeshing the listener in a web of soothing sounds; it represented the speciality of a great artist and resulted from a demand of his own nature, so that it cannot in any way be considered a general rule. The amateur who is carried away by Chopin overlooks these facts, and regards Chopin's style as an important rule of musical performance, which leads to the discovery that keeping to the rhythm means playing without feeling. Let us take another example. In the

---

8 Stephen Heller is reported to have observed that in Chopin's last years the weakness of his health made his playing hardly audible (Frederick Niecks: *Frederick Chopin as a Man and Musician* (London 1888), vol. 2, p. 97), but I have found no one other than Rubinstein who attributes Chopin's use of *tempo rubato* to a physical cause.

topmost register of his voice Tamberlik[9] has notes that are amazingly strong; everyone has heard of his famous top C sharp. The amateur, not taking into account how much Tamberlik must have had to work on his voice to be able to achieve that note and forgetting that only through intensive exercising has his chest developed and his lungs expanded so that he can reach such high notes, nonetheless maintains that he will try at any price to reach that note. It does not occur to him that the most strenuous work, the hardest persistence and patience are the basic preconditions for a good performance.

But the amateur is looking only for satisfaction and embarks only on those tasks which are easy. After hearing a work performed by some famous artist, the amateur sets about playing it himself without any preparatory study. It is not important that his resources will not allow him to do this. Often, not understanding in the slightest even the most basic rules of music, its ABC, he decides to sing the most difficult operatic arias. I consider it pointless to say that here, as in any other case, there are honourable exceptions. Yet there are too few of them for the majority to escape reproof for their all too unceremonious approach to art.

All that I have said about amateurs cannot be blamed on them alone: the main role here is played by parents and teachers. The former, well aware that several years must be spent on a person's intellectual education and resigned to this condition are terribly impatient when it comes to musical education. The pupil might have had only a few lessons, and already they want him to play a piece which makes an impression. Each month they change to a better teacher (fashion in music teachers is even more changeable than fashion in clothes), without paying any attention to the endeavours of the conscientious teacher to instil taste and musical understanding in the pupil. They impose their own opinions on him, and hence they deprive the disobedient teacher of their benevolent grace and favour.

A great many of the foreign teachers who settle in Russia for as long as necessary to enrich themselves and who want to win the favour of parents as quickly as possible teach the dull basic rules of music very superficially, and try only to teach their pupil to play some fashionable piece. All the basic rules, without which one cannot become a musician, are either disregarded completely or studied for the shortest possible time.

It often happens that you are invited to a home which considers itself musical; most of those invited are musicians; every one of them can play something or sing an aria by Rossini, Verdi or Glinka, or a song by Schubert or Gordigiani.[10] But try to get them to play or sing something

9   Enrico Tamberlik (1820–89) was an Italian tenor prominent on the international operatic circuit.
10 This is probably Luigi Gordigiani (1806–60), an Italian composer primarily of works involving the voice.

together – a trio or quartet – and you will find that it is impossible. Most of these artists cannot sight-read four bars, do not understand the time system, do not know which key a work is in, and cannot produce a note until it has been played on the piano.

It is sad when you see this state of affairs in a country where music could attain the highest levels of perfection, because no one will dispute the fact that the Russian people are unquestionably endowed with an aptitude for this art. I would never have allowed myself to pronounce such a definite verdict on this subject were it not for the fact that I head one of the Russian musical societies,[11] and through this am in direct contact with all those involved in all branches of the art. My own experience has convinced me of the lack of solid foundations, and what is more, of the fact that a great deal of good would result if the government[12] wanted to extricate this art from the oblivion in which it has left it until now, that is, if the government gave it the same rights as the other arts – in a word, if musicians enjoyed the same rights as other artists.

Compositions have come into our Musical Society from all corners of the empire. Sometimes there is a great deal of talent in these works, but what is striking is the lack of any knowledge of theory. Amateurs enrol in our Society's choirs who sometimes want to perform individual pieces, but most of our members suffer from a marked lack of basic musical education and a clear inability to learn compositions worthy of inclusion in a serious concert programme.

Many of our amateurs, it is true, want to study – but can they? No, because music lessons are so expensive that you need to be rich to afford them. Yes, and that is not all: the main reason is that there are no Russian teachers of music, and a person who does not know either French or German cannot take lessons. A Russian music teacher cannot make his living from music because to be only a musician means, for a Russian, not to have any civic status. This is why there is such a shortage of Russian teachers of music.

And yet the desire to study music is very widespread, especially among the lower classes. Proof of this can be seen in the fact that when our Society offered free classes last spring there were so many people wanting to join that the Society's resources were insufficient to allow us to accept more than a third of them.[13] In the autumn we started various classes at very moderate

11 That is, the Russian Musical Society.
12 Rubinstein's hope for governmental support is indicative of the degree of bureaucratic regulation of such institutions in Russia, and of the restrictions on individual initiative in such a matter.
13 The Russian Musical Society opened classes in singing in the spring of 1860; there was also a class in the fundamentals of music.

cost[14] and the desire to study has not diminished. A great number of the students we enrolled were merchants or shopkeepers. Does this not prove how great the desire to study art is? But what can be done to remedy this sad situation? I shall tell you: the only answer is to establish a conservatoire.

People will argue that great geniuses have rarely come out of conservatoires; I agree, but who can deny that good musicians come out of conservatoires, and that is precisely what is essential in our enormous country. The conservatoire will never prevent a genius from developing outside it, and, meanwhile, each year the conservatoire will provide Russian teachers of music, Russian orchestral musicians and Russian singers of both sexes who will work in the manner of someone who sees his art as his livelihood, the key to social respect, a means of becoming famous, a way of giving himself up completely to his divine calling, and as a person who respects himself and his art ought to work. If music had taken root in Russia as strongly as it has in, say, Germany, where each little town has its own orchestra, opera, choir school and philharmonic society, I would be the first to advise against founding a conservatoire, which would only add to the number of young people searching in vain along with a multitude of other musicians for enough to make a living. But in Russia, where, except in St Petersburg and Moscow, you never hear music because of the lack of musicians, there is room for not just one conservatoire but even two or three. Even then the whole country would not be filled with musicians, and it would still not be every orchestra or theatre manager in the provinces who would be able to form an orchestra or opera company without difficulty. Yes, create a conservatoire, give knowledge to those who want to devote themselves exclusively to their art, and let the amateurs take an interest in music for their own pleasure. Their influence would not then be fatal, because alongside them would be people who, in the words of the poet, 'eat their bread in sorrow, spend the darksome hours weeping and watching for the morrow, and know ye, you heavenly powers'.

(b) V. V. Stasov: Conservatoires in Russia. Comments on Mr Rubinstein's article. *The Northern Bee*, 24 February 1861, no. 45. Stasov 2, pp. 5–10

Vladimir Vasil'yevich Stasov (1824–1906) was an art critic of formidable energy and range. He completed his studies at the School of Jurisprudence in 1843 and began writing articles on literature, painting and music in 1847. He was in Italy from 1851 to 1854 in the service of a wealthy Russian nobleman and took advantage of the opportunity of

---

14 The subjects taught in these classes were singing, piano, violin, cello, elementary musical theory, and practical composition.

expanding his knowledge of the arts. In the mid-1850s he joined the staff of the Imperial Public Library in St Petersburg, and was head of its Art division from 1872. His career in music ran from the time of Berlioz's first visit to Russia in 1847 until the première of Rimsky-Korsakov's opera *Kashchey bessmertnïy* ('Kashchey the immortal'), the occasion of a speech which was published, in 1905. He was a fervent supporter of Russian art in general, not least Russian music, and exerted a strong influence on the ideas of the Balakirev circle through the suggestion of topics for operas and programmatic works, and then the recommendation of appropriate historical, literary and other sources, and in other ways. With Cui, he was that group's principal press champion; it was Stasov who coined the phrase 'the mighty handful' (see 6(c)). He performed comparable services for many painters, sculptors and others. He wrote almost a hundred items on music alone, to say nothing of archaeology, history or several branches of the fine arts. A voluminous critic, memoirist, editor, biographer and controversialist, his work is now uneven in value, since Stasov did not always allow facts to stand in the way of good argument and sometimes skated on thin ice where musical *technicalia* were concerned. Forcefulness in debate, however, is a common characteristic in Russian discussion of music at this period. Stasov tended to share the views of the Balakirev group: he favoured subjects from Russian history treated in a most detailed and historically 'authentic' fashion; he admired the most modern compositions of Liszt and Berlioz; he preferred originality to sound technique, and, like Musorgsky, truth to beauty. There is little sign that these tastes changed much over a long active career.

The first issue of *The Age* for 1861 contained an article by Mr Rubinstein entitled 'The state of music in Russia' which it would appear is worth looking at. At first glance many people would perhaps not find much in it other than justified complaints about the present state of our music and sensible suggestions pointing to ways in which the situation could be improved. But if you look closer you will find that the whole article is made up of thoughts and reasoning which are so lacking in truth and substance that one cannot commend it to the reading public.

Mr Rubinstein is a foreigner[15] with nothing in common either with our national character or our art (although some musical papers abroad sometimes number him among Russian composers), a foreigner with no understanding either of the demands of our national character or of the historical course of our art. This fact thus to some extent excuses or at least explains the many errors in his article. But there are still other mistakes which occur

15 Rubinstein was born a citizen of the Russian Empire in a Jewish family who converted to Orthodox Christianity in 1831. He considered himself a patriotic Russian, though his opponents were not above exploiting his German surname with Jewish connections and his period of study in Berlin to make him out to be unRussian.

when he is speaking not about Russian art on its own but about art in general. I am not going to take it upon myself to explain these latter errors, but all the same I shall examine them together with the former mistakes, since the two are closely linked, and indeed the latter may be the main source of the former.

Mr Rubinstein states that in Russia only amateurs are involved in music. Let him think that, if he as a foreigner has not managed to discover anything to the contrary! But what conclusion does he draw from all this? He claims that with their operas, songs and other compositions these amateurs hinder the development of music in Russia. Why, one would be justified in asking? This Mr Rubinstein does not explain. It is true that he enlarged painstakingly on his complaints about amateurs without any educational preparation who tackle a subject with which they are not able to cope; that they then remain satisfied with their pitiful attempts and consider them to be great works of art; that when performing they try to equal the great artists, but what they manage to imitate from them is only the inessential and the artificial, and so on. But surely none of this is new; all these are worn-out platitudes about dilettantism, and the reader will still in all probability not be able to grasp what relationship exists between amateurs taking delight in their own achievements and the development of a nation's music. The influence of amateurs in Russia could well be detrimental, but surely only in two circumstances: firstly, if all our society was so blinded by the bad works of these amateurs that it considered their works great and beautiful or, secondly, if the amateurs, not satisfied merely with naive self-delusion, wanted at any price to convince others of their greatness and, with no regard for moral feeling, tried to crush the work of true musical talents. But, it has to be asked, do we come across either of these two circumstances in Russia? No, thank God! Even Mr Rubinstein himself has not been in any position to point them out. Consequently it is no use attacking our musical dilettanti more than the dilettanti of any country abroad. Our dilettante is as innocent and harmless as his English, French or German counterpart. It is possible that he is even more harmless, because he is always more carefree, lazy and apathetic than all the rest. All his work is confined to a close circle of friends and acquaintances, so that it is difficult to point to instances where his work and arrogant pretensions would extend further than the applause of a few drawing rooms frequented by dilettanti just as innocent as himself. Look and see whether many works by our amateurs have even been published. Yet if a few of our dilettanti really published their work at home and abroad; if others were able to have their work performed at concerts and in theatres open to the public; if a majority of them are not well enough versed in the theory of music; if an even greater number of them distort the works of great composers by the way they perform them, or ruin their voices, or overstrain their chests out of an absurd zeal to reach the high note of some worthless but fashionable singer – what of it? All of this will harm them, and them alone. Their performances, like their compositions, are given a correct evaluation by the public, and there is not one of them who is valued more than he really deserves. Why attack them or try to hinder them in an activity they find so pleasant and which is quite harmless to others? Why make them shoulder all the blame when they are guilty in neither body nor soul? And why does Mr Rubinstein not say anything about the compositions of artists who are not amateurs? Having read his article, some, perhaps, would think that only the dilettanti can produce bad compositions and that the artist is somehow immune from them. Mr Rubinstein completely forgot to say that a thousand times more harmful than dilettanti and their works are the bad compositions of non-dilettante musicians, especially when the works have been written by people who are famous for some reason. Sometimes the fame of an artist is sufficient to sway the public's verdict, to set their ideas off on the wrong track and to keep these ideas wrong for a long time. Could the compositions of a dilettante do the same harm?

Besides, it must be noted that our amateurs are far better than the pitiful and despicable picture of them painted by Mr Rubinstein. They are not at all such ignoramuses as he makes out, and if their musical compositions do not reveal any real talent (which, by the way, virtually goes without saying in as much as they are dilettanti), then, at least, they are, generally speaking, incomparably more intelligent than Mr Rubinstein supposes when he says 'especially if they avoid writing a bright melody to sad words'. Whatever they may be like, we are hardly likely to hear from them any of those amazing things that we read in the article 'The state of music in Russia', such as, for example, that romances fall into two categories – those written in couplets, and those written in the artistic style; that dilettanti will never reach the highest level of art because they will be prevented by other work commitments; that a feeling for what is refined, if not instinctive, can be acquired through careful study(!!); that the artist should not do anything without ambition, since the absence of that emotion is the distinctive characteristic of a mediocre nature, which leads to the complete stagnation of intellectual abilities (*what an unfortunate notion to have of art and artists!*); that art will always be cursed by artists who use art to try to satisfy their own material needs; that the indispensable conditions without which a true artist cannot develop are disillusionment, beautiful dreams shattered by life's sad reality, artistic fanaticism unrecognized and ridiculed by an indifferent public (*what amusing ideas, like those in old stories where the main character is an artist!*)¹⁶, and so on. Maxims like these, if spoken by some amateur, would, of course, have suffered the fate which always awaits bad musical compositions: they are regarded first of all with pity, and then forgotten about for ever, out of compassion.

Let us assume, however, that the foreign conceptions of Mr Rubinstein about the state of Russian music are true: that we simply do not have a national school of music standing firm on its own foundations, that it has not created any significant or original works, and that it has as yet no importance in the history of art. Let us for a minute become foreigners like Mr Rubinstein, and imagine that our art needs his concerned care and advice. Let us reflect on the ways of getting Russian music out of the state into which it has been plunged, according to Mr Rubinstein, by the despotism and harmful influence of amateurs. What then? Are the remedies proposed by Mr Rubinstein really the most effective? Give the musicians civic status, he suggests, set up a conservatoire, and everything will suddenly change and work differently, everything will be the way it ought to be. Our homeland will suddenly be full of real artists, and the harmful influence of amateurs will be at an end. Is that enough? Will Mr Rubinstein's remedies actually have the desired effect?

Let us look first at the question of civic status. I seriously doubt that the issue of status would be sure to help the development of music in Russia. Of course it is undeniable that in Russia status is linked with advantages which one can only wish that everyone enjoyed, but this is a blessing to which every member of society should have a right, and not only artists in particular. Human feeling makes us want the most complete and widespread realization for the greatest mass of people of all that will promote their well-being and raise the dignity of the individual. But when such a blessing appears only as a privilege, or only as an exception for some, then, inevitably, it becomes the source only of very mercenary longings. It would be useless to try to associate the idea of the development of art with these longings. A person must benefit from the advantages of status, not because he is a musician or in general terms an artist, not because these advantages are possibly beneficial to his art, but because he has a right to them and because he has a real need for them. If we look at the question of status in the light of its value to the musician, then it suddenly turns into a mere piece of bait which will entice many people to give up an activity where they felt quite happy and were doing something genuinely useful in order to become bad musicians and to increase the number of people who, in Mr Rubinstein's own expression, 'are a curse upon their art', or in order to study

---

16 One example is V. F. Odoyevsky's *Posledniy kvartet Betkhovena* ('Beethoven's last quartet') published in 1830.

music until they win themselves civic status. There are innumerable examples which we can list to corroborate this last fact: how many academies in Europe have given out and continue to give out awards to people studying one form of art or another? When all is said and done, they have created not artists but only people eager to acquire some status or title or some kind of privilege. The creation by means of this well-known lure of a number of musicians does not yet constitute artistic progress. Art moves at its own pace, has its own laws of development and does not bow to any outside pressures. The artificial encouragement of artists remains and will always remain as ineffective for art as the artificial encouragement of factories or trade. Our men of letters were never given any ranks or titles, and yet a deeply national literature has grown up and thriven in our country. Without a doubt this is what should happen with music too. In this field internal life, internal movement and development are all.

The setting up of a conservatoire and the success of art are not at all the same thing; the latter does not depend in the slightest on the former. Even if they open not just one but many conservatoires, nonetheless there may be no real benefits for art. On the contrary, more harm than good might be the result.

It is possible that Rubinstein is not aware of the opinion now deep-rooted in the greater part of Europe that holds that academies and con-servatoires serve only as breeding grounds for talentless people and aid the establishment in art of harmful ideas and tastes.[17] Therefore the best minds search in the sphere of artistic education for means of doing without *higher* educational establishments. *Higher* educational establishments for art are a completely different thing from their counterparts in the sciences, and the two categories should never be confused. There is a vast gulf between the two types. A university and a conservatoire are completely different things. The former communicates only *knowledge*; the latter is not content to do just that and interferes in the most dangerous way with the *creative process* of the artist in training, and extends a despotic power (from which nothing can protect him) over the shape and form of his works, trying to impose on them the conservatoire's bias, to bend them according to a certain academic standard, to transfer to them well-known habits and finally and worst of all sinking their teeth into the young artist's very understanding, foisting on to him opinions about artistic works and their composers, opinions from which it is impossible or infinitely difficult for anyone devoting themselves to art to dissociate themselves subsequently. In view of the very fundamental

17 An instance close to home was the departure in 1863 from the Academy of Fine Arts of the young artists later known as the 'Wanderers', who were not prepared to accept the choice of subject for a painting imposed on them by an old-fashioned institution.

shortcomings of all academies and conservatoires in general, it is now acknowledged as correct to consider them even more harmful than beneficial for the development of art. History shows all too clearly that they have caused entire generations to move backwards instead of forwards. How many musical academies and conservatoires have existed for a good while now, for instance, in Italy and France! Yet they have by no means achieved what people expected of them; they have not raised the musical level of the country, have not enhanced the spread of musical education, and have not even produced the benefit of a school of teachers which had been most hoped for. In Germany the great era of music *preceded* the establishment of conservatoires, and all the best talents were raised *outside* these institutions.

As far as teachers of music are concerned, any teachers we have are all foreigners who were educated in their own countries in conservatoires and schools very similar to that being suggested by Mr Rubinstein. The question arises, therefore, why, despite the huge and constant influx of these people to our country, Mr Rubinstein still has to complain about the poor state of our musical education? If conservatoires were really, as Mr Rubinstein thinks, an effective means of putting down the roots of our musical education, then the hordes of teachers coming to us from conservatoires abroad would surely have done a lot of good by this time and brought about a radical change. Why does Mr Rubinstein suppose that teachers coming from our conservatoires would be any better than those sent out to us from foreign parts? Let us look again at those very amateurs attacked by Mr Rubinstein. Which of them did not study with a famous professor, or at a famous conservatoire? And what of it? Even if they did, nothing emerged other than the amateurs about whom Mr Rubinstein complains so much.

No, obviously it is not a question of just setting up conservatoires. Obviously, Germany is not indebted to conservatoires for the top place she occupies both in the world of music and among a number of other countries with as many conservatoires as she has. Obviously, her supremacy has arisen from other, more deep-rooted reasons which have been able to produce magnificent results *in spite of* the existence of conservatoires.

Ascertaining the real conditions which would help or hinder this development is the main task of every initiative, but it is precisely this which Mr Rubinstein's article has failed to do. In the article Mr Rubinstein suggests only measures for transplanting to our country what already exists elsewhere. But what is the point of that? Each of us knows how many foreign seeds have been transplanted to our country and how little increase they have brought forth. I think that it is time to put a stop to unreasoned transplants and to consider instead what would be truly wholesome and beneficial to our soil specifically, and for our nationality specifically. In this case Europe's experience shows that modest schools limited to giving an elementary education in musical literacy do for the development of art as much good as higher schools such as academies and conservatoires do it harm. Surely this experience will not be wasted on us? Surely we must now emphatically stop obeying and automatically copying everything that exists elsewhere only for the pleasure of boasting about the huge complement of teachers and classes, the futile distribution of awards and prizes, the volumes of worthless compositions and the crowds of worthless musicians? If there is any threat to music it comes from the things I have mentioned, not from the amateurs.

(c) A. N. Serov: The guarantees of genuine musical education in St Petersburg. *The Northern Bee*, 9 May 1862, no. 124. Serov 5, pp. 258–64

To the Conservatoire was soon added the Free School of Music. Founded in 1862, this institution aimed to provide musical training free of charge (that is the meaning of *Besplatnaya* ('Free') in its title), and thus to introduce music to persons for whom the normal fees would be a deterrent. Its first director was Gavriil Lomakin who was known almost solely as a choir-trainer (albeit a highly respected one), and in view of that and the fact that using modern methods it was possible to form singers from a variety of backgrounds into a music-reading chorus quite quickly, the Free School's initial emphasis was on singing and an excellent choir emerged. Balakirev was the other main figure, and his interest (in orchestral music) complemented Lomakin's. The latter retired as director in 1868 to be succeeded by the former until 1873. Although the School continued in existence until 1917, its glorious days barely outlasted the 1860s, when its concerts gave a fillip to the work of modern and Russian composers.

Whatever the sphere of activity, one will always encounter two opposing tendencies in mankind. The first is a self-seeking one, where the individual pays lip-service to the common good whilst striving for his own personal aggrandizement or enrichment. The second tendency encompasses true service to the cause, a fanatical, unselfish service, in which it is only very rarely possible to find a way of somehow reconciling the common good and private gain. Indeed, more often than not personal gain, peace of mind and sometimes even the individual's position in life are sacrificed in the pursuit of that higher ideal.

The Slavonic character exhibits a certain slackness, an excessive compliance and tolerance bordering on apathy in practical, day-to-day affairs. In matters of art and science we Russians, because of the characteristics of our race, are quite willing to stretch out our necks to receive the yoke thought up for imposition on us by some passing trickster who has been smart enough to realize that this virgin soil (in whatever respect) may well turn out to be his *promised* land, believing that if he does not seize this opportunity, then someone else will. *Res nullius cedit primo occupanti* ('property which belongs to no one goes to the first person to take possession of it').

Thus, possessing innate musicality, the utmost natural capacity for the technical and creative aspects of music and for the practical demonstration of musical gifts, we Russians voluntarily yield to the oppression of talentless foreigners, musical Yankels who, as Gogol put it in *Taras Bulba*, are ready to 'lay bare whole provinces'.[18]

We are also aware that these visiting musical educators of Russia are making a mockery of us. Take the following example: a choir is assembled from dilettanti who can neither sing nor read music, under the direction of a pianist who has no understanding of conducting; they immediately perform the choral-orchestral work by Beethoven which is considered to be the most difficult in the world, in front of an audience.[19] It is easy to see that this is tantamount to telling the audience straight to their faces that they are of no consequence, that things are not what they seem, that everything is simply being done for show, and that this whole charade is for the benefit of the Russian and foreign press. Of course we are quite clear about all of this, and we do not even protest about it. On the contrary, for such lovable profanation of art, such blatant mocking of the audience, we allow the great pianist-educator to have laurels bestowed on him in front of that same audience which he himself so crudely ridiculed!

Of course, we are led on like meek little lambs. But we ought to understand that there is no reason why Russia, with its deep-seated flair for music, its musical feeling and sense, should be led in musical matters along the narrow and well-trodden paths chosen by dimwitted French and German teachers of notes.

We ought to be fully aware that if a foreign virtuoso pianist, having ingratiated himself into the protection of our art patrons (!) and winning some influence for himself, founds a musical institution, at the head of

18 In Gogol's story Yankel is a Jewish tavern-keeper who has so enslaved his Slav neighbours 'for three miles in every direction' to alcohol as to have impoverished the whole area. 'And if Yankel had stayed there another ten years, he would certainly have laid bare the whole province' (Gogol, *Mirgorod* (tr. Constance Garnett, London 1928), p. 181). By thus repeating 'Yankel' (a typically Jewish diminutive of the first name Yakov ('Jacob')), Serov is reminding his readers – none too subtly – that Rubinstein too was Jewish.

19 Serov had characterized the performance of Beethoven's Ninth Symphony given at a Russian Musical Society concert conducted by Rubinstein on 1 February 1860 as 'the most unforgivable caricature of this music of the utmost genius in the world' (Serov 4, p. 228).

which he places – apart from himself (a newcomer to conducting, and a layman in the teaching of music) – persons who are not known to the public or even to the pianist himself for their musical prowess, then the founding of such an institution may of course benefit that same pianist's reputation superficially, and . . . help line the pockets of some of his non-musical sponsors.[20] However, Russia itself cannot expect anything but positive harm from this institution, as from everything built upon lies, deceit, ignorance, narrow-mindedness and selfishness . . . We, I repeat, could have seen all this, and, perhaps, we do see and realize it, but . . . we doze on in our Slavonic apathy. Our 'Yankels', however, are not slumbering. On the contrary, they keep all musical activity in both St Petersburg and Moscow under continual siege. Soon, with the founding of the conservatoire they desired for themselves as the future breeding-ground for talentless musical civil servants, they begin to throw their weight around in the province they have acquired in a thoroughly despotic manner, trying to crush any musical talent in Russia that does not spring from within their own Yankel ranks. Out of a hatred of all that is Russian, they are doing all they can to nip in the bud any true and natural development of Russian musical talent.

I have often found myself putting this point of view to the public, and I have always been forthright, making no attempts at diplomacy.

Understandably, my voice has remained a voice crying in the wilderness. Of what consequence are our thoughts, our arguments, even if they are widely accessible, when in the opposing camp we find not words but facts and actions and where extremely skilful chicanery is employed as the ornamental façade for these facts and actions?

Mundus vult decipi ('the world wishes to be deceived'). Every audience in the world loves to be fooled and it appears that our audiences for some reason have a special weakness for it.

But now, thankfully while there was still enough time, the public has been presented, for the good of the cause of justice, with a brilliant instance, which serves as an excellent means of testing the three years of activity of Russia's patented musical educators.

In St Petersburg there have been splendid vocal concerts organized by Gavriil Iakimovich Lomakin,[21] the finest choral conductor in Russia, and

20 The name which contemporary readers would immediately link with this apparently hypothetical pianist is, of course, that of Anton Rubinstein. The art patron is the Grand Duchess Elena Pavlovna, aunt of Alexander II.

21 G. Ya. Lomakin (1812–85), Russian choir-trainer, composer and teacher. He first came to notice through his work with Count Sheremetev's choir, of which he was director from 1830 to 1872. He worked for the Imperial Court Chapel Choir from 1848 to 1859. With Balakirev he founded the Free School of Music in 1862, remaining as its first director until 1868. Serov's description of Lomakin is not necessarily exaggerated to heighten contrast: his work was held in high esteem.

given by a choir composed partly of members of Count Sheremetev's choir and partly of amateur singers of both sexes.

And so, for the first time in many, many years our audiences have heard real performances of secular choral pieces given by a large number of singers who had learned their parts properly and who were directed by a proper conductor. The choir's sound rose from a scarcely audible pianissimo, barely above a whisper for the massed voices, to a deafeningly loud forte. Each sound was distinct and clear where the music demanded it. One could hear thousands of nuances which cannot be expressed in the usual sounds of music and cannot be put into words. One could sense the fusion of this mass of voices into one whole which obeyed the slightest movement of the conductor's hand; there was a complete fusion of the singers with the will of the conductor, a complete and conscious fusion of his will and the spirit of the piece of music. One detected, as one rarely does in St Petersburg, a current of genuine musicality, of the genuine, warm, pure love of music – and the results were glorious.

The audiences of St Petersburg (used to the so-called concerts of the so-called Russian (!) Musical Society and other symphonic concerts) were completely unused to such musical performances of choral works with the appropriate nuances, and became aware in Mr Lomakin's concerts of entirely new delights they had not previously experienced, and applauded furiously.

If only in this case, an exception to the general rule, let us be more consistent in our actions and enthusiasm, our likes and dislikes. Let us dwell on the gratifying and comforting fact of the existence of this great wealth of vocal resources consisting almost exclusively of Russians, of amateurs, gathered together and guided by that great master of his craft, the Russian conductor, without any outside help – indeed, on the contrary, facing considerable obstacles raised by Russia's patented musical educators.[22]

The fact that these brilliant concerts exist speaks for itself, and with the utmost eloquence. Let us hope that this speaking does not remain like a voice crying in the wilderness. Let all those in Russia who truly love music understand that expensive government quarters for the stewards and quartermasters of the patented music colleges are completely without advantage to the genuine good of the cause at present. We have no need of a musical civil service to propagate mediocrity and lack of talent, which sound the death knell for art. We do not need patented judges who will hand out prizes and diplomas to encourage useless activity, because no one who is

---

22 *Author's note*: It was precisely thanks to these obstacles that the orchestra in Mr Lomakin's concerts on 11 March and 11 April was not notable either for its completeness or precision, so that the Overture on Russian Themes, advertised on the poster for 11 April, by the gifted Russian composer Mily Balakirev, could not possibly have been performed.

truly talented will ever wish to submit to the judgement of privileged pedants, ignoramuses and envious people.

Let all those who, in actual fact, hold dear the musical education of Russians starting with the first principles of that education, those who hold dear the spreading of musical literacy, which is necessary if art is to flourish, let them see the high-sounding titles and luxurious grandeur for what they are and give due attention to the institution founded by the same zealous G. I. Lomakin, the Free School of Singing.

The School was opened barely a month ago, on 18 August, in the halls of the Medico-Chirurgical Academy, but already it has more than 300 students.

Attitudes towards musical education and musical study amongst the general public in Russia, it must be said, are still rather barbarous.

Even in the most elementary subjects of study in music, confusion still reigns. Such a mixture of opinions would be unthinkable in any other discipline.

Let us imagine that you charged a teacher with the task of teaching your child grammar – that is, to read and write – and you were not able to follow the progress of the lessons yourself.

After a month or two, you test the child. It turns out that he is unable to read at all, that he can, in fact, scarcely recognize the letters of the alphabet. Instead, he has learned two poems by Pushkin and one by Lermontov off by heart, but he recites them meaninglessly – exactly as instructed by his teacher. It goes without saying that you find this outcome deeply distressing and you would hasten to dismiss such a bright teacher.

Now let us imagine that you wanted your child to study music – either to play an instrument or to sing – and to this end you send him to study with a patented tutor, a 'professor' of music or singing, as all these Yankels like to style themselves.

Not a month, but a year or two go by, and still the successes of your son or daughter are confined to playing or singing a few little pieces, which have been learned *tant bien que mal* ('just enough to get by') under the guidance of the professor himself. Is this not just the same as learning two poems off by heart, instead of attaining the desired level of literacy? If the teacher in question happens to be among the rare ones who value the ability to read music, the fortunate student will be able to read instrumental music for, say, the piano. If the student is learning to sing, this will absolutely never happen, since singing teaching based on currently fashionable Italian methods is limited to learning to sing something.

Italian professors of singing cannot themselves, for the most part, read music, and usually know nothing of musical theory, considering such matters to be unimportant and irrelevant.

As a result of this wonderful state of affairs it turns out that our amateurs who can sing various cavatinas with flair, and arias with pretty grace-notes, are nonplussed when they have to sight-sing in a group even the most simple harmony for two or three voices. They do not have the slightest understanding of intervals, or of the division of time or of the rules of tonality (the knowledge of which forms the basis of accuracy in intonation).

Gavriil Lomakin has been a choral conductor for a quarter of a century and has so developed his aptitude as a teacher in this area as to be able to achieve astounding results.

Every choir entrusted to him learns to sing any piece of music at sight with accurate intonation, and to name just as faultlessly any musical sound.

For musical literacy in choral singing this represents the *ne plus ultra*. And it must be borne in mind that in the singers, alongside this singer's skill, almost unnoticed by them themselves, the talent innate in most Russians for harmony, for a true understanding of modulation, counterpoint and all those combinations on which the most complex music is based, is being developed.

Model performances, such as the ones on 11 March and 11 April which St Petersburg admired, are only made possible by this method of teaching together with boundless confidence in the conductor on the part of the singers.

[Serov compares favourably the work of this new choir with those he has heard abroad, whether in compositions by Haydn, Mozart, Mendelssohn or fifteenth- and sixteenth-century masters of church music; he warmly recommends Lomakin's recently published booklet *Kratkaya metoda peniya* ('A short guide to singing').]

It is time we stopped our practice of marvelling only at visiting experts. The time has come to have the courage to acknowledge the real worth of our own Russian musicians.

It is time, finally, to open our eyes and learn to distinguish genuine service to art from what can only be described as sham.

(d) Ts. A. Cui: A St Petersburg musical chronicle. (The teaching of music at the St Petersburg Conservatoire, its syllabus. The Free School of Music, Lomakin and their concerts.) *St Petersburg Bulletin*, 15 March 1864, no. 60. Cui, pp. 8–11

Tsesar' Antonovich Kyui (César Cui, 1835–1918) was a highly regarded and high-ranking fortifications engineer. Of French and Lithuanian parentage, he had some lessons in music with Moniuszko in Wilna (Vilnius) in 1849 before engineering studies took him to the Russian capital. He graduated from the Academy of Military Engineers in 1857 and went on to teach there for many decades. He met

Dargomïzhsky and Balakirev in 1856 and the Balakirev circle began to form. Cui was a prolific composer who, despite his fourteen operas, was most successful in shorter compositions, such as the song and the piano miniature. In the early years he was viewed as the Balakirev circle's opera specialist, though his own creative efforts were soon surpassed by those of the stronger talents in the group. He appears to be the inventor of the term 'New Russian School', usually with 'Operatic' added, in response, surely to the New German School represented by Wagner and Liszt. It seems ironic that someone whom history has characterized as a Russian nationalist should have composed operas such as *William Ratcliff* and *Matteo Falcone*.

Cui embarked on music criticism in 1864, and continued on a regular basis until 1900. In the 1860s and 1870s he could usually be relied on to support his friends of the Balakirev group, though not completely uncritically. Thereafter his views became less predictable. His final articles, written in the 1910s, are reminiscences or sarcastic commentaries on the latest musical styles. In addition to his over a hundred articles, his *La Musique en Russie*, published in Paris in 1880, helped to make his country's music known abroad.

Until now people have justifiably complained that studying music entails great expense and is completely beyond the reach of the poorer classes; yet among them too there may be wonderful voices, remarkable artistic gifts, and perhaps a talent for composition as well.

These material obstacles have lately been removed to a significant extent here in St Petersburg by the establishment of two musical institutions which, though their aims and methods differ, nonetheless will lead to a broadening and enhancement of musical life.

In 1861 the *Music College*[23] of the Russian Musical Society (known as the Conservatoire) was founded, and in 1862 the *Musical Free School for Singing*[24] was founded. At the Conservatoire (this name was current among the public – hence our use of it) you can study singing, piano and all the orchestral instruments, theory of composition and orchestration, history of music, aesthetics, and declamation (para 2 of the Constitution), at the moderate charge of 100 silver roubles per annum. The choice of instrument depends on the students themselves but in any event they are *obliged* to study choral singing, piano, *the history and aesthetics of music* (para 14). Those entering the Conservatoire must be able to read music (para 9). A director selected by the Committee of the Russian Musical Society is in

23 The terms 'school' (*shkola*) and 'college' (*uchilishche*) were sometimes used in preference to the clearly imported word (and concept) 'conservatoire' (*konservatoriya*).
24 Cui thus marks the sphere of the School's initial pre-eminence; while 'for Singing' was not, as far as I know, part of its formal title, Serov had referred to it in 3(c) as the 'Free School of Singing'.

charge of the College; the director receives a salary determined by the same Committee (paras 4 and 5). The Committee is made up of the five directors of the Russian Musical Society, but these directors are elected by the directors themselves. Here are the actual words of para 8 of the Constitution of the Russian Musical Society: 'After the expiration of the first two years from the day of this Constitution's ratification and then annually two of the directors chosen *by lot* (o blind fate!) demit office, proposing in their stead two new directors who are confirmed in that office by the remaining members of the Committee' (i.e. the directors). And six lines further on: 'Directors demitting office are eligible for re-election'. The Constitution has already made reference to a general meeting of members of the Russian Musical Society (each of whom contributes fifteen silver roubles annually) at which these members are entitled to vote. But the Constitution has nothing to say as to the topics for discussion to which this entitlement to vote relates or to the circumstances in which a general meeting may be called.

The director's work in running the Conservatoire is shared by others under his authority who receive a salary. Financial expenditure is supplemented by available capital, box-office receipts for ten concerts each year, several *matinées musicales*, students' fees, etc.

This is all splendid: the syllabus is comprehensive, and the tuition fee is moderate. But *moderate fees* are a relative concept; for many people moderate means impossible; besides, the requirement to be able to read music before entry is rather inhibiting. What is to be said about the Music School at which anyone at all can learn to sing – *without any payment* and without being able to read music beforehand? The prime movers in this Musical Free School are Lomakin and Balakirev. It has been in existence now for two years and for that period its founders have tirelessly pursued their ends. The School's financial resources are limited; two concerts support it for a whole year [. . .] and the public crowds in to these concerts from all over; the huge hall of the Assembly of the Nobility is always filled to capacity and produces full-house returns at the box office; but nevertheless, except for concert expenses, the resources on which the School exists for a year prove to be quite paltry. But all the while assistants must be engaged – two men are quite insufficient when it comes to teaching several hundred people, and when sheet music has to be prepared for all the students, the hall lit and so on. The utmost unselfishness and profound love for the cause are needed if it is to prosper in such conditions.

The School's syllabus is narrow: only tuition in singing is offered; the syllabus does not embrace 'the art of music in all its spheres'; but on the other hand it is open to everyone. Among its students we find factory workers, sales assistants, shopkeepers and some representatives of the middle class; all their voices blend with amazing unanimity in music's harmonies. Probably the School's framework will expand as its resources increase, but for the moment we can compare the achievements of the School over two years with those of the Conservatoire over three in the field of choral singing. Because of its short period of existence to date the Conservatoire cannot yet form an orchestra from its own students, but the students do take part in the choruses at Russian Musical Society concerts. This choir is weak, as everyone must agree. It is not merely a question of there being no shading, no transitions from loud to soft in their singing – they are weak even in tempo, their intonation is inaccurate, and I have rarely heard them sing a movement decently.

The choir of the Free School has been brought to a pitch of perfection such as we never even dreamed of in St Petersburg. Under Lomakin's direction it constitutes a single whole, like an enormous organ utterly obedient to the skilled hand which plays upon it. The harmonious quality of performance and the fullness of sound are quite out of the ordinary; the listener is astounded when the voices start to swell, grow stronger and finally burst out in a stupendous forte. But perhaps an even stronger impression is made when this enormous choir sings in a whisper: one hears a distant rumble, but a rumble with a definite sound, a prolonged and even rumble. Whether a gradual change from piano to forte is needed, or a sudden strong attack – all these the choir can do uniformly well. And no wonder: Lomakin's well-earned fame as the most excellent *choirmaster* and teacher of choral singing is too firmly consolidated to need to say any more about it; he can scarcely have any rivals in this field – not only here in Russia but abroad – for it is impossible to imagine a choir raised to a higher level of perfection.

[Cui postpones a verdict on the charge that Lomakin is good only in semi-religious andantes, but finds him guilty of incompetence as an orchestral conductor.]

Leaving that aside, Lomakin's services have been colossal: he has prepared extraordinary material which an expert conductor can exploit. And we can expect such a conductor to emerge in the person of Balakirev. In the same concert he proved that he is a masterly orchestral conductor; it is desirable that the conducting of choruses in which the orchestra plays an important part should also pass to him (of course no one could conceivably replace Lomakin in choruses without orchestra or with a slender accompaniment). At this concert the orchestra performed the overtures from A. S. Dargomïzhsky's *Rusalka* and César Cui's *The Prisoner of the Caucasus*[25] and the Second Spanish Overture of M. I. Glinka; in addition Neylissov[26] played Liszt's First Piano Concerto.

[Cui bemoans the preference shown by the Imperial theatres in selecting repertory to *Martha* and *The Bohemian Girl* over *Ruslan and Lyudmila* and *Rusalka*.]

(e) G. A. Laroche: A note on Mr Serov's lectures on music. Letter to the editor of *The Northern Bee*. *The Northern Bee*, 8 May 1864, no. 110, p. 559

Since Rubinstein was opposed to taking part in the press controversy which developed around the establishment of the Conservatoire, his case went by default. While he succeeded in keeping other involved supporters' pens inactive, he failed with one of the students who contributed a letter to the press signed simply 'A pupil of the Conservatoire'. An immediate pretext was given by the views expressed by Serov in a series of ten lectures given from mid-March 1864 on the subject 'The present-day condition of music and musical pedagogy'. The programme of the lectures is in Serov 6, pp. 162–3.

The anonymous author who questioned Serov's assessment of the relative merits of Glinka and Verstovsky, and claimed that Serov's compositions themselves showed the inadequacy of musical knowledge gleaned from the examination of model compositions without technical practice, was German Avgustovich Larosh (Herman Laroche) (1845–1904). The young correspondent went on to become one of the best informed and equipped music critics of the nineteenth century. He graduated from the St Petersburg Conservatoire in 1866 and thereafter taught in the conservatoires of both Moscow and St Petersburg. He tried his hand at composition, and added literary criticism to his activities from 1869 until 1889. His writing on music, which continued until 1900, amounts to over 200 items. It ranges over most of the contemporary repertory, showing tastes similar to those of Tchaikovsky, who, though a close friend, was not immune to criticism of his compositions in the press. Laroche tended increasingly towards scepticism about the more extreme manifestations of modernism in music, sharing Tchaikovsky's idolization of Mozart.

Laroche alludes to Serov's connection with the 'organic criticism' associated primarily with the writer and critic Apollon Grigor'yev (1822–64). The principles of the approach are not very clear, but it seems to have involved regarding art not from a utilitarian perspective, as had become common, but as a natural, whole outgrowth of the society which produced it. Serov and Grigor'yev were friends and admirers of each other's work.

25 This opera was composed in 1857–8 and 1881–2 and premièred at the Mariinsky Theatre on 4 February 1883.
26 I. F. Neylissov (or Nelisov) (1830–80) was a pupil of Liszt who taught at the St Petersburg Conservatoire.

In the tenth lecture which A. N. Serov gave in Mr Kontsky's hall, our gifted critic and composer touched on conservatoires in general and that in St Petersburg in particular. While acknowledging the establishment's noble aim, Mr Serov tried to persuade his listeners that one cannot expect a national Russian development of music from a college in which Germans teach, and in general terms that a school cannot form an artist. Warming to the novelty of his views, Mr Serov pronounced that a true genius develops *of its own accord*; he did not, however, say how this comes about and forced his listeners to think that an artist develops *organically*, like a tree, rather as *narodnost'* developed in the late *Russkaya beseda* ('Russian debate') (the reader will recall the polemic of Messrs Samarin and Chicherin).[27]

This is perhaps the first time that we have heard from someone in a responsible position and apparently seriously such pitiless mockery of the credulity and the worship of a once recognized authority. Mr Serov could count on it that a well-known critic, the composer of an opera which the public enjoyed, would not provoke laughter in his readers when he demanded from a composer as a *conditio sine qua non* the absence of technical familiarity with music, although we should not have believed him had he informed us that a painter must not know how to draw or a sculptor how to wield a chisel. Mr Serov is sweetly oblivious of the fact that all the great composers of all tendencies and periods were in complete control of their technique; he must know that the only exception is he himself, as innocent as a baby 'of dry, scholastic, mechanical, narrowly professional contrapuntal combinations'. The extreme triteness of those parts of *Judith* where he wished to be a contrapuntist, for example the fugato in Act I, serves as splendid proof of this. After many years of campaigning for an opera 'which should not be a concert in costumes', and of refining this very correct but not very new idea in innumerable articles, Mr Serov has suddenly gone over to the camp of certain amateurs who are enemies of serious study of whatever it might be, but who consider themselves specifically Russian composers.[28] It was rather flattering and unexpected for them to see in their midst a *Wagnerian*; *c'était même très chic*; but for the Conservatoire and its unselfish director who is entirely at the service of art, on the other hand, it must be flattering to be accused of lacking talent and so on by a critic who places Verstovsky above Glinka as a *national (narodnïy)* composer, forgetting once more that Verstovsky is national (*narodnïy*) in the same way as Flotow and Offenbach.[29]

27 This involved a Slavophile and a liberal, and may have concerned land tenure.
28 Laroche surely has the Balakirev circle in mind.
29 For Verstovsky, see Chapter 1, note 7. Friedrich Flotow (1812–83), German composer of operas whose *Alessandro Stradella* and *Martha* (of the 1840s) were very popular in their day. Jacques Offenbach (1819–80), an adopted Parisian of German origin, was the master and immensely popular composer of operettas.

We leave it to Mr Serov to dream how good *Kamarinskaya would have been* if composed by Verstovsky instead of Glinka, and we conclude our little article with the wish that the public should not accept as one and the same thing, as an inseparable whole, Wagnerism – that is a broad and free tendency in music applied to ideas and to the general progress of the arts – and hostility to every objective and special theory in art. Not a single autodidact however gifted, not a single youth who all of a sudden imagined himself wiser than all good and bad conservatoires, can turn himself into a true, profound Wagnerian – and it is the education of such immature adherents that Mr Serov seeks, albeit in vain.

(f) V. F. Odoyevsky: Speech at the opening of the Moscow Conservatoire. *Contemporary Chronicle*, 4 September 1866, no. 30, p. 3. MLN pp. 305–7

Prince Odoyevsky was a member of the Consultative Committee of the Moscow Branch of the Russian Musical Society. While that Committee was not at the very heart of preparations for the establishment of the Conservatoire, Odoyevsky personally took a keen interest in the new institution and warmly supported its work. He was a great admirer of its first director Nikolay Grigor'yevich Rubinstein (1835–81), who as a pianist was by some considered not inferior to his more famous brother, and who through personality, dedication and tact enabled the conservatoire in Moscow to put down firmer local roots than its senior sister managed in the capital. He was also more open-minded musically than Anton, and enjoyed much more cordial relationships with musicians suspicious of the conservatoires, such as Balakirev.

Prince Odoyevsky was a prime mover in the inclusion of the history of Russian church music in the Moscow syllabus, and in recommending the first professor, with whom he had long been sharing discoveries on the subject. On the Prince's death his widow presented the musical part of his library to the Moscow Conservatoire and that body resolved to establish a scholarship in his name. In this speech Odoyevsky highlighted Russian church and folk music since it had not occurred to any of the luminaries who had spoken previously to refer to it. He thus touched on the whole field of musicology, a subject studied in Russia in the conservatoires.

Ladies and gentlemen!

I did not expect to be speaking today in this venerable company of friends and I did not imagine that my health would allow me even to be present. And so I must ask you to show indulgence if my speech has too much of artlessness about it. But at this moment I cannot refrain from expressing, though it be in few and simple words, my profound sympathy for that branch of the Moscow Musical Society's activities which has remained almost forgotten in all our artistic and musical associations. In our Conservatoire a scholarly discipline will be taught which is, astonishingly, new to our country – *the history of church music in Russia*; so new is it that one cannot point to a single *published* work which could serve as a text-book or manual on the subject. A kind of singing has been preserved in our church, a chant to which our Orthodox sanctuaries have resounded for over 700 years, a chant which is original, like no other, which has its special laws, its distinctive character and a sublime significance both historical and artistic. Moreover, it is not only the original staveless symbols in which our ancient melodies were represented up to the eighteenth century, but even the church (square) notes on staves still in existence which remain inaccessible to a great many, and the history of our ancient notation was thereby rendered likewise impossible. I cannot help but be glad from the bottom of my heart that the teaching of this subject important, nay, vital, to Russia has been entrusted to that devout and learned man Father Dimitry Vasil'yevich Razumovsky[30], a tireless investigator in the sphere of *our own* musical archaeology whose recent researches have shed significant light on this hitherto unknown area of our country's traditions. Let us hope that in time the Moscow Conservatoire will not leave artistically and historically untilled our *secular* folksongs scattered over the whole expanse of our great Rus'. Such cultivation has hitherto been impossible, and it remains so: we do not yet have a collection of our folk melodies *reliably* transcribed with all their local variants and nuances. So far the majority of those who have transcribed our melodies have tried to make them conform to the patterns of 'general'[31] music, and have even allowed themselves to rectify imaginary mistakes, or characteristic deviations from the generally accepted rules in them. I make bold to think that the *rectifiers* themselves have erred, for folk melodies are a sacred possession of the nation, which should be approached with an innocent sense, without any preconceived theory, without thinking deeply, but [simply] writing down folksong as it is heard in the voice and ear of the people, and then one must try to extract their theory from the tunes themselves as they really are. Why the heart of each one of us should stir when we hear a Russian melody is understandable; but why do we at once unconsciously distinguish the *character* of a Russian melody in the

---

30 D. V. Razumovsky (1818–89), the founder of Russian medieval musical studies. The material of his lectures was published as *Tserkovnoye peniye v Rossii: opït istoriko-tekhnicheskogo izlozheniya* ('Church chant in Russia: an attempt at a historico-technical exposition') (3 vols., Moscow 1867–9).

31 The author frequently uses this term, by which he means the common elements of the idiom used in the major European musical schools – those of French, German and Italian composers.

midst of whatever kind of music it may be, and say involuntarily 'there is something Russian here'? In our time we can no longer be content with mere assumptions; science must investigate this phenomenon, but reliable materials are necessary for science. The *alumni* of the Conservatoire, having obtained a complete musical education, will prove to have an important role in promoting the art of music in this field too; at some future date our *genuine* folk melodies will be collected from all the various corners of Russia through their labours and it will seem possible for science to translate our hitherto unconscious perception into technical language, to define those inner laws which control our folksong. Permit me, ladies and gentlemen, to offer a toast to the success of Russian music as an *art* and as a *science*.[32]

32 Odoyevsky often advanced this idea, seeking to underline the view that philological, philosophical, physical and historical approaches (to name but a few) were a vital complement to the acquisition of executant skills widely recognized as the primary realm of music.

CHAPTER FOUR

New ideas about opera

While the seminal significance of Glinka's operas was by no means unanimously recognized at their first appearance, it was not long before almost all Russian musical figures were paying tribute to it. It is striking that Tchaikovsky and Serov as well as the 'mighty handful' claimed Glinka as their forerunner. The two operas were substantially different, the first showing the combination of features from Russian folklore with elements from contemporary French and Italian styles, while the second displayed a wealth of novel experiment in timbre, harmony and melody, some of it in the context of an oriental realm of the imagination. *Kamarinskaya* was a virtual anthology of Russian folksong treatments. Since the way ahead owed so much to Glinka's pioneering works, it is not surprising that their exegesis consumed so much of the attention of critics.

(a) A. N. Serov: The role of a single motive through the whole of Glinka's opera *A Life for the Tsar*. *Theatrical and Musical Herald*, 13 December 1859, no. 49. Serov 4, pp. 186–92

Serov's discovery of organic connections between different numbers of the opera coincided with his enthusiasm for viewing entities as wholes, and for the 'organic criticism' of Apollon Grigor'yev. The latter was also linked with *pochvennichestvo*, the idea that Russia's destiny lay in the reconciliation of the educated classes with the peasantry (the *pochva* ('soil')) on a religious and ethical basis.

Experiments in technical criticism carried out on the music of M. I. Glinka

Detailed technical analysis of individual sections from both the operas of our great compatriot as well as analyses of others of his compositions (orchestral, piano and vocal) will appear under this heading from time to time. Critical views on the organic unity of Glinka's large-scale works as a whole from the purely technical standpoint (as for instance in the present first case) will also appear under this heading. In so far as *clear visual examples* placed directly in the text and immediately linked to it are useful for articles of this character, to the same extent in my opinion the analyses themselves will be of benefit to those of our readers who are able to regard music not as a source of entertainment, amusement or gratification of the aural sense but as a subject for the loftiest inner life, the object of philosophical thought.

I The role of a single motive throughout the opera A Life for the Tsar[1]

The tragic subject of this opera is Ivan Susanin's feat of heroism in rescuing Tsar Mikhail from the criminal plots of the Poles, a rescue effected at the cost of his own life. One of the supreme merits of the scheme of the opera is that it does not end at once upon Susanin's death. The logic of the drama demanded that the *consequence* of this death be embodied dramatically, and that the spectators be shown the triumphal *sequel* to Susanin's heroism in all its grandeur and splendour – the rejoicing of the Russian people at the crowning of Mikhail Feodorovich as tsar.

The marvellous chorus in the epilogue 'Slav'sya, slav'sya, svyataya Rus'' ('Glory, glory, Holy Rus'!') is one of Glinka's loftiest immortal creations and at the same time one of the fullest expressions of Russian national identity (*narodnost'*) in music. This very simple combination of sounds

1 Although numbered 'I', this article had no sequel. The closest approximation is to be found in Serov's treatment of the songs in 'Vospominaniya o Mikhaile Ivanoviche Glinke' ('Reminiscences of Mikhail Ivanovich Glinka') published in nos. 1–5 of *Iskusstva* ('The Arts') in 1860.

captures the essence of Moscow and of Rus' in the times of Minin and Pozharsky[2]! As far as the actual musical invention is concerned, it shows the same 'lofty wisdom of simplicity' which dictated the theme of the final chorus of his Ninth Symphony to Beethoven. The melody keeps within the very tight limits of the most natural intervals of the C major scale. The harmony, too, by the good proportions of its organism, does not quit the circle of the given tonality, but by the use of two minor triads (A minor and D minor) as integral parts of the tonality of C brings the whole of the music nearer to the character of medieval harmony and that of our church's Byzantine harmony. And it seemed as if it all just happened of its own accord! Those who think to *praise* this 'Slav'sya' chorus inordinately by preferring it to several national anthems 'Bozhe, tsarya khrani!' ('God, preserve the tsar!'), 'God save the King!', 'Gott erhalte Franz den Kaiser!', etc.) are greatly in error.

The 'Slav'sya' chorus belongs to a quite different category of musical works. It is not at all a *separate* song, an individual *anthem* sufficient unto itself – it is a *march-anthem* (*gimn-marsh*), as Glinka himself incomparably called it,[3] a chorus which it is *impossible* to separate from Red Square in front of the Kremlin, covered with crowds of people, from the whole stage movement, from the sound of trumpets and the pealing of bells; moreover, it is not merely a triumphant finale, the conclusion of some tacked-on scene – on the contrary it is an *integral*, a *most capital* part of the opera, the luxuriant

---

2 Minin (?–1616) and Pozharsky (1578–1642) were leaders of Russian military and political resistance to Polish aggression at the beginning of the seventeenth century.

3 *Author's note*: *Facsimile*, beneath a portrait, published by Mr Stellovsky's firm.

flowering of one of its principal ideas – the idea of the *tsar's* greatness, the idea of 'the tsar', as the idea is powerfully reflected in Susanin's soul and as it serves as the basis for his heroism.

Aesthetic conclusions of this sort, if they are not to remain in the sphere of phrase-mongering using big words, which always gives a semblance of rhetoric and windbaggery, must be supported by *facts*.

The facts which are the most convincing in music criticism are musical examples. Let us consider for a little the opera *A Life for the Tsar* at the points where according to the meaning of the scene and the words of the text the idea of 'the tsar' is the dominant one in Susanin's heart, and we shall find that at *every one* of these points the *musical* idea has as its basis the melody of the chorus 'Slav'sya, slav'sya, svyataya Rus'', which is heard *in its complete form* only at the end of the opera.

Had our investigations not led to this conclusion, our faith in the strict organic quality of Glinka's compositions and our faith in his genius would have been severely shaken.

But it is precisely from the standpoint of the strict organic quality of his work that Glinka is boundlessly great, like all truly great creative artists.

Here are the facts.

In the first act after the arrival of Antonida's bridegroom, after his passionate account of the victory, Susanin, depressed about the grave fate of his motherland, is not yet ready to give his permission for the marriage: 'Chto za vesel'ye v eto bezvremen'ye!' ('What kind of merry-making could there be in these hard times!')

But after Sobinin's news that a tsar is already being chosen in Moscow, joy flashed through the patriot's heart as he guessed at once that it was his *boyar* who was being elected:

> Sto pobed ne stoyat takogo slukha!
> Tsar'! Zakonnïy tsar'!
> ('Such a report is worth more than a hundred victories!
> The tsar! The rightful tsar!')

And at the repetition of the chorus (in the middle of the Allegro of the terzet):

The motive of these notes is none other than the opening of the 'Slav'sya' chorus:

Instead of the major third we have here the minor one — firstly, from the purely musical connection with what has gone before and what follows; secondly, also for a psychological reason (something which even if only *unconsciously* is characteristic of the creations of true artists) – the triumphant idea of 'the rightful sovereign' at this point in the opera still seems something distant, in the future, and thus not yet so *clear* as to give rise to the bright major third, which is at the root of the melody of the 'Slav'sya' chorus.

In the second act comes the portrayal of Susanin's happiness in the bosom of his family. He is admiring his daughter and her bridegroom, he blesses their union, rejoices in his children's happiness, and prays:

> Serdtse polno! Budem Bogu blagodarnï.
>
> ('My heart is full! It is to God that we should be grateful.')

The text of the prayer is:

> Bozhe, lyubi tsarya!
> Bozhe, proslav' tsarya!
> Slavoy i milost'yu
> K Russkoy zemle rodnoy!
> ('God, love the tsar!
> God, bring glory to the tsar!
> Fame and favour
> Be to the Russian land!')

The glory and greatness of the tsar in the mind of Susanin and his family have called forth a hint of the motive of the 'Slav'sya' chorus in the music too:

The music here is laid out in two choirs (as in antiphonal singing) with one group formed by the vocal parts and the other by the orchestra. The groups alternate. In the course of the orchestral parts which answer the voices the melody and harmony of the 'Slav'sya' chorus are transposed to the key of G and transferred from quadruple time to $\frac{3}{4}$:

In the wonderfully dramatic scene between the Poles and Susanin in his cottage after Susanin's first attempts to get out of accepting the invitation to take his uninvited guests to where the tsar is, the Poles start to become indignant:

> Nu, nu, nam boltan'ye tvoyo nadoyelo!
> Idi, pred soboy lish' pryamo smotrya.
> Nas vedat' tvoyo li kholopskoye delo?
> Seychas provodi nas k zhilishchu tsarya!

> ('Look here, we're tired of your chatter!
> Off you go, looking only straight ahead.
> Do we need to know your serf's business?
> Take us right now to the tsar's dwelling!')

To these words, uttered with a threat which is already harsh and blatant, Susanin replies calmly and solemnly:

> Vïsok i svyat nash *tsarskiy dom,*
> I krepost' bozhiya krugom!
> Pod neyu sila Rusi tseloy,
> A na stene v odezhde beloy
> Stoyat krïlatïye vozhdi –
> Tak, nedrug, blizko ne khodi!

> ('Lofty and holy is our *tsar's house,*
> And God's fortress surrounds it!
> Under it comes the strength of all Russia,
> And on its walls in white attire
> Stand winged leaders –
> So, foe, do not draw too near!')

It is precisely in the rebuff to the rudeness of the Poles whom Susanin hates that the idea of the grandeur and unattainable sanctity of the tsar's house arises here with special significance. The notion of 'sanctity' (which, by the way, is rendered here by the librettist in a highly poetic manner – it is one of the best passages in the text) must lend the musical expression a hint of mystery and reverence. The composer sets the whole *future* melody of the 'Slav'sya' chorus a semitone higher, in the mystical tonality of D flat major, which, as the lower third from F is organically linked with the previous loud cries of the Poles, Susanin sings in the broad calm tones of the bass register (in his middle range) and a smooth solemn $\frac{3}{4}$ rhythm; the orchestra of string instruments accompanies this singing with full harmony of a religious character from the future 'Slav'sya' chorus, but *pp*, and this embodiment of the dramatic moment is majestically accomplished in this music thus:[4]

4 *Author's note:* later on p. 289 of the complete piano part with the vocal line.

In order to convince readers fully that the passage of the opera which I have cited (ending with the words 'Rusi tseloy' ('all Russia')) really does not contain *a single chord* which is not taken from the future 'Slav'sya' anthem, I attach the music of the anthem, after transposition to D flat major and the bass register, and I ask you to compare it note for note, chord for chord, with the excerpt I have quoted (disregarding, naturally, 'rhythmical' changes):

In the scene of the catastrophe, that is the scene of the Poles and Susanin in the depths of the forest, the character of the dramatic style, which is swifter and shows Susanin's soul racked by anguish and suffering, did not permit a direct calm repetition of the entire solemn melody of the anthem, but more or less explicit hints of this melody may be encountered very frequently in this scene in the forest also.

In the big Cantabile 'Tï pridyosh', moya zarya' ('You will come, my dawn')
(D minor) the second phrase:

borrows its harmony from the 'Slav'sya' chorus because the text of the aria
is concerned with the struggle in Susanin's heart between *duty*, summoning
him to self-sacrifice, and human weakness. It is hard to be parted from life!
The notion of duty, the heroic deed naturally is clothed in the solemn
sounds of the tsar's majesty.

The melody to the words:

> Rumyanaya zarya
> Promolvit *pro tsarya* . . .
> ('The rosy dawn
> Will speak *of the tsar* . . .')

is once more closely *related* to the motive of the 'Slav'sya' chorus:

Finally, Susanin's exclamations immediately the dawn's rays break through:

> Zarya! Zarya! Spasyon *nash tsar'!*

> ('The dawn! the dawn! *Our tsar* is saved!')

exclamations which Susanin will repeat later under the blows of Polish
sabres until his last moment, are, once more, the *first sounds* of the
'Slav'sya' melody:

Was I entitled to claim that just as the idea of the tsar is fundamental to the *aim* of the opera, so in the opera's music the 'Slav'sya' motive is the *fundamental* one which is organically built into the principal moments which are concentrated around the fundamental dramatic idea?

Opinions about the very same music, in fact the very same notes, notes which one would think would appear identical to everyone with eyes and ears, can vary greatly.

The celebrated director of the Brussels Conservatoire [Fétis][5] also noticed certain repetitions in the scene of the Poles in the cottage from what had gone before (from the chorus in the introduction, for example), but he held it against Glinka that this showed poverty (!) of invention. Opinions vary, as I said.

There is also a printed Russian analysis of the opera *A Life for the Tsar*,[6] which contains, of course, not a single merest hint about the *inner* artistic *organic* quality of the opera, clear, small examples of which I have provided here.

In my opinion only such a *comparative anatomy* of music can provide a solid buttress for music criticism, revealing for it realms of inexhaustible riches which are as yet scarcely touched. Artists such as Glinka and Wagner, consciously and unconsciously, have by the force of their innate genius outstripped the Fétises and his like by at least a hundred years. Criticism, in other words, will have its hands full just *catching up* with art at its present stage of development.

(b) A. N. Serov: *A Life for the Tsar* and *Ruslan and Lyudmila*. *Russian World*, 1860, no. 67. Serov 4, pp. 285–312

After Glinka's death the relative merits of his two operas were much debated, each work finding proponents and antagonists. Among the important texts in this long-running discussion were Stasov's 'Mikhail Ivanovich Glinka' published in the *Russian Herald* (*Russkiy vestnik*) in 1857, October, book 2; November, books 1 and 2; and December, book 2; the present article by Serov; his '*Ruslan* i Ruslanistï' ('Ruslan and the Ruslanists'), which appeared in *Music and Theatre* (*Muzïka i teatr*) of 1867, nos. 1, 2, 4, 5, 7, 8 and 10; and Laroche's magisterial 'Glinka i ego znacheniye v istorii muzïki' ('Glinka and his significance in the history of music') which was published in the *Russian Herald*,

---

5 Serov wrote in response to Fétis in 'Russkiy khudozhnik i frantsuzskaya kritika' ('A Russian artist and French criticism') in *Teatral'nïy i muzikal'nïy vestnik* ('Theatrical and Musical Herald'), 1858, 12 and 19 January, nos. 2 and 3, and in 'M. Fétis et Michel Glinka' in *Le Nord*, 1858, nos. 187 and 188.

6 Serov refers to Rostislav's *Podrobnïy razbor operï M. I. Glinki 'Zhizn' za tsarya'* ('A detailed analysis of M. I. Glinka's opera *A Life for the Tsar*') (St Petersburg 1854).

1867, no. 10, and 1868, nos. 1, 9 and 10. By the 1860s discussion of opera took place against a background of compositions and theories richer than those of the 1830s and 1840s. It is evident where Serov stood in the controversy surrounding the ideas of Richard Wagner.

The venom with which Serov pursues his quarry, Stasov, in this article may not be explained solely by the intrinsic weight of the issues. The view which he attacks was put forward by his erstwhile close friend, now mortal enemy, a dislike probably intensified by the break-up of Stasov's relationship with Serov's sister. A venomous tone on the part of Serov is not, however, peculiar to this article alone.

As creations of the highest degree of artistry and as the works of the sole Russian composer *of genius* hitherto, the operas of M. I. Glinka furnish an extensive field for critical investigation from all possible angles. Our whole theory of national identity (*narodnost'*) in operatic music has to rest on Glinka's works as its foundation-stone. The entire future development of the art of music in Russia is intimately and inseparably bound up with Glinka's scores. But the more elevated and important the object of investigation, the more profound and proficient must be the investigations themselves. Fundamental music criticism, in my view, is inseparable from purely technical details, and thus from musical examples.

It is obvious that the real place for all this can only be in individual books or in a journal which specializes purely in music.

Readers of the *Russian World* (*Russkiy mir*) therefore, are not expecting the article on Glinka's operas offered to them here to be an extended analysis of both operas with a dogmatic purpose in mind.

No: the present drawing of a comparison between Glinka's two works has a character which is purely *polemical*, and it has been provoked by another article in another journal about the very same subject. [Serov explains how he came upon the article.]

The article written and signed by V. V. Stasov and placed in the 1st of April instalment of the *Russian Herald* (*Russkiy vestnik*) for 1859 (*Sovremennaya letopis'* ('Contemporary Chronicle') pp. 234–44)) is entitled in the original not 'an opera which has suffered much' but 'an opera which has sufferated (?) much' (*mnogostradatel'naya opera*).

The contents of the article are no less strange and awkward than its title, and fully earned the sympathy of the Abyssinian maestro.[7] V. V. Stasov's opinions on Glinka's music, on the significance of that music both for art as a whole and for the demands of the operatic ideal are remarkable in the

---

7 A. V. Lazarev (1819–?). Composer. His many travels extended to Abyssinia – hence his nickname. His writings include *Lazarev i Betkhoven. Tvoreniya ikh i muzïkal'nïye zaslugi* ('Lazarev and Beethoven. Their works and their musical merits') (St Petersburg 1860). Understandably, Lazarev frequently attracted Serov's fire.

extreme and provoke objections with nearly every line. But since a polemic of this kind must necessarily be based on a rather substantial *comparison* between Glinka's two operas and is moreover closely linked with many aesthetic questions which engage the contemporary musical world, I consider it beneficial to share my remarks directed against V. V. Stasov's article written some six months ago with the public in the conviction that discussion of Glinka's operas will always be opportune and *relevant*.

> His reasons are as two grains of wheat hid in two bushels of chaff: you shall seek all day ere you find them: and when you have them, they are not worth the search.   *Merchant of Venice*, Act I, Scene 1

In view of the roughness of the language and sometimes the complete inability of the author to set out his stock of ideas in any coherent or elegant fashion, ideas in which one occasionally glimpses a confused flash of truth, it is fairly difficult to guess what the author of the article 'An opera which has suffered much' is trying to say. What did V. V. Stasov have in mind?

We are concerned with Glinka's second opera *Ruslan and Lyudmila*. This opera, in the opinion and the expression of V. V. Stasov, is said to be 'an artistic martyr' (?) (p. 239), since it has been haunted from the very moment of its creation until now by particular misfortunes and persecutions, troubles and failures, 'such as *not a single other* artistic work has ever experienced in Russia' (p. 235).

Meanwhile, this opera deserves not this fate, of course, but the most brilliant one which awaits it in the distant future as an opera immeasurably superior to Glinka's first opera *A Life for the Tsar* (pp. 240–2); as an immortal opera, 'after the creation of which Glinka has only two rivals in the world of opera – Gluck and Mozart' (p. 242).

To everyone familiar with operatic music in general and the operas of Glinka in particular the incorrectness of V. V. Stasov's views is *obvious* right from the start; but since there is not an opinion which when uttered with confidence and pretension to being serious thinking could not find adherents, but also so as to avoid the charge of pronouncing sentence without judgement being passed, one must examine in sequence each of the three main points which may be found in the article, and we must therefore consider:

1 to what *special* alleged misfortunes did the opera *Ruslan* fall victim between 1842 and 1859?
2 wherein lies the *indisputable superiority* of *Ruslan* to *A Life for the Tsar* claimed by V. V. Stasov?
3 can the opera *Ruslan* occupy beyond dispute the supreme place on the operatic horizon of the nineteenth century assigned to it by V. V. Stasov?

I

'One must start off from the fact', says V. V. Stasov, 'that when Glinka had merely begun to think about his opera he could not cope *with the very simplest matter* – finding a librettist.'

One must start off from the fact, say I in turn, that finding a subject to one's taste even for an opera whose plan has been conceived previously, finding a wholly obedient and talented librettist – is a matter by no means 'of the very simplest' (?!), but always *very difficult* and *very rare*. Everyone who has written or embarked on writing opera whether in Russian, German, French or Italian – it is all the same – can vouch for this to V. V. Stasov in a decisive manner. The laments and complaints of composers about the insufficiency of texts and authors of texts for operas have been heard and continue to be heard everywhere. Literary men avoid collaborating with composers, for they consider setting verse *to* music and writing verse *for* music ungrateful and even degrading work. It was partially thus when the text of an opera was regarded as the *lining* of a musical dress, or as a canvas for musical patterns, when even the plan of an opera as a play was regarded with utter contempt because the whole point of the matter lay, it was said, not in the play but in the music. At the same time, of course, they forgot that the world's best operas, the most successful operas, emerged thus precisely on account of the given subjects being propitious for music (all the operas of Gluck, and even *Don Giovanni, La Vestale, Les Deux Journées, Der Freischütz*, etc.); and conversely the very best music could not redeem operas with texts which were absurd (Weber's *Euryanthe*, Mozart's *Così fan tutte*). In Russia, thanks to the small number of literary men and their unmusicality in general, capable librettists are a – *cosa rarissima*!

It would be interesting to know how V. V. Stasov came to the conclusion that finding a libretto was *'the very simplest* thing'! His logic is pure Lazarev.

In relation to *Ruslan* the difficulty is increased further – only not *accidentally*, as V. V. Stasov puts it, but as a result of the character of the creative act in Glinka himself.

On account of the depth and breadth of his genius, Glinka of course could not have been content with any sort of routine, commonplace nonsense (that is, had people *been able* to fabricate easily such nonsense as is found in the libretti *di dieci scudi* prepared for Bellini and Donizetti, to say nothing of rhetoricians of depressing memory such as Metastasio and da Ponte). But on the other hand as Glinka contemplated various musical ventures he had most inadequately mastered the *ideals of opera* and the relationship of an operatic text to music. Glinka completely separated the composition of the libretto as a literary job from its inner *musical* demands when in reality there must be *not the slightest* separation between the two.[8]

Many people must take the blame for the incoherent text of *Ruslan*; this opera's libretto turned out to be a patchwork or a mosaic not because Glinka was *unable* to find a librettist but because Glinka himself, creating this opera in separate scenes more or less inspired by Pushkin's long poem (*poema*) and, in consequence of the immaturity of his operatic ideals, paying very little heed to the whole opera *as a stage play*, tried merely to find versifiers prepared to stitch something together almost to the composer's dictation and to music which was in part already written. The difficulty in the relationship between the libretto and the composer of an opera can be resolved in our day *exclusively* on the pattern of uniting the author of the text and the author of the music in *a single person*. Glinka lived in a time of transition. But had even the *plan* of the libretto for *Ruslan* been a good one, the details of the working-up of the verses by *several* hands would scarcely have done any harm.

Thus the *first* of the *failures* enumerated by V. V. Stasov as having hung over *Ruslan* proves to be purely imaginary, and the shortcomings of the libretto of *Ruslan* cannot in any way be attributed to the realm of chance.

Then come in V. V. Stasov's article 'the exceptionally sad circumstances of Glinka's personal life at the time of composing *Ruslan*'.

The influence of *external* circumstances on the activities of an artist and on his actual work is a most problematic matter about which nothing at all has yet been proved. The difficult time for Glinka when *Ruslan* was being composed is of some importance for Glinka's life and for his biography. In relation to this opera itself, when it was nevertheless created, nevertheless written, domestic circumstances had, maybe, no significance *whatsoever*.

Only the Ulïbïshevs[9] of this world dare to assert that Beethoven's last three symphonies, last five quartets and his second Mass – that is, the most sublime music he ever created – *suffered*, allegedly, in their composition because Beethoven was involved at that time in an unfortunate lawsuit on account of his nephew.

And was Glinka alone in experiencing suffering and afflictions in the midst of his artistic career? Only people with wires instead of nerves undergo no suffering in this life, but such people, of course, do not bestow operas or

8 The 'original plan' of the opera, first published in 1871 and unknown to Serov, in fact shows Glinka making a close connection between the literary and musical tasks. The solution practised by Serov's hero Wagner was, of course, for the same person to create both the libretto and the score.
9 A. D. Ulïbïshev (1794–1858). Music-lover and patron of Balakirev in his early days. He was the author of a pioneering *Nouvelle biographie de Mozart* (Moscow 1843) and of the more controversial *Beethoven, ses critiques et ses glossateurs* (Leipzig and Paris 1857).

symphonies on the world, and perform exceptionally badly when they start even to discuss music.

Later on V. V. Stasov enumerates the reasons for the *failure* of the opera *Ruslan* at its first performances. There is much truth in these reasons, and the explanation of the fact is accurate. But again the fact in itself cannot be of any special significance either for us or for the opera.

It is true that the failure of *Ruslan* after the significant success of *A Life for the Tsar* was the cause of great bitterness for Glinka himself, and that it left a deep wound in his soul. But after all Gluck's *Alceste* was nearly a failure in Paris at its first performances in spite of the colossal Parisian success of *Iphigénie en Aulide* by the very same Gluck, and that only shortly before *Alceste*; but after all, Mozart's *Figaro* and *Don Giovanni* enjoyed no success at their first performances in Vienna; after all, one of the most inspired operas there is, Beethoven's *Fidelio*, was first performed in Vienna during the siege of that city in 1805 to an audience of . . . French officers to whom both the play in German and Beethoven's music could only have been ridiculous, like double Dutch.

The immense fame of *Fidelio* began some thirty years after the composition of the opera, that is when there appeared an inspired performer of the leading role – Schröder-Devrient.[10]

For the most lofty, inspired music for the stage (and not only for the stage!) it is almost a general rule that it must not expect immediate success. The *happy* exceptions (such as *Iphigénie en Aulide*, *Die Zauberflöte*, *Der Freischütz* and *A Life for the Tsar*), that is, operas which were successful from the very beginning, *despite* the inspired quality of the music, owe this success to special circumstances which came about advantageously irrespective of their scores' merit. The best ally of genius is time. If *Ruslan* meets all the conditions for a long-lasting permanent radiance on the operatic horizon, then the ephemeral failure of this opera's first performances will be only an *ordinary, normal* phenomenon of history. Thus, V. V. Stasov, in taking the normal order of things to be an exceptional case, in making out the failure of *Ruslan* to be *a special victimization of this opera by fate* (?), does not know what he is saying even from his own standpoint (that is, considering *Ruslan* a miracle of art). In calling the roll of the productions of the opera *Ruslan* (or parts of it) which have been staged at various times up to the present, all the while bemoaning the general lack of sympathy for this work (which is again in the nature of things) and for the exploits of the performers who decided to protest through their performances against this unjust (though also very natural)

10 Wilhelmine Schröder-Devrient (1804–60). This soprano in fact sang the part of Leonore in 1822. She also appeared in the early Wagner operas.

coldness on the part of the public, Mr Stasov comes to O. A. Petrov's[11] benefit performance in November 1858 in the *Teatr-Tsirk* (Theatre-Circus). Complaints of the most basic kind about the many 'tortures' to which the opera *Ruslan* was subjected at its most recent production, especially as regards the arbitrary cuts in the music, the disfigurement of the instrumentation for the wind band, the distortion of tempi by the conductor who did not go into his important task with sufficient care, all this was said in print in a specialized journal at the time, long before Mr Stasov's article.[12]

The same article said: 'How can one treat so barbarously music of genius such as our country should be proud of?'

V. V. Stasov's variations on someone else's theme are useful, for they are carried in a big journal for a different and far wider circle of readers, but V. V. Stasov is here again wrong to a high degree to present cuts and distortions in the tempo and the performance as among the *persecutions of fate* (?) which have allegedly rained down predominantly on *Ruslan* alone.

It is very easy to demonstrate by some hundred technical examples that the opera *A Life for the Tsar* too has been distorted in almost the same way (the finale, for instance, of the Polish ball has up to now never been performed in the theatre *in the least* like the manner in which Glinka wrote it in the score; most of the tempi are wrong, and so on).

All the best operas in the world (to say nothing of Wagner's) suffer more or less seriously from arbitrariness, carelessness and illiteracy or stupidity on the part of singers, producers and conductors. Is *Don Giovanni* on either Italian or German stages the same opera as is in the score? (The huge finale to Act II which Mozart wrote is not performed *anywhere*.) What do the Italians turn *Freischütz* into? What have the French made out of *Euryanthe*? In what kind of wounded war veteran's state do all audiences

11 For O. A. Petrov, see Chapter 1, note 17.
12 *Author's note*: In the *Musical and Theatrical Herald*, no. 46 of 23 November 1858, *immediately* after Petrov's benefit performance, and not six months later at the time of the fire in the Theatre-Circus. In all the technical matters V. V. Stasov simply repeats my comments made at that time in 'Ruslan i Lyudmila, opera M. I. Glinki (Benefis g. Petrova, 12 noyabrya')' ('*Ruslan and Lyudmila*, the opera by M. I. Glinka (Benefit for Mr Petrov, 12 November)').

In my article it says: 'In music in such a style as that of Mr Glinka, the singers represent only one aspect of the performance; the other, which is perhaps more important, is the *orchestra*. The demands made by this score are great, immense, so that so much more circumspection, assiduity and labour are required of the person in whom are concentrated all the orchestra's forces – I mean the conductor.'

In Mr Stasov's article we read (on p. 237): 'But putting the opera across does not depend on the singers alone – that is only one half – the other half lies entirely in the orchestra, that is in the conductor.'

I said: 'A tempo even slightly slower or fractionally faster than that intended by the composer can wholly pervert the character of the music being performed.'

Mr Stasov (by imitations *en écho*): 'It is well known that in a musical performance the meaning and physiognomy of a composition can be completely altered by a change in motion' and so on.

everywhere encounter an opera which is delightful and inspired in a thousand respects – Rossini's *William Tell*?[13]

Once again, then, a bitter fate, an evil fate, there is no dispute, but for all splendid operas – it is their common lot! It is not a *special* victimization by fate, as if with the help of the sorceress Naina, which has befallen *Ruslan*!

Finally, V. V. Stasov recounts with special horror the wretchedest of the disasters which has overtaken his 'artistic martyr' – 'the fire in the Theatre-Circus' (26 January 1859).[14]

'Among the objects destroyed by the fire', V. V. Stasov cries plaintively, '*the whole opera Ruslan and Lyudmila* was consumed! The present destruction of this opera has a significance completely different from the destruction of all the others, because it entails consequences such as the destruction of not a single one of all the other operas performed in the Theatre-Circus can have.'

Let us investigate this jeremiad more closely. Let us look more intently: what is this *present destruction* of *Ruslan* which has a different *significance* and different consequences from the *other destructions*, etc.? Apart from the amusing clumsiness of the phrase, we shall see that there is in all this an insufficiency of sense as well. What is the meaning of '*the whole opera* was consumed'?

Fires have indeed sometimes assisted in the destruction of musical works and there have been irretrievable losses – in those instances, of course, when *the only copies* of scores, whether in the composer's manuscript or in copies not further reproduced, have gone up in flames. That was the case, for example, with a round hundred unpublished scores by Adolf Hasse which were destroyed by fire in the bombardment of Dresden in 1760; that was the case with a whole pile of unpublished scores of comic operas by Joseph Haydn; that was the case, as is written, with a score most interesting and perhaps now forever lost to criticism and musical history, that of the opera *Undine*[15] by the celebrated writer of fantasies and expert on music E. T. A. Hoffmann, for which the author of the short story (Baron de la Motte Fouqué) himself wrote the libretto.

Fortunately, nothing like that happened in the fire at the Theatre-Circus. Among several items of sheet music, hand-copied and printed, the orchestral *parts* for the opera *Ruslan* and *one* of the official copies of its score were lost. (Likewise the costumes and sets for the most recent production.)

---

13 Serov discussed this matter in his articles 'Nechto o vandal'stve v otnoshenii oper' ('Something on vandalism in regard to operas') in *Theatrical and Musical Herald*, 1857, 20 October and 3 November, nos. 41 and 43, and 'Eshcho neskol'ko slov o vandal'stve v otnoshenii oper' ('A few more words on vandalism in regard to operas'), *ibid.*, 1857, 17 November, no. 45.
14 The theatre subsequently built on the site was the Mariinsky.
15 It is untrue that this music is lost, though the story was long believed.

But in his article V. V. Stasov himself lists the other complete copies of this score (unfortunately still not published in its entirety either engraved or lithographed); it turns out that there are three copies in St Petersburg and one in Berlin.[16]

The score of *Ruslan* and the orchestral parts have long since been recopied in the music office of the Theatre Directorate.

The sets and costumes (which were by no means magnificent in the most recent production) will also be ready in time for the renovation of the Theatre-Circus, probably in a more splendid form, and the opera will take its course. Where is 'the destruction' (?) of the opera, and what does that mean? Where is the wicked disaster, the terrible persecution of this opera by fate? What purpose was served by Marius's lament over the ruins of Carthage?

II

Moving on to the polemic against V. V. Stasov's critical opinions of Glinka's talent and the significance of each of his operas in the destinies of operatic music, I must make an essential digression concerning myself; I must explain the difficulty of my situation in the present instance when I am obliged to do battle with blind idolatry of Glinka – to stand apart from the convictions of those who worship him alone – and consequently seem to be *not on the side of* our single musical genius hitherto, but to move into the camp of people who hold him in low esteem.

I hasten to say that only ignorance, thoughtlessness, an inability to grasp the real meaning of printed articles, or else overt calumny and ill-will could cause me to be accused of having little sympathy or insufficient love for the creations of M. I. Glinka!

The whole long conflict, for example, with Rostislav Feofilovich [Tolstoy] arose simply from the fact that I was indignant at his most shallow, dandyish critique of the inspired opera *A Life for the Tsar* (in the *Northern Bee* of 1854) and published a critique of his critique in the *Muscovite* (*Moskvityanin*) (in the book for the same year, no. 24).[17] From any article in the *Musical and Theatrical Herald* (*Muzïkal'nïy i teatral'nïy vestnik*)

---

16 *Author's note:* Or was it not one of the article's secret purposes to inform the public, by the way, about 'domestic matters', that is that D. V. Stasov (the brother of the article's author) has, so it is said, a complete copy of *Ruslan*, presented to him by the composer's sister? Bobchinsky [in Gogol's *Revizor* ('The government inspector')] asked Khlestakov to report to the tsar that in such-and-such a city there lives, so it is said, Pyotr, son of Ivan, Bobchinsky.

17 The article is entitled 'Neskol'ko strok o broshure Rostislava "Podrobnïy razbor operï M. I. Glinki Zhizn' za tsarya"' ('A few lines about Rostislav's pamphlet "A detailed analysis of M. I. Glinka's opera A Life for the Tsar"').

(over the course of four years) among the many devoted to detailed analysis of works by Glinka, and also from my article in *Le Nord* (6 and 7 July 1858) denouncing the crass ignorance and childish technical blunders made in every word uttered by the renowned (!) Fétis[18] about Glinka's two operas, those willing and able to see the truth can easily discern all my constant enthusiasm for the music of our great compatriot.

If in the last two years I have happened more than once to state many things which were not to the advantage of the opera *Ruslan and Lyudmila* as a *stage-musical* work, then I regard that as an obligation of impartial, balanced criticism, an obligation which does not in the least inhibit me from understanding and appreciating the musical treasures contained in the inexhaustibly rich score of *Ruslan* right down to its minutest details; it does not inhibit me from going into raptures about these treasures one whit less (if not far more) than, for example, even V. V. Stasov.[19]

The great and manifest defects in *Ruslan*, especially as regards the play, I always recognized from studying this opera with unusual love from the very first rehearsals (in 1842), but I did not speak out about these defects in public because . . . I did not need to turn to discourse and did not wish to offend the composer's touchy sense of artistic self-esteem as I was acquainted with him on the basis of friendship. And now it is the case both that the time has arrived and also that, in contrast with *music dramas* of the most recent time closely familiar to me, the weak aspects of *Ruslan* stood out for me with particular clarity. That was why I had to say what I think about them, without being constrained by unfounded rumours or the danger of being misinterpreted. In that spirit I shall defend my opinion here too.

In comparing Glinka's two operas V. V. Stasov ascribes all the advantages to *Ruslan* as a work which is in all respects maturer and far more powerful.

---

18 See note 5 above.
19 *Author's note*: The same article on the benefit for O. A. Petrov which brought the indignation of Glinka's admirers upon me contains, by the way, the following judgements about the music of *Ruslan*:

'This opera has many aspects of the entrancing treatment of harmony, rhythm and orchestration, new aspects, which in my opinion are capable of giving rise to whole treatises not without advantage to the progress of art.'

'In orchestration our Glinka occupies one of the most brilliant places on the universal musical horizon. In the power, diversity, careful planning and charming strikingness of his orchestra, especially in *Ruslan* (as well as in *Kamarinskaya* and the Spanish fantasies), Glinka equals music's supreme heroes.' – The entr'acte before Act II is a marvellous symphonic work, with which only Beethoven's music can compare! The ballet in Act IV is one of the most capital creations of the most modern art! What breadth and boldness of brush! From the very first sound of Chernomor's march there appears a special kind of fantastic world – *le fantastique grotesque*, just as there is a graceful fantastic element – for instance, in the ravishing chorus of flowers, one of the episodes of the previous aria and so on. [Source: see note 12 above].

From the standpoint strictly of the musical *forms*, from the standpoint of the technical execution of the music, no one who understands these matters could fail to give the advantage to *Ruslan*.

But should *all* discussions about an *opera*, which after all is a work involving drama, the stage and music, really begin and end with *these* standpoints alone?

It goes without saying that in a fairly detailed comparison of the plots and the merits of Glinka's two operas even V. V. Stasov has much to say about the gratefulness and ungratefulness of one plot and the other, about the theatrical effectiveness (*stsenichnost'*), the characters and the dramatic quality (*dramatizm*).

Unfortunately, all these 'words' remain merely 'words' (words, words, words)! Sundry expressions, technical terms and words which are more or less familiar have some *meaning* only when they are used with understanding, when they state a positive idea which is logically formed and comprehensibly put across. There is nothing of the kind in V. V. Stasov's article! One could lay a bet of a million roubles that no one could explain to himself by attentive reading of the article what V. V. Stasov understands by the words 'dramatic quality', 'theatrical effectiveness', 'the epic element in a play' and what he imagines 'the operatic ideal' to be . . .[20]

In the second half of this nineteenth century of ours a very great deal is said about the operatic *ideal*. From philosophical debates, comparative critical conclusions and the practice of artists, an aesthetic apophthegm has been worked out among people who are musically educated which is acquiring more and more the status of an *axiom* from one day to the next:

> 'Opera must be *first and foremost* drama.'

And let not Mr Stasov think that I am here merely repeating the motto of the theory and practice of the latest genius whom people who do not understand him have mockingly nicknamed the *Zukunftist*.[21] No, the formula I have quoted may be encountered in the work of a musical aesthetician who has not yet transferred to the ultra-progressive camp, in the work of a

---

20 *Author's note*: This inconsistency and vagueness about concepts is a symptom common to many of V. V. Stasov's articles. In 1858 he placed in a Leipzig musical newspaper (the *Neue Zeitschrift für Musik*) a series of investigations into *plagal* cadences in the works of Chopin. A famous artist and refined, enlightened judge in musical matters (Mr Stasov had *dedicated* his profound inquiries to him and another celebrity of the musical world) expressed himself to me about these articles thus: 'On ne sait pas précisément ce qu'il veut dire par ces articles. Il lui manque la gouverne.' [Serov is passing on the comment of Liszt. Stasov's work was entitled 'Über einige neue Form der heutigen Musik. Ein Brief an Dr. Franz Liszt in Weimar und Prof. Dr. Adolf Bernhard Marx in Berlin', and was published in vol. 49, nos. 1–4.]

21 In this reference to a *Zukunftist* ('Futurist'), Serov alludes to his championship of Wagner, whom the latter's opponents took pleasure in describing so.

theorist exceptionally respected by V. V. Stasov himself, in the book *Musik des XIX. Jahrhunderts* by the Berlin professor A. B. Marx (pp. 108, 165 and 184).[22]

In another of his books (*Beethoven*, Band I, S. 327), writing about Beethoven's *Fidelio*, Marx observes:

> How do musicians usually set about composing an opera? They only follow their natural bent. To the realization of their desire to create an opera they bring their talent, their ability, the best will in the world – in a word – *their whole selves* as musicians. But then *opera is not simply music* ('eine Oper ist nicht *blos* Musik'), it is a drama set to music ('sie ist ein Drama in Musik'), the realization of its dramatic content *on the stage* is essential, and the stage has its own requirements.

The whole *history* of operatic music can testify in favour of the formula-axiom I have quoted better than all possible theoretical authorities, that is the history of the gravitation of opera towards musical drama, a gravitation which was more or less clearly conscious, and the history of the *obstacles* to this tendency.

One of these obstacles is widely known, and it is familiar even to V. V. Stasov as far as we can judge from his scornful reference to the trend in the Italian operatic school (p. 243); I understand the virtuosity of the singers of both sexes and the composer's ministering to these virtuoso aims to be to the detriment of the coherence and sense of the drama.

Gluck protested against this obstacle and through his great reforms he achieved a good deal – he opened up the truest and most auspicious way ahead for art; but later – alas! – male and female songsters in coalition with the public's sensuality came out on top again, and art once more took to twisted paths. Pure service to art was in part preserved only in the German operatic school, where the operatic ideal was not forgotten entirely. All these matters, I repeat, are generally known.

But there is another obstacle to the operatic ideal which arises not from singers or the public but strictly from composers themselves, an obstacle no less pernicious, although it is not in itself so pernicious and has still scarcely been exposed by anyone. I mean *compositional* virtuosity, showing off through the very *composition* of the music, showing off compositional skills *apart from* the main aim of a work of art, apart from *the stage, stage drama* and *the meaning resulting from it.*

One of the most important composers of our time, Hector Berlioz, contemplated writing music on the subject of Goethe's *Faust*, not in the form of

22 Marx (1795–1866) published *Die Musik des neunzehnten Jahrhunderts und ihre Pflege: Methode der Musik* in Leipzig in 1855, and his *Ludwig van Beethoven: Leben und Schaffen* in Berlin in 1859.

an opera but as a 'dramatic legend' (for performance at concerts). Something of the main idea which had inspired Goethe still remained in the text of the French symphonist's legend (*La Damnation de Faust*), but it remained in a very disfigured, distorted form. The main thing for Berlioz was not *the idea of the whole*, not the *idea* of 'Faust', but the *details* which captivated the French composer in the German poem. Berlioz was so attracted by these details (with the addition of some further ones in accordance with his personal taste) that the awkwardness of the plan of his *Faust* is in its own way a masterpiece of a curiosity. For example, the *entire first* part of the legend (made up of four movements) consists in Faust wandering along the banks of the Elbe and listening first to the villagers' round dance (*Ronde champêtre*) and then to a Hungarian march (the Rákóczy march, to a melody national to the Magyars). As Berlioz himself *naively* explains in his preface, he forced his Faust to stroll across Hungary *solely* in order to provide the music with the opportunity for the Hungarian march, whose melody appealed to Berlioz. The march is wonderfully developed and orchestrated, to be sure! But incoherence remains incoherence. The dramatic thread of the legend seems of so little importance even to the composer himself that he is very fond of performing *excerpts* from his *Faust* at concerts which he himself conducts. The beauties of this score gain precisely when taken *separately*, because the whole work is intolerably dull as a result of its incoherence.

Just the same 'naive' and in our day unforgivable *rhapsodic* quality, the same awkwardness, disfigurement, monstrosity of *plan* occurs too in Glinka's *Ruslan*. Here a Finnish song; there a Persian chorus; now a chorus in honour of Lel'; then a *lezginka*. And why exactly is there a *lezginka*, a local *Caucasian* dance, in Chernomor's fantastic castle? How did the Caucasus become involved? The reasons are the same as those for Hungary and the Hungarian march in Berlioz's *Faust*. And what is the point of the opera itself? Better not to ask! It is like programmes for the pantomimes in a fairground.

It is obvious that in conceiving *Ruslan* the composer's ideal amounted to nothing more than to write a rich score for a *big* opera on the model of French *grand opéra* – in five acts, with two ballets and luxurious sets in which could be included various musical pictures, various *displays of virtuosity* in colouring and all possible aspects of a composer's skill (without despising various ingenious marvels, the scale of six whole tones, the 'Karabakh'[23] scale, the *gusli*, bells and so on); where musical shapes and colours which had by then ripened powerfully in our artist's talent could find an outlet. The overall resulting idea of the play – the relationship and sense of the scenes – these matters were of less importance to Glinka when he was

23 Karabakh is a region in Azerbaijan with a predominantly Armenian population; I have not discovered its supposed connection with the whole-tone scale.

composing *Ruslan* than the subject of *Faust* meant to Berlioz. The plot of the opera was only a thread upon which Glinka wanted to string his musical pearls and diamonds.[24]

But I pose a question to all who are not lacking in logic: on the scales of strict *organic criticism* can a necklace like this strung arbitrarily on one thread from pearls and stones which are precious certainly but alien one to another, can such a necklace match the inexhaustible profound treasures of *an organic unity* in a creation which is poetic, which has grown up and blossomed forth magnificently from one creative idea, as from a seed?

The difference between the beauty of an entire artistic organism, of a whole world enclosed within itself *together* with the beauty of its component parts, and an agglomerate of beautiful details, is no doubt beyond the understanding of those gentlemen for whom an opera's music is *the sweets* and the libretto *the dish* on which the sweets are served.

That is why V. V. Stasov too, in talking about the shortcomings in the characters and actions of the opera *A Life for the Tsar*, in talking about the *ungratefulness*(?) of that plot from the dramatic point of view and on the other hand on the *gratefulness*, the *richness* (!) of the plot of *Ruslan*, does not notice the mere 'trifle' that Glinka's first opera is *that which* an opera *must be* – a drama on a full, profound, natural, organic basis, whereas *Ruslan* is not a drama, not a play, and therefore *not an opera* but a fortuitously formed gallery of musical pictures. The coldness, the artificiality of this opera's conception *as a whole* are reflected in it everywhere and cannot be redeemed by any inspired details. The opera cannot fascinate anyone, and if it cannot do that, why even raise the curtain for it?

Even if one were to agree with V. V. Stasov that *A Life for the Tsar* contains only *two* active participants – Susanin and the detachment of Poles (which is not true, as we shall soon see), that there is allegedly only *one* scene – the scene in the forest (which is also untrue, as we shall soon see), even then the most unsophisticated logic would tell us that having *two* active participants in a theatrical work is better than having *not a single one*, and *one* scene with genuine dramatic action is better than *not a single one* (in a play in five acts).[25]

24 This idea is contradicted by Serov citing the words of Glinka in his 'Reminiscences of Mikhail Ivanovich Glinka' (see note 1 above): 'At the end of the opera, in the course of the finale, I wished there to be shown a series of *tableaux vivants* to provide a characterization of various districts of Russia.'

25 *Author's note:* And besides, is it possible that V. V. Stasov does not know or has forgotten that among the dramatic works which are universally renowned as exemplary there are many of the kind where the main action and the main interest are concentrated *in a single scene*, on the mental conflict of one or two characters? Everything else in the play is either a preparation for or the consequence of a single principal factor. I am ashamed even to select examples, so widely familiar are they.

The content of the opera *A Life for the Tsar* is pure tragedy: the heroic exploit of Ivan Susanin. V. V. Stasov calls this deed of heroism '*passive* self-sacrifice', but of course he would be hard put to it to cite an example of self-sacrifice which was 'active' (?!). Without 'passivity' no voluntary sacrifice in the world can be accomplished, and the sacrifice of one's *life* as a result of profound mental *conviction* is the highest pathos, the highest tragedy, straightforward heroism, which can compete with any kind of 'activeness' at all. Glinka took upon himself the task of 'hymning Susanin's exploit' and he did so magnificently.

To give some poetic body to this fact of the exploit, the contrast of Susanin's *happy* family life from which he was suddenly torn away by the Poles swooping down on a peaceful family was a necessary one.

In his superb rules for tragedy (which were understood the wrong way round by the French pseudo-classicists), Aristotle demands that tragic heroes be shown to the spectators *beforehand* in the midst of happiness and contentment. There in the midst of happiness grief suddenly comes down upon them and ties a knot over their heads such as they cannot untie. Courage, strength of heart – these are what the struggle requires of them – and they bravely, steadfastly look destiny, death itself, in the face! . . .

Susanin's is that kind of tragedy!

> Vo pravde dukh derzhat' –
> I krest svoy vzyat'!
> Vragam v glaza glyadet' –
> > I ne robet'!

> ('In truth keep up your spirits –
> And take your cross!
> Look your enemies straight in the face –
> > And do not flinch!')

Only 'active cowards' are capable of not feeling sympathy for this sort of tragedy! We can see, then, that Susanin's *daughter*, whom he loves dearly and who loves him dearly, is not at all a superfluous character, and as a means of increasing Susanin's family happiness his daughter's imminent marriage is a very natural and successful ingredient of the opera.

A young man close to Susanin – whether a son or an adopted son is all the same – is essential to inform the tsar secretly of the Poles' plans. Vanya is thus essential to the play's economy, and V. V. Stasov is mistaken in saying that Vanya does nothing other than weep and complain. Vanya, who is a *contralto*, is the main representative of the *elegiac* element in the play, and that is extremely artistic; and the elegiac element is brought about by the tragedy and the gloomy northern colouring of the drama itself.

By what right could one banish the *elegiac quality* from the opera merely because it is *elegiac*, or banish *suffering* merely because it is suffering?

There are among famous tragic plots some in which sobbing and weeping form the *fundamental*, the *main* mood of the play. In accordance with Mr Stasov's views one would have to call the aim of the *Alceste* of Euripides and Gluck 'sickly' and 'sentimental'!

Looking through the opera *A Life for the Tsar* scene by scene, we shall find both action and diversity in it, notwithstanding the unchanging organic quality of all its parts.

The scene of the magnificent Polish ball is extremely relevant and cuts across the idyll of Russian country life which, though very poetic and accurate, is yet rather meagre in its colours.

In the form in which it is now staged in the theatre, the ball scene does indeed have the appearance of an extended interpolated *divertissement*, as V. V. Stasov observed. But should Glinka take the blame for that? His idea was different. The principal accent in this scene must lie not on the dances of Mesdames Koshevaya and Lyadova[26] but on the interruption in the dances caused by the unexpected news that Mikhail Feodorovich Romanov has been elected tsar. In the big finale the Poles are *exasperated* by Romanov's election, and then, after a vainglorious and purely Polish escapade of sending a detachment of bold spirits (to the music of the boastful mazurka heard previously with double orchestra), their indignation subsides:

Tucha moskovskogo zla
Shutkoy vesyoloy proshla!

('The storm-cloud of Muscovite ill-fortune
Has gone by in a cheerful *jest*!')

The Poles again continue their dances and feasting in carefree fashion.

That is not how all this is done on the stage. On the stage the mazurka which in the score is broken off at the sudden entrance of the messenger is brought to a conclusion and rounded off, just like an ordinary number in an interpolated *divertissement*; the final chorus of this scene is not sung at all. But, I repeat, should Glinka take the blame for that?

After the interruption of Susanin's quiet family happiness by the sinister arrival of the Polish detachment in the marvellous scene of Susanin with the Poles in his cottage, the Polonaise and the mazurka become integral parts of the tragic action alongside the struggle going on in Susanin's heart. You see what profoundly dramatic scenes occur long before the final catastrophe! By what reckoning does V. V. Stasov calculate that there is only *one* such scene?

26 A. D. Koshevaya (?–1921), a ballerina in the St Petersburg Bol'shoy Theatre. V. A. Lyadova (1839–70) was a character dancer and later an operetta singer.

Antonida's parting from her father, Antonida's uncontrollable weeping and the wonderfully poetic contrast of these sobs and wails with the calm and cheerful chorus of girls who knowing nothing of the misfortune in Susanin's house come for the *devishnik* [part of the elaborate ritual preparations for a wedding, where the bride's girlfriends gather]; finally, the commotion throughout the village and the savage cries of the crowd of peasants who with axes and knives, stakes and staves, rush to rescue their village elder from the hands of the adversary – all this is once more the genuine, profound, vital *dramatic quality* of the same class which is justly and universally renowned for example in Cherubini's *Les Deux Journées*, except that Glinka, who equals Cherubini in the dramatic quality of these scenes, significantly excels him in the originality of his forms – the forms of *Russian* music appearing in the theatre for the first time.

The gloomy chorus of the Poles in the forest, without abandoning the character of a mazurka, now sounds somewhat funereal; the howling of the Russian blizzard, the wild cheerless backwoods, form a marvellous background for the grave drama between the Poles, enraged like a pack of wolves, and the unshakeable steadfastness of the martyr Susanin, himself doomed to perish and taking the Poles with him!

The stern, tragic character and the snowdrifts of this scene are not to the taste of those gentlemen who seek blue skies and Florentine gardens everywhere, regardless of the subject (just as trifling dilettanti seek mellifluous tunes and cabalettas *throughout* all music, even when the composer's purpose was to depict Ugolino's[27] suffering in the turret of hunger).

Finally, the epilogue: Moscow rejoices while Susanin's family grieves. One could anticipate *a priori* that in an organic realization of these two aims of the epilogue there would be *two* elements, neither more nor less, that is one element where the family's *sorrow* is in the foreground, and the people's jubilation in the distant background; and another element where the jubilation is in the foreground and the doleful memory of Susanin emerges only episodically in order to turn into an apotheosis and to be drowned in a noisy hymn of exultation and joy.

This is exactly how it was carried out by Glinka, and both elements are realized in an *equally inspired way*.

V. V. Stasov passes over the first scene of the epilogue in complete silence, and probably relegates it to the *ungrateful* parts of the opera upon which in his view 'pressed the weight of the subject with its melancholy and mournful colouring'. Persons who are not so short-sighted in their critical activity and who are responsive to the truly dramatic character and the true

27 Ugolino was starved to death with his four children in a tower in Pisa. Dante: *Divine comedy, Inferno*, Canto XXXIII.

profundity of feeling in the music of this element in the epilogue in addition to the beauty of the Russian march (when detachments of troops cross the stage en route to the celebrations), which later, in the concluding hymn, will resound in all its grandeur, in addition to the amazing, miraculous transition from these sounds of celebration to the gloomy terzet of the heroic martyr's family, can see delights of the utmost genius in the terzet itself, in Vanya's account of Susanin's death. This bitter, inconsolable and purely Russian elegiac quality is one of Glinka's greatest achievements. Lyricism, epic, drama and national character (*narodnost'*) are there blended.

V. V. Stasov accords the honour of a panegyric to the chorus 'Slav'sya, slav'sya', but . . . he goes into raptures about it from entirely the wrong point of view. V. V. Stasov treats the music of this chorus as if it were a separate national anthem and credits it with superiority over all existing national anthems, 'like a colossus beside small insects' (p. 242), when in fact the chorus 'Slav'sya, slav'sya svyataya Rus'' ('Glory, glory, Holy Rus'') should be understood in no way other than together with the whole opera and with the movement *on stage*. This is nothing like a single anthem (like 'God save the King', 'Gott erhalte Franz den Kaiser', or 'Bozhe, tsarya khrani' ('God, preserve the tsar'), it is not a separate self-sufficient song – it is a march-anthem (*gimn-marsh*) as it was called with the greatest accuracy by Glinka himself.[28] To an educated musical taste this march-anthem cannot be dissociated from Red Square covered by crowds of the simple people, from the sound of the trumpet and the pealing of bells. This is by no means a separate 'musical bagatelle' but rather a most inspired frame for the historical drama of Susanin. Glinka liked to say with pride that this chorus (and the whole epilogue) provides a successful *mounting* for the whole opera. And Glinka was right – perhaps much more so than he thought. No opera in existence to date contains a final chorus which is so closely united with the aim of the musical drama and which uses such a powerful brush to portray the historical picture of a certain country at a certain epoch. The Rus' of the period of Minin and Pozharsky[29] can be heard in every sound. Meanwhile, the musical motive of this march-anthem serves as the basis of very many melodies during the opera itself long before the epilogue – it permeates the entire opera.[30]

Now compare Mr Stasov's judgement upon this epilogue: he says that 'despite the inspired character of the wonderful chorus, the whole epilogue is an *insertion* which is not in the least dramatic' (p. 241), and say honestly

28 *Author's note*: Facsimile beneath a lithographed portrait, taken from a photograph – published by Mr Stellovsky.
29 See note 2 above.
30 *Author's note*: I demonstrated this factually, i.e. in music examples, in the *Musical and Theatrical Herald* in 1859 [see item (a) above].

whether V. V. Stasov understands anything at all of the meaning of the opera *A Life for the Tsar*, of operatic *drama* in general or of the shaping of operatic music?

By bringing out the profound dramatic quality in the whole organic structure and in all the main scenes of *A Life for the Tsar*, to a point beyond dispute, I did not in the least intend to prove thereby that Glinka had a natural vocation for stage drama or for musical drama.

His first opera turned out to be a satisfactory drama as a result of the subject which was felicitously chosen to form an organic unity on the stage, and of the integrity of the conception and inspiration; perhaps in consequence of a certain mistrust of his own powers in his first attempt at a big national opera, Glinka stuck closely to the *idea* of the play like a guiding thread, and did not sacrifice the play to other purely musical ends, and thus created a superlative work as a whole and in its parts.

Sensing that his genius extended to new broader and mightier powers, and fully trusting in precisely these very musical powers, Glinka then turned away from the true, direct path to the hearts and minds of his listeners, forgot all about the aim and integrity of opera as a stage-cum-musical work, and wrote something which was inspired but to some extent also deformed.

A hundred years before our time one of Gluck's zealous defenders against Piccinni's party, the abbé Arnaud,[31] made fun of Italian operas by calling them concerts for which the play was a mere pretext ('les concerts, dont le drame est le prétexte'). In the trend taken by his operas Glinka is beyond doubt extremely remote from unconscious Italianism. *Ruslan*, however, emerged also as a kind of concert piece, or as something which finds a place neither on the concert platform nor on the stage, because the stage is superfluous to this opera.

V. V. Stasov imputes to Glinka the great merit of having once 'selected a subject grateful (?) to opera from Pushkin, giving the opera a completely new meaning, a completely new colouring, which was not present in Pushkin's playful, very light folk tale'.

It is true that the general character of the opera *Ruslan* is not *in the least* similar to the general character of Pushkin's magical tale; but is this a matter of pure gain for the opera itself? That is the question.

Magic in general terms may lie at the basis of a poetic work either as a serious *mythical* or *mystical* environment for a profound spiritual drama (such as Wagner's *Tannhäuser* or *Lohengrin*), or for its own sake, as a motley series of inconceivable happenings, comic or entertaining, and inevitably turning the whole subject towards mischief-making with flashes now of

31 François Arnaud (1721–84), French scholar and writer whose support for Gluck's operatic reforms earned him the nickname 'the Gluckists' high priest'.

sentimentality, now of mockery and satire. That is, either the author forces us to *believe* seriously in the supernatural foundation of the subject, or the author plays games, makes fun by his invention and his heroes. Pushkin's long poem (*poema*) fundamentally belongs to precisely this category – magical, mischievous, comic. It contains not a single factor which could *touch the heart*. We cannot feel any sympathy with any of the *dramatis personae*, who are glimpsed fleetingly and succeed one another like figures in a magic lantern. The characters in the long poem (which is definitely not a strong piece and not in the slightest folklike) remained sketches drawn boldly and with genius, a canvas upon which the youthful poet traced out his Ariosto-like patterns. Everything good in the long poem, its whole charm, was destroyed irrevocably as soon as the thought of taking this mischievous nonsense *seriously* (!) entered someone's head, as soon as the lightness of its approach was turned into *heaviness*. All the enchantments of the poem have been preserved in the opera, but the work *as a whole* has not been imbued even to the slightest degree with any colouring of myth or the Russian folk-tale; the comic outlook on the world has been taken away; the rainbow prism of light satire has been taken away; the capricious smile through which Pushkin shows us the adventures of Princess Lyudmila, the heroic knights who are her suitors, the love of the old woman Naina for the old man Finn, the philandering of the terrible dwarf Chernomor have all been taken away, but *in their place* we are not given even a glimpse of an idea of any sort of deep feeling of pathos. No, that means that we have no tears, no laughter, no warmth, no irony anywhere in the whole course of a huge opera. As a result we are left with an impression of dramatic nonsense and ponderous, soporific boredom.

I shall cite one example (using the words of my article in the *Musical and Theatrical Herald* (*Muzïkal'nïy i teatral'nïy vestnik*)) to demonstrate to what extent one must completely distract one's thoughts from the stage in order to enjoy the beauties of the music in this five-act 'miscalculation':

> Ruslan's bride has disappeared at the very time of the wedding – that is the dramatic *datum* of Act I.
>
> In the second act the curtain opens on Finn's cave. For no reason at all Ruslan comes up to him, and after the most cursory questioning of Ruslan the talkative old gentleman recounts to him in detail the long story of *his own* unhappy love (a ballad of one hundred lines). Is it of interest to the knight who in excruciating impatience is searching across the whole world for his beloved bride, nearly his wife, to hear the story of how some Finnish wizard, a complete stranger to the knight, fell in love with a capricious Finnish beauty forty years before? . . . Glinka fell for the poetic beauties of this narrative in Pushkin (a narrative which *in the poem* has a different significance from that in the opera and which moreover has a *comic* twist at the end) – that is understandable, and like the great artist he was he reproduced these beauties through the very

same musical enchantments, not leaving out anything; the music reflected as in a mirror the stern picturesqueness of the Finnish landscape, and the shepherds, and the pirate fishermen, and the enigmatic grey-haired sorceresses, and the tender passion and powerful magic! Astounding musical pictures follow one after another, but this *is not an operatic scene* at all because even when well performed by the singer this lengthy ballad cannot possibly make any deep impression *in the theatre*. It is a different matter if it is performed in a room as a separate item. When the composer himself sang this ballad with piano accompaniment it had a magical effect, it seemed like a marvel of marvels. The orchestration adds further incomparable beauties, but in the theatre even all this does not make up for blind obliviousness to the laws of the stage.

In the last scene of Act II Ruslan is again obliged to listen to the lengthiest narrative from Polkan's *head* (a chorus of tenors and basses in unison). The impossibility of this narrative on the stage was perceived by Glinka himself after the first performance. This scene, among many others, was cut out by the composer himself. But the cut only intensified the nonsense in the planning of the whole opera.

V. V. Stasov computes the shortcomings in the plot of *A Life for the Tsar* in respect of *action* and *characters* (we have seen how sound these views are). In defiance of the facts and common sense Mr Stasov finds that the plot of *Ruslan* 'contains no such *shortcomings*'. That is, in *Ruslan* Mr Stasov sees both 'action' and 'characters'! Just as you wish!

From V. V. Stasov's point of view (taking the text of the opera as a 'saucer' for holding musical sweets), there are in fact quite sufficient 'characters' when the *dramatis personae*, costumed variously and in motley colours (and not in peasant *kaftans* like Susanin), appear one after another on the stage, sing each his aria and then go out to call on other people; from the same point of view, there is quite enough '*dramatic action*' as well, when, for instance, Ruslan plunges a spear into the cheek of Polkan's head (probably *because* it is always growling in a most unmusical way) or when a doll-Ruslan at the back of the stage flies through the air holding on to a doll-Chernomor by its beard. What a spectacle indeed! Even the puppet theatre affords no greater prodigy . . .

During *A Life for the Tsar* we are variously happy, bitterly miserable and mourning, we enjoy ourselves at the *devishnik*, we grieve with Antonida, suffer with Susanin, celebrate with the people of Moscow in Red Square. Is there even a ghost of these impressions in *Ruslan*?

Praising *Ruslan* as a 'play', V. V. Stasov finds that this opera has 'content which is purely *epic*'. There is another big word – used without the least meaning in this case![32]

32 One might, on the contrary, think that the heroic characters (*bogatïri*), the musical ideas and the slow pace of *Ruslan* provided justification for the description 'epic'.

The concepts of epic and drama are of course closely related and often in poetic works they merge. And this merging must often take place precisely in *opera*, since it is drama with special musical characteristics. Do not Antonida's lament, Susanin's scenes in the forest and the epilogue of the whole drama have an inherently epic character? But if you commissioned various people in ancient Greek costumes to read in turn lines from Homer's *Iliad* on the stage, no drama, play or opera would come into being as a result, however. The *purely epic* contents of the opera *Ruslan* in other words turn out to be: *antidrama* (*antidramatizm*) and *antitheatricality* (*antistsenichnost'*) – that is to say, the quality adduced by V. V. Stasov in praising the opera has precisely the opposite effect.

V. V. Stasov himself admits that 'Glinka is almost entirely without the capacity for theatrical effectiveness', but how do you think he excuses this capital shortcoming in the composition of *Ruslan*? First of all, by the fact that the very first of musical dramatists, *Gluck* and *Mozart, supposedly* suffered from precisely the same shortcoming (this would be a good reason if the fact were correct), and, secondly, by the fact that one should not confuse *the quality of being dramatic* (*dramatichnost'*) with *theatrical effectiveness* (*stsenichnost'*); that is, that the reproaches levelled at Glinka of the absence of stage action are based precisely on such a 'thoughtless' confusion of two different concepts, whereas *strictly within the music itself* Glinka is always very dramatic. (To clarify the matter, I am giving the sense of V. V. Stasov's beliefs without repeating his phrases exactly – 'His reasons are . . .'.)

Once again all the ideas are muddled in the extreme, and V. V. Stasov's knowledge of the operas of Gluck and Mozart, as is clear, has served only to impair the accuracy of his judgements.

In those places in the operas of Gluck and Mozart where the music is *strongly* dramatic the stage impression is also unusually strong. The scene of the Scyths and the scene of the Furies with Orestes in *Iphigénie en Tauride*, and the scene of Orpheus in Tartarus, are staggering in both music and action, and take your breath away also by the external plasticity of effect (given an intelligent and elegant production). The introduction to *Don Giovanni*, the Act I finale and both scenes with the Commendatore's statue – likewise.

All these scenes when performed not in a theatre but at a concert lose *almost all* their force. Mozart's music for *Figaro* in a concert in our day and age can seem somewhat pale and wearisome. In the theatre it is perfectly fascinating. It could not be otherwise.

The examples V. V. Stasov cites from Gluck and Mozart of 'lack of theatrical effectiveness' (*nestsenichnost'*) (a few arias which were worked out over a long period from the purely musical point of view, the Allegro from the sextet in *Don Giovanni* and so on) testify only to the immaturity of the operatic *ideal* in their day (half a century before *Ruslan*), and about the concessions which Gluck and Mozart made to music and to the singers to the detriment of the drama. Whatever logic, other than that of V. V. Stasov, deduces a distinction between dramatic quality (*dramatizm*) and theatrical effectiveness (*stsenichnost'*) (?) in the talents of the very first of operatic creators from this category of *misfortune* and *obstacle* attending musico-dramatic works?

In poetry there can be rare instances of drama deliberately not conceived and created for the stage (Byron's *Manfred* and *Cain*, Goethe's *Faust*) – but an *opera not* written *for the stage* – what could that be? What is the right place for it?

If V. V. Stasov's ideas about drama in opera were not so amazingly mixed up, he could without bothering the colossus Gluck (whose forms are already obsolete) or Mozart (with whom our Glinka in his whole nature has very few points of contact) have found a parallel to excuse *Ruslan* which was nearer to hand and more precise – that of Weber's *Oberon*. This opera, which enjoys excessive renown and celebrity among the Germans, is taken from a poem by Wieland, which is also far removed from the folk-tale element, also written in a jokey, erotic-mischievous way; the text of the opera is clumsily tailored from the poem (with an admixture of something from Shakespeare's world of fantasy); it was written for the amusement of the tasteless London public, as a pretext for the most opulent sets and for Weber's music at the time when he had just become famous for his truly immortal *Freischütz*; it intermingles and weaves together all sorts of odds and ends from the realms of both fantasy and romance, from the oriental world, the world of elves and paladins – all without the least connection, without the slightest sense. V. V. Stasov has probably not seen this opera on the stage, or with his love for vivid colours and his motley of operatic aims he would certainly have felt sympathy for this magnificent nonsense (*Spectackel-Stück*), which is extremely similar in its general aim to Glinka's second opera. V. V. Stasov would have been made sincerely happy by the abduction of a Baghdad princess by pirates after a storm, the shipwreck and the sunrise; and the patrol of harem guards in Baghdad with their enormous Turkish drum on the stage; and the dances of elves and sirens by moonlight; and the ballet of odalisques in the harem at Tunis; and the dance of the Bey of Tunis and his slaves to the accompaniment of Oberon's magical horn – all this is so 'colourful', so full of charm and stage 'life'! And what about sense, meaning, general idea, the general impression resulting from the play, the closing chord left in the mind after the opera has finished? What is the *point* of it all?! Is all this not superfluous in such a simple, *trifling* matter as an opera libretto? Were there the music alone, nothing else need be asked.

Happily for art, people nowadays who understand *music* and understand *opera* look at this matter rather differently from V. V. Stasov with his retrograde and shortsighted point of view.

The recognition of *musical* drama as the operatic ideal is putting down deeper roots with every day that passes among both musicians and thinkers about music. Nowadays even someone as lacking in discrimination when choosing texts and poorly educated as Rubinstein would not have set himself such nonsense as *Oberon* or *Ruslan* as a goal for his operas.

III

An assessment of the libretto of *Ruslan* in comparison with the subject of the opera *A Life for the Tsar* may serve as a close and natural transition to the third point of my objection, to a critique of V. V. Stasov's conviction that the opera *Ruslan* occupies a very high position on the operatic skyline as a whole.

After all that has been said and from the very essence of the matter this part of my thesis can be developed more briefly than the preceding ones.

Let us repeat V. V. Stasov's words of conclusion (p. 242):

> After the creation of *Ruslan* Glinka has only two rivals in the world of opera – Gluck and Mozart. In our century Glinka stands entirely alone, remote from those incomplete or false, narrow or restricted aims and forms, *in* which and *for* which all the other operas of our time have been created.

Tell me, readers – could anyone possibly give you a serious analysis of the judgements of a literary critic who in a paroxysm of rapture over Lermontov, for example, inserted into his laudatory dithyramb the following phrase:

> After the creation of Lermontov's *Maskarad* ('Masquerade'), he has only two rivals in the world – Aeschylus and Shakespeare?

And you will surely agree that V. V. Stasov's opinion is strongly reminiscent of an adolescent's innocent and amusing passion.

Let us forget for the time being that V. V. Stasov expressed his thoughts in 1859; let us suppose, rather, that this opinion of *Ruslan* had been advanced not now but immediately after *Ruslan*'s appearance on the stage, that is in 1842.

Anyone who knew music and the art of drama, who loved and visited opera houses regularly, would then in astonishment turn to V. V. Stasov with a very modest question: 'I can't understand, my dear sir, in exactly what respect you regard this opera so immeasurably highly and why you crush to dust beside it the works of Spontini, Cherubini, Méhul, Rossini, Weber and Beethoven? If you mean the whole opera *Ruslan* as a unity, as a stage-musical work, then it cannot rival either the first-rank operas of *our* own century, such as *La Vestale, Joseph, Les Deux Journées, Fidelio, Freischütz, Euryanthe, William Tell* or even Auber's *Fenella*, Meyerbeer's operas, even those of Marschner, or the lesser ones of Auber and so on.

'As a work for the stage *Ruslan* is a clumsy opera and beneath all criticism. If, my dear sir, you divert your judgement entirely from the theatre, from the stage, and look at Glinka's work as a 'score' only, then, while doing the fullest justice to the music, while going into raptures about its inspired beauties, no one will venture to say that this score by its virtues decisively outweighs once more *Freischütz, Euryanthe, Les Deux Journées, Joseph, Tell* or *Fidelio*! Does *Ruslan* contain a single number which speaks to the heart as much as the trio in Act I of *Der Freischütz*, or the duet of the gravediggers in Act II of *Fidelio*, or the Andante of the terzet in Act III of *William Tell*, or even the fifth act of *Robert*?

'Surely the purpose of the music lies in this language of the *heart*. If everything could be expressed in words, what is the point of music, what is the point of opera?

'You can give any opinion you like in *speech* or *writing*, the strangest, the wildest. Paper tolerates anything. But would you mind, my dear sir, *demonstrating* to the musical world that the opera *Ruslan* as a score puts, say, *Freischütz* or *Fidelio* completely in the shade? In respect of pathos, expressiveness, dramatic quality, comparison is to me impossible because in *Ruslan* dramatic quality and pathos are missing from the very aim of the opera. In respect of simple *beauty of sound*, beauty of musical forms, both Weber and Rossini, I think, will vie strongly with Glinka (keeping in mind the differences in style, inclination and period), and in the face of Beethoven Glinka himself would at once lay down his arms. Would you mind comparing the overture to *Ruslan* with the *Leonora* overture, for example, or with *Coriolan*?

'If you raise the objection that *Ruslan* shows a more pure striving for objectivity in the music itself, without concessions to external consider-ations, then I shall tell you that there is no truth in that at all. In both the operas of Weber and *Fidelio* there is far more of the strictest objectivity than in *Ruslan*; it would even somehow be strange to have to give proof of it! And if in Beethoven and Weber there are here and there glimpses of small concessions to the taste of the public of their time (the jailer's couplets in *Fidelio* or the type of aria which has bravura tricks) then *Ruslan* sins incomparably more in that respect. Lyudmila's cavatina in the first act relies to a great extent on the prima donna's flirtatious virtuosity. Lyudmila's other aria, in the fourth act, has the whole stamp of big virtuoso arias. The third-act ballet is an insertion adjusted to fit all the choreographer's patterns and not a whit above the level of commonplace ballet music; especially in the second half of these dances, whose beauty is very dubious. Does not the Allegro of Ratmir's aria 'Chudnïy son zhivoy lyubvi' ('A lovely dream of real love') rely directly on a solo effective with the public which takes the form of a waltz where our own A. Ya. Petrova[33] could excel?

'The world, my dear sir, does not yet contain, unfortunately, any operas in which the composers aspired to a pure realization of the musico-dramatic ideal divorced from *all* external considerations drawing art away towards aspects which are alien to it and which are more or less unaesthetic. As is clear to everyone, *Ruslan* is not in the least exceptional in this regard; why do you wish to attach such great importance to this opera alone, above all others? There are points of comparison where the primacy remains with Glinka in *Ruslan* over all previous operas (sparing neither Mozart nor Gluck), there are other points again where not only model operas but even mediocre operas outweigh the Kievan *bogatïr'* [legendary hero, i.e. *Ruslan*] to such an extent that he need not be measured against anyone in those respects. In respect of the homogeneity, unity of impression, then of course *Ruslan* will be still further removed from the operatic ideal than for example *Fidelio*, *Freischütz* or Glinka's first opera, which displays high artistry precisely in respect of the blending of music with its dramatic purpose, in respect of the wholeness of the idea and its embodiment in an organic musical entity.'

That is the rejoinder one might have given V. V. Stasov had he pronounced his notorious verdict eighteen years ago.

Now, in 1860, one must add to all this that if for someone embarking on a discussion of operas from an aesthetic angle, and weighing up operas from the standpoint of characters, dramatic quality, objectivity, etc., it is *unforgivable to forget* the earthly existence in our century of Beethoven's opera and Weber's operas, then it is still *more unforgivable not to know* or 'to appear not to know' what has happened and has been happening in this field in the last decade-and-a-half.

Fifteen years after the creation of *Tannhäuser* it is time that everyone concerned with operatic music knew that there are already in existence musical works for the stage in which the strictest ideal of musical drama is *fulfilled*. It is time people knew that in the noble soil of German opera in direct, intimate kinship with such fragrant flowers of that soil as *Fidelio*, *Freischütz* and *Euryanthe* there have appeared creations which are marvellously poetic and complete, where the music is determined by the dramatic

33 For Vorob'yova-Petrova, see Chapter 1, note 18.

action, from the main general idea down to the slightest details, and the drama is called forth by its musical realization, from the main idea down to its subtlest nuances; where in addition to the purity and chastity of the style of Gluck, Beethoven, and Weber are enlisted all the magnificent achievements in musical characterization and expressiveness made through the colours of the orchestra since Beethoven and Weber by Rossini, Meyerbeer, Mendelssohn and Berlioz; wherein the endeavours to blend poetry with music, and word with sound, are just as rationally conscious as in Gluck, who strove for a musical embodiment of tragedy – except that in Wagner the poetry is not a repetition of the rhetorical commonplaces of French pseudoclassicism but the dramatic poetry of our own era reared on Aeschylus, Sophocles and Shakespeare and extracting its inspiration from the rich springs of medieval German legend. And the blending of poetry with music, drama with singing and the orchestra in the present case has been carried out organically, naturally, without any barriers, because in these works the composer of the music and the librettist are one and the same person, has been carried out without the least concessions to the taste of the crowd, because the great poet-musician is at the same time also a great thinker.

It goes without saying that the system of musical sweets along with the dish on which those sweets are served is now out of place. That is why, perhaps, this trend in operatic music, this fullest realization of Gluck's dreams, is not to V. V. Stasov's taste, although he is consistently extolling Gluck and his dramatic truth. To like Gluck's style and ideal yet protest against Wagner is the height of senselessness.

Wagner's ideas in their inviolable logical consistency, and the captivating, spell-binding realization of these ideas in his musical dramas of magical beauty, all this is so triumphantly inspired that it would be the highest pane-gyric to our Glinka to say with pride that ten years before the Wagnerian revolution there was in Russia an artist of genius who succeeded in creating on Russian national soil an opera which approaches the Wagnerian ideal *very closely*.

Unfortunately, the second opera by the same artist, which is maybe more mature on the musical side, inclines again towards the empty, meaningless type of magnificent spectacles accompanied by excellently worked music, but by no means towards conscious musical drama. It is remarkable that Weber could toil over *Oberon* after creating *Freischütz* and *Euryanthe* . . . (For Gluck, Beethoven and Wagner such inconsistencies in their work are not possible.)

The bankruptcy of the opera *Ruslan* as a stage-musical work is evident to everyone who has heard this opera in the theatre, and has also been sufficiently shown in the present article.

In order to justify his belief to the contrary, V. V. Stasov has now to prove:

1 that when Beethoven and Weber created their operas 'their *aims* and *forms* were *incomplete* or *false, narrow* and *restricted*' in comparison with Glinka's *Ruslan*;
2 that all the music in *Ruslan* is higher and better in absolute terms than all the music in *Freischütz, Euryanthe, Joseph, Fidelio, Fernand Cortez, La Vestale, Les Deux Journées, Mosè, Otello, Semiramide* and *William Tell*;
3 that Wagner's ideals (the flower of the philosophy of art) are an absurdity, and his music dramas (astounding living organisms in every word and every note) are utterly worthless.

Until all this has been *demonstrated* by *facts*, the absurdity remains on the side of V. V. Stasov.

In the meantime, in all naïveté or innocence, as if Wagner and the revolution brought about by him did not exist (*tanquam non esset*), in the year 1859 V. V. Stasov can exclaim: 'The future is unknown (!), unknown too are the new paths by which art may (!) progress moved by the powerful hand of future talents (the attempts (!) which have so far been made to establish theatrical effectiveness (*stsenichnost'*) on the operatic stage have been most satisfactorily realized only in comic opera; outside that field they have led so far almost exclusively only to melodramas (?) and external material effects).'

These are exactly the judgements of Ulïbïshev who in his book on Mozart printed in 1843, that is exactly twenty years after Beethoven's creation of his Ninth Symphony, calmly speaks about the ideals of the *symphonic style*, in conformity with only the symphonies of Mozart, and makes fun of Beethoven's innovations, which are of the highest genius, as pathetic *attempts* which have only *perverted* art (*Biographie de Mozart*, vol. 3, pp. 233–70).

To the narrowmindedness, one-sidedness and short-sightedness of these gentlemen's view is added an inert obstinacy which covers up their eyes and ears. They live at some point in the past; what everyone else takes as a *present-day fact*, something as indisputable as the rays of the sun in the sky on a cloudless day, is to them playing the part of the distant 'unknown future'.

Later on V. V. Stasov states the very well-known truth that, whatever the art of the future may be like, the great earlier creations will never cease to shine like brilliant, life-giving stars, and predicts the very brightest future for the opera *Ruslan and Lyudmila*.

In V. V. Stasov's words this opera must stand, undoubtedly, in our theatres and in public opinion, on the indestructible pedestal which by rights it ought to have. 'And what a time that will be!' exclaims *Ruslan*'s panegyrist.

> Then Russia will understand that Glinka is the same for us as Gluck and Mozart are for Germany; that we must take pride in his *Ruslan* as one of the loftiest works of art to date; that this opera together with a few other works of Glinka's final period is the foundation of the future independent Russian school; that this opera, once established on the stage, will never leave it, so that it can be constantly before the eyes of new rising generations; that this national work should be *projected* (?) (does he mean *produced?*) in Russia with the same brilliance, opulence and care, from the choruses to the military orchestration with the same artistic integrity and even *archaeological faithfulness* (!) with which Shakespeare's tragedies are mounted in England and Sophocles' tragedies and the operas of Gluck and Mozart in Germany; finally, that after creating *Ruslan*, Glinka should belong to the company of people to whom monuments are erected. What a time that will be!

If V. V. Stasov in his proud confidence as an expert on art in all its branches were not deaf and blind to what is happening on Germany's operatic stages *now* he would have saved himself from acting out a ludicrous role: perching on his professorial chair to propagate backward notions and prophesying the future while looking *only* at the past.

Being used to *retrospective* views is probably a most valuable attribute in an *archaeologist*. And it may well be that as an archaeologist V. V. Stasov is, as people say, on sure ground. For that he has books in his hand. But music criticism is emphatically not his forte. The finest proof of this lies in his curious article about 'an opera which has suffered much'.

For someone who wants to be a *real* judge of musical and music-theatre matters (and not merely to 'pass' for a musical Aristarchus[34] in a group of . . . architects and engravers), for such a person 'retrospection' and admiration confined to individual parts, bits and pieces of an opera, one number here, one phrase there, a chord somewhere else, various musical odds and ends unconnected *to all the rest*, is not *nearly* enough.

On the contrary, the first requirement of a true critic of art is to observe the object as a unity, as a complete organism, to judge this organism and its circumstances in comparison with the demands of the age in which the work was created, and with the demands of his own day. To a true critic the future of art cannot remain *closed* or appear in a *false* light. Like the Janus of the ancient Romans, the art critic casts a sure eye over both what has been and what is to come. One opposed to progress is not in a position to be a critic.

---

34 Aristarchus (*c.* 217BC – 145BC) was regarded by Cicero and Horace as the supreme critic.

There is no doubt that Russia should be proud of such a score as *Ruslan*; there is no doubt that Glinka is the founder of the Russian school in musical art; there is not the least doubt that Glinka is a great artist, worthy of monuments (though he is not in need of them: his best monuments are his compositions); there is no doubt that the opera *Ruslan* just as much as *A Life for the Tsar* must be performed on the Russian stage with all due zeal and thoroughness (although to look for 'archaeological accuracy' in an opera with a frivolous fairyland for its subject is to make an inappropriate and even ludicrous claim), but *Ruslan*'s blessed time to which V. V. Stasov looks forward will not arrive, alas, *ever*.

By its very nature this opera is an odd, even a freakish phenomenon. It is both a heroic knight (*bogatïr'*) and a dwarf at one and the same time. The music in the score was some twenty years ahead of its time, so that its ties with the music of Chopin and Schumann and the last works of Beethoven must even now in the 1860s arouse the greatest sympathy in people whose musical taste has either matured or been acquired naturally; as an *opera*, that is as a stage-musical work, *Ruslan* did not have the strength to stay alive even at the moment of its birth. A puppet show of that kind would perhaps have amused an audience at the time when *Dneprovskiye rusalki* ('Water-sprites of the Dnepr')[35] and *Chertovïye mel'nitsï* ('The devil's mills')[36] were refashioned from the German originals (although even those had more point and coherence). But even in 1842 no one could have shown the least sympathy with *Ruslan as a play*. Everyone just shrugged their shoulders. Now, when even Italian operas show an incontestable striving after strong drama, when there is a general tendency in opera towards drama, when the Russian public too knows, when it admires *A Life for the Tsar*, what real opera means in the complete blending of drama and music, how can one wish for taste to turn back to trifles from the *real thing*?

A Life for the Tsar will be an adornment of the Russian operatic stage for many, many decades to come ('for ever' in the strict sense hardly applies in this field of art). The beauties of the opera *A Life for the Tsar* which result from its permeation by the general idea of the aim, drama, and from its closeness to the Wagnerian ideal, will not pale before any other nation's treasures in the world. The opera *Ruslan*, on the other hand, is not in a position to hold the stage anywhere. If you are to stand on your feet, to walk, you need legs, and this opera was born crippled, without any legs. The more that public taste develops musically, the better the public is able to appreciate the treasures so generously scattered through the score of

35 *Dneprovskiye rusalki*: see Chapter 1, note 44 and Chapter 2, notes 19 and 21.
36 *Chertovïye mel'nitsï*, a Russian version staged in Moscow in 1816 of *Die Teufelsmühle am Wienerberg*, music by Wenzel Müller, premièred in Vienna in 1799.

Ruslan by Glinka, the more will that same public *regret profoundly* that all these musical pearls and diamonds are wasted; that all these are in essence wonderful colours, incomparably inspired études, caprices, escapades, toys, foppery using the skills of a composer, but still *nothing like a true opera* by comparison with Gluck, Mozart, Beethoven, Weber, Wagner or Glinka's matchless *first* opera!

V. V. Stasov (p. 240) cites the general opinion, the general verdict on *Ruslan*, that it has become common to place that opera immeasurably lower than *A Life for the Tsar*, to consider it an utterly unsuccessful, extremely tedious opera which has over-reached itself, whose *few* fine parts are unable to redeem its basic internal worthlessness.

But how has V. V. Stasov *refuted* the justice of this general verdict? You have only to remove the word *'few'* before 'fine parts' for the verdict to express the most accurate assessment of the opera *Ruslan*. Almost *all* its parts are extremely good and some are astoundingly inspired; all that is lacking (a mere bagatelle!) is an *inner idea*, a living dramatic organic quality. That which is without life cannot live.

The matter speaks for itself, and the best answer to V. V. Stasov's article is the facts which directly contradict his groundless complaints (about the imaginary destruction (!) of the opera *Ruslan*, about this opera's imaginary persecution by fate), his retrograde beliefs and unrealizable prophecies.

But a printed article of that sort, which was particularly disgraceful for its self-confident tone, just had to call forth a printed article in rebuttal.

A polemic like this is certainly of benefit to the public as well. The aesthetics and criticism of music are hardly yet much developed in Europe as a whole. Here in Russia this is all nearly virgin soil.

Everyone in this field is free to proclaim whatever comes into his head, to preach all kinds of fables and 'Gothamisms', hoping with impunity that no one will come out with objections. But for that very reason everyone in his turn who recognizes that he possesses some strength in such matters is *under an obligation* to expose muddleheadedness and ignorance.

(c) P. I. Tchaikovsky: The revival of *Ruslan and Lyudmila*.
Russian Bulletin, 17 September 1872, no. 201, pp. 1–2.
Tchaikovsky, pp. 47–53

Pyotr Il'ich Tchaikovsky (1840–93) made some sixty contributions to the literature on music in the form of reviews of concerts and theatre performances; there are, besides, his theoretical works and his prodigious output of letters. His work as a journalistic critic was mainly accomplished between 1868 and 1876, concluding with several reports on musical events in Bayreuth in the latter year.

The most important texts in the debate about *Ruslan and Lyndmila* are listed in the introduction to item (6) on pp. 104–5.

This article shows that Tchaikovsky could have forged a successful career as a writer of words had not notes taken a tighter grip on him. The first night of this Moscow revival was 12 September 1872.

While the leading lights of Russian music criticism are unanimous in placing Glinka's name at the head of the independent Russian school and thus alongside the names of the greatest composers of all times and peoples, they are in sharp disagreement about the two greatest works of our brilliant composer – his two operas. One group, led by Serov, openly take the side of the first opera, *Ivan Susanin*. In a whole series of articles entitled 'Ruslan and the Ruslanists' the late Serov tried to demonstrate that however beautiful the music in *Ruslan*, however mature Glinka's mastery in that work, however rich in delightful melodic invention, splendour of instrumentation and abundance of contrapuntal wit, nevertheless that work must be considered the unsuccessful creation of a muddled artist, albeit of a great one. Serov's opinion derived from the proposition which was the motto of his whole career as a critic, the Wagnerian principle that 'opera is musical drama'. There is no drama in *Ruslan*, Serov showed. The opera's libretto is a motley of shreds and patches hastily sewn together. The great number of unconnected individual episodes which follow one another without any logical sequence; the absence from the action of characters and dramatic situations; the insubstantial quality of the libretto, both in a purely literary sense and as regards historical and social truth – such features deprive the listener of complete artistic enjoyment, for he finds them tiresome and disturbing. *Ivan Susanin*, on the other hand, includes the tragic situation of Susanin where the interior struggle between family feeling and patriotic duty is concluded in the moving triumph of the latter, and leads the opera's hero to unconditional self-sacrifice for the sake of his country; the contrast between the two hostile nationalities offers interest too; in short, despite the weakness of the libretto as regards literary technique this opera has – in addition to a wealth of musical elements summoning so many unfading beauties from the depths of a great artist's soul – dramatic movement in accordance with the laws of aesthetics, which constantly increases in complexity and ends with the all-reconciling action of dying. Thus, in the opinion of Serov and his disciples *Ivan Susanin* is an opera, and what is more a superlative one, whereas *Ruslan* is a more sequence of delightful illustrations to the fantastic scenes of Pushkin's naive poem.

The other group of representatives of our musical world, whom Serov calls 'Ruslanists', assert the complete opposite. This party, which has its voice among music critics in the form of the musical columnists of the

St. Petersburgskiye Vedomosti ('St Petersburg Bulletin'),[37] without relying on any philosophical principles or going into aesthetic abstractions, has decided that *Ruslan* is not only Glinka's better opera but the best opera of the whole lot, that is to say the opera of all operas, the wearer of the operatic crown, the ruler of the whole operatic realm. In *Ruslan*, say these columnists who are ardent but known for their paradoxical nature, Glinka displayed by comparison with his first opera the highest creative power; in *Ruslan* he was in full possession of mature mastery and was moving along new artistic paths which he was the first to lay out. In their opinion, in *Ruslan* Glinka proved himself a bold innovator who cast off the bonds of routine and convention, whereas in *Ivan Susanin* he was still subject to the old forms and only within the limits of those outmoded forms showed a strong, original but not yet completely developed creative gift.

In comparing these two sharply conflicting views and trying to reconcile them, it is impossible to avoid the conclusion that Serov's criticism is the more profound and the more rational. Taking a specifically musical point of view, Serov does not in the least deny the undoubted advantages of *Ruslan*; the amount of musical material in the latter opera is greater, and it is of higher quality. But everyone knows that major works of art are evaluated not so much by the strength of the immediate creativity shown in them as by the perfection of the forms into which this strength is cast, the balance of parts, the successful fusion of an idea with its external expression.

After all, Beethoven is rightly considered incontestably the first among composers, although every musician is aware that Mozart and even Schubert possessed no less, if no more, intensity of musical inspiration. If we look for Glinka's place in the musical pantheon, then by virtue of the strength of his powerful creative genius alone he can stand beside the greatest representatives of his art; but the point is that providence did not furnish him with the environment, the conditions of development which he needed if his immense gift was to reach its fullest flowering. [. . .] One has only to read Glinka's *Memoirs* published in Mr Semevsky's journal[38] to understand the extent to which the environment, the spirit of the age and its social conditions combined together to hinder the brilliant artist's conscious advance along the path indicated to him by his richly gifted nature. Like the *bogatïrs* of the fables, he possessed a degree of strength which he did not realize and could not channel appropriately. The character of his musical nature made Glinka primarily a lyrical symphonist, but he left us hardly a single purely symphonic work; to judge by several episodes in both operas

---

37   This is a reference to Cui and Stasov.
38   The *Memoirs* (*Zapiski*) appeared in *Russkaya starina* ('Russian antiquity') (founded by M. I. Semevsky) in 1870.

he could have given us inimitable models in that sphere. Lacking the encouragement provided by a highly-developed musical environment, and not finding proper backing and support (Prince Odoyevsky's authority could not suffice), Glinka sought an outlet for his inspiration and, falling for some detail in the subject in hand, went after it with all the impulsiveness of an artist bursting with ideas, without weighing up, without calculating all the conditions necessary for the success of the projected work. Thus, for example, *Ivan Susanin* arose as the result of the circumstance that Glinka was captivated by the impact of the contrast between the three-beat rhythm of the mazurka and the long-drawn-out dolefulness of Russian song. *Ruslan* was composed for the sake of some fantastic scenes which genuinely did evoke musical inspiration, but the inspiration of a symphonist. Thus it came about that *Ivan Susanin*, written to a fortuitously successful scenario, turned out to be a superb opera; *Ruslan*, on the other hand, made up of a series of unconnected short fantastic scenes written at various times by several people, on account of the inorganic quality of its construction and complete absence of dramatic motives cannot be numbered among model operas; it is only a magic spectacle accompanied by the most distinguished music. There is no doubt that if our repertory of operas were rich in splendid works, or if Glinka had managed to write two or three more operas which satisfied the demands of the stage and dramatic interest more than *Ruslan*, then *Ruslan* would have been staged more seldom than other operas and would have belonged for the most part to the concert repertory, alongside such wonderful operas as, for example, Weber's *Oberon* or Schumann's *Genoveva*, which only rarely if ever appear on Germany's operatic stages.

If one examines *Ruslan* from an exclusively musical point of view, one cannot but be amazed by the variety and wealth of its musical delights. The overture, fervent, fiery and brilliant, festive and gay – and its effect clouded only right at the very end by the whole-tone scale hinting at Chernomor's spells – introduces a sequence of outstanding musical pieces which, unfortunately, are not linked by any unity of dramatic movement. The restricted space of a newspaper column does not allow me to enlarge on the music of *Ruslan*; an extensive article would be necessary for that. I shall therefore confine myself to a brief indication of the best parts of the opera.

Among those, first of all, is the grand introduction, epic in character, to Act I, with Bayan's charming song accompanied by harp and piano. [. . .]

Then the ensemble later in this act, in which the passionate melody of the Khozar prince 'Breg dalyokiy, breg zhelannïy!' ('Distant shore, longed-for shore!'), makes an enchanting impression, is wonderful. After Lyudmila's abduction with its accompaniment of thunder and sudden darkness, there follows a canon in which the characters express their common feeling of horror and bewilderment with staggering truthfulness. Here Glinka gave an amazing sample of his enormous technique; this entire canon is built on a pedal, that is an E flat held on in the bass during the whole piece, which periodically appears on the second beat of the bar in the pizzicato of the cellos and basses.

Act II consists of three episodes: the ballad of the good magician Finn, the scene of the coward Farlaf with Naina, and finally Ruslan's big heroic aria in the dead ground guarded by the giant's head. Of these three numbers, the first, Finn's ballad, is particularly remarkable. As the theme for the ballad Glinka took a short little Finnish song which he takes through a long succession of many variations full of contrapuntal interest and decorated moreover with all the riches of the most brilliant instrumentation. But the virtues of all these three numbers pale in comparison with the profoundly inspired short prelude which opens Act II. In the compressed, wholly original form of this entr'acte Glinka was able with the sweeping powerful strokes which typify only great creators and with striking artistic truth to depict for us at one and the same time: Farlaf's fear of the old sorceress, the languor of the melancholy Ruslan and the grief of the giant's fantastic head. Had Glinka composed nothing but this short piece, the musical judge would be compelled by it alone to place him in the very front rank of musical talents.

In Act III I shall mention the chorus of maidens in Naina's castle, which like Finn's ballad consists of a series of superb variations on a single theme, and also Ratmir's famous aria 'I zhar i znoy' ('Both heat and sultriness') which Glinka succeeded in colouring, the Andante of the aria especially, with pure oriental voluptuousness and passion.

Act IV transports us to the bewitched world of Chernomor's magnificent garden. The music of this act presents us with a succession of musical wonders which entirely overwhelm the listener. Both of the yearning Lyudmila's arias interrupted by the offstage chorus of flowers, Chernomor's march, the maidens' dances, the *lezginka*, the chorus 'Kto pobedit' ('Who will be victorious') – all these are first-rate, inimitable specimens of musical creativity. [. . .]

In Act V I shall note Ratmir's aria, the charming chorus *Akh ti, svet Lyudmila* ('Oh you, dear Lyudmila') and the opera's finale, which is massive, festive and rejoicing.

One must recognize as among the relatively weak parts of the opera Lyudmila's first aria and the dances in Act III which, though nicely written, are still in the conventional ballet style. These two small black marks on the bright face of Ruslan's music pass almost unnoticed. Far more important is a general shortcoming of Glinka's opera which stems from its very virtues.

I am saying nothing especially paradoxical if I observe that Glinka's music is too good. One cannot with impunity renounce the practical conditions of theatrical effectiveness, ease of vocal performance and a multitude of other small considerations which nonetheless have a very powerful influence on a work's success. And the greatest artists must be able to contain their unbridled inspiration if it lures them too far beyond those conventional forms on which ease of execution and hence success too are founded! Thus, for example, Glinka completely lost sight of the fact that our singing per-formers are very rarely sound musicians; but his ensembles are exceedingly difficult, and for successful performance require either infallibly secure singers or else such a number of preparatory practices and rehearsals as is impossible with our theatre dispositions. As an example, I can point to the trio in Act III, where the inconsistent accompaniment in quintuplets and the complexity of the modulations make things extremely difficult even for the ablest singers, and still more difficult for such as our Moscow ones. This results in some sort of mess in the orchestra and the chorus which reflects badly on the music itself, which in this instance is filled with combinations of the utmost interest.

Or take, for example, the chorus of flowers. What ideally graceful specimens of humankind, what choice collection of selected voices must make up the chorus if this divinely poetic, ethereally limpid music is to be performed in any degree satisfactorily! For the singing of flowers must be like the depiction in music of their fragrance. How sweet must be the fra-grance personified by our plump chorus ladies! If someone such as Offenbach conceived the notion of composing, for instance, a chorus of pumpkins, car-rots and turnips or come what may, these products of the kitchen garden industry could perhaps find worthy representatives among our chorus ladies; but roses, jasmine, lilies – and these mature ladies with their good-natured bourgeois appearance – there is a terrible mismatch. You will say to me that the chorus sings offstage. But in the first place the vulgarly commonplace timbre of our ladies' chorus matches exactly their external appearance and secondly, however great theatrical illusion may be, I recognize them all the same, and from the sides I can even see our assiduous but voiceless chorus ladies crowded behind the scenes conscientiously working through their flower parts.

There is no point in enlarging specially on the performance and the production as a whole. In any case they are little in keeping with the poetic quality of the work itself, although some of the artists show a very diligent attitude towards their roles. [. . .]

The orchestra this time was the opera one, and for that reason things went far better than in *Ivan Susanin*. The overture was played with great animation and particularly successfully. As regards the general course of the opera, the ensemble, it naturally left much to be desired, although there was not the same fabled chaos to which the Russian opera treated us at the revival of *Ruslan* last year.

Mr Finocchi's[39] benefit was nearly the Russian opera season's swansong. The opening of the Italian productions is almost upon us, and my soul was gripped by an ill omen when in the middle of this opera the tall skinny figure of the controller of Muscovites' pockets, Signor Merelli,[40] appeared in one of the stalls boxes. His face showed calm self-confidence and from time to time a smile played on his lips – a smile not quite of disdain and not quite of crafty smugness. What was the cunning Italian thinking about? Probably about the impact on the public of the poster due to appear soon with the names of Mmes Mallinger[41] and Di Murska[42] added again, and about how sweetly naive our public is, believing in Lucca,[43] Mallinger and Di Murska when it will never hear either the first, the second or the third. And why should he not smile when thinking thus! Our blessed Moscow is the promised land for Mr Merelli. Crude charlatanism and a persistent system of naked swindling are rewarded here not by ignominious banishment but by tightly stuffed pockets and even by something else more honourable.

---

39 L. Finokki was a bass who performed at the Bol'shoy Theatre from 1870 to 1881. He had earlier sung in Italian opera in Moscow.
40 Eugenio Merelli was an impresario who staged Italian opera in Moscow from 1868.
41 Mathilde Mallinger (1847–1920). A Croatian soprano who worked in Munich (where she was the first Eva in *Die Meistersinger*) before settling in Berlin.
42 Ilma Di Murska (1836–89). Croatian soprano. She sang in opera in Vienna, London and other important centres.
43 Pauline Lucca (1841–1908). Austrian soprano. A successful career took her to Prague, Berlin, London, New York and Vienna. She sang in Russia in 1868 and 1869.

CHAPTER FIVE

New operas

Against a background of debate about the principles underlying the relationship between music and drama, new operas were composed and produced. The works of Serov the composer enjoyed the greatest popular success even while they were at odds with the ideals promoted by Serov the Wagnerite critic. The 1860s saw the completion of the 'mighty handful', the group of talented disciples of the magnetic if autocratic Balakirev. This was the time of their greatest cohesion as a group: in the next decade each went his own way. The example of Dargomïzhsky, especially in the setting of words to music outside the framework of the number opera, in *The Stone Guest*, was a crucial supplement to the example of Glinka and current ideas of realism in the development of the concepts of the New Russian Operatic School as articulated by Cui in the press. Cui also played a modest role as the composer of *William Ratcliff*. Dargomïzhsky died in 1869 and Serov in 1871, leaving the 1870s to the next generation, which included Musorgsky, Rimsky-Korsakov and Tchaikovsky.

One musical event has left no trace in these articles. On 29 October 1862 the world première of *La forza del destino* took place in St Petersburg. It represented the final instance of the conspicuous Russian consumption of Italian musical products, a taste acquired in the previous century. Henceforth, the impetus lay with Russian compositions, though the decline of Italian performers still had a long way to go.

(a) P. I. Tchaikovsky: Dargomïzhsky's *Rusalka*, The Italian opera. *Russian Bulletin*, 14 September 1873, no. 198, p. 1. Tchaikovsky, pp. 131–5.

Here Tchaikovsky supplements his estimation of Glinka's operas in the previous chapter (4(c)) with his assessment of Dargomïzhsky: both *Rusalka* and *The Stone Guest* are considered. 'Our city' is, of course, Moscow.

About five months have passed now since I last conversed with readers of the *Russian Bulletin* about our city's musical affairs. A dead calm has reigned during this significant gap in my observations on music; it is true that in the capital's closest environs the cascading sounds of the Offenbach repertory have rung out ceaselessly along with other piquant wares of Parisian musical manufacture; it is true that posters have daily proclaimed musical festivities in one club or another, but all this enters not at all into the programme of my chronicles, since music in all places of entertainment of that kind is a secondary matter and is accepted only as a traditional accessory to pleasures of an entirely non-aesthetic character. I am very well aware that even during the opera and concert season Muscovite musical talent is in the majority of cases no more than an illusion of hugely comical scale and duration, and that except for the concerts of the Russian Musical Society, all the events of our musical life are either disgraceful or ridiculous; but I am obliged to speak about them, I cannot disregard them, since in any case they attract public attention to a highly significant extent and offer abundant material for my modest observations.

In fact, is not the Italian opera in Moscow a topic which swallows up almost exclusively the attention of the majority of the public over the winter season? Is not great care taken over it? Is it not spoken of a great deal? Does there not exist for it an extensive and complex administration with an entire horde of theatre functionaries from the higher and lower ranks? Yet look closely at or better listen attentively to the result of all this bustling activity by so many people, perhaps highly capable, conscientious people, and you will become convinced that our Italian opera is the sheerest illusion. There is an excellent theatre with an extensive stage equipped for effects of all kinds, such as deafening thunder when bad weather must be represented, such as traps for characters of demonic features, with electrical and other lighting, with huge and often beautiful sets, with machines, costumes and props. We have an orchestra, and choruses, and a ballet, but in the sense in which the word is understood in western European capitals, we have no opera. We cannot understand the action on the stage, whether as a result of unfamiliarity with the language or of the high cost of the libretto, which by the way is very poorly translated; the sets, costumes and props almost always constitute astounding anachronisms, sometimes of an extremely comical nature; the orchestra is so feeble and plays so limply and out of tune that the proper musical effect is not achieved; the choruses go completely unheard, or if the wheezy sounds which they make do reach the ear it is only to lacerate the auditory nerves located there; it is true that the beautiful, sometimes phenomenally beautiful, voices of Italian singers can captivate the ear, but only for an instant, for as soon as they start singing together then they will without fail go out of tune and do it not one bit better than Mrs Turchaninova[1]

---

1. M. D. Turchaninova. I have been unable to discover any information about this performer. In subsequent such cases, of which there are several in this chapter, there is no footnote at all.

who, let me say *en passant*, has attained the highest degree of musical mastery in the matter of musical confusion. Now tell me: is not all this one vast illusion, one which is the more astonishing because the great mass of the public treats it as if it were something entirely serious? But that's enough about Italian opera for the moment; I shall have to speak about it time and again in the future both in general terms and as regards its astounding manifestations in Moscow in particular.

I shall move on now to an account of the recent revival on our Russian operatic stage of Dargomïzhsky's delightful opera *Rusalka*.[2] Our Russian opera is dragging out an even more miserable existence in Moscow than the Italian one. Interest in the latter is maintained to a significant extent by the appearance of a large number of soloists who are either already familiar to the public or else entirely new to them, who are often quite wonderful both in the beauty of their voices and their artistry. In the Russian opera, which has for long now been performed by the very same more or less respectable and conscientious, although ageing, singers, it is the superb music of our few but nonetheless first-class operas which constitutes the only interest. So fascinating is the music of these few operas by our best operatic composers that for its sake you sometimes forget the disgrace of the frightful performances! By virtue of all its melodic charm, its warmth and artless inspiration, the elegance of its cantilena and recitative, *Rusalka* without doubt holds the first place among Russian operas after the unattainable genius of Glinka's operas. Unfortunately, the superlative qualities of this exceptionally sympathetic work are overshadowed by its significant shortcomings, stemming from the sad circumstance that the late Dargomïzhsky did not receive a thorough technical education, and as a result, despite the effervescence of his talent, he offended by a dilettante's lack of the finishing touch and an absence of critical self-consciousness which are reflected, unfortunately, on every page the gifted composer wrote. Speaking of Glinka on the occasion of the revival of his *Ruslan and Lyudmila* last year,[3] I pointed out to readers the unhappy circumstances deriving from the composer's position in society but to a still greater extent from the course of his life and the customs of those bygone days which prevented Glinka from emerging in the forefront of Europe's leading lights in the art of music.

The same unfavourable circumstances, that is the undeveloped artistic environment, affected the entire artistic evolution of the highly talented Dargomïzhsky in wholly equal measure. It was only by the amazingly refined flair of his richly endowed, highly characteristic individuality that Dargomïzhsky attained in some aspects of opera a summit of artistic perfection reached only by a tiny handful of the elect.

2 The first performance of the revival took place on 2 September 1873 3 Cf. Chapter 4, item (c).

It is well known that Dargomïzhsky's strength lies in his astoundingly real and at the same time gracefully singing recitative, which imparts to his magnificent opera the fascination of inimitable originality. The late composer apparently recognized the predominant strength of his creative gift, and this recognition, alas unsupported by a firm critical buttress, moved him to the strange idea of writing an entire operatic work made up of recitative alone. To this end, Dargomïzhsky selected the text of Pushkin's *Kamennïy gost'* ('The stone guest') and, without changing a single letter in it, without adapting it to the demands of opera as is usually done when a literary poetical work is taken as the groundwork for broad musico-dramatic forms – strung recitatives over every line of the original text. It is well known that recitative, lacking a fixed rhythm and a clearly outlined melody, is not a musical form – it is only the cement binding the different parts of the musical building together, necessary on the one hand as a result of the simple stipulations of stage movement and on the other as a contrast to an opera's lyrical moments. A sad delusion on the part of a bold talent without the guidance of an aesthetically developed artist's sober understanding! Composing an opera without music – is that not the same thing as writing a drama without words or action?

To return to *Rusalka*. I repeat that the predominant merit of that opera lies in the unusual truthfulness and elegance of its recitatives, and also in the beauty of its melodic outlines. As regards harmonic and orchestral technique, in these respects Dargomïzhsky stands far below not only Glinka but also the majority of other Russian composers. Perhaps for that reason he was much less successful with the fantastic element in the opera than with the depiction of scenes from real life. Here what is required to reproduce the *rusalkas'* underwater world successfully is a refined flair for musical colours expressed in brilliantly coloured instrumentation, but that ability was missing in Dargomïzhsky.

His orchestra is inert, dry and ineffective; his harmony, while now and again interesting, lacks the mastery of polyphonic part-writing which is characteristic of Mozart, Gluck and other great creators in the realm of fantastic opera.

Of the performance of *Rusalka* on our stage, I can say that it was of a kind which can be heard nowhere else but Moscow. The most complete disorder reigned in the ensembles, the orchestra played weakly and flabbily, the chorus as always sang mercilessly out of tune, and the production was careless and pitiful in the extreme.

[Tchaikovsky discusses the merits of two new singers.]

Moscow's Italomanes are rejoicing. A season promising a long series of delights opened on Monday with *Il trovatore* which has long bored everyone [else]. Among old acquaintances Messrs Rota[4] and Marini[5] appeared this time. The former has lost nothing of his splendid vocal technique for all that his voice has suffered significantly during the time when we have been deprived of the pleasure of hearing him. As regards Mr Marini, it seems to me that he is moving quickly in the steps of his predecessor Mr Stagno[6] who, as everyone knows, shouted away his fine voice for the amusement of the visitors to the gods and, it should be said, for most of the rest of the public. Apart from sonorous chest Bs and Cs, Mr Marini has nothing left which is worthy of the attention of true connoisseurs of the vocal art. Instead of singing – a kind of hoarse squeak; instead of acting – an automatic waving-about of the arms; instead of expressiveness – a sickly-sweet stretching-out of notes in the falsetto register. But Muscovites have a weakness for crude effects of force and fail to notice all these little shortcomings, and as soon as Mr Marini hits his chest note go into a frenzy of enthusiasm as if this extremely anti-artistic yelling was the desired aim of their diligent visits to the Italian shows.

Of the new members of Mr Merelli's[7] company, one cannot fail to speak in praise of Mrs D'Angieri,[8] who possesses a strong ringing soprano voice, clean intonation and a handsome technique. But Mrs Bernardi, who very conscientiously gave herself airs in the role of Azucena, turned out to be a very poor singer with a cracked voice and a complete absence of correct method. Except for the noisy success of Mr Marini's chest notes, the performance moved in a very limp fashion and the audience astonished me by their coldness, which was completely incomprehensible for the affecting celebration of the opening of the Italian season.

(b) Ts. A. Cui: Musical chronicle. Mr Serov's *Judith*. Cui 1918, pp. 183-97

This notice was published in the *St Petersburg Bulletin* of 26 January 1865, no. 22. *Judith* was composed between 1861 and 1863 and premièred at the Mariinsky Theatre on 16 May 1863. Its subject is taken from the Apocrypha's account of the Jewish heroine who slays the Assyrian leader Holofernes and thus releases her people from a protracted siege.

4 One Giacomo Rota sang the baritone role of Fra Melitone in *La forza del destino* at La Scala in 1869.
5 This is *not* the Ignazio Marini who was the first Oberto in 1839 and the first Attila in 1846 and who sang for the Italian opera in St Petersburg from 1856 to 1863.
6 Roberto Stagno (1836–97), a tenor who impressed Tchaikovsky when he heard him in Rossini's *Otello* in 1868.
7 For Merelli, see Chapter 4, note 40.
8 This may be Anna d'Angieri, the soprano who was the first to perform Amelia's role in the revised *Simon Boccanegra* in Milan in 1881.

In recent years – to be precise, from the time when [Dargomïzhsky's] *Rusalka* was produced on the stage of the Russian opera – works by Russian composers have begun to appear rather frequently, whereas before *Rusalka* the only pieces performed regularly were *A Life for the Tsar* and Verstovsky's opera-vaudeville *Askol'd's Tomb*. Even *Ruslan* was abandoned after two seasons, to be revived only in recent years.

[Cui argues that a new production of *Rusalka* is a practical proposition.] After *Rusalka*, [as I said], works by Russian composers began to appear on the Russian operatic stage rather frequently. Mr Vil'boa's[9] *Natasha* is a childish work, which does not manage even to attain the levels of Varlamov's[10] Russianisms; Mr Fitingof's[11] *Mazepa* is an outrageous mixture of Verdi and Dargomïzhsky scored in the ballet style, something like Mr Pugni[12]; Dyutsh's[13] *Kroatka* ('The Croatian girl') is far from being an untalented opera, but is written in too routine a fashion and is too rich in borrowings from the works of others; Mr L'vov's[14] half-baked *Undina* is without rivals in thinness and insipidity; and finally, in the spring of last year, Mr Serov's *Judith* appeared.

Mr Serov has long enjoyed in Russia a significant reputation for his music-critical articles where he has demonstrated his splendid musical abilities and knowledge, but his creative powers were revealed only in the past year by his opera *Judith*; prior to *Judith*, we had heard several successful arrangements by Mr Serov for orchestra, but no one so much as suspected him of being the future composer of a large five-act opera. As one should have expected of such an expert musician, Mr Serov is a champion of new musical ideas and aspirations, and he has tried to embody in his opera these strivings for the greatest possible dramatic power (*dramatizm*), picturesqueness, and freedom of form. And in this respect *Judith* is a phenomenon remarkable in the extreme, since it is the first conscious attempt in Russian opera to realize the contemporary view of art. Unfortunately, Mr Serov's *creative* abilities are restricted: to say nothing about the complete absence of distinctiveness and originality, the musical implementation in general of his good intentions is not always successful. *Judith* is a wonderfully intelligent outcome of all that music has achieved up to the present, but Mr Serov has not spoken any new word of his own in *Judith*. The influences of Wagner

9 K. P. Vil'boa (1817–82) was a composer and conductor.
10 For Varlamov, see Chapter 2, note 41.
11 For Baron Fitingof, see Chapter 2, note 43.
12 C. Pugni (1802–70) is best known as a composer of ballet scores. He composed 300 of them, thirty-five as official composer of ballet music for the imperial theatres in St Petersburg from 1851.
13 Otto Dyutch, or Dyutsh, or Dütsch (c. 1823–63). Composer and conductor of Danish birth and German musical education who settled in Russia in 1848. His *Kroatka* was staged in St Petersburg in 1860.
14 For L'vov, see Chapter 2, note 28.

and Glinka are the ones most clearly visible in this opera. In all those places where Mr Serov wishes to outline more graphically the national identities of Hebrews and Babylonians we encounter musical devices and harmonic traits the prototype for which is to be found in the Hebrew song in [Glinka's music for] *Prince Kholmsky* ('S gornïkh stran' ('From mountainous lands')) and Chernomor's march in *Ruslan*. In a good half of what remains we see a striking similarity to Wagnerian forms, with his colourful use of the orchestra and constant modulations (which are not always necessitated by the idea itself) with which he tries to conceal his lack of ideas. Besides Glinka and Wagner, the influence on *Judith*, although to a significantly lesser extent, of other composers as well is noticeable, as I shall indicate shortly.

In my view, the choice of subject is very unsuccessful; it is entirely founded on religious ecstasy and steadfast faith; of all the characters, only Holofernes is animated by passion, while the others – Judith, Ozias, Charmi and Eliachim – inhabit lands beyond the clouds, pray and go into religious ecstasy. The chorus, one of the most important elements in opera, *whines* throughout the first and fifth acts, and plays an insignificant role in the third and fourth acts. It was strange to rely on one's own powers for the successful realization of such a subject which is monotonous in the extreme, which over the course of five acts presents only two situations: in the first, second and fifth acts the Hebrews weep and pray, and in the third and fourth acts Holofernes drinks heavily and blasphemes. It is not easy to rouse a biblical and religious mood in oneself, especially for a man of the second half of the nineteenth century; how is one to sustain such a mood over the course of three acts?

The first act is preceded by an introduction written entirely in the style of Wagner's *Vorspiele*. This introduction ends with a beautiful musical phrase depicting the excruciating, miserable moral state of the Hebrews in the besieged city. It is curious that Mr Serov paid no attention to this beautiful phrase (they are few and far between here) and did not base a chorus of Jews upon it or at least recitatives for Ozias and Charmi instead of those insignificant ones with which the opera opens. The lament of the people begins, the elders' admonitions and the threats of Eliachim the priest. The free fugue which the chorus sings is mediocre in both theme and treatment, and falls far short of expressing the irritable and highly-strung state which the Hebrews, tormented by hunger and thirst, ought to be in. The speeches of Ozias and Eliachim are pervaded by the fear of God and by faith, and here already, from Act I onwards, Mr Serov's bankruptcy of inspiration by religious ecstasy is shown: Eliachim sings in the Italian style (especially at 'smirite skorb' i upovayte' ('subdue your sorrow and put your trust [in God]')); Ozias' uninteresting recitatives are accompanied by beautiful instrumentation very reminiscent of the sound of the Catholic organ, or more accurately the Protestant one, which does not suit an elder of the Jews at all. Achior's narrative and particularly his song ('V sud'be svoyey narod evreyev' ('In its fate the Hebrew people')) are very good. The original, splendid harmonic turn (the Hebrew song from *Kholmsky*) and the beautiful instrumentation – these are the distinguishing features of this number. In the narrative which follows it I shall mention the originality of purpose in constructing a recitative on the sound of timpani alone and the successful portrayal of Holofernes in the brass instruments' chords. There follows a chorus of Hebrews appealing to God. The end of this chorus is charming; it is the best passage in the whole opera. The point is that Mr Serov holds the listener for a very long time on the two minor chords of E and A with a seventh above; on the notes forming the final chord, Eliachim moves to the upper register, Ozias descends to the lower one, and then, adding in the bass the lower fifth, the chorus shifts to G major. All this, together with the marvellous instrumentation, and with the picture of the people at prayer, makes a most gratifying impression on listeners. This is the *one and only* place where prayer is portrayed musically in an adequate manner. Only it was in vain for Mr Serov to modulate again to the minor: it spoils the effect, and is moreover out of place: hope has come to the people praying.

Act II opens with Judith's recitatives. Her address to her late husband is quite warm. The famous 'Ya odenus' v visson' ('I shall put on the byssin')[15] is effective in Mrs Bianki's performance, effective in instrumentation and its many high notes, but the music in itself does not amount to anything apart from pretty harmonies and modulations akin to Liszt's. When Judith 'in the highest ecstasy' appeals to God, the music changes to a bad Mendelssohnian march and ends with seconds in the wind instruments which represent fairly well the words 'Krïlami angelov pokroyet' ('He will cover with angels' wings'). Avra's recitatives are written wholly in the manner of Dargomïzhsky. The first phrases of Avra in Yaila's song begin in a strange and ugly way, but the middle and end of each couplet are very good: the harmonization is powerful and the idea full of energy (the Hebrew song from *Kholmsky* again serves as the prototype for this number). The ending for two voices is disgraceful: Judith and Avra manufacture *fioriture*. Here Mr Serov has abandoned musical truth and striven exclusively for effect. This reminds one of the appallingly bad duet of Susanin and Vanya in *A Life for the Tsar*. The scene between Judith and the elders is pretty inert, though with some good turns of phrase, such as, for instance, 'Molit'sya stanu ya za vsekh' ('I shall begin to pray on behalf of all'). The act ends with a duet between Judith and Avra. First comes 'I shall put on the byssin' for two

15 This refers to 'fine linen' as worn by kings and priests.

voices. Mr Serov should have finished with that; it would have been highly effective; because the Allegro which follows it:

Tï u grudi moyey vzrosla,
Chto mayskiy krin tï raztsvela

('You grew up at my breast,
You blossomed like a spring lily')

is so feeble and melodically pitiful that one might think that it had been extracted from some quintet by Onslow.

In Act III we are in the camp of the Assyrians, where the songs of the odalisques are mixed with their dances. An excellent musical task, the intention perfect, the atmosphere authentic and poetic, and had there been ever so slightly more inspiration and creative talent it would have turned out miraculously. The Assyrian march is very full of colour: Mr Serov wished by means of this march mainly to depict savage conquerors. The march is strongly reminiscent of Chernomor's march, its instrumentation even containing purely comic effects (wind instruments staccato in a high register) which scarcely entered the composer's intention. The chorus-scherzo of Assyrians as they run in is of middling quality, but too monotonous in rhythm, especially taking account of its substantial length. In the recitatives which follow, intelligence is to be seen everywhere, but they do not contain any special musical virtues. The large *morceau d'ensemble* which comes after the recitative is entirely of the Wagnerian kind: it has an Italian melody, rather *recherché* and strained, with modern harmonies, appoggiaturas and minor-key episodes, scored with the utmost unctuousness, which all adds up to a whole which is cloyingly sweet and perverted. The chorus with which this act concludes is a periphrasis of the Assyrian march in $\frac{3}{4}$.

Act IV opens with an orgy in Holofernes' tent. The music is completely identical in character, worth and power to the beginning of the third act: that is why the bewildered spectator sees in this scene a pointless and tedious repetition of what he has already seen earlier. The difference is, however, in actual fact considerable: in the preceding act the odalisques and almehs[16] are merely trying to dispel Holofernes' boredom, whereas here a desperate general drinking-bout and orgy are in progress. But this difference of situation entirely disappears as far as the spectator is concerned, because the composer has not managed to express it adequately in his music. Vagoa's Indian song is unsuccessful in the extreme. It is the weakest number in the whole opera. In spite of the harp chords, the splendid harmonies and the flutes' ritornello, what has emerged is something forced and incoherent to the utmost degree. The martial song of Holofernes which ensues is excellent.

16 An *almeh* or *almah* is an Egyptian dancing-girl.

In the gloomy tread of the basses, in the melody itself and its development, in everything, one can hear the energy and thirst for blood of the Assyrian leader. The scenes which follow until the very end of this act are interesting for the course of the drama, but not for their music, all of which is intelligently written and in accordance with the situation on the stage but contains no inspiration, no passion, no purely musical interest. Among Holofernes' ugly snarls the phrase 'ti ostayosh'sya, o golubitsa' ('you will stay, oh, my darling'), taken from the orgy, stands out more sharply and is accompanied by violin passages which make an impact.

The fifth act is musically the feeblest of all; it contains nothing interesting at all. The people *moan* and Eliachim threatens. The popular rejoicing at Judith's arrival is represented by music in the style of Cherubini ('Spasen'ye, spasen'ye! Gospodu slava!' ('We are rescued, rescued! Praise be to the Lord!')) and this piece stands out very conspicuously and inappropriately from all the rest of Mr Serov's music. The final hymn of Judith with the chorus is written in the same manner and is of the same worth as the *morceau d'ensemble* of Act III: it is a Wagnerian-Italian Andante strained and stretched with a great pretension to breadth of scale.

The whole of *Judith* is delightfully scored: with great taste, remarkable intelligence and talent. Mr Serov's instrumentation most closely resembles Wagner's in character. I even prefer Mr Serov's orchestra – it is more delicate, elegant, varied and less ornamental.

There are in *Judith* many more slight defects which stem from the composer's lack of experience and which are inevitable in a first composition. Although they will of course disappear of their own accord in subsequent works, it may nevertheless not be entirely useless to point them out. Thus, in the fugue the words 'nashi skorbi, nashi muki' ('our griefs, our torments') repeated often in a fast tempo make an impression which is almost funny. Thus, in *recitatives*, Mr Serov sometimes mistakenly repeats one and the same line of text. Thus, it is misguided that Holofernes has only to mention trumpets for trumpets to ring out at once in the orchestra. Thus, recitatives in duet must be avoided, as for instance between Ozias and Charmi. The most significant defect is the clumsiness of the part of Judith herself: it is written very high, tends towards screaming, and is awkward for the voice; the performance of a part like this is extremely difficult for a singer and harmful for her voice. To say nothing about the hymn in Act V in which Judith in the heights must out-shout the entire chorus, to say nothing about the end of 'I shall put on the byssin', even the recitatives are all written in too high a register.

The general impression which *Judith* makes on the spectator is a painful one. Weariness sets in from Act II on and, constantly intensifying, weighs upon you right to the very end of the opera. This results from a subject which evokes little sympathy in present-day man, from its being stretched out over five acts when it could have been contained within a more compact framework; from the fact that the opera has just two characters: all these factors unavoidably render a large five-act opera monotonous. This monotony is significantly increased by the music, by the *constant* andante and, the most important consideration, by want of creative abilities, which cannot be replaced by either skill, or intelligence, or the best of intentions, of which there is so much in Mr Serov's work. There are few of the musical treasures which might have revived the listener, and even those go for nothing in the midst of a long, intensely serious opera. At any rate, Mr Serov's labours have produced a work which is worthy of respect and remark, standing prominently and sharply apart from the voluminous trash which is being written both abroad and here in Russia. *Judith* is not an entirely successful attempt, but it is the *first attempt in Russia* to realize *consciously* the contemporary view of art in opera, and it is impossible to stress this merit sufficiently.

[Cui has praise for Mme Bianki[17] as Judith, but cannot accept the unmusical shouting, presumably sanctioned by the composer, of the talented Sariotti[18] in the role of Holofernes.]

Judith had great success[19] and in less than two years ran to twenty-nine performances, but on all the most recent occasions the theatre was very empty. What usually happens in Russia is that if a piece enjoys success it is given very frequently to begin with, and after about two years it goes out of the repertory. This way of going about things is excellent as regards bad pieces which are indebted for their success to fortuitous temporary circumstances. But it strikes me as mistaken to deal in this way with solid works such as *Judith*: it ought not to leave the repertory; but in order that it show a profit, it must not be performed too often. With twenty-nine performances in under two years it is no wonder that the public has become tired of it, and one cannot put on a piece which does not attract spectators; but the fact of the matter is that the last-named circumstance stemmed not from the opera itself, but from too frequent performances of it initially.

---

17 Valentina Bianki (Bianchi) lived from 1839 to 1884. She was born in Wilna, studied at the Paris Conservatoire, sang on the stages of the Mariinsky (1862–5) and Bol'shoy (1865–7) theatres, and died in Kandava (in Latvia). She created the title role in *Judith*.

18 M. I. Sariotti (1839–78), high bass. An artist of the Mariinsky Theatre from 1863, he was the first Holofernes in Serov's *Judith*.

19 *Author's note*: A highly comforting phenomenon in that it means that the public is capable of feeling sympathy for the most recent musical opinions and that in embarking on work which is practical, serious and well-considered one need not despair of success.

(c) G. A. Laroche: On *Rogneda. Contemporary Chronicle*, 1869, no. 2. Laroche 3, pp. 19–26

Serov's *Rogneda* was composed between 1863 and 1865 and first performed in the Mariinsky Theatre on 27 October of the latter year. The libretto was the work of Serov himself with some verses contributed by D. V. Averkiyev. The action of the opera is set in the tenth century, when Prince Vladimir, ruler of Kiev, was converted to Christianity, and following his example eventually all of Russia. The story involves priests of the old religion trying to induce one of his wives, Rogneda, to murder him. The opera ends happily after a series of improbable adventures with both husband and wife still living.

The author sets the appearance of this opera in the context of Russia's musical development, and of current theories about music and drama. Serov is the unnamed target of the opening sallies, with Wagner's shadow behind him.

Over the last decade a great deal has been said about musical drama. By this term was meant not the opera which exists at present, not those works to which our public is indebted for so much enjoyment in which young composers search for living models, towards which the critic studying them adopts a reverent attitude – no, the 'musical drama' advocated to us with ardour and passion is the fruit of philosophical speculation, prophecy for the distant future. Opera – so the musical press has repeatedly educated us to believe – is an error, since its principal purpose, that is, drama, is always being lost sight of inasmuch as it is a musical work, a set of musical numbers embellished by means of ballet and décor but lacking any grand idea and integrity. From a desire to please the vulgar crowd, composers have supposedly filled their operas with arias, duets, quartets and so on without paying any attention to the demand of the plot and the dramatic goal; from a desire to please the crowd they have demeaned themselves by writing easily remembered (that is bold and beautiful) melodies which are capable of immediately appealing to the uneducated taste; from a desire to please the same crowd they have chosen plots which are rich in effect and colour, with pretensions in the direction of history, but which are incoherent and just cobbled together anyhow using coarse, stunning effects. Meyerbeer is the particular target of this criticism; his operas certainly do indeed reveal a striving for historical characterization (a striving which in many respects, even in its failings, is similar to that which we can see in the novels of Sir Walter Scott); moreover, they are exceptionally effective, affect the public strongly and enjoy huge popularity. But the theory of 'musical drama' is ultimately criticizing mercilessly not particular composers but a whole genre of opera for the incoherence and emptiness of its libretti, for giving in to the demands of singers, that is, in other words – with long arias which halt on high notes, with *fioriture* and embellishments, and as a result of the collection of effects which make no contribution to the drama's contents.

There is no doubt that in general the adherents of this ideal and of truth, dissatisfied with present reality and thirsting for a better future, have been guided by the most pure and honourable motives. There is no doubt that the critics who have set their 'musical drama' as such a lofty and remote ideal – the harmonious combination of all the arts, the complete subjection of the means to the idea, the chaste renunciation of external frills and allurements – there is no doubt that these critics have been animated by fervent love for art and a firm faith in their ideal. They could not count on the sympathy of opera-lovers when they all attacked every Italian opera without exception which had brought the majority of these devotees so many moments of enthusiastic enjoyment; they could not convince specialist musicians as long as they treated the classical authorities with condescension; to both the former and the latter they exposed the immaturity of some and the backwardness of others and thus aroused mainly bewilderment and displeasure. Consequently, they wrote entirely unselfishly. One needs to have a strong conviction to be constantly telling the reader things which are most unflattering to him; the reader who sees how far distant he is from the author's intentions and wishes and puts up at every turn with powerful reproofs and pungent sarcasm does not, however, always believe in his own [mental] bankruptcy, and indeed sometimes develops an animosity towards the author and turns into a determined opponent.

There remains only one consolation then for the author – faith in his ideal and the hope of being understood one day in the fullness of time. Our prophets of 'musical drama' were placed at precisely this disadvantage and thus displayed all their disinterestedness and selflessness. While simple mortals, who in their intellectual development had not yet attained complete philosophical denial, continued to admire that kind of opera which circum-stances allowed them to hear, the musical prophets chastised this opera familiar and dear to everyone with their thunderous indignation, chastised it in the name of a 'musical drama' which no one knew, which did not even exist, which had still to be. While concert- and theatregoers continued to love music, and to admire its development which is such a recent thing in Russia, the musical oracles prophesied that all kinds of music in general as a separate art have become out of date since the time of Beethoven's Ninth Symphony, that from that time onwards – that is from the 1820s – music has been striving to merge with the other arts, that it can merge with the other arts only in drama and that drama can be nothing but musical. Let the ignoramuses carry on staring at the fairground wares with which they have got used to being content; let charlatans carry on pulling the wool over their eyes with their unworthy conjuring tricks; only a few, but those unshakeable in their faith, recognize the whole vanity of the entertainments and amusements around them which are falsely called music, poetry, drama; these believers have obeyed the letter of the new doctrine, have meekly followed it and renounced for ever the sinful passion for Mozart and Weber, Rossini and Donizetti, Auber and Meyerbeer, Glinka and Gounod. These strict ascetics, who reject music other than the dramatic kind and condemn most severely of all dramatic music in the form in which it exists now and existed before, cannot spare new talent either pursuing the same path which they have forbidden. And here is where this virtuous ardour with which they rejected everything in existence in the name of something which does not exist drew them further than they could have foreseen and perhaps have wished. The first appearance in Russia of the theory of 'musical drama' coincides with certain facts which testify that music, at least in this country, has not yet reached the age of self-negation or, what amounts to the same thing, of slavish subjection to another art. On the contrary, in fact, the first gleams of independent music have only just started to appear in Russia.

The death of Glinka (as often happens with the deaths of great persons) drew attention to him once more. Musicians and the public alike remembered the great artist when he was no more, and his immortal although unfortunately extremely few works gradually began to attract the affection of ordinary listeners and the inquisitiveness of specialists.

In St Petersburg on the stage of the Mariinsky Theatre they have revived *Ruslan*,[20] a work long abandoned and thus unfamiliar to the majority; the *Russian Herald (Russkiy Vestnik)* has published a fine biography of Glinka written by his friend Stasov;[21] the very activities of the Russian opera which was for a long time inhibited by the Italian opera livened up with the appearance on the stage of Setov,[22] and the sorry place which it had held up to then in St Petersburg has been changed by the attention and sympathy of the public and the improvement in repertory and performance. Thus not only could the works of Glinka be performed for the public if not in a version worthy of them then at least in a tolerable manner, but also an arena for Russia's compositional forces was opened which formerly had either to disavow their nationality or to dream about performing Russian opera somewhere in Berlin (which even Glinka himself tried to obtain for his

---

20 The revival took place on 6 September 1864.
21 V. V. Stasov's *Mikhail Ivanovich Glinka* was published in the *Russian Herald*, 1857, nos. 9–12.
22 I. Ya Setov (1826–93), tenor, producer and theatrical entrepreneur. He made his début in 1855.

A Life for the Tsar). At almost the same time the [Russian] Musical Society was being founded in St Petersburg, which later opened branches in Moscow, Kiev and Khar'kov.[23] This Society's concerts gave composers a new opportunity of coming before the judgement of the public, of hearing their own works performed in orchestral guise and of making artistic progress (prior to this, access to concerts was very difficult for [the works of] Russian composers). The Conservatoires which the RMS opened laid the first foundation for that full and systematic study of music without which the formation and continuous existence of orchestras and choirs which rise above a workmanlike and amateur level are inconceivable. At long last (thanks to the increased performances of musical works) Russian composers for the orchestra and the stage have emerged as well. What could be said about this by people who saw in the concert and the opera an evil and who felt themselves called to do battle with this evil? Paying no attention to the public's voice, they rushed boldly into the struggle with that living art which they had condemned to death. Blows rained down on Glinka, on the Musical Society in the person of its founder Anton Rubinstein, and more than anywhere else on the Conservatoire. A great creative artist who had so recently opened up new musical horizons, a gifted and energetic public figure who had undertaken to advance and develop musical talent in Russia; a new institution which had to respond to the newly awakened demands of the public for musical education – none of this could in any way fit in with a theory which declared that music as an independent art was in its last days.

While the school of criticism which made a hobbyhorse of 'musical drama' carried on retailing its stale news, the young, fresh growth of the art moved ever forwards. The division between theory and reality became still deeper. The critics had to deal with the most diverse phenomena, which demanded from them the most varied approaches; but always and everywhere the critics of the tendency mentioned above applied one and the same yardstick. In the most heterogeneous species they recognized the very same old enemies of their truth, the very same inveterate pagans. At the same time as the theorists of 'musical drama' were repeating over and over again that music as an independent art was antiquated, young composers with significant talent began to appear in Russia, and each of them represented new evidence that music in Russia had barely entered its adolescence. But our young composers kept to spheres alien to this theory, to the spheres of symphonic music and the romance. Of course the romance and the symphony had no right to exist – such was the teaching of the supporters of 'musical drama' – but music's principal ill lies not there but in opera void of

23 These branches opened in 1859, 1863 and 1864 respectively.

dramatic meaning and unity written to enable singers to display their voices and pockmarked with stage effects irrelevant to the main business. The chamber and concert works of our young composers were unconvincing to the theorists of 'musical drama'; their speciality was opera, and it was only in the field of this speciality that they could suffer a decisive defeat. Would Russian operas bear out theories which had been preached so ardently for so long? Would the main attention in our operas be directed towards the concept and towards unity? Would the singing be only strict declamation, without any reliance on sweet melodies and high notes? Would those colourful and not always logical effects to which Meyerbeer and his imitators had accustomed us be banished? One had to be afraid lest having heard so many sermons about truth and the ideal (as our Wagnerites understood the truth and the ideal), our operatic music might indeed enter on that severe ascetic path upon which it would scarcely be rewarded with the public's attention and sympathy.

The appearance of Serov's *Rogneda* has dispelled all these misgivings. His opera has proved again that Wagnerism's dreamy theories are groundless – in our country more than anywhere else. First and foremost this can be seen in the theatrical construction of the libretto. The effective and absorbing plot of *Rogneda* is entirely without the integrity and 'organic quality'[24] which the Wagnerites placed first among their requirements. The principal character after whom the whole opera is named comes before us in a short scene in Act I and then in Act IV carries out her criminal attempt on the prince's life without taking any part in Act II or Act III and without acquainting us to the slightest extent with her personality. The fact of the crime can be seen but the entire psychological development which preceded it remains concealed from us. All the situations, and thus the whole plot as well, are based on a series of coincidences: the unexpected arrival of the prince in Act I where he saves Rual'd's life; Rual'd's unexpected help when they are hunting bears, help which saves the prince's life; the unexpected intervention of Izyaslav in Act V, which saves Rogneda's life. But the opera's essence does not lie at all in these hastily strung together adventures to which the characters are subjected. The essence of *Rogneda* is the epic rituals and the historical costumes: the greater part of Act I and all of Act II are devoted to choruses and dances which have nothing whatever in common with the plot of the opera, which could have been performed, for instance, in [Verstovsky's] *Askol'd's Tomb*, and *Rogneda* without these two acts would have retained all of its plot, though it would have lost the greater part of its charm. In the remaining acts too it is precisely the most attractive numbers, the ones which are most carefully worked out, the ones

24 Laroche here refers to Serov's allegiance to both Wagnerian and *pochvennik* ideas.

which most attract the public's attention, which are independent of the dramatic content and belong in the background among the props. It is impossible not to see this too as a sign of the times. The demand that drama show 'unity, organic sense', as our Wagnerites have expressed it, is in principle not open to argument. But over the course of development of the literature one sometimes detects a striving towards extreme strictness in this respect, sometimes a tendency to a view which is unrestricted and condescending. If one takes all the literature of our century, it is obvious at once that a free attitude towards dramatic unity predominates in this age. Thanks to their knowledge of Shakespeare, thanks to the Romantics, thanks to historical drama, present-day dramatists have broadened extraordinarily the framework of their works, but have at the same time lost the conciseness and clarity which distinguished the earlier stage. Whatever judgement a strict aesthetic view might have passed on such a fact of art, this freedom and this multi-coloured variety (introduced into opera above all by Meyerbeer) had a beneficial effect on opera: these qualities gave music scope to develop and display itself, they obliged it to search for brilliant and sparkling colours, and they thus enriched the musical substance. In this as in everything else the Wagnerites' zeal was misplaced when they demanded that all effects not essential to the plot be removed from an opera and that the plan of a libretto should be in accord with the strictest logic. In his freedom of construction and the accumulation of diverse effects Serov has departed a long way [from his ideal]. The sorcerer's cave, the sacrifice to the idol, the ballet, the *skomorokhs'* dances,[25] the Fool and his songs, the hunting with horses and dogs, the pilgrims' singing, the assembly of the people (the *veche*)[26] – all this is picturesque and absorbing, but perhaps it is rather lacking in coherence.

Apart from their doctrine of organic unity, our Wagnerites had another hobbyhorse: their view of melody. As everyone knows, every opera contains lyrical moments during which the action comes to a halt and the mood of one or more of the characters or of a whole crowd is expressed (an aria, ensemble or chorus). In order to express itself and explain itself in a wholly artistic way, the artist's mood seeks a musical form which is complete and rounded, comprehensible and elegant. The Wagnerites rose in revolt against this: the musical drama which they pictured in their dreams had to consist only of recitative, and all the more musical forms and all cantabile phrases were banished from operatic music for ever. The critics poured ridicule on the arias and ensembles in, for example, Italian operas, in which the

25 *Skomorokh* – an itinerant Russian professional actor, musician and general entertainer.
26 *Veche* – popular assembly in Rus' from the tenth to the fourteenth centuries, and for longer in Novgorod and Pskov. Such a meeting is depicted in *The Maid of Pskov*.

dramatic movement did indeed come to a stop at every turn so that a singer, male or female, could sing a beautiful and effective melody. The supporters of 'musical drama' demanded that music precisely reproduce declaimed speech and, applying a purely intellectual yardstick to every aria or cavatina, considering that it would be absurd to *speak* in the way that people *sing* in arias, reached the following verdict: any melody which requires long drawn-out syllables, word repetition, changes in word order, in a word – a melody constructed in accordance with musical rather than rhetorical laws is harmful to opera and turns it into a 'concert in costume'. A persecution was launched against 'melody'. Beautiful and outstanding melodies won the attention and sympathy of the public more than anything else: almost every opera contains favourite passages (*morceaux favorits*) upon which the listeners' interest and the performers' zeal are always concentrated; most of these favourite excerpts have been published in the most varied adaptations; very often they have been made into dances. That is the public's attitude towards melody, but such melodies too (clear and approachable) have provided the Wagnerites with a topic for their witticisms and mockery. Here too (as in the matter of dramatic unity), Serov turns out not to be on the side of the negative critics. *Rogneda* is an opera extremely far removed from the endless, even if truth-filled, recitative which the Wagnerites promised us. On the contrary, *Rogneda* contains very many agreeable and easily accessible melodies. Some of them are exceptionally advantageous to their singers who can use them to show off their voices and skill; others are entrusted to the chorus or the orchestra. Both kinds have an irresistible effect on the public which prefers music to have pleasant sounds rather than a profound idea. It is true that some of these melodies are reminiscent of Verdi's style (the part of Rual'd the Varangian) while others recall Varlamov's[27] style (in Act II); but they redeem the deficiency in outstanding originality by their good musical development, particularly in the orchestral colours, of which Serov is a master. Some of the melodies I have mentioned, moreover, sin excessively against the character of the time: thus in Act II the prince's Fool sings a fairy-tale ('Za morem, za sinim' ('Beyond the sea, the blue sea')) the theme of which is strikingly similar to the Annen Polka of Strauss, but harmonized in the style of the newest salon piano pieces (as the well-known and much-loved *La prière d'une vierge* is harmonized, for instance).[28] There are some among the public, and a very significant part, to whom a theme appeals and whom its aptness does not concern, but in Kiev and in the tenth century this theme is a strange arrival.

27 For Varlamov, see Chapter 2, note 41.
28 *The Maiden's Prayer*, composed by Tekla Bądarzewska-Baranowska, first published in Warsaw in 1856.

Serov's *Rogneda* is obviously written not for a small group of bold thinkers and reformers; it is written for the public, and the public was so quick in appreciating and falling in love with this light playful element in *Rogneda* that only a little while after its first performance in St Petersburg a polka and a quadrille on themes from this opera appeared. One must not lose sight of the fact that together with these popular sides the music of *Rogneda* possesses extremely serious merits too. I have already mentioned its orchestration; it shows an experienced and skilled hand, a subtle understanding of sonority, but at the same time it reveals a rather one-sided taste, an exceptional weakness for dense, massive sonorities and contempt for more refined colours. But Serov's multitude of vivid effects demonstrates that this contempt is by no means the product of ignorance but that it was intended by the composer. The critic is also under an obligation to point to the first-rate variations of which the chorus 'Zhaden Perun' ('Perun is athirst') in Act I consists. The theme, which is at first sung in unison, then goes through a series of harmonic and instrumental modifications – a technique of construction borrowed as a whole and in some of its details from Glinka, but applied tastefully and painstakingly. The jaunty, devil-may-care theme 'Barïnya, sudarïnya' ('Madam, your ladyship') in the Fool's song with chorus (in Act III) is worked out excellently. The combination of several themes at the end of Act II is not so successful: these themes follow on one after the other rather than going along simultaneously, and thus they acquire the appearance of an attempt to solve a great technical problem which however remained unsolved. The final chorus of Act I is put together with the highest skill, although its basic theme is of no significance; this chorus is an excellent specimen of constant growth. Other numbers (especially in Acts IV and V) are written with significantly less care and are of no technical interest. But from the numbers I have mentioned it is obvious enough that Serov is trying to achieve a thorough and elegant technical polish. Here too we see him parting company in the practice of his art from the Wagnerites. It behoves the Wagnerite to show scorn for musical technique; he considers the *art* of harmony and counterpoint to be a shameful *craft*. In his tendency as a composer Serov is just as free from the Wagnerites' contempt for technique as he is from their views on 'organic unity' and 'absolute melody'.

One must add, however, that in his conservative tendency Serov sometimes goes too far. A grain of truth underlies the phrases of the Wagnerites. Drama must indeed be the content of opera. A series of effective pictures not connected to one another by the common action of a plot which gradually unfolds is not yet an opera: and a complete *laisser-aller* here is just as injurious as stiff purism. Music must indeed as far as possible reflect the character of the place, the time and the characters; when it neglects this aim, when it pursues only euphonious themes it assumes a character which is now already outdated.

(d) G. A. Laroche: The new Russian opera *The Voyevoda* by Mr Tchaikovsky. *Contemporary Chronicle*, 9 February 1869, no. 6, pp. 10–11. Laroche 2, pp. 23–6

The Voyevoda was Tchaikovsky's first opera and his third official opus. Written in 1867–8, it was first staged at the Bol'shoy Theatre on 30 January 1869. It is based on Ostrovsky's comedy *Voyevoda*, also known as *Son na Volge* ('A dream on the Volga'). The libretto was a joint venture by playwright and composer. The opera survived for five performances. The composer later destroyed the score (having prudently saved a considerable part of its material for use elsewhere), though it was reconstructed and performed in Leningrad in 1949.

Another new opera has enriched the Russian repertory, another name has been added to the number of our operatic figures and this time Moscow is seeing the début of a composer new to the world of drama.[29]

The composer of the new opera, given for Mrs Men'shikova's benefit,[30] P. I. Tchaikovsky, is well known to the public, particularly to that of Moscow, amongst whom he set out on his career as a composer. His works, which have been played mainly at the Russian Musical Society's concerts, have always been rewarded with success, and some of them (such as the second and third movements of his symphony, performed at the Society's concert on 3 February last year)[31] even with a success beyond the normal run. And truly they displayed excellent aspects which promised a great deal for the future. Besides their technical merits, besides their varied, subtly well-considered instrumentation, a general tone prevails in them, they had a general imprint, a musical personality was expressing itself through them. Soft and graceful lines, a warm feeling of feminine tenderness, nobility, free from hackneyed triviality – these are the characteristics of the best of Tchaikovsky's works which we have heard and which outline the character of his talent. Where from the nature of the task he was not able to give expression to these predominant sides of his talent, he has often lapsed into coldness and artificiality, which usually occurred in places intended to be of an energetic quality; but his capital artistic personality excused its negative sides by its positive ones, and was amiable and sympathetic even in its one-

29 *The Voyevoda* was first performed at the Bol'shoy Theatre on 30 January 1869.
30 A. G. Men'shikova (1846, or 1840, –1902). She was a soprano at the Mariinsky Theatre from 1869 until 1880, after which she sang with private companies.
31 They were performed under those auspices on 11 February 1867.

sidedness. That was how we came to know him from his symphonic works; now he is embarking on an operatic career and in this broader field he further justifies the opinion we came to from his instrumental compositions. First and foremost we must take note that the libretto which he has selected has placed him in a most disadvantageous position for a composer writing for the stage. A musician sometimes, in a moment of unfocussed thought and an incomplete, confused mood chooses for himself words or a plot doomed to futility and begins his composition, is carried away by his work, is inspired in a purely musical way but ascribing his inspiration to the words and the plot, gradually gets used to and identifies with his false goal, the further away from which he gets, the more powerless he is to give it up. Something of this kind has happened with Mr Tchaikovsky, who selected as the plot for his first opera Ostrovsky's[32] drama *The Voyevoda* or *Son na Volge* ('A dream on the Volga'). This play is based on the most paltry, hackneyed plot-outline, which, without interesting or confusing a soul, is hidden beneath a welter of motley details of everyday existence. This environment is exceptionally interesting and Ostrovsky's first-rate language endows it with that real tangible colour which mark out all this writer's works. In the opera libretto reworked from the drama and serving for Mr Tchaikovsky's music, this everyday milieu is entirely dispensed with. Only the plot-outline has stayed – there remains the idea that Nechay Shalïgin stole Mar'ya from Bastryukov, and Bastryukov stole Mar'ya back again from Shalïgin. Several touching encounters and farewells, and among them several Russian songs arranged for orchestra – those are the entire contents of the opera known as *The Voyevoda*. For this incoherent and uninteresting material music has been written which fully confirms the opinion expressed above about Mr Tchaikovsky's talent, an opinion which was based on his previous compositions, but adds to it several new features. Mr Tchaikovsky is a composer who is most attractive in his own musical sphere, but, as far as we can see to date, not capable of going outside it. Gentle, beautifully moderate, nobly elegant outpourings wherever they were possible, have turned out very successfully in *The Voyevoda*; to this category belong the first half of the overture, the first aria of the tenor Bastryukov, the Andante of his duet with Mar'ya, the middle cello phrase of the dances in Act II and the quartet in Act III. On the other hand, the energetic and passionate places, such as for instance the first finale, are forced and ugly in the extreme; the affected boldness which can be heard in the noisy orchestration sharply contradicts the shallow impotence of the contents. To speak generally, one senses a

32 A. N. Ostrovsky (1823–86) is best known as the author of plays set among the merchants of Moscow. The operas *The Power of the Fiend*, *The Snowmaiden* (which is not of that sort) and *Kát'a Kabanová* are based on plays by him.

further weakness: Mr Tchaikovsky has been reared too exclusively on German models; one can clearly hear in his style its affinity with the most recent imitators of Schumann, and with Anton Rubinstein in particular. Whatever the shortcomings of Ostrovsky's *Voyevoda*, it is in any case beyond dispute that this play is permeated by a purely Russian tone. Mr Tchaikovsky's music, which sways between the German style (the predominant one) and the Italian style, is most of all devoid of this Russian imprint. Given the slender development of musical composition in Russia, and given the necessity first and foremost of assimilating what has been done in the west, this absence of a national (*narodnïy*) style would not necessarily have been such a great misfortune. But from time to time Russian folk (*narodnïye*) songs occur in *The Voyevoda* which the composer takes as themes for extensive development and works out with undoubted taste and gracefulness. These songs more than anything expose the lack of national character (*nenarodnost'*) of all the other numbers. They appear foreign in the midst of this whole environment so little related to them. After a song like 'Solovushka' ('Little nightingale'), which Mar'ya Vlas'yevna sings in Act II, the melody of which belongs among the most sublime manifestations of our national (*narodnoye*) musical creativity, how much more keenly and unpleasantly one feels any reminiscence immersed in Mendelssohn, Schumann or their imitators. Mr Tchaikovsky shares a bias towards the orchestra and indifference to the human voice with the latest German composers; the former is polished assiduously, with delicate deliberation and with heartfelt love, whereas the latter is dealt with negligently as if it were of no significance. The dense, beautiful instrumentation very often completely drowns the characters' voices, and in such cases all the spectator can do is to look at his libretto and try to guess what precisely they are singing about.

Mr Tchaikovsky's opera is rich in individual musical treasures. But in its general dramatic course it reveals in the composer a limited ability to adapt himself to the varied problems of word and situation, the absence of the Russian folk (*narodnïy*) element and an inability, or, to be more accurate, an unwillingness, to subordinate the orchestra to the voices and to elucidate the latter not for purposes of egoistical virtuosity but for the sake of the demands of the poetic idea.

I shall say a few words about the performance of this score on our stage, [which he judged very mixed.]

(e) Ts. A. Cui: *The Stone Guest* of Pushkin and Dargomïzhsky.
St. Petersburg Bulletin, 24 February 1872, no. 55. Cui, pp. 194–206

Pushkin's *The Stone Guest* (*Kamennïy gost'*) is a variant of the story
used in *Don Giovanni.* In this opera Dargomïzhsky abandoned almost
throughout the usual divisions into numbers. Except for a few set
pieces, the music flowed continuously in a melodic style between
recitative and arioso. The work was experimental in retaining the text
of Pushkin's 'little tragedy' almost without modification. The opera's
compositional progress was watched over by the Balakirev group, who
regarded it as a great step forward, as this article explains. The work
was indeed a milestone on the road to *The Maid of Pskov* and *Boris
Godunov.* When the composer died, leaving the work incomplete,
Cui added the few bars missing and Rimsky-Korsakov orchestrated
the whole opera.

At the present time the choice of a subject and text for an opera is a matter
of prime importance. True, up to now the majority of the public has looked
on the voice as a special instrument with a quality of sound peculiar to it,
but has regarded the text as a means of easing this instrument into operation.
The public has been schooled in this way of thinking by French and principally by Italian composers and above all by Rossini. To him a subject and
a text were regrettable necessities, mere pretexts for sounds which had
nothing in common with them. But now many people are beginning to form
a more sober view on this question. If the voice were no more than an
instrument, concerts would be quite sufficient on their own, and dramatic
performances with singing would be meaningless. Many people are starting
to acknowledge that music and words can complement one another, that
music may lend to the expression of passion the depth, force and fascination,
can express the internal psychological state, of which words are incapable,
and that, on the other hand, words may lend music a fixed meaning which
it does not have on its own. It is recognized today that drama united with
good music must make an especially strong impression, that an idea
artistically expressed in words united with inspired sounds must create an
irresistible effect. Consequently, the choice of a subject and text for an
opera is a matter of prime importance.

Dargomïzhsky has always been notable for choosing subjects for operas
successfully. *Esmeral'da*[33] (from Victor Hugo's novel *Notre-Dame de Paris*)
served as the subject for his first opera; for the second it was Pushkin's
Rusalka, with some deviations from the original, some changes in the text
and – the main thing – with significant additions; and for the third – Pushkin's
The Stone Guest, without any alterations. (Among these successful choices

33 This opera was composed between 1838 and 1841 and staged in Moscow in 1847.

Torzhestvo Vakkha ('The Triumph of Bacchus')[34] constitutes an exception: this is an opera-ballet in which the choreographic ventures are of the most banal and the subject is of no interest; one can only suppose that in the case of *The Triumph of Bacchus* Dargomïzhsky was won over by the quality of the text and the charms of Pushkin's verse.) The theme of Pushkin's *Kamennïy gost'* ('The stone guest') was the same Spanish popular legend from which Mozart's *Don Giovanni* was quarried. The theme is the same, but what an endless variety of differences separate the treatments of Pushkin and Lorenzo da Ponte! Da Ponte's version is anecdotal in nature and many characters who are not essential to the development of the action are introduced; in Pushkin the subject is executed with wonderful power and conciseness, there is no one and nothing superfluous, and only one extraneous character is brought in, and that is Laura, whose function is to provide an immediate, incisive characterization of Don Juan. In da Ponte Don Juan fights and kills the Commendatore in consequence of his attempt upon the virtue of his daughter Donna Anna; in Pushkin Donna Anna is the Commendatore's wife, Don Juan kills him before he makes her acquaintance, and wins her love in spite of the fact that he is her husband's murderer. In da Ponte Don Juan invites the statue of the Commendatore to supper; in Pushkin he invites him to be on duty at his widow's door at the time when Don Juan will be with her. Need one say anything about the inimitable Pushkinian poetry in which *The Stone Guest* is written, or about its uncommon beauty and euphony, or about the wealth and the strength of the ideas which it contains, or about its succinctness, which cannot find room for a single extra word? The plot of *The Stone Guest*, with its planning of the scenes and incomparable verses – three component parts of every libretto – nothing better than this could be desired for an opera.

But on the other hand, in the form in which Pushkin wrote it *The Stone Guest* presents significant shortcomings for use in an opera. Since it was not written for music, certain requirements of music have not been met. Firstly, there are no choruses, for the choir of Laura's guests singing one line 'O, bravo! bravo! chudno, bespodobno' ('Oh, bravo! bravo! lovely, superb') cannot be considered a chorus. Of course, there can still be opera without choruses (there are some examples); but the chorus is a powerful musical resource which in addition provides a good contrast with the singing of individuals. Secondly, *The Stone Guest* contains few lyrical moments – the most advantageous for music – and many prosaic, commonplace conversations – the most unfavourable subject for music. Then there

---

34 This work was composed as a cantata in 1843–6 and performed thus in St Petersburg in 1846, and then as an opera-ballet, with revision carried out in 1848, first performed in Moscow in 1867.

is the question of whether Dargomïzhsky was right in deciding not to deviate one inch from Pushkin, despite these shortcomings which, as he knew, were bound to be reflected in the music of *The Stone Guest*, or whether the composer should have reworked the play. If he had wanted to use this theme for a routine, conventional opera in which the text plays a secondary role, then, of course, *The Stone Guest* should have been reworked, cut up into arias and duets, a chorus of monks and a chorus of village girls made up and so forth. But if one wanted to make a deliberate attempt at a full and serious realization of the ideal of an opera-drama in which the text played a part of equal weight with the music, then there was no question of touching Pushkin. And who would have been the one to rework Pushkin? Some run-of-the-mill librettist? What comparison would there have been between the verses of Pushkin and the verses of a librettist? And is it conceivable that the librettist's lines could have had the same inspiring effect on the composer as Pushkin had? Maybe *The Stone Guest* is not entirely suitable for music, but it either had to be taken as it was or not at all. And where could one find another subject like it, written complete by a great poet? I repeat again – it was a question not of an opera in the usual operatic forms, but of an opera-drama in which the text and the music would merge into a single whole.

From his earliest years Dargomïzhsky displayed a remarkable aptitude for and aspiration to the embodiment of words in music, to faithful, good, natural word-setting. To become convinced of this it is worth looking through his very first romances. This aptitude and aspiration are less in evidence in *Esmeralda* since that opera was written to a French text, and the French language with its *e muet* is not much conducive to musical word-setting; the Russian translation was fitted in later – not badly, admittedly – but still just fitted into existing music. In the recitatives of *Rusalka* Dargomïzhsky shows himself a great, inspired exponent of word-setting. For each phrase of the text he finds a corresponding musical phrase which is deeply felt, alive and passionate. Dargomïzhsky's strength in recitative becomes still clearer if you compare it with the shameless banalities of recitative with which all foreign operas are filled, and particularly Italian ones. Recitative in those operas is mere ballast, unbearable alike to the public and the composer; and since the most dramatic points in an opera require exposition precisely in recitative then either they are done for as a result of being debased by these routine, impossibly tame sounds, or else we behold on the stage sworn enemies with their swords at the ready, holding forth in song for a quarter of an hour, first with the Andante, then the Allegro of an operatic number.

Dargomïzhsky can identify the dramatic situations in an opera and he strives to embody them in music; to him, recitative which is musical, expressive and melodious is the very heart of the matter. The best music of *Rusalka* is in its recitatives; the remainder of *Rusalka* is more or less fine, but sooner or later will date and be forgotten; but its recitatives are immortal, like the truth and inspiration which gave birth to them. In creating his recitatives in *Rusalka*, Dargomïzhsky could not fail to realize that all the dramatic scenes in that opera should be written in that way. But he did not have enough strength and courage for that then; he decided not to break away so sharply and radically from generally accepted operatic forms, and we find in *Rusalka* many misplaced rounded numbers some of which did not stand up to criticism even from the general operatic point of view (e.g. the Andante of the Act II finale, where the chorus plays the unfortunate role of accompanying instruments).

After *Rusalka*, produced in 1856, a prolonged lull occurred in Dargomïzhsky's musical activity; it was accompanied by appreciable hesitation caused as follows: in the first place, his impressionable nature was strongly affected by the then dubious success of that opera and the indifferent attitude of the public and the theatrical world towards him; secondly, he could not but be aware of the disparity which existed between the matchless dramatic music in *Rusalka* and its distinctly mediocre operatic numbers. He decided, therefore, not to embark immediately on a new opera; he wrote a lot of romances some of which – for instance, *The Old Corporal*, *Paladin* – represent the acme of perfection both as declamation and as music; he wrote his humorous orchestral fantasies: *Kazachok*, *From the Volga to Riga*, and the Finnish Fantasy; he wrote two choruses for a fantastic opera *Rogdana*[35] which he conceived but did not work out in detail, and, finally, he wrote individual dramatic scenes from Pushkin's *Mazepa* (the duet of Kochubey and Orlik) and from *The Stone Guest* in a strict style of word-setting. But when Dargomïzhsky composed these separate scenes (in 1865) he did not then envisage it being possible to sustain a whole opera in the same style; he did not consider it possible to make an impression on the public with music of that kind; he supposed that operatic falsehood had taken root with the public too strongly for truth to be able to make its way. But fortified by reflection, by the success of the first trial scenes and by the powerful impression made by those trials, he resolved to undertake the great task. In 1868 he set about composing *The Stone Guest* with unusual energy, and in less than a year, despite his sickly condition and the closeness of death, he composed almost all of this opera, this *first attempt* at an opera-drama maintained strictly from first to last without the slightest concession to the earlier falsehood and routine. How

---

35 Some work on this projected magic opera was done in the early 1860s.

gratifying it was to visit Dargomïzhsky at the time he was creating *The Stone Guest!* What vitality and animation he exuded, what strength and firmness of conviction! Happy is the artist whom death catches at the fullest growth of his creative powers, in the awareness that he is accomplishing something new and great!

Operatic music requires accurate word-setting (*vernaya deklamatsiya*), musical outlining of the characters involved, musical colouring for the time and place concerned and above all *music*, that is to say that technical and rational realization of the three points mentioned above is insufficient: inspiration is required, beauty of sound is needed and the musical phrase elucidated by the text needs to make an impression by means of its melody and its harmonic structure.

There is no reason to enlarge on the perfection of Dargomïzhsky's word-setting in *The Stone Guest*. Not only is the stress observed correctly everywhere, but it is always found on the word which is most important in a given phrase; rising and falling vocal intonations are often observed faithfully and naturally. Such is Dargomïzhsky's strength in the setting of words, and such also is the power of his music, that a fairly ordinary performer, even one of little talent, could merely by accurately singing the notes written and observing the tempo mark and the rhythm turn into a good communicator of the sung text (*deklamator*) and make a favourable impression. Music in which the word-setting is good spares listeners the torments to which they are doomed when listening to dramatic works performed by people without talent. The word-setting in *The Stone Guest* is the summit of perfection from start to finish; it amounts to a *codex* which vocal composers ought to study constantly and with the utmost zeal.

The personalities of the characters are shaded in and kept up to the same extent as in Pushkin. Leporello and the monk are characterized more sharply than the rest; the former is comic through and through with a hint of impartial malice directed against his master; the latter is permeated by an unprofound, superficial religious mood. The remaining characters are less sharply distinguished one from another; but once you have looked into their musical speech more intently you will find that each character has his own peculiar features; you will be able to recognize the ardent, passionate, thoughtless Laura as distinct from the colder, sensible, careful, restrainedly coquettish Donna Anna. You will be able to distinguish among her guests the ordinary one (the first one) and the stupid one with his one and only set phrase (the second one). You will be able to distinguish the noble, sincere Don Carlos from Don Juan about whom there is a barely noticeable suggestion of something false, of phrase-making, of stiltedness in the midst of the most passionate impulses, despite the fact that he enjoys his own play-acting.

There is no musical colouring-in of a given period in *The Stone Guest* because there is no specific period – it is not a historical drama. Spanish local colour is depicted by Dargomïzhsky only in Laura's two romances; the remaining music is of the common sort. This happened because *couleur locale* is expressed most vividly in the people, in folk movements and songs; but in *The Stone Guest* there are no choruses; it is drama through and through, and the language of the passions is a common language in which the lines between different nationalities are shaded off and wiped away.

The Stone Guest is musical almost throughout, and melodious almost throughout. But before we can obtain assent to that statement, let us decide what we mean by melody. Melody is any succession of sounds not limited by duration in time or linked with any form. Melodies may be good or bad, long or short, but any succession of sounds forms a melody. (Dividing them into actual melodies and melodic phrases is vague and leads nowhere.) In actual fact, except for Laura's two romances, *The Stone Guest* contains no melodies like Italian ones, eight-bar melodies with an answering phrase and an obligatory reprise, that is, the repetition of the first phrase, melodies recalling couplet construction with constant repetition of the same four-line verse. In *The Stone Guest* the melodies are indissolubly connected with the words and are dependent upon them. Like the phrases of the text, they are sometimes longer, sometimes shorter and are almost never repeated; they flow uninterruptedly one after the other. Without the text each of these musical phrases has its own beauty and significance, but on the whole there is no absolutely musical connection about their sequence, no abstract development in musical logic, because this is not absolute, symphonic music but applied music, vocal music; its development and sequence depend on the text, the music must be listened to only with the text, and in that case its power is immense. In the harmonic respect *The Stone Guest* is also extraordinarily remarkable.

The Stone Guest also has some shortcomings which are mainly derived from the shortcomings in a text not composed, as I have already remarked, with music in mind. This opera, as I said, has no choruses, no masses of people, no popular movements – there is none of that powerful musical resource, that striking contrast with the depiction of the inner drama [of the individual]. This shortcoming is felt little, however, because *The Stone Guest* is a very concise and short opera. The text of this opera contains few lyrical moments lending themselves to the rich and broad growth of melody, and as a result one can detect here and there an excessively fragmentary quality in the musical phrases, but only here and there, only on occasion. Here and there in *The Stone Guest* one can detect also a shortage of musical interest – to be specific, in those places where Dargomïzhsky had to write music for the most prosaic phrases of everyday conversation. What kind of musical interest could one attach, for instance, to conversational phrases along the lines of – Laura: 'Where have you come from? Have you been here long?' – Don Juan: 'I have just arrived, and am lying low.' Or – Laura: 'You were passing by chance and saw the house.' – Don Juan: 'No, my Laura, ask Leporello.' The frequent interruption of these fatally cold phrases by warmer phrases is a disadvantage for the purposes of music. Finally there are here and there, on occasion, in *The Stone Guest* oddities of modulation and harmonic audacities which reach the point of ugliness, even harmonic impurity. The first is typical of *all* of the music of Dargomïzhsky, who has one of the most original of musical physiognomies. The second has occurred, one must suppose, because he did not have time to complete and score this opera; he would probably have smoothed out a few things while he was scoring the work, and the people to whom he entrusted the completion of the opera allowed themselves to tamper with Dargomïzhsky's work only in two or three places, in cases of direst necessity, and then only in the most insignificant fashion, such as one note in the harmony and so on.

With such capital merits and the insignificant, barely noticeable shortcomings I have indicated, *The Stone Guest* satisfies entirely the present-day operatic ideal in its forms, without the slightest slip or compromise, without the least transgression. From beginning to end the music illustrates the text incomparably and merges with it organically. Just as thoughts arise one after another in the minds of the characters, so musical ideas give way to one another in Dargomïzhsky's mind; nowhere is there the slightest delay in the action, or any kind of halt in the psychological drama, for the sake of conventional outpourings of music; thus is the opera written and maintained from beginning to end. There is melodious, inspired, simple, truthful musical speech throughout.

There is no need to say much about the details of *The Stone Guest*. With other operas one can dilate upon each act and each number. Alongside such a shameful act as Act II of *Les Huguenots*, we can find significant musical merits in Act IV. But *The Stone Guest* is written evenly, it is all kept in the one style, so that after indicating its general character I shall limit myself to just a few points about individual scenes.

Act I Scene 1 presents an animated conversation between Don Juan and Leporello in which the personalities of the characters are excellently delineated: the passionate and poetic vitality of the former, and the ironic humour of the latter. In the midst of this conversation the warm, sincere, beautiful episode about Inesa stands out, the more so as Leporello's mocking phrases such as 'Inesu, chornoglazuyu!' ('Inesa, the black-eyed one!') or 'Chto zh? Vsled za ney drugiye bïli' ('So what? there were others after her') make it stand out with special boldness. The characteristic figure of the monk makes its mark in this scene also; it is based on wide-spaced chords of a religious temper. Here again what a striking contrast there is between the monk's powerful, gloomily calm phrase 'razvratnïm, bessovestnïm, bezbozhnïm don Zhuanom' ('the depraved, unscrupulous, godless Don Juan') and Leporello's crafty speech 'Ogo, vot kak! . . . . Otshel'niki khvalï emu poyut!' ('Aha, that's it! . . . . the recluses sing his praises!'). All of this scene is impeccably well done, but it does not offer outstanding musical interest on account of the prosaic nature of the text.

The second scene (at Laura's) is superlative and full of musical virtues. In it Laura sings two romances. The first – 'Odelas' tumanom Granada' ('Mist enveloped Granada') – was written by Dargomïzhsky a long time ago, was published, and was merely inserted into the opera by him. The second – 'Ya zdes', Inezil'ya' ('I am here, Inezil'ya') – was written specially. Both of these romances are not bad; they are impassioned, lyrical and in a good performance with good vocal resources they are highly effective. But the musical strength of the scene at Laura's does not lie in these romances: it lies rather in the dramatic places. Let us recall Don Carlos's angry outburst: 'Tvoy Don Zhuan bezbozhnik i merzavets; a tï – tï dura' ('Your Don Juan is an atheist and a scoundrel; and as for you, you are a fool') and Laura's still more furious outburst: 'Ya seychas velyu tebya zarezat' moim slugam' ('I shall order my servants to cut your throat'). What passion and force reside in the amazingly truthful sounds in which these words are put across. Let us recall Don Carlos's kindly, noble speech: 'Skazhi, Laura, kotorïy god tebe' ('Tell me, Laura, what age you are'); what melodic beauty, richness and sincerity it has. It is one of the few lyrical moments in Pushkin's text and how superlative it has turned out in Dargomïzhsky!

Let us recall the two musical scenes which follow that: the scene of the magical Spanish night, filled with aromas, freshness and intoxicating charm, and the scene of the bad weather in Paris where you can almost feel the leaden sky, the drops of rain and the gushes of wind. Let us recall Don Juan's hot-tempered entrance after that; his altercation with Don Carlos and their duel, the most realistic of all duels, in which you can hear the passes and the sound of rapiers crossing. After Don Carlos's death Pushkin has a rather long conversation between Don Juan and Laura on everyday topics. Until the opera's production on the stage these cold sounds of little musical potential always made a dampening impression on me; but on the stage their rational insincerity has an aching effect. The scene ends with the short instrumental apotheosis of Don Carlos. Apart from its excellent conclusion, Dargomïzhsky had little success with this apotheosis; he always found it difficult to control well-proportioned symphonic forms.

Act II – in the cemetery – represents a series of musical wonders unbroken from beginning to end. This act is superbly framed by two comic scenes with the statue of the Commendatore (the second has an admixture of the most powerful tragedy). In the first scene Don Juan is cheerful and makes a joke of the contrast between the gigantic statue of the Commendatore and the Commendatore himself, who 'was small and puny' and who died on his dagger 'like a dragon-fly on a pin'. The music of this short scene is filled with genuine, subtle comedy. With Donna Anna's entrance Don Juan changes and starts on his declaration of love. This scene with Don Juan and Donna Anna is almost the most incomparable, the most ardent, the most impassioned of all such scenes in the whole of operatic music. Don Juan's speeches are full of such seething passion, such fascination, that it is impossible to resist them, yet for all that falsehood can be heard in them in places ('U vashikh nog proshchen'ya umolyayu', 'At your feet I implore forgiveness') and stiltedness (*smerti*, 'death'). In this lengthy, brilliant scene we should especially note in Don Juan's speeches the phrases 'Ya tol'ko izdali, s blagogoven'yem' ('I only from afar, with reverence') as of unusual subtlety and beauty, the phrase 'O pust' umru seychas!' ('O, may I die now!') for its burning hot and splendid music, the phrase 'Kogda b ya bïl bezumets' ('When I should have been mad'), repeated three times with constantly increasing energy, and finally the phrase 'Lish' ne gonite proch'' ('Only do not send me away') – which is loving and caressing. After Donna Anna's exit Don Juan in an unruly display of joy plays the fool with Leporello and orders him to summon the statue to Donna Anna. Leporello's cowardice and his comic, timorous, abrupt speech are portrayed with the utmost success by Dargomïzhsky. Don Juan addressing the statue has an air of self-assured swagger. But almost the most remarkable thing of all is the characterization of the Commendatore, which Dargomïzhsky carries over into the next act as well. The Commendatore's principal phrase, which is developed in many ways and from many angles, consists of five notes rising and falling in whole tones. These whole tones lend the Commendatore special originality, and the harmonies Dargomïzhsky has invented convey a severe, wild picture of him with sepulchral, irresistible power.

The third act is just as incomparably created by Dargomïzhsky as the others, but its first half makes a weaker impression on listeners because on two occasions the tension is damped down by the text: the first time is when Donna Anna five times pesters Don Juan with the prosaic question 'chto takoye?' ('What's that?'); the second time is when after his avowal of love Donna Anna inquires how he was able to reach her and how he was to get away? Such unmusical questions weaken and nearly efface the favourable impression made by such wonderful episodes as the lovely opening of the act, Don Juan's effective, ardent avowal of love, Donna Anna's fainting fit, which are so poetically depicted by Dargomïzhsky. But right from the appearance of the statue of the Commendatore until the very end of the act there is the most superb music. Here also it is constructed from the same whole-tone phrase, but in its development Dargomïzhsky has here endowed it with overwhelming power which reaches the uppermost limit in the definitive, grandiose, mighty theme, astoundingly harmonized in whole tones, to which the statue enters. The Commendatore himself sings his few phrases on only two notes, which increases the grave-like terror of this scene still further. The entire ending of this act of unprecedented novelty and marvellous power is crowned by Don Juan's exclamation 'O, Donna Anna!', full of pain and tragedy.

The Stone Guest was not completely finished by Dargomïzhsky. Several times before his death he expressed the wish that the opera be completed by Cui and orchestrated by Rimsky-Korsakov. This wish was carried out. Cui finished the last ten-and-a-half lines at the end of the first scene of Act I (the only place which Dargomïzhsky left unfinished), beginning at Don Juan's words 'Slushay, Leporello, ya s neyu poznakomlyus'' ('Listen, Leporello, I'll make her acquaintance'); he also composed the introduction to the opera, which was absolutely vital since Don Juan's first phrase was preceded only by eight bars of $\frac{2}{4}$, so that, who knows, the raising of the curtain would have had to begin before the start of the music. But in composing the introduction he wished to make it as short as possible so as to add as little music by someone else to Dargomïzhsky's music. Therefore Cui took only two characters for his introduction – the Commendatore and Don Juan – and at that only the latter's relationship to the statue – constructed the introduction on the Commendatore's whole-tone theme and Don Juan's theme when he approaches the statue, and subjected these themes to a little development, joining them together contrapuntally and ending the introduction with the entrance of the statue at Donna Anna's.

Rimsky-Korsakov orchestrated the opera in his usual talented way. The scoring of *The Stone Guest* is marked by simplicity, restraint, transparency, beauty and also variety of colours. Korsakov gave the monk a fine organ-like quality and thereby contributed to the bold relief in which that character is portrayed. To Laura's songs he gave a brilliantly effective Spanish colour resembling the orchestration of [Glinka's] *Jota aragonesa*. He imbued the Commendatore with a fateful, sepulchral air of irresistible doom, and so on. We should pay particular attention too to the fact that there is not a single place where Korsakov's orchestra drowns the singers' voices – something extremely important in opera, which unfortunately not everyone observes everywhere.

The Stone Guest receives an outstanding performance; it has been studied with the utmost diligence. Despite this work's difficulty in performance, there is scarcely another opera which goes so harmoniously and perfectly in our theatres. But the difficulty amounts really only to learning securely some intervals which it is not easy to sing in tune and melodic phrases which are not always readily memorable. As far as expressiveness of performance is concerned, the difficulty there is more apparent than real, because for all the unprecedented novelty of *The Stone Guest*'s operatic forms, even a mediocre artist who has learned his part securely and sings accurately what is written will create a good impression and will astonish everyone with Dargomïzhsky's splendid word-setting, in whose music the main portion of expressiveness is contained.

[Cui reviews the achievement of each singer.]

The Stone Guest was given for the first time for Napravnik's[36] benefit performance. Our conductor received a most enthusiastic reception and he was given a great many presents. And there is hardly anyone more deserving of these ovations than Napravnik, who through his tireless activity, conscientiousness, energy, talent and expertise has done so much to achieve the high level at which the Russian opera company now stands. To appreciate Napravnik's services you have only to recall the degree of excellence to which he has brought the orchestra of the Russian opera and what warm, precise and effective playing, rich in subtlety, he obtains; you have only to recall how many operas, and significant operas, he has already managed to put on, and to put on so superbly.

Enormous ticket prices were fixed for this benefit performance, but there was not a single empty seat, and the takings exceeded 5,000 roubles. If you remember that it was found to be impossible to pay 3,000 roubles for *The Stone Guest*, and you compare that sum with the total of the takings at a *single* performance – takings which can only be explained by the intense interest in *The Stone Guest*, you start to feel strange and uneasy. Fortunately, the story connected with *The Stone Guest* cannot take place again, however: *The Stone Guest* is the last opera to be acquired by the Theatre Directorate for 1143 roubles; the law establishing the maximum remuneration for a

36 E. F. Napravnik (1839–1916). Conductor of Czech birth and education who settled in Russia in 1861. He became first conductor at the Mariinsky Theatre in 1869, remaining in that appointment until his death. He was credited with raising musical standards to the highest level. Besides conducting the premières of a large number of significant Russian operas, he conducted the international repertory of his time and directed orchestral concerts as well as composing.

Russian composer at 1143 roubles, as readers know, has been repealed, and repealed probably on account of *The Stone Guest* which brought the question to light.[37] Yet another historic service rendered by this opera!

[...]

[The] attitude of the public who were little prepared by previous works for the new trend so radically realized by Dargomïzhsky in *The Stone Guest*, must be regarded as a victory for the new trend. If Act II was capable of arousing unfeigned enthusiasm, it means that power and truth reside in this way of writing dramatic music. From the point of view of style *The Stone Guest* really is the summit of perfection, a superb, inimitable model, and one cannot adopt any other attitude to the question of opera at the present time. But while admiring the style of *The Stone Guest*, and commending it as a model to all opera composers, one must on the other hand avoid texts which, though perfect in language, poetry and ideas, were not written for music; one must avoid rational, prosaic conversations and look for a little more lyricism, suitable for broader melodic developments; one must look for crowds of people who are alive and play an active part in the drama. Continuous dialogue and nothing but dialogue becomes in the end wearisome, and if *The Stone Guest* were longer, listening to it would be heavy going, for all its inspired qualities. *The Stone Guest* is a superlative specimen of an opera which is short, intimate, domestic; it makes the deepest impression, but it is not the only kind. An opera in which the inner life of individual characters was linked with the inner life of the masses of the people, an opera in which the people were portrayed with the same truthfulness and talent as the individual characters in Dargomïzhsky – an opera of that kind would be even more grand and would make a still deeper impression.

In any case, *The Stone Guest* is Dargomïzhsky's best composition. After *The Stone Guest* Dargomïzhsky's genius is not open to doubt. Without genius it is impossible to create a work which is entirely new, mature and irreproachable in general conception, the more so since previous attempts were timid and incomplete; without genius it is impossible to be such a bold and decisive reformer who not only shatters what is old but also creates something new. *Ruslan* and *The Stone Guest* are the two greatest operas in existence – *Ruslan* primarily on account of the inspired music of which it

---

37 Dargomïzhsky's heirs requested a payment of 3,000 roubles from the Theatre Directorate in return for the right to perform the work. The Directorate pointed to a regulation of 1827 which precluded the payment of any more than 1,143 roubles to a Russian composer. Following a press campaign waged by Stasov and Cui in which they drew attention to the injustice of restricting fees paid to Russian composers when those of other nationalities could receive substantially greater sums, the total amount was gathered by public subscription, the score was purchased from the heirs and presented to the theatre authorities. (See R. C. Ridenour: *Nationalism, Modernism, and Personal Rivalry in Nineteenth-Century Russian Music* (Ann Arbor, Michigan, 1981), p. 199.)

contains so much, and *The Stone Guest* primarily because of the trend which is so brilliantly realized in it; *Ruslan* and *The Stone Guest* are the highest points to which a youthful operatic cause has been taken up to the present; *Ruslan* and *The Stone Guest* are the points of departure and at the same time the basis, the foundation on which opera, at least Russian opera, will achieve new, broad, splendid growth at the hands of talented composers in the future.

(f) G. A. Laroche: Serov's *The Power of the Fiend*. *The Voice*, 1872, no. 184. Laroche 3, pp. 88–92

Serov's *Vrazh'ya sila* ('The power of the fiend') was completed by his widow with some help from N. F. Solov'yov. Its evolution from Ostrovsky's play *Ne tak zhivi, kak khochetsya, a tak zhivi kak Bog velit* ('Live not just as you like but as God commands') was troubled. The final libretto was the work of the playwright himself, P. I. Kalashnikov and A. F. Zhokhov, with the first two taking leave of the project on bad terms with the composer. The opera was written between 1867 and 1871, and premièred at the Mariinsky on 19 April 1871. The plot, set in the Moscow merchant milieu, involves love and the murder of a spouse, with the Devil prompting the crime but God exacting retribution.

The late Serov was a remarkable musical phenomenon. I do not know of another composer who came before the public so late. He did not learn before their very eyes, did not fumble along and make blunders as usually happens with musicians who begin publishing their songs, piano pieces and so on from the age of twenty. Thanks to the success of his opera *Judith*, he at once occupied a conspicuous and honoured position. At that time he was over forty; his début as a composer was preceded by long years of solitary and earnest toil. *Judith*'s success was deserved; one could even say that it was less than the opera deserved: had this opera had a little more individuality of style, it could have been called classic. The absence of a powerful, distinctive creative impulse, for all the multitude of musical virtues, led to the result that *Judith* appealed far more to the so-called experts than to the mass of the audience. Serov conceived the idea of writing a piece such as would by impressing the experts attract the mass of the public as well: the consequence of this aspiration was *Rogneda*. But when he wanted to please everyone, the composer had to betray his own principles to a significant extent. He had preached an extremely strict aesthetic faith by virtue of which all extraneous embellishments, all effects which did not derive from the idea of the composition were expelled from musical drama: such things as bravura arias, inappropriately sweet melodies, *divertissements* fitted in to the play from outside it, the effect of scenery, machinery, lighting and so on. By expounding this puritanical theory in the press in a long series of excellently written articles, Serov acquired a quite significant number of supporters among the reading public; these supporters came predominantly from among those who are always drawn by boldness of language, by the 'integrity' of a tendency, by a spirit of opposition and by the casting-down of authorities. But Rus' contains few gentlemen who read musical reviews; for an opera to succeed it has to satisfy those who do not read them and even to keep in mind those who do not read anything. For the public of this kind it turned out to be necessary in *Rogneda* to amass pleasant popular melodies, *divertissements*, effects of scenery, machinery and lighting – in a word, everything to which those who attend *grand opéra* are accustomed. As if by design, the plot of *Rogneda* lent itself to the inclusion of all these effects with extreme difficulty: they had to be pasted on from outside, sewn on using white thread, and the outcome was a highly variegated and rather characterless potpourri not without routine features and in places descending to triviality. For all that, in his preface to the libretto the composer repeated his musico-dramatic creed and even stated it with especial emphasis and solemnity, which in view of the uncommon chasing after effects displayed in the opera itself made a fairly comical impression. These contradictions did not escape the notice of the press, who made *Rogneda*'s composer into a laughing-stock; but he could easily draw comfort from the fact that the public was in raptures over his new work. It placed Serov on a pedestal, where he wrote his third and last opera. This position was not entirely comfortable: a great many literary men, publicists and artists, finding themselves on a pedestal, are excessively filled with concern lest they fall off, and, like the archbishop in *Gil Blas*,[38] would like to bid farewell to the public while still at the zenith of their fame. I think that considerations of this sort explain the slowness with which Serov embarked on his third big work, and his repeated vacillation in choosing a subject (he rejected two subjects after starting work on them). He settled finally on *Ne tak zhivi, kak khochetsya* ('Do not live just as you please'), and one cannot deny that this was a successful choice. Ostrovsky's[39] drama, one of the most integral and poetic of all his dramas, abounds in musical elements and is very suitable for reworking as an opera. The libretto of *Vrazh'ya sila* ('The power of the fiend'), as Ostrovsky's work is called in its new form, is incomparably more coherent, logical and vital than the libretto of *Rogneda*. It is clear in general that in his heart of hearts Serov was in agreement with the many reproaches which opponents directed at his own *Rogneda*, and conscientiously tried to avoid them in *The Power of the*

38 Novel by A. R. Lesage (1669–1747). In Book 7, Chapter 3 the archbishop asks his servant to tell him when he sees his powers waning; when the servant does so, the archbishop sends him packing.
39 For Ostrovsky, see note 32 above.

Fiend. One of the most capital failings of *Rogneda* lay in the absence of the national (*narodnïy*) Russian element, in whose place the skilled and experienced composer offered nothing but a collection of the most cheap banalities, thus confusing 'vulgar' (*poshlïy*) with national (*narodnïy*). In this important respect *The Power of the Fiend* is far more serious than *Rogneda*. It is true that it too is not without banality, which appears every time it tries to portray the Orthodox people making merry; but at least these banalities lack the salon-European, the secular, perfume-drenched character which one sees at times in *Rogneda* (for instance in the Fool's fairy-tale) and are written as if in mockery of the national (*narodnïy*) content of the words. I shall say more: Serov's attitude to national identity (*narodnost'*) remained the same in *The Power of the Fiend* as it had been in *Rogneda* – external and mechanical. He was a fanatical supporter of Beethoven and Wagner who thought and felt more in German than in Russian.[40] But the difference resides in the fact that this experienced musician with his multi-faceted musical education, with his painstaking study of our national (*narodnïy*) songs, *imitated* the tone of national (*narodnïy*) Russian music in *The Power of the Fiend* with obvious diligence and in places rather adroitly; *Rogneda* shows no trace of this conscientious effort. All the same, the two operas *Rogneda* and *The Power of the Fiend* are striking in the uncommon decline in the composer's creative powers after *Judith* and moreover in the decline in the composer's good taste. Even Serov's technique of instrumentation seemed to weaken and decline as soon as he had finished *Judith*. In *Rogneda* and *The Power of the Fiend* the orchestration is taken to the highest point of sophistication: in nearly every bar the composer has, as they say, racked his brains to make sure that the orchestra sounds rich, succulent, deep and vivid; the combinations of the instruments are almost always very complicated; but for every nine carefully thought-out combinations there is only one which really turns out to be successful; the others vanish unnoticed. The following instrumental device is particularly intolerable: Serov very often (especially in the accompaniment of a recitative) uses chords in the lowest registers of the cellos and double basses, and furthermore for the most part gives the cellos double-stopped notes and divides the double basses into two and even three parts. In my view these thick, low and unclear sounds are more like loud snoring than anything musical. I shall observe further that the misuse of brass instruments is greatest in ours of all epochs, and it is greatest in Serov of all the composers of our epoch: their thunder rings out so frequently in his works that in the shortest time it loses its threatening character and then for the whole evening it only induces tedium and disappointment.

[Laroche turned finally to the performance.]

40 It is most unlikely that Serov thought in German.

CHAPTER SIX

The 1860s, opera apart

This decade witnessed a considerable increase in the number of concerts in both St Petersburg and Moscow thanks to the work of the Russian Musical Society; in the former, the vitality of musical life was further enhanced by the opening of the Free School of Music. With Rubinstein and the conservatoires' staff engaged in composition and Balakirev persuading his disciples to take up the challenge, the repertory expanded considerably. While the resources at the disposal of opera had been visibly to hand before (even if inadequately made available to Russian composers), the prospect of frequent and adequate performances of orchestral music acted as a spur to composers. This chapter records the growth of this repertory, formerly consisting of a handful of pieces by a few composers. The visits of Wagner in 1863 and Berlioz in 1867–8 made Russians more aware of what the modern orchestral conductor could obtain from his forces. Music publishing expanded also. The important new firms of Gutheil (Moscow, founded in 1859), Jürgenson (Moscow, 1861), Bessel (St Petersburg, 1869) and Zimmermann (St Petersburg, 1876) are indicative of new commercial activity.

(a) Ts. A. Cui: A St Petersburg musical chronicle (the musical part of the celebration of the 300th anniversary of Shakespeare). *St Petersburg Bulletin*, 10 May 1864, no. 103. Cui, pp. 28–31

This concert took place on 23 April 1864.

Independently of his worldwide literary significance, Shakespeare has had and will continue to have a permanent influence on artists and through the other branches of art: he has inspired painters, sculptors and musicians; his scenes and characters have served as an object of study and have often been reproduced using the chisel or the brush or in the sounds of music; through his art he has given rise to further art. An enviable lot, given to very few. Let me observe, moreover, that Shakespeare has had a greater influence on music than on painting or sculpture; in their quality too the musical works far surpass the pictures painted on Shakespearean themes. Here are some of the musical works inspired by Shakespeare: *A Midsummer Night's Dream* prompted Mendelssohn to compose music for it, and it is his best work. Schumann wrote an overture to *Julius Caesar*. Berlioz (by this time Victor Hugo had made Shakespeare fashionable in France) wrote a symphony with choruses on several episodes from *Romeo and Juliet*, a fantasy on *The Tempest* (an excerpt from the monodrama *Lélio*) and an overture to *King Lear*. Gade has a *Hamlet* overture – an insipid work, like all of Gade's; Liszt has a symphonic poem *Hamlet* – one of his weak works, though it preserves Liszt's usual character. Of the Russians, Balakirev is indebted to Shakespeare for his most significant work, which is fully worthy of the best of the works mentioned above. He has written an overture, entr'actes and a triumphal procession (in Act I) for *King Lear*.[1] Operatic composers have frequently also taken their subjects from the Shakespearean world, but the results there have been caricatures, especially from Italian composers. And could it have been otherwise? Can a superficial Italian for whom the subject is merely a pretext for his music, which is also superficial, can he be joined to Shakespeare, whose subjects cannot be reshaped without significant disfigurement? But what does it matter to Italians? – they would at least have their subject. Thus, the sentimental Bellini debased the poetic personalities of Romeo and Juliet with his sighs; in Rossini Otello and Desdemona suffocated to the sounds of impassive *fioriture*; and the bloodthirsty Verdi made Macbeth and his witches into pure Punch and Judy figures. Just as Shakespearean themes call forth the happiest inspiration in serious composers, so Shakespeare gives birth to the very worst operas written by Italians. It is odd that Beethoven, the only musician who can stand comparison with Shakespeare (their natures had much in common in their comprehensiveness and gigantic strength), wrote nothing on Shakespearean themes, whereas he used themes from Goethe, Schiller and even *Kotzebue*!![2] One must suppose that Beethoven knew little of Shakespeare; it is no wonder, if we recall that Beethoven lived and worked at the beginning of the present century.

The musical part of the Shakespeare tercentenary commemoration[3] consisted, firstly, of Schumann's *Julius Caesar* [overture and the Queen Mab scherzo from Berlioz's *Roméo et Juliette*. Cui found the former mediocre but could not praise the latter highly enough, especially as regards its

---

1 This music was intended for a performance of the play in St Petersburg in 1858 but not completed in time. The overture was premièred in St Petersburg on 15 November 1859; the remainder was completed by 1861 and first performed at this concert.

2 August von Kotzebue (1761–1819). This German playwright attracted such scorn from Cui, perhaps, because his assassin believed him to be a Russian spy.

3 This celebration in the capital was something of a damp squib. The musical programme formed the weighty second part of an ill-attended evening otherwise made up of readings of speeches, poems and a translation, some read out on their authors' behalf. See Yu. D. Levin: *Shekspir i russkaya literatura XIX veka* ('Shakespeare and Russian literature of the nineteenth century') (Leningrad 1988), pp. 199–200.

instrumentation.] Balakirev's Overture and entr'actes to *King Lear* are deeply pervaded by their subject and convey excellently all the sorrow which has accumulated in the breast of the unhappy old Lear. This feeling grips us more and more as the overture draws nearer to its conclusion; and the final chords (taken from the introduction), quiet and peaceful, reconcile us with the lot of the sufferer whose earthly disasters are now at an end. The entr'actes prepare the spectator in the best possible way for what is about to happen on the stage. The first and third entr'actes are slightly weaker – the Andante written using an English theme. In this Andante Balakirev's personality is lost, as if someone else had composed it. But the fourth and especially the second entr'actes are good beyond reproach. In the latter the heath, the storm and the fool are represented superbly; the peals of thunder from the basses ending with the blast of the trumpets make a staggering impact. *It is particularly good* that the young generation of Russian musicians, of which one must regard Balakirev as a representative, seeks inspiration in profound works of genius. Are this very seriousness and the artistry of their direction not one of the guarantees that our hopes for an immediate and great future for music in Russia will be realized? This evening ended with Mendelssohn's hackneyed march from *A Midsummer Night's Dream* – greatly to the point for the audience's dispersal.

This same evening displayed Balakirev to us as a superb and *fully mature* conductor. *Queen Mab* is an excellent touchstone for a conductor's virtues; with one person this scherzo goes well enough; for another there are no orchestral difficulties at all. The frequent fermatas, the unusually fast tempo ($\frac{3}{8}$), the peculiarity and unaccustomed originality of the orchestra – all these things considerably complicate the performance of this scherzo; but the task was carried out irreproachably by Balakirev, with all the nuances and with immense fire. There is no need to enlarge on how important it is to have in St Petersburg for concerts an *excellent* conductor-musician in the face of the complete lack of them, whereas we have a superb orchestra. Let us not forget that Balakirev was on the platform for only the fifth time – and so far he has conducted everything by heart. These facts alone, without any commentaries, are indicative of the huge musical gifts he possesses. *Queen Mab* greatly appealed to the listeners and was repeated at their request – a fact which demonstrates that now is exactly the time for the Philharmonic Society to invite Berlioz to St Petersburg to conduct their concerts next Lent.[4] [. . .]

4 When Berlioz next visited Russia, it was at the invitation of the Russian Musical Society in 1867–8.

(b) Ts. A. Cui: The first concert for the benefit of the Free School of Music (The first Russian symphony by N. Rimsky-Korsakov.) *St Petersburg Bulletin*, 24 December 1865, no. 340. Cui, pp. 66–8

The Free School of Music enabled Balakirev to promote the performance of composers he favoured and who were sometimes neglected by the Russian Musical Society. Besides his compatriots, these composers included Schumann, Berlioz and Liszt. This review is of the first version of the symphony – before its key shifted from E flat minor to E minor.

During all the time when I have found myself writing about happenings in the musical life of St Petersburg, I have never before taken up my pen with such pleasure as today. For today it is my quite enviable lot to be writing about a young Russian composer, a beginner, who has made his first appearance before the public [on 19 December 1865] with an extremely talented composition, the *first Russian symphony*.[5] The public listened to the symphony with increasing interest and after the Andante and the finale loud applause was supplemented by the usual calls for the composer. And when the composer came on to the platform, an officer in the navy, a young man of about twenty-two, everyone who responded to his youth, talent and artistry, everyone who believed in his great future among us, everyone, finally, who does not need to have an authoritative name (often that of some mediocrity) to go into raptures over a fine composition – everyone stood as one man, and the sound of a loud, unanimous salutation to the young composer filled the hall of the City Council.

Perhaps I too will be allowed to salute the composer at the start of his career[6] and tell him how much we expect from him and what great hopes we place on him. I do not know how his career will take shape, I do not know to what extent the circumstances of life will promote the development of his talent; but it is certain that at the present time his talent is already extremely remarkable; it is certain that in any of life's sorrows and in all difficult circumstances he will find solace and support in his art and in sacred and unsullied service to music. Let Mr Korsakov not forget that we too are in need of such solace and support, let him strengthen his talent by

5 *Author's note:* Mr Rubinstein's symphonies are wholly German works, like the symphonies of Mendelssohn. Count Viyel'gorsky wrote only the first Allegro of his symphony, which is a dry piece rather like Cherubini. [For Viyel'gorsky, see Chapter 1, note 6. T. Shcherbakova in *Mikhail i Matvey Viyel'gorskiye* (Moscow 1990) lists two four-movement symphonies by the former, written in 1821 and the 1830s respectively (p.110), and reports a performance of the Second Symphony on 7 January 1861 at a Russian Musical Society concert conducted by Anton Rubinstein (p.49). Alyab'yev (see Chapter 1, note 5) had also composed a symphony in E minor in 1850. Cui ignores Bakhmetev's contribution to the genre: cf. Chapter 2, item (a).]

6 Prior to this symphony, Rimsky-Korsakov had written six piano pieces and between two and four songs.

continual musical labours and bestow upon us more often moments of pleasure such as we experienced while listening to his symphony.

It is fascinating to follow the growth of a young talent through his compositions, to follow him as he grows more self-reliant with each step that he takes, and thus to form an opinion of the direction in which his taste is moving, which composers he liked and what music he has been studying. Mr Rimsky-Korsakov's symphony represents an interesting case-study of this sort. It is written in the usual symphonic form and consists of four movements; each movement marks a significant step forward in relation to the one composed before it. The exposition of the first Allegro is extremely simple: there is nothing special about it apart from the two main themes, which are not bad, though still slightly childish. But starting with the central section one feels that these are not timid beginnings but a clear, precise expression of the musician's thoughts: a phrase from the first theme is transformed into a charming pastorale, and then is interrupted by chords from the whole orchestra where it gains considerable power.

The conclusion begins with a pure Beethovenian effect – with an immediate shift from E flat major to D flat major, and after harmonic intensification in the orchestra it ends most effectively with a three-note phrase in the horns and trumpets and alternating major and minor chords accompanied by a scale in the basses; by this means the composer has most successfully avoided the usual tonic and dominant ending. The first Allegro is preceded by an introduction, obviously written later, which is in the style of Schumann, short, but full of substance and profound, utterly sympathetic ideas; this introduction surpasses the actual Allegro in musical worth. The scherzo, which is fiery, full of life, and absorbing, reflects in places the influence of Glinka and Schumann; the last entr'acte from [Glinka's incidental music to *Prince*] *Kholmsky* gave Mr Rimsky-Korsakov the idea for those superb chords (with the basses wavering between one constant note and a series of descending notes) with which he ends the second limb and the scherzo itself at the big, dark crescendo. The trio is in the manner of Schumann's trios in $\frac{2}{4}$ time (Overture, Scherzo and Finale) – it is sweet, graceful, intimate and perfectly orchestrated with very effective pizzicati in the violins.

The Andante is entirely independent and wholly new in form; by this time there are no outside influences (it was written last). The beautiful Russian folksong which serves as the basis and is the *one and only* idea in this Andante, is treated with wonderful originality and bewitching poetry. It would be hard to find anything more fresh and sympathetic than this Andante; to demonstrate this it is enough to recall all the charm of the second part of the theme which is built on a pedal and adorned with the most magical and original harmonies, or the very end of the Andante. There is one more place of uncommon power: I mean the development of the same phrase in the middle section, when thrice-repeated descending chromatic thrusts from the horns lend it a gloomy quality, and finally violins at fortissimo sing the first phrase of the Andante on top simultaneously; it is impossible to avoid falling for the charming animation of this moment. The finale was written earlier than the Andante and is also *superb*, though less independent – Schumann's influence is noticeable here, and the exposition of the second theme is even rather conventional. In the central section, nonetheless, we can find the strength and power lacking in the symphony's other movements, so that after the Andante this is the best movement.

Mr Korsakov's music is distinguished in general by simplicity, healthiness, power, ease of invention, the free flow and profound growth of thought, and by variety. If his music has to be compared with something, then it most resembles that of Glinka, which has the same qualities in the highest degree. It is precisely the complete absence of morbidity, over-refinement and a forced quality in the composition which compel me to have high hopes for Mr Rimsky-Korsakov's future, who right from his first work to be performed in public seems to be a fully-fledged composer. This symphony is very good, by even the strictest criteria; but if one takes into consideration that it is the first work of a young man of twenty-two, then one has to admit that *not a single* composer has had such a beginning. The symphony is orchestrated unpretentiously, without superfluous orchestral colouring, and quite meticulously, but the Andante is scored with wonderful elegance, taste and knowledge of the character of orchestral instruments. It was performed with Mr Balakirev's customary mastery and fire; if one wanted to carp at any price about the performance, then the only thing one could say was that the two wind chords which end the first limb of the scherzo were a little late. I cannot help returning by way of conclusion to the truly joyful impression made on the public by the appearance of a new Russian composer in the person of Mr Rimsky-Korsakov, cannot help again foretelling a great future for him if the circumstances of his life turn out favourably for his further musical development.

(c) V. V. Stasov: Mr Balakirev's Slav concert. *St Petersburg Bulletin*, 13 May 1867, no. 130. Stasov 2, pp. 110–12

This notice celebrates the upsurge in Russian music. Stasov makes the most of Balakirev's recent successful performances of Glinka's operas in Prague, draws attention to the wealth of Russian creative talent, and uses the phrase 'the mighty handful' for the first time. The concert, on 12 May 1867, came under the aegis of the Free School of Music.

Mr Balakirev's Slav concert today[7] was, one may say, a continuation of yesterday's Slav dinner. Our dear guests from the Slav West encountered in the hall of the Duma, marvellously decorated and glittering with innumerable lights, the same triumphal welcome as in the Hall of the Noble Assembly, which must be evidence to them as to how much importance their first visit here has for us. The coats of arms of all the Slav nationalities and the flags with their national colours were disposed along the whole length of the gallery; the platform for the orchestra was entirely hung with festoons of three-coloured curtains, and groups of three-coloured banners stood at both ends of the stage; above a portrait of His Majesty the Emperor placed at the back of the hall banners were also arranged, but these ones had the Russian national colours.

Thus, the Hall of the Duma presented an extremely brilliant and lively appearance. Not all of our Slav guests were able to be there in time for the start of the concert: some of them were today at a dinner given by the Minister of Education; but when they arrived and came into the hall loud applause and cries of 'Hurrah for Rieger![8] Hurrah for Palacký!'[9] greeted them. The calls went on for quite a while, and it was only after these representatives of the Slav deputies had replied from their places by bowing to the public and the applause and shouts of hurrah finally ceased that the concert could continue.

As our readers are already aware from newspaper announcements and posters, Mr Balakirev's concert was made up of pieces each relating to one or other of the Slav nationalities. Thus, the representative of the Great Russian element was Glinka's *Kamarinskaya*; representing the Ukrainian element was Dargomïzhsky's *Kazachok*; the Czech element was represented by Mr Balakirev's Overture on Czech Themes; the Serbian by the Overture on Serbian Themes of Mr Rimsky-Korsakov, the Slovak by the Fantasia on Slovak (incorrectly called Hungarian) Themes of Liszt,[10] and the Polish by an aria from an opera [*Halka*] by Mr Moniuszko. Apart from the last piece, all the remainder, the major pieces in the concert, were, thus, instrumental works. This has a profound significance of its own; the majority of the most

7 This concert was held during a congress for which representatives of several Slav nationalities gathered. While some of the participants may have felt genuine pride in belonging to a wider pan-Slav family, the event served Russian political interests where they clashed with those of the Habsburg monarchy. A sceptical note is sounded by Serov in item (d). The programme also contained the following works not mentioned by Stasov: L'vov's overture to *Undina*, Dargomïzhsky's romance 'Moya milaya' ('My dear one') and Rimsky-Korsakov's romance 'Yuzhnaya noch'' ('Southern night').
8 F. L. Rieger (1818–1903) was a leading figure in Czech nationalist politics.
9 F. Palacký (1798–1876) – the founder of modern Czech historiography and a leading political figure.
10 There are cross-influences between the folk music of southern Slovakia and northern Hungary (*NG* 5, p. 135); while the Slovaks are Slavs, the Hungarians are not.

notable musical works created by the Slav genius consist of instrumental compositions. The Slavs agree in their tastes here with unusual speed, they understand one another here most quickly of all, they merge in a single common feeling, a single common enthusiasm. *Kamarinskaya* was demanded twice, it was the same with the Overture on Serbian Themes, and it seems likely that but for the fear of tiring both orchestra and conductor terribly, all the other instrumental pieces would also have been repeated. It was heartening to run one's eye along the lines of Slav guests seated in the first two or three rows of the hall: all the faces were animated, one did not find a single vacant, bored or indifferent face. You saw at once that the people sitting there were ones to whom music is a precious national art and to whom its language is their native one. One had only to look at all these southern, energetic faces with their wonderful sparkling eyes, to see the expression on these faces, to know in advance that in a minute, when one piece or another came to an end, then the hall would be filled with endless bursts of shouting and applause. You will rarely find a gathering of such listeners in the theatre or at a concert in Russia, even if they played the same *Kamarinskaya*, the same *Kazachok*, even if the same Balakirev conducted with the same mastery, energy and passion as today. After pieces which struck them especially favourably, the Serbs would shout their *Živeo! živeo!* ('Bravo! bravo!'), and the Czechs their *Sláva, sláva!* ('Hurrah, hurrah!'). One can probably say that today's concert will be of particular significance for all of them: where could they hear in one evening so many superb, so many fascinating creations of the Slav musical imagination? Where else could they be present during such a highly artistic leading of an orchestra by the hand of a Slav conductor as today? And they readily recognize it; the Czechs, who so recently found out how fine an opera the Slavs now have in *Ruslan and Lyudmila*, conducted by Mr Balakirev,[11] the Czechs brought with them from Prague a wonderful gift for their favourite Russian *kapelník* ('conductor'): Rieger and other Czechs with him rose from their places before the beginning of the second half of the concert and presented to our first and best conductor, Balakirev, a conductor's baton, carved all over, made of ivory, and of such marvellous workmanship that this item would probably occupy a conspicuous place at the Universal Exposition in Paris. At the bottom 'Prague, 1867' is written in prominent letters. A little further up, on the handle, is 'Pushkin, Glinka'. From there to the top are the names of all the main characters in the opera *Ruslan and Lyudmila* on a winding ribbon. On the superlative box made of wooden, unusually elegant mosaic is written in carved letters 'To the Slav *umělec* ('artist') M. A. Balakirev'. Our readers may easily imagine what deafening, unending

11 These performances took place on 4/16, 5/17 and 7/19 February 1867.

applause broke out in the hall at this presentation. But after the Overture
on Czech Themes, its composer, Mr Balakirev, was also presented with a
large laurel wreath, interwoven with gold ribbons and held in by a carved
gold agraffe, with a portrait of M. I. Glinka and round it the inscription
'To M. A. Balakirev, 12 May 1867'. If I am not mistaken, the little hands of
St Petersburg ladies tied up this wreath with the gold ribbons. It would
appear that Mr Balakirev cannot be displeased with his first instrumental
concert. The good fortune fell to his lot that this concert of his was the first
all-Slav concert, and that delegates from all the Slav lands gathered to
admire his talent and to express their fellow-feeling for him.

It remains for me to mention in conclusion the three soloists in this concert.
Mr Kross[12] performed the difficult solo part in Liszt's impassioned and fascinating Fantasia on Hungarian Themes in masterly fashion, with the greatest
subtlety and also energy; Mr Petrov[13] sang as, of course, none but he in
St Petersburg ever will, 'Nochnoy smotr' ('The midnight review'), one of the
most inspired creations of our great Glinka; finally, Mrs Platonova[14] gave our
public with all her customary elegance and taste the chance to learn the little
piece by Mr Balakirev *Zolotaya rïbka* ('The little golden fish'), a romance to
words by Lermontov, a charming piece but unfortunately too little know, too
little appreciated here. Everything about it is staggering: the wonderful beauties
of sound, and the passion, and the fascinating, magical depths of feeling.
There are few such musical creations in the whole of European music.

I shall finish my remarks with a wish: may God grant that our Slav
guests will never forget today's concert; may God grant that they retain for
ever a recollection of how much poetry, feeling, talent and ability is
possessed by the small but already mighty handful (*moguchaya kuchka*) of
Russian musicians.

(d) A. N. Serov: The seventh Russian Musical Society concert. *Music
and Theatre*, 1867, no. 15. Serov 1895, 4, pp. 1841–5

The peak of Balakirev's career was reached with his appointment (with
Berlioz) to conduct the orchestral concerts of the Russian Musical
Society. It represented a considerable change of direction on the part
of that institution to engage a known champion of modern and
Russian music who, while not without admirers, lacked the stature of
Anton Rubinstein, whom he succeeded; the latter's resignation from

12 G. G. Kross (1831–85) was a pupil of Henselt and Anton Rubinstein who taught the
piano at the St Petersburg Conservatoire between 1867 and 1885.
13 For Petrov, see Chapter 1, note 17.
14 Yu. F. Platonova (1841–92) was a lyric-dramatic soprano who sang at the Mariinsky
Theatre between 1863 and 1876. She created the roles of Dasha in *The Power of the Fiend*,
Donna Anna in *The Stone Guest*, Ol'ga in *The Maid of Pskov*, and Marina Mniszek in
Boris Godunov.

the Conservatoire and pursuit of his international career created the vacancy. Diplomacy was foreign to Balakirev's nature, and his personality was in part responsible for the parting of ways which took place after two seasons. For a time, however, he swept all before him: in the autumn of 1867 he took up his conductorship with the Russian Musical Society, and in 1868 he replaced Lomakin as director of the Free School of Music. In this article Serov raises some searching questions, as usual from his own independent standpoint. It is the first version of the orchestral work *Sadko* which he writes about here.

As an exception (to allow Berlioz to rest, or for the sake of variety to give the public a programme including some *Russian* music?) this concert [on 9 December 1867] was conducted by Mr Balakirev.[15]

The programme was rather interesting because of two novelties: an orchestral fantasy by Mr Rimsky-Korsakov, being performed for the first time, and Mr Balakirev's Overture on Czech Themes, which had been heard before only once at the concert given by the 'Slav' composer and conductor for the 'Slav' guests.

Mr Rimsky-Korsakov's remarkable talent for orchestral colouring was spoken of here in connection with his Fantasy on Serbian Themes. The same thing may be said of his new work as well: it is *Sadko*, a musical *bïlina*.[16] That the sounds of the orchestra contain here a boundless wealth of what is not just common-Slavonic but also *truly Russian* and that the composer's palette sparkles with distinctive, original richness – these are unquestionable. Only – and this is precisely in consequence of the 'programme' chosen by the young composer – one may permit oneself to adopt towards this piece a standpoint which is more exacting and critical than towards the 'Serbian' Fantasy.

'Sadko – the wealthy merchant' is an ancient Novgorod *bïlina*, one of the gems of our *folk*, unwritten literature which is not so rich in monuments.

It is included in Rïbnikov's collection[17] in several variants which supplement one another, though the last one (Part I, pp. 370–80) is the most complete and integral.

This tale is a coherent long poem (*poema*) with charming details; it is in character Russian and epic.

This legend is full to overflowing of the element of music. It all just asks to be set to music, since the hero himself, the rich Novgorod merchant, Sadko, is also a *guslyar*, a virtuoso player of the *gusli*,[18] who captivates by

---

15 It had been intended from the start that the work would be shared between the conductors.
16 A *bïlina* is a Russian folk epic song-narrative recounting the deeds of *bogatïri* (heroes).
17 P. N. Rïbnikov (1831–85), folklorist and ethnographer. His *Pesni, sobrannïye P. N. Rïbnikovïm* ('Songs collected by P. N. Rïbnikov') was published in Moscow (vols. 1 and 2), Petrozavodsk (vol. 3) and St Petersburg (vol. 4) between 1861 and 1867.
18 The *gusli* is a Russian folk instrument of the box zither or psaltery type.

his music the king (*tsar'*) of the sea to such an extent that he gives Sadko one of his daughters in marriage (the river Chernava). The secret intervention of an unknown venerable old man (who turns out to be St Mikola) saves Sadko from the danger threatening him of remaining forever at his father-in law's court at the bottom of the sea.

The myth outlined in the fantasy of the folk (*v narodnoy fantazii*) – so fully and circumstantially – may of course and indeed should become the property of our *art*, given the present so legitimate striving for rootedness (*pochvennost'*)[19] and national identity (*narodnost'*).

The choice of subject is excellent.

But a small proviso arises: to wit, the *integrity* of this legend, typical of its kind, as the basis or canvas for musical pictures.

Who has any right, in taking, for example, Pushkin's *ballad Rusalka* as the subject for a piece of music, to dwell in an entirely arbitrary way on, let us suppose, the line

'Na vodï stal glyadet' monakh'

('A monk began to gaze upon the waters')?

This would be an 'extract', to which one could not give the title 'Ballad by Pushkin, set to music by so-and-so', without profaning Pushkin's creation, which is charming in its *integrity*.

But it is in just this way that Mr Rimsky-Korsakov has proceeded. He has chosen a small part of the Sadko legend as the programme for this piece of music; not the very beginning, not the dénouement and the end, but an episode from the first half (*only* that episode, where to Sadko's playing on the *gusli* the whole underwater kingdom, the king and queen and all the members of their household break into *a dance*, the entire sea is stirred up). Meanwhile, he has boldly christened his piece with the full (and first-rate) title of 'musical *bïlina*'.

This is an inexactitude which is important not because the title has turned out to be inaccurate (that's a small misfortune!) but because it gives an opportunity to take a look into the composer's mental laboratory, and clearly it displays no particular carefulness about the *idea* behind the music which he writes with so much talent.

Had Mr Rimsky-Korsakov called his piece (maybe) *the first part* of a musical *bïlina* we could only have felt sorry as to why *all* the other parts of the *bïlina* had not been written or not been performed at the concert as a whole.

Now it is an extract, a torso, which, if offending against both the idea and the convictions of the composer himself it passes for an integral finished thing, *contradicts* the text of the subject itself.

19 For *pochvennichestvo*, see Chapter 4, item (a).

In no circumstances can the *bïlina* about Sadko *end* at the moment when, as Sadko plays, *the strings of his* gusli *suddenly break* and the dance suddenly ceases. In the legend all this has a motivation, its own beginning and end, and is not a whimsical episode. From the angle of the actual music, the episode is very interesting.

It is perfectly understandable, however, that in the musical circle which, to his misfortune, Mr Rimsky-Korsakov has joined, there is positively *no* concern about the *idea* governing musical creativity. It is as if there are sounds both male and female, i.e. musical colours, and a palette ready with some hint of a subject – and that is the end of it. But where, and when, is a 'palette', however brimful of treasures, of a significance equal to a well thought-out 'picture'? A capacity for vivid colouring – surely that cannot be everything, cannot be the ultimate aim of art? Surely such a gifted musician as Mr Rimsky-Korsakov could not be content with the reputation of a 'musical Ayvazovsky'?[20]

It is a pity, but one must presume that the answer is 'yes'! For the idol of the group mentioned above, Mr Balakirev, a 'remarkable composer (?)' (according to the verdict of Mr * * *),[21] whose overtures both to *King Lear* (!) and on Russian and Czech themes, for all their praiseworthy music-technical qualities, display a pathetic lack of controlling intellectual thread – simply, a lack of *any idea* as to the '*content*' of the given sounds.

The overture on Czech songs is not a whit better than the earlier Russian 'potpourri overtures' of the same composer. He has taken three Czech folk motives – he could have taken six or ten and strung them along one arbitrary little thread in just the same way out of a desire to write a short piece of music. The result would have turned out similar: some good work, rather pretty orchestration in places, monotonous in other places (in general not to be compared with the colourfulness of Mr Rimsky-Korsakov's music); and the general impression: nothing but tedium.

Imitating Glinka *in the superficial devices* of his overtures does not mean creating Slav music.

Had Glinka himself written nothing apart from a few romances and the overtures – let's say to *Prince Kholmsky*, or the second Spanish one, hardly anyone – besides Mr Balakirev's circle – would have recognized Glinka as a 'great', let alone a 'remarkable', composer. Meanwhile, the 'Slav'sya' chorus is just one line, but, of course, by its truthfulness of expression and the depth of its historical idea, it outweighs heaps of works by the Russian Schumannists who saunter along without themselves knowing where they are going, taking a path which – in our times – is entirely false and unlit by

20 I. K. Ayvazovsky (1817–1900), a painter renowned in particular for his seascapes.
21 * * * was the symbol used by Cui to sign his reviews.

reason. What is the significance, for instance, of the participation of the harp in the Czech overture (and in the Russian one, which uses Volga songs)? Where do these sounds come from and why are they there? After all, it is not Italy or Spain, and it is not a fantastic world. And what about the very form of a separate overture (that is, an introduction to something which 'does not exist') – is it worth continuing with it in our day and age? It is essentially nonsensical and cannot and should not enjoy the right of citizenship in art for long.

Thus, with these works too Mr Balakirev has confirmed the opinion of him formed earlier as a *composer*. No one would think of denying that he has workmanlike abilities in musical matters. But in our times that is extremely little for a 'composer', far less for a 'remarkable'(!) one. One needs also a mere 'bagatelle': one needs the *capacity to create*, but it does not usually arise in a head which is incapable of *thought*. From figures of that kind music gains absolutely nothing. They are not architects but stonemasons, not painters but colour-grinders.

There was little of note in the remaining pieces in the concert, [which were: Act V, scene I of *Ruslan and Lyudmila*, the Fantasia on Hungarian (or 'Slovak') themes by Liszt, songs by Schumann and Pauline Viardot-García,[22] and Schumann's Third Symphony. Serov appears determined to find no merit at all.]

The trumpeters of Mr Balakirev's fame write in the newspapers that he was given the *same* reception as Berlioz. The public who gathered in the Hall of the Assembly of the Nobility on 9 December in not very large numbers can testify to the usual 'truthfulness' of our newspapers in this case too.

(e) A. P. Borodin: The Free School of Music concert. The seventh and eighth concerts of the Russian Musical Society. *St Petersburg Bulletin*, 20 March 1869, no. 78. Borodin, pp. 26–36

The association of Aleksandr Porfir'yevich Borodin (1833–87) with Balakirev began in 1862. Before the time of this review Borodin found relaxation from his labours in medical chemistry by composing most of his best songs, his First Symphony, and an opera-farce, *The Bogatïrs*, which used music by leading composers of the day and was performed at the Bol'shoy in 1867. The première of the symphony occurred on 4 January 1869, and that was the year in which he began work on Stasov's scenario for an opera to be called *Prince Igor*, a project left unfinished at the time of his death. Being a cellist and pianist who played in chamber music, Borodin composed in that genre too – one

---

22 Pauline Viardot-García (1821–1910). This mezzo-soprano, composer and friend of Turgenev visited Russia frequently from 1843.

otherwise neglected by the Balakirev circle. This article is one of only three of its type written by this author.
The version of *Antar* under discussion is the first.

The concerts of the Free School have always held a conspicuous place among concerts whose significance is truly musical. They have been notable not only for good performances of orchestral and choral things but also for the extraordinarily interesting choice of repertory. The programmes have been made up of many wonderful works of lively current interest for the art of music which are largely unfamiliar to our public or else very rarely performed here. In spite of the brief existence of the School and the small number of its concerts, it has already succeeded in acquainting the public with many excellent works of unquestionable importance for the development of the art of music, but which have until now been the property of only a very small group of inveterate enthusiasts and connoisseurs of music. The School has thus done much for the spread of musical education among the mass of the public and has ensured for itself a place as a serious musical institution. The present concert [held on 16 February 1869] belongs among its most remarkable. This time the Free School gave us the opportunity of hearing in an excellent performance one of the most interesting and fundamental works of contemporary art – the *Te Deum* of Berlioz.

[It emerges from a long and detailed critique that Borodin was not uniformly impressed by the work, considering the first and last movements ('Te Deum laudamus' and 'Judex crederis') the most effective, though no section was without some praiseworthy aspect. The performance, by contrast, was apparently beyond reproach. Beethoven's Pastoral Symphony was performed at the same concert.]

Let us go on now to the seventh concert of the Russian Musical Society [held on 22 February 1869]. The concert opened with the first Allegro [moderato] and the Andante [con moto] of the Unfinished Symphony (in B minor) by Franz Schubert. Both movements were receiving their *first* performance in Russia. [Borodin judged the quality of this work to be variable, but implies that the composition was quite good for a modern 'German' composer.]

After this the Fantasia on Finnish Themes by A. S. Dargomïzhsky[23] was played, also for the *first* time. As we know, he has several orchestral pieces of a comical character based on folk (*narodnïye*) themes (for instance, the 'Ukrainian *Kazachok*'). The prototype of this kind of music is Glinka's inspired *Kamarinskaya*, familiar to everyone. The Fantasia on Finnish Themes too belongs to this genre. But while the music of the 'Ukrainian *Kazachok*' still reminds one somewhat of *Kamarinskaya*, then the Fantasia

23 This composition was written between 1863 and 1867.

on Finnish Themes has nothing in common with the last-named. It is based on Finnish folk (*narodnïye*) themes and depicts Finns who have lost their inhibitions and taken to going on drinking bouts, who first strike up one of their doleful songs (introduction in F sharp minor, $\frac{5}{4}$), then, cheering up, break into a dance, at first a moderate one but gradually flaring up to the extreme limits of Finnish daring and fervour, sluggish, sickly, clumsy and funny in the highest degree (Allegro, A major, $\frac{2}{4}$). It is utterly impossible to convey in words all the humour and comicality of this charming little musical picture. Dargomïzhsky is here the very same great musical genre-painter as in his comic songs ('Chervyak' ('The worm'), 'Titulyarnïy sovetnik' ('The titular counsellor') and so on). As regards the technical beauties of the music, the Fantasia on Finnish Themes, despite its small scale, offers rich material for study. It is filled to overflowing with wholly distinctive new devices and effects – harmonic, instrumental and rhythmic. Musical curiosities of the most unprecedented, most varied sorts occur at every turn; to list them in detail is absolutely impossible – one would have to stop at every bar in the piece. And the whole thing sparkles with the most unfeigned wit and humour. Of Dargomïzhsky's orchestral pieces the Fantasia on Finnish Themes is positively the very best. The impression which the piece made on the public was clearly reflected in the unanimous applause and cries of 'encore', after which the piece was repeated.

[The Piano Concerto of Schumann and two excerpts from Baron Shel's[24] opera *Demon* ('The demon') followed.]

The concert came to an end with the overture to Wagner's opera *Die Meistersinger von Nürnberg*. It is difficult to imagine anything duller and more insipid than this music! If only there were one fresh idea in the whole overture! If only there were one flash of inspiration! And what clumsy, forcible theme combination! What intolerable orchestration! The brass bellow incessantly – throughout the whole overture, and simply reduce one to despair; thus, one is glad of every bar where one of the trumpeters or trombonists stops to draw breath. The inordinate aridity, the solemnity and the abundance of brass instruments might make one think that this is the *Vorspiel* to some highly undistinguished oratorio depicting the fall of the walls of Jericho, whereas it is nothing more than the overture to a *comic* opera from a nation's (*narodnïy*) everyday life. Imagine the music for a national (*narodnaya*) comic opera without the slightest trace of life and humour! How much blind trust must one place in authorities before failing to see the complete lack of talent in music like this!

Let us move on to the eighth concert [, which took place on 10 March 1869].

24 For Baron Fitingof-Shel', see Chapter 2, note 43.

The main interest in this concert was concentrated, without any doubt, on Mr Rimsky-Korsakov's new, second symphony, *Antar*.[25] This symphony is a work remarkable both for the novelty and beauty of its music and for the astounding brilliance and colourfulness of its orchestration. It belongs as regards form to the kind of symphonic compositions created by Berlioz. That is, it is a symphony in several movements written on a definite subject with the division into movements and the construction of each of them determined not by the conventional framework of the sonata but exclusively by the contents of the subject itself. The subject of Mr Rimsky-Korsakov's symphony is an oriental fairy-tale whose contents I shall try to convey in a few words. Antar has conceived a hatred for people because they have repaid him for good with evil, and he has decided to forsake them forever. He withdraws to the Shama desert where the ruins of the city of Palmyra[26] lie. There, all of a sudden, he sees a gazelle running. Being tortured by hunger, he chases it with a spear. But at that moment a terrifying noise is heard: a monstrous bird is flying behind the gazelle and wants to tear her to pieces. Antar now feels sorry for the gazelle, changes his intention in an instant and strikes the bird instead of her. The wounded monster disappears with a crash into an abyss, and then such a storm arises that Antar cannot stay on his feet and falls unconscious. When he comes to again, he finds himself in a luxurious palace where a host of male and female slaves serve him and enchant him with songs, dances and victuals. It turns out that this is the palace of the tsaritsa of Palmyra, the Peri, who disguised as a gazelle sought escape from attack by the evil sorcerer who assumed the form of the monstrous bird. By defeating the monster Antar has saved the Peri. In gratitude for her rescue the Peri promises to make his life full of pleasures, warning him, however, that each pleasure will leave a bitter taste afterwards which can be cured only by a different pleasure. Then the charm wears off and Antar finds himself in the desert as before. That is, strictly speaking, the plot of the first movement of the symphony. The remaining three movements portray the three pleasures to which Antar gives himself up in turn. The first of them is the sweetness of vengeance (the symphony's second movement). After revelling in vengeance Antar wishes to experience the sweetness of power (the symphony's third movement); on being satiated with that, he requests the sweetness of love which he finds in the embrace of the Peri herself who turns into a Bedouin beauty. But the Peri reminds Antar that this pleasure is the final one and that the bitter taste which it leaves cannot be cured by anything. Then Antar implores the Peri to take away his life at the first signs of this bitter taste. The Peri fulfils this request too.

25 *Antar* was composed in 1868 and revised in 1875 and 1897.
26 Palmyra was a city-state in Syria.

And so after prolonged mutual happiness Antar dies beside her immediately the poison of satiety begins to penetrate his soul (the symphony's fourth movement).

The oriental element, the fantastic details of the subject, the character of Antar and the variety of situations in which he finds himself offer the composer abundant nourishment for his fantasy. And one must say that Mr Rimsky-Korsakov has exploited all the elements in masterly fashion.

Every particular of the plot is reproduced in music with uncommon sharpness of relief and inimitable accuracy. How fine, for example, is the depiction of the desert (chords from three bassoons, etc.) at the beginning and end of the first movement. How picturesque is the portrayal of the gazelle running, where not only is the running movement (rhythmic figures in the violins) accurately conveyed, but the personality of the Peri herself disguised as a gazelle is partially outlined (the flute's figures; these flute figures form elements of the theme which characterizes further the poetic personality of the Peri in the fourth movement). How much originality there is in the depiction of the monstrous bird whose heavy flight is communicated so expressively by the strings. The unusual harmony, which is entirely distinctive, could not better suit this fantastic monster whose predatory nature can be heard in the winds' characteristic pecking. How much languor and ethereal grace are in the music by which Antar is charmed in the Peri's palace. Let me note in passing that the dance theme in this music is a genuine Arabian one[27] which is arranged excellently. And through all of this runs a melancholy theme depicting the disappointed Antar. As regards descriptive music the first movement of the symphony is the summit of perfection and is particularly remarkable for its unusually pictorial communication of the most heterogeneous details of the plot. The second movement is just as faithful to the plot, but conveys Antar's general mood of revelling in vengeance rather than depicting individual details of revenge. For that reason it does not present such a motley and varied character in its musical elements such as distinguishes the first movement. It is also more rounded and complete in form. The music of this movement is uncommonly fine, and breathes oriental passion, energy and an unbridled ferocity which fully matches the programme. The theme which portrays Antar runs through this movement too, but its colouring is quite different from the one it had in the first movement. Scored for brass it acquires awesome power. The music of the third movement portrays the magnificent trappings of power in the East. It includes a solemn military march; it includes the dances of female slaves as well as rejoicing. Antar's theme itself

27 For Arabian themes in this work, see N. A. Rimsky-Korsakov: *My Musical Life* (London 1974), pp. 92–6.

has acquired here yet another new colouring – a bright and grand one. One of the themes here (the second one) is also a genuine Arabian one, reminiscent of the Persian chorus in *Ruslan* but still more beautiful. But musically this movement is somewhat weaker than the first two, especially the end. The music of the fourth movement is extremely likeable and is based mainly on a genuine Arabian theme, one full of love and delicate languor. This theme is taken first by the cor anglais, accompanied by clarinet and bassoons; later it is in the cellos and violins where moreover it takes on a more passionate character. Just as amazingly attractive is the second theme representing the personality of the Peri. What grace, warmth and sadness it has! Whereas the first movement only hinted at the theme, here it appears fully developed. The theme of Antar himself acquires here a character which is soft, tender and filled with profound melancholy. The ending of this movement is uncommonly fine and poetic – for harps, flutes and violas.

All four movements have a completely oriental colouring in both harmonization and orchestration. With regard to orchestration *Antar* is positively one of the most perfect and most distinctive works in contemporary music. It is impossible to enumerate all the astounding orchestral effects with which every movement of the composition is filled to overflowing, and there are very few places which are orchestrated in an ugly way (for example at one moment in the second movement the horns are so used, and so on). And how new and colourful all this is! How much fantasy of the most capricious and sumptuous kind!

There is not even a suspicion of anything routine or ordinary anywhere in the whole symphony. *Antar* in general is new evidence of the unwontedly powerful creative talent of Mr Rimsky-Korsakov, whose work as a composer represents an extremely gratifying occurrence in our musical world. In speaking of this symphony's virtues I must also indicate its weak sides. One can level at the composer the reproach that the theme representing Antar himself is not entirely original; that in the third movement there is insufficient vastness and grandeur; that in the fourth movement the music is in places rather cold; that the symphony offends rather by the variety of elements in the details; but the last circumstance finds partial justification in the subject itself.

[After this came the Henselt[28] Piano Concerto.]

After that followed Glinka's Spanish fantasia *A Night in Madrid* [*Souvenir d'une nuit d'été à Madrid*]. The beauties of the first order and the originality of it are so familiar to the public that it would be superfluous to analyse them in detail. This piece was repeated by public request.

28 For Henselt, see Chapter 2, note 3.

Then Mrs Khvostova[29] sang three romances of the most varied character delightfully: Schumann's *Waldesgespräch*, Musorgsky's *Evreyskaya melodiya* ('Hebrew melody') and Gounod's *Sérénade*. The romance by Musorgsky was repeated.

Mendelssohn's overture *Athalia* was played in conclusion. This overture is also too familiar, even to those who hear their music only at the Pavlovsk[30] pleasure-gardens.

(f) V. V. Stasov: A note on P. I. Tchaikovsky's article. *St Petersburg Bulletin*, 14 May 1869, no. 131. Stasov 2, pp. 184–6

Russia's musical spokesmen react to the dismissal of Balakirev from the conductorship of the Russian Musical Society concerts.

Moscow has anticipated us. The Moscow press has had its say earlier than ours about a matter which is of particular concern to us who live in St Petersburg but which in all fairness must be regarded as our common cause. The following extremely important note was published the other day[31] in *Sovremennaya letopis'* ('Contemporary chronicle').

'It has happened before that a young man, full of love for the truth and of energy, with the rosiest hopes, has embarked on the career which seemed most appropriate to his abilities. His gifts were recognized, his qualities appreciated; he began, as they say, to get on in the world, but suddenly a whim of his boss all at once destroyed the situation patiently and honestly won, and the insulted victim of a superior's arbitrariness perished in an abyss of inactivity, in a tavern or a hospital. Something similar to this has taken place in the last few days in the capital city of St Petersburg, and in what field? In the peaceful field of art, where, one would think, a greater or lesser degree of success must depend solely upon a greater or lesser degree of talent. A few years ago there arrived in St Petersburg M. A. Balakirev, in search of a position in the musical world commensurate with his talent. This artist earned an honourable reputation as a pianist and composer very quickly. Full of the purest and most unselfish love for the art of his native land, M. A. Balakirev proved himself an energetic man of action in the highest degree, *specifically in the field of Russian music*. Pointing to Glinka as the great model of a purely Russian artist, M. A. Balakirev in his artistic activities advanced the idea that the Russian people, richly gifted in music,

29 A. A. Khvostova, dedicatee of Tchaikovsky's romance *None but the lonely heart*.
30 This final station on the Tsarskoye Selo railway line became the centre of St Petersburg's musical life in the summer months. A concert hall was built in 1838, and for the next forty years music of a lighter character was performed. This was where Johann Strauss conducted in the 1850s and 1860s.
31 In fact, on 4 May 1869.

must contribute their mite to the common treasure-house of art. I am not going to enlarge on what this superb musician has done for Russian art: his services have long been evaluated at their true worth by all who love music; but it will not be superfluous to indicate a few of them, so that the St Petersburg public can understand what it is being deprived of with the loss of such a remarkable artist as an indispensably useful member of the Russian Musical Society. Without touching upon Mr Balakirev's importance as a first-rate composer, let me mention only the following facts. M. A. Balakirev has collected and published an excellent collection of Russian folksongs,[32] opening up for us in these songs the richest material for future Russian music. He has acquainted the public with the great works of Berlioz. He has reared and educated several highly talented Russian musicians, of whom I may name N. A. Rimsky-Korsakov as the most outstanding talent. He has, finally, given foreigners the opportunity of satisfying themselves that Russian music and Russian composers exist through putting on Glinka's immortal opera *Ruslan and Lyudmila* in Prague, one of the musical cities of western Europe. Doing justice to such brilliant gifts and such meritorious services, the enlightened directorate of the St Petersburg Musical Society invited Mr Balakirev two years ago to become one of the conductors of the Society's ten annual concerts. The directorate's choice was justified by the most complete success. The remarkably interesting way the programmes of these concerts, have been compiled, programmes where sometimes a small place was even allocated to Russian compositions, the excellent performance of the orchestra and the well-trained chorus attracted to the Musical Society's meetings a large public which enthusiastically declared its sympathy for the tirelessly energetic *Russian* conductor. As recently as the last concert (26 April), Mr Balakirev, as I have read, was the object of endless noisy ovations from both the public and the musicians. But how great was the astonishment of this public when they found out shortly after that the above-mentioned enlightened directorate for some reason finds Mr Balakirev's activities perfectly useless, even harmful, and that someone[33] has been invited to join the conductors who is as yet unbesmirched by a penchant, forbidden by those who would enlighten us, for our national music. I do not know how the St Petersburg public will respond to such unceremonious behaviour towards it, but it would be very sad if the banishment from the supreme musical institution of a man who constituted an adornment to it were not to provoke a protest on the part of Russian musicians. I take upon myself the courage to assert that my modest voice acts in the present case as

32 This collection was published in St Petersburg in 1866.
33 Napravnik is meant. For him, see Chapter 5, note 36. Ferdinand Hiller (1811–85) was also invited to conduct four concerts in the hope of lending international allure to the season.

the spokesman for the very painful feeling common to all Russian musicians, and I shall say in conclusion that M. A. Balakirev is not at all in the position of those insulted and aggrieved of whom I spoke at the beginning of my short article. The less encouragement this artist finds in those spheres from which the decree dismissing him came down upon him, the greater the sympathy with which the public treats him, and that despot [the public] deserves to have her opinion reckoned with since, in the battle with forces hostile to her chosen artist, she will remain the victor. Mr Balakirev can now speak as spake the father of Russian literature when he received the news that he had been expelled from the Academy of Sciences: "One can dismiss the Academy from Lomonosov", said the inspired toiler, "but it is impossible to dismiss Lomonosov from the Academy."'[34]

This note was written by Mr Tchaikovsky, one of our gifted composers and professors at the Moscow Conservatoire. Yes, Moscow has anticipated us in communicating to the public that sad event which occurred among us the other day; but Moscow will not surpass us in the feeling of indignation and consciousness of the insult now inflicted on us. People who are not capable of assessing artists of true talent are suddenly dealing with the fate of both those artists and the entirety of our Russian musical affairs on the basis of unaccountable caprice! Why do they have to cause damage by their lack of understanding in an important matter full of serious significance for the future – what business is it of theirs? They belong to the German pseudoclassical musical party,[35] and apart from their own petty, trivial interests, they do not think about anything else. And now the German musical party is triumphant in St Petersburg; the Russian party headed by Balakirev is humiliated and spurned. What a triumph! Surely the *Russian Musical Society* was set up here for precisely this? So the name is there for no special reason – just as a pretext? Yes, as long as this Society had no character at all, no independence, while it kept within the limits of complete insipidity, while it performed works by a whole host of undistinguished composers of all sorts, all was well, there was not so much as a squeak of discontent from anyone. But as soon as there appeared a person of talent and energy who knew deeply and respected all that was talented in music, but who strove to promote the talented school of Russians as well – then reproaches and complaints rang out on the part of all that there is of the

---

34 M. V. Lomonosov (1711–65) was a Russian universal man who made substantial contributions to the arts and sciences of his time, becoming the first Russian full member of the St Petersburg Academy of Sciences in 1745.

35 This refers to Rubinstein whose education and tastes justified the description, Stasov felt. The Grand Duchess Elena Pavlovna, a prime mover in these events, was German (see Chapter 3, note 20); there may be an implicit hint about her manner and conduct when Stasov sets up the public as a (would-be rival) despot later.

most backward and benighted in our musical world, and now Balakirev has fallen victim to German routine and ignorance. Every kind of nonentity has moved against him, to replace him or to inveigh against him in the press. Neither talent, nor knowledge, nor the most ardent, wonderful aspirations – nothing helps. But perhaps one day justice will catch up even with the German musical party.

(g) Ts. A. Cui: Rubets's collection of Ukrainian songs. Newly published compositions by Balakirev, Borodin, Rimsky-Korsakov and Musorgsky. *St Petersburg Bulletin*, 12 November 1870, no. 312. Cui, pp. 167–75

The raw material of folklore was a matter of some importance to composers making use of it by quotation or imitation in their own works. How folksong was gathered, and how it was treated once collected, were questions arousing increasing curiosity. Besides its uniquely musical features, folksong was significant because to the Slavophiles it seemed, as an organic product of the common people, preserved, transmitted and developed without the contaminant of 'civilized' society, to offer clues to the thinking of the overwhelming majority of Russians (which the peasantry constituted), and thus to outline a distinctive path ahead mapped from the past. By people of various socio-political outlooks, folklore was viewed as a precious heritage of great artistic wealth. Most of those writing about it in its musical aspect idolized the rural form at the expense of the urban variety, which they regarded as a suspect hybrid of the oral with the classical tradition. Odoyevsky and Serov in particular studied folksong, publishing articles illustrated with music examples; Balakirev, Tchaikovsky and Rimsky-Korsakov produced collections (or arrangements) in 1866, 1869 and 1877 respectively, in common with many lesser lights. This article reviews one collection, and sheds light on the state of knowledge in 1870.

The spring and summer of this year have seen the publication in St Petersburg and Moscow of rather many musical works, to some of which the attention of readers must be drawn.

1. Sbornik ukrainskikh narodnïkh pesen ('Collection of Ukrainian folksongs'). Compiled by A. Rubets.[36] *St Petersburg, A. Cherkesov*

As early as 1866, in no. 348 of the *St Petersburg Bulletin*, in connection with Balakirev's collection of Russian folksongs, I spoke of the great importance of good folksong collections. The inexhaustible treasures of folk (*narodnoye*) creativity, the folk (*narodnïy*) genius, lie in folksongs; these

36 A. I. Rubets (1838–1913), folklorist, composer and textbook writer.

songs, which are frequently first-rate in their own right, are also significant in the further respect that a composer of genius, by studying through them the spirit, character and attributes of folk music, by taking them as the basis of his art, by applying the whole perfection of musical technique to them, by bringing to bear the entire breadth of a developed, profound view, founded on the study of all existing music of all schools, creates immortal, colossal and wholly national (*narodnïye*) works. And these works, on which the generation of the future will be raised, will strengthen national (*narodnïye*) forces within them, and will impart vitality and stability to them.[37]

I admire the idea of common humanity and cosmopolitanism in the arts; but even in the arts national identity has its peculiarities, the result of geographical and historical development, which cannot be eradicated by violent means without inflicting wounds which are not easily healed.

Good collections of folksongs are the more important at the present time in that folksongs are becoming ever more distorted with every day that passes. Folksongs have really almost ceased to exist in western Europe and in Russia, thanks to barrel-organs, accordions, *khutorki*[38] and *sarafans*[39] – in a word, thanks to the banally (*poshlo*) and falsely civilizing element they are being smoothed out, stripped of individuality, and amalgamated with the undistinguished rubbish composed by separate individuals.

It is not easy to compile a good collection. The collector must be a good connoisseur of folk music in order to be able to distinguish a real folksong from a forgery; he must be a good musician, but without pedantry, in order to be able to write down a song accurately, with all its peculiarities and, from the conventional point of view of the Conservatoire, incorrectnesses; the compiler must love his job, work at it patiently and be free from the tempting ideas of purely monetary speculation. All these considerations account for the fact that there are very few good collections. Rubets's collection can be included among the quite decent collections. It contains twenty songs, and the selection is very successful. [Cui considers the contents in considerable detail.]

---

37 *Author's note*: Many works by Glinka, Dargomïzhsky, Beethoven and Schumann will exert an influence of this sort, because national identity (*narodnost'*) is united in them with breadth of enlightened outlook. Rossini and Verdi, Auber and Offenbach are also extremely national (*narodni*), though their works exert only a bad influence on national (*narodnoye*) development, since in them national identity is accompanied by self-willed narrowness of outlook and a lack of wide-ranging, solid musical education.

38 *Khutorok* ('The small farmstead') is the title of a popular romance by the pianist and composer A. I. Dyubyuk (1812–1897/8).

39 *The Red Sarafan* is a popular romance composed by Varlamov, for whom see Chapter 2, note 41.

*2. Islamey, oriental fantasy for piano by M. Balakirev. Moscow,
P. I. Jürgenson*

A brilliant concert piece for piano. The fantasy is constructed on two oriental themes opposed in character: the first theme is energetic and impetuous, while the second is gentle, tender and poetic. But in the later development Balakirev lends the second theme too the same energetic and impetuous character, so that as a whole this fantasy permeated by oriental colouring is startling in its unusual passion and violence to the point of savagery. Chromaticism plays a large role in the fantasy; it contains many highly subtle, rapidly changing harmonic features; it is very difficult, in the fastest tempo; that is why in performance it will always lose a great deal for people who are not familiar with it in advance. In reading it through, apart from the talented, splendid, impassioned music, one cannot fail to be carried away by the multitude of elegant, original harmonic turns, the remarkable taste, and the unusual degree of polish. It is also noteworthy from the standpoint of piano technique; it contains many new and excellent piano effects which are worthy of Liszt.

*3. Sadko, musical picture by Rimsky-Korsakov. Score and four-hand
piano arrangement by Purgol'd.*[40] *Moscow, P. I. Jürgenson*

This fresh and colourful musical picture has been discussed in the *St Petersburg Bulletin* on about two occasions[41] when it was performed at concerts, and I am not going to repeat now what was said then. I shall remark only that the publication of the score of *Sadko* is very important for all musicians in that Korsakov is a very talented orchestrator and now, thanks to the score, everyone can see what orchestral colours, what combinations of instruments he has used in order to achieve his many fascinating effects. Purgol'd's four-hand arrangement is superb. Despite all the difficulty of conveying on one piano the modern orchestra's complex effects (it is easier to make an arrangement for two pianos), Purgol'd has emerged victorious from all the difficulties, and her arrangement when well performed makes a big impact; it displays that she has both a knowledge of piano technique and a sound knowledge of the orchestra which is as yet so little spread through Russia where she represents a solitary exception as a woman. The Secundo, i.e. the part for the player on the left, is of moderate difficulty; the Primo – the part for the player on the right – is difficult, though it would scarcely be possible to manage without these difficulties in

40 N. N. Purgol'd (1848–1919), pianist and composer who married Rimsky-Korsakov.
41 In fact, in the issues no. 355 of 1867 and no. 322 of 1869.

faithfully communicating the orchestral effects; moreover, the number of good pianists is increasing every year. In only one place, on p.13, I suppose, could one have avoided a very awkward crossing of the hands and obtained the same effect in an easier manner.

4. *Six Romances by Rimsky-Korsakov*.[42] *Moscow, P. I. Jürgenson*

'Ti tam, gde mïsl moya letayet' ('It is to you that my thoughts are flying')[43] – the weakest of the six. It is rather fine in its harmonies, but quite ordinary in musical idea, and Korsakov has lent it a conventional, rather banal romance character by creating a very perceptible couplet form as a result of the twice-repeated exclamation 'Gde tï, gde tï' ('Where you are, where you are'). But it would not have been difficult to avoid this: it would have been necessary to strike out 'Gde tï' ('Where you are') only, and to join up what was left to the musical phrase preceding it, changing it, of course, to make it conform to this plan. In addition, the high opening of the phrase 'Gde tï, tam samïy den' svetleye' ('Where you are the day itself is brighter') is uncomfortable for the performer, as are the inappropriate pauses separating almost every phrase from the others.

'Noch'' ('Night'), words by Pleshcheyev, is a charming, perfumed small picture full of unusual freshness and beauty, one of the most fascinating musical landscapes which have the significant advantage over painted ones that a whole series of consecutive moments can be depicted in them, whereas a painting is able to portray only one of them. It is well known how much talent Korsakov has for this kind of music, and 'Night' is among his happiest inspirations. Under the bewitching influence of Korsakov's music, and not being a poet, you feel yourself in a thick forest, you breathe in the bracing smell of fir resin, you hear the flowing of the stream, the sounds of the nightingale are borne to you through the silence of night, with a starry sky overhead and air aplenty . . . The music of 'Night' is permeated with a sense of Russian national identity (*narodnost'*).

'Tayna' ('The secret')[44] is a romance of the same character as the previous one, slightly more impassioned and slightly less beautiful. The beginning and the very end are wonderful, very simple and very original in harmonization, reminiscent of Dargomïzhsky. The lines 'V tu noch' zvezda odna upala' ('That night one star fell') are expressed more feebly; but beginning at the words 'volna veslu progovorilas' ('the wave blabbed to the oar'), despite the comical preciosity of the text, first-rate music comes again, continually intensifying, becoming more and more ardent.

42 These romances are the composer's op. 8 nos. 1–6.
43 The poem is by an unknown author.   44 The poem is after Chamisso.

'Vstan', soydi, davno dennitsa' ('Rise, come down, the dawn long ago'), a Hebrew song, words by Mey, is an exceptionally graceful and elegant romance constructed entirely over a single pedal. The melody is very plain and might have seemed monotonous were it not refreshed by the most varied harmonies and tasteful counterpoint of oriental character, which continues right to the very end of the romance. All these factors together: the simple, natural idea, the constant pedal, the harmonic interest and the effect of a flute cascading above, make up a captivating whole.

'V tsarstvo rozï i vina pridi' ('Come into the kingdom of the rose and of wine'), words by Fet,[45] is a Bacchic, passionate song. It has a handsome accompaniment which is harp-like nearly throughout. It has a good deal of fire and animation, particularly the phrase 'Utishi tï, pesn', toski moyey' ('Comfort my anguish, you song') and those following it. It sings superbly.

'Ya veryu, ya lyubim' ('I believe she loves me'), words by Pushkin, is an extremely beautiful romance as regards its harmonies, the accompaniment and the melody (the phrase 'stïdlivost' robkaya' ('timid bashfulness') is especially charming), but unsure in its general conception. Korsakov treats it as if it were two couplets – with different music, it is true, whereas the text demands a completely different structure. The first lines 'Ya veryu, ya lyubim; dlya serdtsa nado verit' / Net, milaya moya ne mozhet litsemerit'' ('I believe she loves me; for the heart's sake one needs to love. / No, my sweet girl cannot dissemble') require recitative speech and fit a smooth melody awkwardly, even if the melody is retarded a little by the exclamation 'Net!' ('No!'). And only later on, at 'Vsyo nepritvorno v ney: zhelaniy tomnïy zhar, stïdlivost' robkaya' ('Everything about her is unfeigned: the languorous ardour of desire, the timid bashfulness') and so on, can the words be represented in a strictly melodic form. Of course, had this romance been written by someone other than one of our younger, powerful talents, then one could not have admired it sufficiently, but the most rigorous, the most exacting scale must be applied in the evaluation of compositions by Balakirev, Korsakov, Borodin and Musorgsky.

5. Three Romances by Borodin. Moscow, P. I. Jürgenson

'Spyashchaya knyazhna' ('The sleeping princess') – a fairy-tale (*skazka*), text by Borodin. Its contents are as follows: a princess sleeps a bewitched sleep in an enchanted forest; a noisy swarm of witches and wood-demons rushes over the forest but is not capable of waking the princess. At some point a mighty hero (*bogatïr'*) will appear, break the spell and destroy this bewitched sleep; but year follows year, the hero does not appear, and the

45 A. A. Fet (1820–92). Lyric poet of nature and the human heart.

princess continues to remain in her bewitched sleep. Borodin's 'fairy-tale' is the most superlative little musical picture, remarkable alike for the richness and maturity of its ideas and for the elegance of its external finish. In his 'fairy-tale', as everywhere, Borodin is the most subtle harmonist, full of good taste; by means of unprecedented harmonic combinations peculiar to him alone he endows his music with a wholly distinctive character. The entire accompaniment of the 'fairy-tale' is based on an alternation of seconds imparting to the sounds a kind of mysterious, magical quality. The vocal part is simple and beautiful, and in the episode of the expected mighty hero attains remarkable force and power. The words of the late Dargomïzhsky provide the best description of the 'fairy-tale': he said of it: 'It is like one of the beautiful pages of *Ruslan* not on account of any resemblance of the music of the "fairy-tale" to Glinka's music but because it has the same delicacy, beauty and magic . . .'

'Fal'shivaya nota' ('The false note'), text by Borodin. 'She would always be assuring me of her love. I did not believe, did not believe her: a false note sounded in her heart and in her speech . . . And she came to understand that.' To this text in the manner of Heine Borodin has written charming music in the manner of Schumann. Apart from the beauty and elegance of the musical idea this romance is noteworthy for the following external feature: the note F is never silent throughout the accompaniment, and on this upper pedal Borodin builds his diverse, original harmonic progressions.

'Otravoy polnï moi pesni' ('My songs are filled with poison'), words by Heine, is an inspired outburst of extraordinary passion and extraordinary talent. This romance is so good, in every bar, beginning with the two capricious bars of introduction, so much truth can be heard, such a wail is heard from a heart which has suffered much, that one has no wish to notice even the slightest speck of imperfection. Yet such a speck exists. In the lines 'Ne malo zmey v serdtse noshu ya, i dolzhen tebya v nyom nosit'' ('I carry not a few snakes in my heart, and must carry you in it as well') Borodin puts a slightly stronger emphasis on the word 'malo' ('a few') than on the word 'zmey' ('snakes') and, besides, a tiny halt is desirable between the words 'noshu ya' ('I carry') and 'i dolzhen' ('and must'). In a good performance this is of course unnoticeable, and, given Borodin's generally perfect word-setting, this romance makes the strongest impact on a sensitive listener.

All the works mentioned above, with the exception of Rubets's 'Collection', have been published in Moscow during the current year by Jürgenson.[46] All honour to him for his energetic and worthwhile publishing activities, the

---

46 P. I. Jürgenson/Yurgenson (1836–1903/4) opened a music shop in Moscow, began publishing sheet music in 1861 and books on music in 1867, and established a music printing plant in 1867. Expansion continued by acquisition, with a Leipzig branch opening in 1897.

more so as his publications are very good: the paper is excellent, the print clear, the title-pages handsome, the misprints few; if they are not as good as foreign publications, they far surpass in elegance all the St Petersburg music publishers without exception.

6. *Three Romances by Musorgsky. St Petersburg, Bessel*

'Klassik' ('The classicist') is a very witty and very successful lampoon of the classical tendency which has revealed itself partly in our musical journalism and partly in the direction taken by the concerts of the Russian Musical Society in the past season. The text is also by Musorgsky. At the beginning and the end the 'classicist' sets out his *profession de foi*: he is 'prost, yasen, skromen, vezhliv, v meru strasten, uchtiv' ('simple, lucid, modest, polite, in moderation passionate, courteous')[47] and he sets all this out in sounds which are just as simple, lucid, modest and reminiscent of the banal works of the Mozartian era, with the inevitable classical trill at the end. In the middle section all the hatred, all the horror felt by the 'classicist' towards the contemporary movement in art, whose irresistible power he senses, is very successfully conveyed in sounds. Also very amusing is the ending of the romance with the excessively humble chord of the third repeated three times. 'The classicist' is also noteworthy in that it is the first experiment in Russia, and a successful experiment, in polemics in sound, sound ridicule, parody.

'Detskaya pesenka' ('A child's song'), text by L. Mey, is a very sweet, fresh, graceful work; it is naive and yet at the same time it is full of that originality which is characteristic of all but every note of Musorgsky.

'Sirotka' ('The orphan'), text by the composer. A starving wanderer trembling from the cold, pursued by people's indifference, abuse and blows, appeals with a wail to a passer-by for help. That is what this song is about. The music of 'The orphan' is superlative: severe, heart-felt and not without depth; it is a cry bursting forth directly from a sore heart, and at the same time a shy, timorous cry; the music of 'The orphan' is, besides, very dramatic and, in a talented performance, capable of having a very powerful effect on the listener. I cannot refrain from citing among the details the exclamation 'Barinushka!' ('Dear mistress!') after the words 'szhal'sya nad bednen'kim, gor'kim, bezdomnïm sirotochkoy' ('take pity on a poor, wretched, homeless

---

47 *Author's note*: Musorgsky accurately anticipated Famintsïn's speech against Stasov. [Cui refers to the court action taken by the critic A. S. Famintsïn (1841–96) against Stasov in respect of his articles 'Muzikal'nïye lgunï' ('Musical liars') and 'Po povodu pis'ma Famintsïna' ('On the subject of Famintsïn's letter'), appearing in the *St Petersburg Bulletin* (1869, nos. 154 and 165). Stasov was acquitted of libel but found guilty on a lesser charge and fined twenty-five roubles.]

orphan') – it is so truthful and dramatic! It goes without saying that Musorgsky's perfect word-setting throughout increases still more the merits of this remarkably talented little piece.

Bessel''s publications are neat and tidy, but no more than that: they are significantly less good than the Moscow publications of Jürgenson and slightly less good than the St Petersburg publications of Iogansen.[48]

The reader can see from this short review of works published this spring and summer that our young talents are not sitting with their arms folded but are working busily, the more so as Musorgsky has completed and submitted *Boris Godunov*[49] to the Theatre Directorate and Korsakov will probably finish his *The Maid of Pskov*[50] for next season. With all our composers mentioned above, their outlook on art and direction are correct, their attitude towards and love for their cause are of the most serious, their talent remarkable. One cannot help rejoicing when one looks at what they have already done, one cannot help but hope for still greater things, one cannot help but acknowledge that at the present time music in Russia is in a first-rate condition and that the Russian school created so maturely all at once by Glinka and Dargomïzhsky has brilliant representatives in the persons of our young composers.

48 A. R. Iogansen (1829–75) was a St Petersburg music publisher. His firm issued the weekly newspaper *Muzïkal'nïy sezon* from 1869 to 1871.
49 It was, of course, rejected on this occasion, reaching the stage only in 1874 in a revised version.
50 This opera was completed only in 1872 and first staged in 1873.

CHAPTER SEVEN

Opera in the 1870s

It was in this decade that some of the most familiar Russian operas (*Boris Godunov* and *Eugene Onegin*) came to the stage. *The Maid of Pskov, Boris Godunov* and *The Oprichnik* all mine the same vein: that of opera on a historical subject, with ample scope for evocation of *couleur locale* in song, instrumental music, dance, costume and sets, albeit with intimate personal relationships intertwined with the powerful thread of political conflict. If this scheme owes something to *A Life for the Tsar*, it owes more to *grand opéra* with its interweaving of private passion with religious or political clashes and ready exploitation of imposing spectacle. What is distinctive, however, is the Russians' attempt to deal with their own nation's past and to do so (at least in the first two cases) while creating a more continuous, more dramatically flowing texture unimpeded by the conventional division of the music into sections of recitative, arioso, ensemble etc. The New Russian School made its mark with *The Maid of Pskov* and *Boris Godunov*. These works are examined in Richard Taruskin: '"The Present in the Past": Russian Opera and Russian Historiography, ca. 1870' in Malcolm H. Brown (ed.): *Russian and Soviet Music – Essays for Boris Schwarz* (Ann Arbor, Michigan 1984), pp. 77–146.

A quite different vein is mined in *Eugene Onegin.*

(a) Ts. A. Cui: Rimsky-Korsakov's opera *The Maid of Pskov. St Petersburg Bulletin,* 9 January 1873, no. 9. Cui, pp. 215–24

This notice contains a substantial exposition of the operatic theory of the New Russian Operatic School (for instance, on the question of when folksongs may appropriately be used and when not). In format it resembles that used by Rimsky-Korsakov earlier for his review of Cui's *William Ratcliff.*

The translation 'the Dread One' refers to Tsar Ivan, known as 'the Terrible'.

On the very first day of the new year our gifted artiste Platonova[1] presented a gift in the form of her benefit performance to the public which so admires

1 For Platonova, see Chapter 6, note 14.

her – the first production of *The Maid of Pskov*, a new Russian opera and
the first opera to be newly performed on the Mariinsky stage in the present
extremely thin and unsuccessful season.[2]

The plot of *The Maid of Pskov* is taken from Mey's[3] drama of the same
title, [and may be summarized as follows. The maid referred to in the title
(Ol'ga) is a daughter of Tsar Ivan whose paternity has been concealed. The
action takes place as reports of the savage treatment meted out by the
dreaded *oprichnina*[4] to the people of Novgorod at the tsar's behest reach
Pskov. Act II is a popular assembly (*veche*)[5] held to decide how to respond
to Ivan's anticipated arrival. At the urging of Tokmakov, the governor-
general, a hospitable welcome is resolved upon; the chief protagonist of a
hostile reception is Tucha, who is in love with and loved by Ol'ga; her
hand, however, has been secretly promised to the unappealing Matuta. In
Act III the tsar is received in the town, but keeps the populace in suspense
as to his intentions towards them. He meets Ol'ga, and, recognizing in her
his daughter, spares the town. In Act IV, after some time spent in the
presence of a thoughtful tsar, Ol'ga is abducted by Matuta, and is killed in
the confusion of a battle between her rebellious lover's followers and the
tsar's forces. The tsar is heartbroken at his daughter's death.]

The plot of *The Maid Of Pskov* is splendid and suitable for serious
operatic purposes. Much space is devoted to the people and their passions;
alongside them is placed the severe, unbending personality of the Dread One.
That sharp, powerful personality appears in the most dramatic situation:
meeting his daughter, who does not know him to be her father, but knows
the tormentor, who loves Tucha the rebel and plotter. If we add to this the
honest personality of Tokmakov, the scoundrel Matuta, the bold, indomit-
able Tucha and the gentle, poetic Ol'ga, then all this together forms a
wonderful operatic subject, the selection of which for his first opera shows
Mr Korsakov to be a fully formed, developed musician with an extremely
serious attitude to his work. The exposition of this subject, that is, the
scenario, is also constructed well, simply, without forced, unnatural effects,
and boldly in places with deviations from generally accepted operatic traditions (the ending of Act I with Ol'ga's phrase of recitative, or the ending
of Act II with Ivan's phrase of recitative). Only two episodes strike me

2 Cui's complaint concerns the absence of Russian operas of which he approves from the
   repertory, the loss of key personnel, and poor organization. The same complaints were
   repeated in item (d) below.
3 L. A. Mey (1822–62), poet and dramatist. The opera *The Tsar's Bride* is also based on his
   work.
4 *Oprichnina* denotes the administration of lands directly under the control of Tsar Ivan IV,
   and, more commonly, the new armed force established to run this territory, a force
   associated with cruelty and terror.
5 For *veche*, a popular assembly, see Chapter 5, note 26.

disagreeably in this scenario. Firstly, Tucha, who was left for dead by Matuta during Ol'ga's abduction, immediately recovers and launches an attack on the Tsar's headquarters – and singing, moreover, and thereby announcing his approach from afar – in other words, he himself does all he can to ensure that the attack does not succeed. Secondly, the presence of the chorus in the Tsar's headquarters, lamenting over his daughter's corpse, is out of place; which of Ivan the Dread's retainers would be so brave as to force his way into the Tsar's tent at such a moment to stare at such a spectacle? Both these episodes were called forth, obviously, only by musical considerations, and thus the blame for their inappropriateness falls squarely on Korsakov. As far as the text of *The Maid of Pskov* is concerned, it is superlative; after *The Stone Guest* and those lines of *Rusalka* which came from Pushkin's pen, it is the best operatic text. It is full of national character (*narodnost'*), power, character, ideas; it lacks the banalities common to all operas, and it is moreover expressed in short, rhymed lines. This text is written partly in blank verse, partly in prose – an innovation which has a big future, especially in folk scenes.

[Cui compares the plot with that in its literary prototype.]

I pass on to a critique of the music.

The Maid of Pskov satisfies present-day operatic demands as regards its forms; but its composer displays only a judicious submission to these demands, not a striving to take their development further, or to bring them to the utmost expressive power (Act II constitutes an exception). *The Maid of Pskov* contains no separate numbers in the conventional forms, no ensembles with the characters lined up along the footlights, no sacrificing of logic to music, no repetition of words. All this has disappeared for ever from the works of the New Russian Operatic School. But at the same time, *The Maid of Pskov* contains no uninterrupted flow of musical speech, as, for example, in *The Stone Guest*; there is no indissoluble link between a word and a musical phrase, one detects the subjection of the text – not the meaning – to the music, and one detects an aspiration to lend the music symphonic development. *The Maid of Pskov* was composed by a symphonist who recognizes perfectly the requirements of operatic music but to whom the symphonic forms are more familiar and more dear. Thus in *The Maid of Pskov* all the choruses are incomparable, but the dramatic and lyrical scenes for individual characters are significantly weaker.

The musical characterizations of the *dramatis personae* in *The Maid of Pskov* are partly successful and partly unsuccessful. Matuta is outlined best of all – the most fully and consistently. One could hardly convey the miserably vile and cowardly soul of this scoundrel in sound better or more accurately. For this purpose Korsakov has had recourse to chromaticism, to the augmented fifth and by means of a logical series of these intervals and harmonies has achieved a remarkably artistic and wholly new portrayal of a person of worthless, sickening personality. But since the scenes in which Matuta is the principal character are very short, no discomfort arises from the piling-up of these nasal harmonies. The Dread One is also splendidly outlined – through sharp, strong, sombre features. The nurse too has a musical physiognomy which is well sustained. Ol'ga's portrayal is weaker; one can observe an excess of German sentimental diffuseness in her characterization. Apart from the *veche* scene, Tokmakov and Tucha are pale.

The music of *The Maid of Pskov* is strongly national (*narodna*). It is all, with only the most insignificant exceptions, Russian in musical ideas, their development and harmonization.

The music of *The Maid of Pskov* is notable in its entirety for its uncommon beauty and nobility, a beauty which is melodic, harmonic and in timbre; in the whole opera you will not hear a single sound which is even in the slightest trivial, not a single platitude in the chord progressions; an astonishing purity spreads throughout this four-act opera. Apart from that, its music contains much freshness, delicacy, gentleness; it has enchanting, often new harmonizations of the utmost refinement and elegance; one often encounters a highly poetic mood, and energy, power and passion frequently manifest themselves.

The main fault in the music of *The Maid of Pskov* lies in its rather monochrome character (Act II is an exception), which arises from the small variety of musical ideas in the opera, most of them related to one another, from their frequent repetition, from the monotonous way they are developed, mainly canonically and contrapuntally, involving combinations among themselves; from the monotony of rhythmic movement in the opera's individual numbers; and finally, from the use of phrases in pairs, to which Korsakov is very partial. He likes repeating every musical phrase twice: the exposition gains a great deal from this in roundedness and clarity, but it becomes tediously monotonous and if such repetition is appropriate in symphonic music it is less suitable for operatic music. *The Maid of Pskov*'s second fault lies in its recitatives, which are superb in some places but not without sin in their very basis in others. Quite often Korsakov entrusts the principal musical idea, outlining a character, to the orchestra, and against this background constructs recitatives on notes of the harmony, recitatives which are perfectly faithful in word-setting but of no musical interest. This device is good for conversations which are mundane (and it is impossible to avoid them in opera); but where passion plays a role, where drama comes into play, this device is false. In such cases the main musical idea must be entrusted to the singer, not the orchestra, because all the listeners' attention is focussed on the character, and they pick up every sound he makes and they allow sounds made by the orchestra to pass by almost unnoticed. Besides, this device is applied in *The Maid of Pskov* to all the characters, and it smooths out their characterization and paints it all in the same colour. I must add that in *The Maid of Pskov* these recitatives are very often interrupted by pauses, sometimes short ones, which make the speech of the characters abrupt almost throughout, and sometimes prolonged ones, with the only music in the orchestra, which slows the musical speech down and sometimes places the singers in the highly embarrassing position of not knowing what they should be doing on the stage. In places these recitatives have too rich an accompaniment. In order to point out all the failings of *The Maid of Pskov*, even the slightest ones, I shall add that here and there one could do with a greater sense of passion in the music, especially in the love duets, that here and there Korsakov is too protracted in his dissonances and here and there he uses the voices awkwardly (particularly for Tucha and Ol'ga): too high and at the same time too low, and also with intervals characteristic of orchestral instruments but unnatural for the human voice.

After thus indicating the general character, the general qualities and failings of the music in *The Maid of Pskov*, I shall now survey briefly each act scene by scene.

The overture is powerful and passionate, bursting forth immediately, with brutal and unbridled harmonization; it depicts the battle between Ivan and the Pskov outlaws, in the midst of which Ol'ga's calm and gentle image is glimpsed fleetingly. (At the first performance of the opera the public could make nothing of this overture because during it the theatre was still filling up, there were banging noises as chairs were moved, boxes unlocked and so on.) The game of catch (*gorelki*) is an attractive and graceful scherzo of exceptional lightness and subtlety. (This scherzo too went for nothing with the public: for almost all of it they were busy applauding Platonova whose benefit it was.) In the following scene the song 'Po malinu' ('Gathering raspberries') is notable for its melodic freshness and bright mood; it is cut short by the beautiful, typical speeches of the nurse, among which the story of the pillage of Novgorod is particularly good. 'Skazka pro tsarevnu Ladu' ('The tale of the Tsarevna Lada') is the finest number in this act and one of the best passages in the whole opera. It shows the natural way of speaking of a good-natured old woman, a manner which is in part sceptical, in part suggesting belief in what she is saying, and is based on captivating, magical music full of new sounds taken from some mysterious fairy-tale world. Tucha's song, which cuts this fairy tale short, is charming: it is beautiful, in pure folk style; it can be heard first in the distance, to begin with on its own without the orchestra, then it draws nearer accompanied by muted strings in octaves, and finally in harmonized form. This song makes a marvellous sound amidst the trees' greenery on the empty stage, in the twilight, and gives rise to a very poetic atmosphere. The second half of the first act, that is, the duet of Ol'ga and Tucha and the scene of Tokmakov and Matuta, is far weaker: the inadequacies of Korsakov's recitatives make themselves felt; they wipe out the good impression made by the successful episodes to which I have directed the reader's attention. Ol'ga's little descending scale in the duet is beautiful; it is repeated several times and ends with a warm phrase, warmly harmonized (in C sharp major); but this phrase does not make its effect on the stage because it is at a low pitch where it is awkward for the voice. The same qualities of beauty and warmth recur to a still greater extent in the middle of the duet, before the second part (at Ol'ga's words 'A ezheli vo vsyom emu pokayus'' ('And what if I confessed everything to him'), and derive from the overflowing cello phrase and principally from the enchanting modulations (A major on the dominant, C sharp minor, A flat major). For the second part of his love duet Korsakov has taken the theme from a folksong in Balakirev's collection (no. 27), an inspired, peerless song; but Korsakov's basis for this device is false.

Why should one not make use of folksongs when they provide such rich material? Why not develop that material when it can impart such marvellous local colour? That is true; but nonetheless one should note that folksong can be given to a chorus of the people, or to individual characters who are singing a song, but the feelings of individuals cannot be given vent to in the sounds of a folksong. Here Ol'ga and Tucha speak of their love and of what they feel, and at such a moment it is not appropriate at all to put a folksong into their mouths. Moreover, Korsakov treats the folksong in an unfortunate manner, monotonously, the combination of the voices is ineffective, the part movement is unnatural, here and there the soprano is lower than the tenor and consequently completely inaudible. Only at the very end of the duet does the scale rising over a pedal form a fascinating, original harmonic combination, of the type of which Korsakov is such a master. In the matter of harmonic subtlety, taste and beauty, he has few rivals. In the final scene Matuta's musical character is already being hinted at by some deft strokes; Tokmakov's unison phrase 'Ya uzh starenek' ('I am old') is not bad; Ivan's theme occurs for the first time very dramatically at Tokmakov's words about Ol'ga: 'A ottsa ne znayem' ('But we do not know who her father was'); the ending of the act with Ol'ga's phrase to the sound of the *veche* bell is effective. The first act is a weak one in the opera, but even it contains many beauties – I point again to the game of catch, the song 'Gathering raspberries', Tucha's song, and especially the fairy tale of amazing newness.

The second act – the *veche* – is the best act in the whole opera. All Rimsky-Korsakov's failings as a composer of opera have disappeared as if by some miracle, and all his merits turn out to be present in abundance. The act opens with the same peals of the *veche* bell as ended the first act, artistically portrayed in the orchestra by brass chords with tam-tam and violin figures. Starting with the very first bars and going right up to the very end of the act, the musical interest grows, the sequence of musical ideas is stunning in its power and truthfulness and absorbs the listener in its vitality and fervour. Everything in this act is beyond compare: the herald's speech, which is gloomy and without hope, the wailing of the people of Pskov as they learn of Novgorod's ruin; the fits of frightful despair as they contemplate their own fate, and Tokmakov's speech, full of the nobility and tone of a high official, pervaded by the decency of honest conviction; Tucha's speech, furious, impetuous, of unrestrainable passion, punctuated and accompanied by exclamations from the people; the agitation of the people driven to the uttermost degree of distraction; the daring, inspired outlaws' song to which Tucha abandons his country; the profound numbness which overcomes the remaining inhabitants of Pskov as they hang their heads; the fateful peals of the *veche* bell which bring the act to an end; and more than all these things the vital truth which permeates this entire act and makes an irresistibly powerful impression on the spectators. You forget that it is a stage in front of you with chorus-members who are presenting a more or less skilfully constructed folk scene; you see before you reality, the living people, and all that is accompanied by incomparable music rich in substance from beginning to end. Not a single previous opera has yet contained such a folk scene as this. If all the rest of *The Maid of Pskov* were utterly paltry, then this *veche* scene would be sufficient for this opera to be of significance to the history of art and to occupy a prominent place among the most noteworthy operas, and to put its composer among the best composers of opera. The song to which Tucha leaves with his Pskov outlaws is a Russian one, a folksong, also taken from Balakirev's collection (no. 30); here this borrowing is entirely appropriate: the people withdraw to the accompaniment of a song – let its sounds be drawn from the creations of the people, the more so as this particular song is a thing of genius.

The first scene of the third act opens with an excellent, superbly devised chorus of citizens of Pskov awaiting the Dread sovereign, which is built out of one theme. This chorus faithfully and powerfully conveys the profound grief and despondency of the morally crushed mass of the people. Ol'ga's arioso which follows is warm and pervaded by a significant mental anguish, but Rimsky-Korsakov sticks to it too insistently, and carries on too persistently with the dissonance of a major seventh and its inversion the minor second, and then even adds a dissonant pedal to it. In consequence of this device, there is mixed in with the painful impression made by the music of the arioso an unpleasant doubt as to whether the singer and orchestra are on the right notes. The nurse's replies in this scene are sweet and nurse-like. The Dread One's entry is wonderful. The splendidly grandiose theme, developing gradually, with the choral and instrumental masses accumulating, passing through several tonalities of ever-increasing solemnity, blending with the ceremonial peal of the bells, makes a strong impression and is fully worthy of the event it describes: the entry of a stern tsar, come to decide the fate of 'mighty Pskov' at his discretion.

The second scene is primarily devoted to giving a musical characterization of Ivan. This characterization is founded on a three-bar phrase of extremely strong character and remarkable power and depth. This phrase is repeated constantly whenever Ivan speaks; it occurs with varied harmony and the most diverse orchestration but without any changes in its rhythmic and melodic contour. It is only at the words 'v Moskvu, v gosti k nam' ('to Moscow, as our guest') that this phrase is replaced by another one, also splendid, which is two bars in length and of a half-joking character. Ivan's speech is constructed from these two phrases, partly out of their melodic outline but incomparably more often out of the notes of the harmony, in other words without any musical substance in the voice. Three episodes occur in the midst of this characterization. First there is the little folk theme with two variations for the orchestra alone during which Ol'ga and the girls bring Ivan honey and sweetmeats (*zakuski*). (Although this little theme and the variations are very nice, one of the last ones prolongs this orchestral prelude too much, so that for a time the stage remains in a state of expectation, which is disagreeable for both the spectators and the artists on the stage.) The second episode – Ol'ga's tiny speech 'Tsar' gosudar', s toboyu tselovat'sya' ('Tsar, sovereign, let us embrace') – is poetic and charming in a feminine way. The third episode is a very characteristic brief women's chorus of girls singing the tsar's praises. Despite the presence of these three episodes, one senses in this scene a rather tiresome uniformity of tone, since the entire personality of Ivan is based exclusively on two phrases, and in developing these two phrases Korsakov has not had recourse to changes of tempo or bar-length, nor to rhythmic changes, nor to lengthening of the themes, nor to shortening of them.

The final act is preceded by an entr'acte portraying Ol'ga, an entr'acte of wonderful delicacy, beauty and elegance. The unison chorus of girls moving across the stage consists of a theme and three variations; this third brief women's chorus is just as good as all the choruses in *The Maid of Pskov*; it is noteworthy for its national character (*narodnost'*), fine theme, its original, good and beautiful harmonization. Ol'ga's short scene in the forest is full of poetic charm; it is one of those little pictures of nature of which Korsakov is such a master, a short scene which is all the more captivating for the fact that to describe it he has used all the bewitching charm of his magical orchestra. The second love duet of Ol'ga and Tucha is better than the first; it contains, besides Korsakov's usual prettiness, real animation; but sadly this animation is expressed in phrases which are too delicate and short, and the proper effect of this duet is vitiated again by the uniformity of rhythm and the sometimes unfortunate use of the voices (they are too low and inaudible). The end of the duet is amazing: it conveys profound happiness, as if in premonition of imminent and inescapable death. In the final part of this scene (Matuta's attack) we find that uncommonly original and complete characterization of Matuta of which I spoke earlier. One could wish only for more energy in the cries of the attacking serfs and less scrappiness in Matuta's speech, unless Korsakov wanted to portray him running out of breath, that is to outward appearances as comic, which is pretty unlikely: Matuta is too serious a scoundrel for that.

In the final scene of *The Maid of Pskov* the musical characterization of Ivan is far richer than in the fourth scene; here, apart from his main, basic phrase, there are also some new ones which are not inferior to it in power, and there are some very characteristic harmonic alternations. Ivan's whole scene on his own and with Ol'ga is first-class as regards its music; it is not inferior in musical quality to the *veche* scene; the episode in which Ivan sings 'Chem chashche: bukoy al' tsaryom Ivanom tebya pugali?' ('Which did they scare you with more often – the bogeyman or Tsar Ivan?') is so powerful that it can rival the creations of the very greatest composers in this genre; if this whole scene had been a symphonic picture for orchestra alone, it would have made the strongest impression; yet on the stage the word which imparts a quite specific meaning to a scene does not deepen an impression but rather lessens it, and the reason lies in the sometimes false and clumsy use of the voice. First of all, the voice sings a melodic phrase abruptly which in consequence of that goes for nothing. (May I remind you how pleasing Ivan's phrase 'Ne plach', ya ne medved', ne lyudoyed kosmatïy' ('Do not weep, I am not a bear or a shaggy cannibal') sounds – not because it was any better than the others but because it was sung with the full power of the voice.) Secondly, because Ivan's speech is in places too fast and uniform in rhythm, rather chopped up (take for instance 'kto zhitiyem vo istinu molchal'nïm' ('who by the silent way of life in truth') and the following lines), whereas Ol'ga's speech is too slow and diffuse because of the many pauses. (It is analogous in character to Liszt's *Saint Elizabeth*.) Thirdly, the placing of the voice is not adroit enough to enable it to augment the strength of sound continuously, yet that is essential to augment the impression.

But, I repeat, musically this is a most outstanding scene. Matuta's episode is just as successful as in the previous scene, and acts like its continuation. At the moment when the song of the Pskov outlaws can be heard off-stage as they attack the Tsar's headquarters, we encounter one of Korsakov's blunders in stagecraft, an especially damaging one. At this point Ivan ought either to continue his conversation with Ol'ga heedless of this song, or else he should pay attention to it and immediately summon someone to find out what is happening. In Korsakov's version Ivan is evidently alarmed by the song but does not call anyone, rushes around the stage, taking up now his staff, now his sword, until Prince Vyazemsky enters the Tsar's headquarters on his own initiative. The fight too is unfortunate in stage terms: as music it is good, but it is all built up so correctly, measured out so precisely, two bars by two bars, conducted so evenly and cold-bloodedly from start to finish, that not only is there no fight in it, there is not even any swordplay. The final chorus, whose inappropriateness in terms of the stage I spoke about when surveying the libretto, is musically profound and thrilling. This scene, which surpasses the fourth scene in musical quality to a significant extent, has a more wearisome effect, however, on the listener, who has already been tired out by the monochrome music of the preceding scene and the second half of the first act.

The Maid of Pskov is orchestrated with the qualities of mastery, inventiveness and taste which everyone recognizes Rimsky-Korsakov to possess. Among other things, the fairy tale and the *veche* scene are particularly striking for their instrumentation. In the latter the use made of percussion instruments, the bass drum and side drum and cymbals is astounding. These instruments impart a great deal of brilliance, but a measure of banality is usually indissolubly associated with them. In Korsakov's hands, though, they are uncommonly noble, they make their peculiar effect but at the same time are so completely blended with the other instruments that they go almost unnoticed.

The only thing to be said against the orchestration of *The Maid of Pskov* is that it is in places too delicate and not brilliant enough, almost as if it were intended for the concert hall rather than the theatre.

Such is the work which Rimsky-Korsakov has bestowed upon us. As the reader has seen, this opera is not without shortcomings, which lie partly in the nature of the composer and partly in the problems linked with a first work for which the composer does not yet have sufficient experience.[6] But

6 *Author's note*: Glinka apart, there is not a single composer whose first opera comes anywhere near the merits of *The Maid of Pskov*.

in spite of all that, *The Maid of Pskov* represents a most gratifying event in our artistic life: it enriches our repertory with a solid and extremely talented work, it offers new proof of the seriousness of the course, the strength of conviction and significant future of the New Russian Operatic School, and Korsakov's *veche* is a step forward for art; it will have a very long life, it will long serve as a splendid model for other composers writing folk scenes, and it will long continue to captivate listeners profoundly.

[Cui next evaluates the performance.]

Finally, one cannot fail once more to rejoice in Mr Korsakov's work, and to wish that the composer takes further firm steps forward towards the ideal along the creative path which he has so far followed with such honesty and such brilliance.

(b) G. A. Laroche: Mr Rimsky-Korsakov's *The Maid of Pskov*. *The Voice*, 1873, no. 10. Laroche 3, pp. 105–12

In the narrow circle of Russian composers N. A. Rimsky-Korsakov occupies nearly the most brilliant position at present. It is a rare composer who makes such a successful début: his first composition (a symphony performed in 1865 at a Free School concert) was greeted sympathetically by everyone. The energetic and superbly organized party of our musical progressives (the only musical party in Rus' to deserve this name on account of its tightly-knit personnel and its concerted way of operating) immediately recognized him as their own, which guaranteed Rimsky-Korsakov the invariable and enthusiastic praises of the musical *feuilleton* of the St Petersburg Bulletin.[7] The readers of that newspaper found, alongside scornful judgements of Bach and Handel, Haydn and Mozart, forever new evidence of the lofty qualities of Rimsky-Korsakov as a composer, and thus gradually accustomed themselves to the idea that the creator of *Sadko* was greater than Bach and Handel, Haydn and Mozart, a position which Rimsky-Korsakov shared with Musorgsky, Borodin and some others, a strained and not entirely advantageous position, as it has its due share of the comical. The language of this tight circle is incomprehensible to the naive majority, and when the circle's regular judges view their own people through a magnifying glass and all others through a reducing one, then the violation of proportion, imperceptible to themselves, may cause the outsider to laugh. One must add that at the beginning of Rimsky-Korsakov's career relations between our musical progressives and the public were worse than they are now, and the number of adherents of this school incomparably fewer. Not a single one of the disadvantages of this position, however, has rubbed off on Rimsky-Korsakov.

---

7 The author of this *feuilleton* was Cui.

He was praised by a publication antipathetic to the majority (*massa*), but they found the composer himself sympathetic. Every new step he took in the symphonic field was met by the majority with amicable applause: it was as if he had found the talisman which enabled him to combine sharing his friends' exclusive aspirations with having an irresistible impact on people who had no desire even to hear about these aspirations. Thus, the compositions of Balakirev, which in many respects served him as training-ground and model, never enjoyed the sympathies of the majority; it saved up these sympathies for his fortunate imitator. The majority were followed by the specialists. People who could not speak about the musical heresies of the *St Petersburg Bulletin* without a shudder, people disposed to consider everything described as bad in the *feuilleton* of that newspaper to be good, unwittingly softened their anger when conversation turned to Rimsky-Korsakov. Without feeling any sympathy for the tendency to which he belonged, they could not deny his talent and even when they found it impossible to be reconciled with the substance of his ideas they were astounded by the skill of his colouring. The new talent really did have many winning aspects. He shared with the musicians of his own circle the quest for what was of the Russian folk (*k narodno-russkomu*) in melody and rhythm, he shared the choice refinement of sumptuous harmonies, their love of energetic dissonances, and the motley play of modulations in rapid succession; but he surpassed all the others with the dazzling brilliance of his orchestra and, what is far more important, by his fecundity, the ease with which he worked, by his relative fluency and naturalness. It seemed that this brilliant and sympathetic talent was short of individual physiognomy; it seemed that the influences of other people showed themselves too directly in his scores; but this shortcoming was easily explained by the composer's youth. Often he displayed an inclination to reminiscences and unintentional borrowings from the repertory closest to him or his school: phrases and devices from Schumann, *Ruslan and Lyudmila*, later from Richard Wagner, and most frequently from Liszt could be glimpsed more often, perhaps, in his works than in those of other members of his circle; but one must not forget that he wrote more than they did, and therefore was more often able to lapse into this shortcoming to which, strictly speaking, the particular features of their outlook and musical education were bound to dispose them. A more serious defect lay in the predominance of the surface and of sensuality which undoubtedly manifested itself in all his works. Their weakest part was always the melodic contour; apart from the absence of originality, Rimsky-Korsakov's melodies were not conspicuous for their distinctness of outline or easily-memorized melodiousness. The harmony was more interesting, and most interesting of all was the instrumentation. Not producing remarkable ideas but sparkling with the luxuriant play of instrumental colour, Rimsky-Korsakov's works vividly reminded one of the pictures of a famous Russian painter who was dazzlingly rich when it came to portraying air and water but powerless to create human figures.[8] Thus, the composer of *Sadko*[9] and *Antar*[10] is a representative of materialism in art – a trend which is very widespread in our time but which rarely occurs with such onesidedness. On the other hand, the relative ease with which he works, the relative fertility which I mentioned always made Rimsky-Korsakov seem less of a dilettante than the other members of his circle. Through the false tendency which compelled him first and foremost to seek new forms and forms which were not in use, one could see his innate capacity to connect and group ideas, an innate searching for symmetry and roundedness. The struggle between the school's harmful influences and his sure innate flair constitutes one of the most interesting aspects of this sympathetic talent, and because of this struggle his works have always been of double significance: apart from the more or less attractive music which they contained, they conveyed the promise of other, freer and more perfect works in which their composer's rich powers would emerge, finally, from the vicious circle of fanatical doctrines.

This was the musician whose opera, announced and withdrawn several times,[11] the public awaited with highly excited and sympathetic impatience. The composer's entire prior career had shown him primarily, if not exclusively, as a symphonist; his romances, of which there are very many, occupy a very secondary place in his activities. The innate abilities and acquired habits of a purely instrumental composer are not always useful and are sometimes even an impediment in composing operas; on the other hand, musical drama is one of the main objects of attention and concern of that critical school whose influence has so far made such a strong impact on Rimsky-Korsakov: one has only to recall *The Stone Guest*, which he orchestrated, in order to imagine the close link between this school of criticism and practical attempts at reform in the field of opera. Curiosity must have been powerfully aroused by the question of how the gifted symphonist and advocate of new paths in musical drama would cope with the new task he had set himself.

The reception with which the public honoured the opera at its first performance [on 1 January 1873] (I was not present for the second, on 7 January) could not be called simply sympathetic: it amounted to a series of ovations. The composer was called out at every change of set – sometimes two or three times. A large part of this enthusiasm must, of course, be

8 For Ayvazovsky, see Chapter 6, note 20.
9 For *Sadko*, see Chapter 6, items (d) and (g).
10 For *Antar*, see Chapter 6, item (e).
11 Illness among the cast caused the postponement of the première.

attributed to the fate of the première of a new opera; there have been occasions in the Mariinsky Theatre when operas rejected by the public after five or six performances were accorded noisy expressions of sympathy at the première. But however much one reduces the success of *The Maid of Pskov* given for Platonova's benefit, there nevertheless remains in this success a very considerable portion of sincerity and seriousness. The author was helped here above all by the subject which offers a very great deal which is interesting and fascinating. [Laroche outlines differences between play and libretto.] Even in its present form [i.e. lacking some of Mey's more poetic passages], *The Maid of Pskov* is attractive, apart from the music, for the personality of Ivan the Terrible, the contrast between the horrors of his reign and the independent spirit of a free city, the picture of the *veche* and popular revolts, and also for the situation of a young, defenceless girl speaking boldly to the Dread Tsar and arousing in him not anger but a feeling of tenderness and compassion. Both the historical background and the exceptional peculiarity of personal fate in *The Maid of Pskov* cannot fail to strike the imagination and to provoke sympathy. Good operatic subjects are of the greatest rarity, and we are dealing with one in the present case. Music sometimes comes to the assistance of these qualities in the text; sometimes it weakens their effect.

All of the music for the new opera is too recherché in respect of harmony, too full of choice dissonances and uncommon modulations, too rich in oddities, too stilted and stiff for a drama taken from historical life and presenting a crude age with simple feelings and passions, with people not tormented by reflection. In the extremes of harmony, in expressing the sharpest and harshest dissonances, in unexpected combinations and chord devices Rimsky-Korsakov has taken a significant step forward by comparison with his previous works, which imparts its extremely morbid character to the opera. This is the kind of music, I think, which should have been written for an opera taken from Dostoyevsky's *Crime and Punishment*. I suppose that before the composer's imagination rose the horror and grief which seized the Russian land during the Dread One's reign, that he wanted to reproduce the physical sufferings of tortures and executions, the moral torments of terror, sorrow, humiliation and hopelessness, and this is how I explain, for example, the general mood of the overture (apart from the fact that part of it returns at the end of the opera as a musical illustration of a fight). But this manner of writing has also spread to such parts of the opera where there is no thought of any sort of terror – to be more accurate, to almost the entire opera; and in addition through these innumerable dissonances the character of sickly whim predominates over that of awesome power. If I add that the composer modulates too often and without any need, that these modulations quickly following one another over the course of four acts weary the attention and deaden feeling, then I shall be uttering a reproach which applies equally to *The Maid of Pskov* and to any other opera of the newest trend; it is just a pity that Russian composers are falling into this defect when the folksongs which they treat ought to be teaching them sober and sensible diatonicism. One must make the very same observation about pedals as about modulations: it is in accordance with the custom of our times which is particularly highly developed in the circle of Russian musical progressives. At every turn Rimsky-Korsakov stops the bass on a single note and over this long-sustained note amasses complex and dissonant harmonies. A large part of his opera is made up of such pedals, and their misuse in its turn, of course, dulls feeling just as much as the incessant modulation. Faithful to the new trend in opera, Rimsky-Korsakov has written almost all of it in recitative, and what is more in so-called 'dry' recitative, so that one rarely encounters those half-lyrical, half-declamatory phrases which being introduced by Glinka and Dargomïzhsky represent a peculiarity of Russian recitative. *The Stone Guest*, for example, consists mainly of such phrases, which often lend it a great deal of distinctive charm. Their rare use by Rimsky-Korsakov must have been provoked by the idea that he considered recitative not as the crux of the opera but as a dark background, that in his work, as in an earlier school, in supplement to conversation pronounced at the speed of speech, there occur rounded melodic cantilenas; but this expectation was not realized: the place of such cantilenas is taken by the choruses, of which there are very many in the new opera, and which by their musical beauties overwhelm all the rest decisively. I shall further comment about the recitative in *The Maid of Pskov* that because of the perpetual modulations accompanying its harmony, it is often based on chromatic intervals which are antimelodic and awkward to memorize, as a result of which it resembles a middle part in some complicated and involved harmony.

I have just said that the new opera contains no melodic cantilenas; I must enter a reservation that there is one exception and this exception stands out sharply from the entire opera: it is the duet between Ol'ga and Tucha in Act I. The composer has taken a fine folksong ('Uzh tï pole, moye pole chistoye' ('You field, my clean field'), no. 27 in Balakirev's collection) for this duet. Performed by the tenor in a high register, this song makes and will continue to make an undoubted effect; there is also a poetic kinship between the original text of this song (it speaks of a young Cossack who is lying, dying, in the middle of the battlefield and orders his horse to convey greetings to his young wife) and the situation of Tucha who in the ecstasy of love and happiness has no premonition of an imminent and glorious death. But as regards music, the effect of this song is a false and inappropriate one; its epically peaceful, smooth and almost idle tone contradicts the mood of a moment full of animation and passion. In general terms one can scarcely justify the insertion of a folksong in an operatic monologue or duet (it is a different matter if the song occurs as a hint in the orchestra as, for instance, in Ratmir's recitative in Act III of *Ruslan and Lyudmila*). A collective unit has its say in the song, an entire nation (*narod*) is having its say; in consequence, the song is in a certain sense impersonal, and nothing can be more contrary to those supreme moments of drama where individuality is outlined with all its one-sided force. One must remark that the expression of individualities, the delineation of characters, is the weakest aspect throughout the opera. The Dread One is more successful than the others, and the worst is Ol'ga, whose moral torments gave the composer the idea of a special duet between her and the nurse (in Act III), where the unprecedented, ruthless harshness of the dissonances surpasses everything known to me of this sort. What is most remarkable of all is that these dissonances are arranged entirely symmetrically, forming a sequence: they thus give the impression of a mathematical operation on the chords undertaken without paying the slightest heed to how they will sound. In reality, the composer obviously aimed for those harrowing sounds which he achieved, and his sharp harmonic relishes, these burning hot pickles of musical gastronomy, testify to the terrible artistic satiety derived from his constant study of the most recent music. The chords which accompany Ol'ga's abduction by Matuta and later the scene between Matuta and Ivan belong to the same category. Far more pardonable than these unhealthy contrivances are the unintentional reminiscences from which the composer could not protect himself even in his new score. Even if in the first chorus of Act III the accents on seconds and the notes alternating in the middle and low register recall the 'Pogibnet' ('Let him perish') chorus in *Ruslan*; even if the effective scene of Ivan's entry is a print taken from the 'Slav'sya' chorus (both here and there we have the oft-repeated diatonic theme on a few notes, the gradual increase in power, the military orchestra, the sustained high G in the violins, during the repetition of the theme; there is a certain resemblance in the two themes as well); even if the orchestral phrase after Ivan's words 'Pritupim mechi o kameni, Pskov khranit Gospod'' ('Let us blunt our swords on the stones, the Lord will preserve Pskov') is similar to the cemetery scene in *The Stone Guest*; even if the introduction to Act IV is reminiscent in harmony and scoring of the introduction to Liszt's *Saint Elizabeth*: I should wish that there were four times as many such reminiscences if at the same time those new and unprecedented things which from time to time occur in the harmony were to disappear.

To put an end to the shortcomings of *The Maid of Pskov*, I shall point out one device introduced, I think, by Wagner, and exploited by Liszt particularly – a device which has caused terrible devastation in the most modern music and which shows the steep decline in the art of composition, a device which is not infrequent in Rimsky-Korsakov. It consists in shifting a short musical phrase (two, three or four bars) in its entirety a third higher or lower; in the main the transposition is not confined to one third, however, but goes on several times in succession. This device is inimical to any internal organic development of an idea: it is a simple mechanical repetition seasoned by the effect of the sudden appearance of a new tonality. The duet of Ol'ga and Tucha in the first act is based on this device (where, however, the transposition is accompanied by variations in the harmony), and the beginning of the duet of Ol'ga and the nurse, which I mentioned on account of its dissonances, is constructed in a way similar to this; the scene in which the Tsar enters Prince Tokmakov's quarters opens in the same fashion; we meet the same device a few pages later when the Tsar invites Ol'ga to go to him in Moscow; to these one must add the many shifts of a minor second which call forth a similar method of composition, and also the interchange of dominant sevenths a minor third or a diminished fifth apart – an effect plentifully used in Act II.

Rimsky-Korsakov's opera is infected with all the shortcomings of the musical environment in which he grew up, and some of these shortcomings display themselves in extreme form. But here too one can see the gratifying spectacle of talent triumphing over circumstances most unfavourable to its development. The choruses in *The Maid of Pskov* are in the main good; they are not only simpler and more natural but also more alive and inspired than anything given to individual characters. The girls' chorus in Act IV ('Akh, tï dubrava' ('Ah, you leafy grove')) – a simple melody written by the composer, but successfully imitating a folksong – is worthy to stand with Rimsky-Korsakov's best works by virtue of its fragrant grace. The prime section of the opera is Act II (the *veche* scene). Here integral and rounded musical construction is combined with successful characterization of the *dramatis personae* (the herald, Tokmakov, Tucha), and the choruses of the worried people contain a violent heat which grips the listener irresistibly. The song to which the Pskov outlaws leave (tenor solo and male chorus) makes a staggering impact; its theme is a folk one (also taken from Balakirev's collection), but this in no way detracts from the composer's merit: the art in choosing it, its deft placing (the contrast of its broad rhythm with the preceding $\frac{3}{4}$ in a fast tempo), the beautiful harmonization and the contrapuntal combination of it with another theme (the phrase which Tucha used earlier to address the citizens of Pskov) – all this is the composer's work and reveals not only a skilful hand but also genuine inspiration. A person capable of creating such a dramatic passage possesses the strength to throw off the chains of conventional views, present-day diseases and the enthusiasms of a small circle. Less than any other contemporary composer has Rimsky-Korsakov uttered his final words: all his work to date, not excluding even this opera, has, in my eyes, only preparatory significance: he has still not emerged from the period of conflict and ferment. I think that the sickliness of his present works is no more than a transitional phase, on the expiry of which his creative talent, expanding to its full power, will present the reconciliation of the newest brilliance and wealth with the plastic completeness of former days.

The performance of the new opera made a most agreeable impression on me. The choruses go excellently, and the orchestra, to whom, as one ought to have expected of Rimsky-Korsakov, the most advantageous role in the whole piece is entrusted, leaves nothing to be desired. [Laroche here considers the singers individually.] The harmonious ensemble performance showed (despite the fact that it was the first one) that our artists had studied the new work with love and zeal. The opera's production is first-rate. If one adds to all these factors in the success the charm of Rimsky-Korsakov's name and the talent bursting forth from his music in spite of all its shortcomings, then the brilliant reception which the public accorded *The Maid of Pskov* becomes easy to explain.

(c) G. A. Laroche: Mr Kondrat'yev's benefit performance at the Mariinsky Theatre (excerpts from M. Musorgsky's opera *Boris Godunov*). *The Voice*, 1873, no. 45. Laroche 3, pp. 119–24

This article is notable for showing Laroche against his will recognizing expressive power in scenes from Musorgsky's opera. This lapse was temporary, as may be seen in 7 (e).

Musorgsky's new work was hardly awaited by the public with the same feelings as Rimsky-Korsakov's *The Maid of Pskov*. The composer of *The Maid of Pskov* was well known to regular attenders of symphony concerts, and in St Petersburg these concert-goers represent a very significant number of people. Rimsky-Korsakov often enjoyed brilliant triumphs at these concerts, and over several years the composer's musical personality won a certain appeal as a result of which many music-lovers were persuaded in advance that an opera by such a musician would be excellent. The composer of *Boris Godunov* did not have the advantages of such a position; possibly he too was a celebrity, but only among the tiniest coterie.[12] Pieces by Musorgsky were rarely performed at concerts, indeed there were almost

12 Laroche had the Balakirev circle in mind, presumably.

none of his pieces suitable for public performance. As a matter of fact, those of his compositions which had appeared in print were unsuitable for any kind of performance at all, and it was difficult to explain why and for whom they were published.[13] They consisted in the main of a moderate number of romances (about twenty) or, to be more accurate, of excerpts written on three staves (one for the voice and two for the piano) and entitled romances, although these excerpts were quite radically different both from all romances known hitherto and also from what is generally known as music. For the most part they consisted of successions of unmelodious cries which were abstruse to the ear and awkward for intonation, accompanied by something or other on the lines of chords or chord figurations whose cacophony, whether naive or malicious and intentional, passed all description. In musical technique this accompaniment represents a sight unprecedented in the annals of art. The most elementary schoolboy blunders – parallel octaves, parallel fifths, unresolved dissonances, the appearance of new tonalities without any modulation, spelling errors in sharps and flats, incorrect barring – all these things stared the performer in the face and tortured the listener's ear no less than the 'exceedingly spry' insects which spoiled Chichikov's night spent under Nozdryov's hospitable roof.[14] It would be easy for these mistakes to determine the composer's musical age; only a child could write like that. But various conceits of chromaticism and dissonance, attempts at complexity, strikingness and so-called 'new paths' gave signs of unusually early depravity in this child. As I played through a work by Musorgsky I would always be thinking of the need to establish a corrective refuge for juvenile musical offenders. In the midst of the furious orgy of incoherent and ugly sounds in his songs there would sometimes be a patch with not a bad idea, with a felicitous turn of word-setting, a melodic scrap in the spirit of the best folksongs, three or four chords in a successful progression – in short, beneath a thick crust of ignorance and pretension to originality one could sometimes detect a musical nature which was not without flair and talent. But these gleams were extremely rare and disappeared in the midst of the trash surrounding them.

This was how Musorgsky struck me in his romances. The reader will not be surprised if I say that I set out for the theatre on 5 February with the strongest prejudice against the new music which I was expecting to hear. I had applied to Musorgsky beforehand the epigram on the French composer Rameau composed in the middle of last century:

---

13 Musorgsky's publications up to 1873 were: four short piano pieces, fifteen individual songs plus 'The nursery' and 'The peepshow', and the choral work *Porazheniye Sennakheriba* ('The destruction of Sennacherib').
14 In Gogol's novel *Myortvïye dushi* ('Dead souls').

Distillateur d'accords baroques
Dont tant d'idiots sont férus,
Chez les Thraces et les Iroques
Portez vos opéras bourrus.
Malgré votre art hétérogène
Lully de la lyrique scéne
Est toujours l'unique soutien.
Fuyez, laissez-lui son partage,
Et n'écorchez pas davantage
Les oreilles des gens de bien.[15]

But the composer whom I had intended to advise to take to flight amazed me by the totally unexpected treasures in his operatic excerpts, so that after hearing the scenes from *Boris Godunov* I was compelled to alter my opinion of Musorgsky significantly. True, these excerpts contained features which vividly recalled the very romances which had inspired my genuine fear of Musorgsky's muse; true, the complete absence of technique and schooling makes itself felt wherever the composer makes an attempt to write in a rounded form, and his indefatigable search for savour and novelty fractures and mangles this form still more; but the ratio between these faults and the spiritual power which breaks through underneath is quite unlike the one I found in the romances. I profoundly regret that Musorgsky's scenes were not repeated at Leonova's[16] benefit performance which took place several days later; I profoundly regret that I thus heard and saw them only once, the more so as I did not have the opportunity of getting to know them either at a rehearsal or at home at the piano. I am convinced that the favourable impression which these excerpts made on me would have been strengthened considerably by a more thorough acquaintance with them.

Three scenes from *Boris Godunov* were performed at the theatre on 5 February: the inn on the Lithuanian border, Marina Mniszek's boudoir, and the love scene by the fountain. Of these scenes, the central one (in the boudoir) seemed to me the most negligible; the prolonged mazurka which Marina sings during it is some kind of double extract from Chopin, recherché and ungracious, awkwardly written for soprano (too low) and in lack of melodic beauty worthy to stand alongside Musorgsky's published works. The women's chorus which precedes this mazurka does not stand out particularly in any way; I am not going to make up my mind about the

15 This poem is attributed to Jean-Jacques Rousseau.
16 D. M. Leonova (1829, or 1834, –1896), contralto who sang on the imperial stages of Moscow and St Petersburg. She created the roles of the Princess in *Rusalka*, Spiridonovna in *The Power of the Fiend*, Skul'da in *Rogneda*, Vlas'yevna in *The Maid of Pskov*, etc. Glinka dedicated songs to her, and Musorgsky was her accompanist on a concert tour in 1879.

scene with the Jesuit which follows it on the basis of one performance. But the remaining two excerpts from the opera – the tavern scene and the scene by the fountain – staggered me by the brilliant musical and dramatic talent which they showed. The tavern scene is a superb étude in the comic style; the action is so spontaneous that at the performance a considerable part of the public were laughing in that uninhibited way which is provoked by good comedy. The musical characterization of the monk Varlaam, the tavern-keeper and the police officer shows the composer's aptitude for that individual expressiveness which is so hard to obtain in music; unfeigned humour comes to light in many separate moments, especially in the majority of Varlaam's phrases. But in my opinion the most remarkable part of this scene is the song 'Kak vo gorode bïlo vo Kazani' ('As happened in the city of Kazan'') which Varlaam sings holding a bottle of vodka. Immense power can be sensed in both the melody and the diverse instrumental variations of the song in this scene; the turns of harmony are marked by an elasticity and brilliance which I least of all expected of Musorgsky, and in the mood of this whole number something wild and terrifying is conveyed by the composer with poetic animation. The same animation prevails in the scene by the fountain: this scene is full of splendid sensual charm and languor which it was quite impossible to expect from the composer of *Boris*, to judge once more from the published examples of his work. Also extremely remarkable is the bold, heroic melody in high notes which the Pretender sings at the end of this scene. The melody is *national* (*narodna*) in the highest sense of the word; it is evident that the element of Russian folk music not only appeals to Musorgsky but that he has a close familiarity with it. I may add that he could realize the ideal of Russian national identity (*narodnost'*) in his music far more often if (his contrapuntal clumsiness apart) he were able to free himself from his extraordinary passion for mannered augmented and diminished intervals in declamatory melody and for intervals based on the augmented triad and on several other dissonant chords which he favours. All these bad habits of his melodies are antipathetic to the spirit of Russian song in the utmost degree; nor can it be allowed that intervals of that kind were necessary if the word-setting was to be accurate.

But let me return to Musorgsky's scene by the fountain. I cannot say that this whole scene satisfied me equally. A polonaise is placed in the middle of the scene (and placed, by the way, extremely awkwardly, without any connection with the action, so that Meyerbeer's scenic effects, which have always been attacked by the champions of strict musical drama, among them Musorgsky's admirers, represent the height of logical and aesthetic consistency in comparison with this polonaise). The music of this number is in the highest degree strained, incoherent, completely lacking in grace and in that festive magnificence which is a main characteristic of a real polonaise; in this dance number Musorgsky discloses that he has little flair for instrumental music and no technical training at all. But if the art of instrumental composition were restricted to the art of *instrumentation*, then Musorgsky would have to be recognized as a master in that kind of composition: all three of the scenes performed on 5 February, particularly the third (by the fountain) are scored splendidly, with variety, clearly and extremely effectively, so that one wonders why an artist who has obviously taken a lot of time and trouble to study the orchestra's resources and the rules of writing for it, has not taken even a little time to acquaint himself with harmony, counterpoint and the theory of form. However, in giving my frank assessment of the merits and shortcomings of Musorgsky's music I certainly do not intend to give him any sort of advice. I regard him as a *fait accompli* and I suppose that for him to turn from the true path and fill in the gaps in his education would be incomparably more difficult than for Rimsky-Korsakov, firstly, because the composer of *Antar* possesses far greater reserves of knowledge as it is, and it is well known that new knowledge is the more easily acquired the more knowledge one has already, and, secondly, because the composer of *Boris*, on the other hand, possesses far more distinctiveness and originality of imagination, as a result of which it must be more difficult for him to submit to some external oppressive discipline, such as that of the rules of the strict contrapuntal style. What is missing from Musorgsky's musical education can scarcely be made up at some later date, and if there should have been on his own part any doubt about his artistic maturity, it must have been dispelled on 5 February by the brilliant reception given to his work. Although he is far less well known to the public than Korsakov, the composer of *Boris* enjoyed a success little less than the composer of *The Maid of Pskov*, especially if you take into account that excerpted scenes cannot make as much of an impression on the public as a whole opera. The public liked the tavern scene best, and on this occasion I am entirely on the side of the public.

[Laroche goes on to assess the performance.]

Boris Godunov is an occurrence of the utmost significance. This opera has revealed that among the small group who form the extreme left wing of our musical world there exist qualities for which this circle was not noted until now: original invention and independent substance. Up till now this circle has produced mainly imitators, although very capable ones. Balakirev copied Glinka and Schumann, and later Liszt; Cui copied Auber and Schumann; Rimsky-Korsakov copied Glinka, Schumann, Balakirev and later Liszt as well; Borodin too copied Schumann; in short, for all its many good qualities, the group was constantly short of an individual physiognomy with strong features. Now this deficiency has been filled by Musorgsky, and it is highly characteristic that this exalted position in the group has been occupied by the least knowledgeable and expert of its members. Nothing could better outline the aspirations and spirit of the group: that the upper hand should have been gained in it eventually not by completeness of knowledge, not versatility of development, not artistic elegance, not breadth of horizon, but by crude, powerful nature. The group always sought the emancipation of the instinct and arbitrariness, the triumph of elemental power over tradition, history, knowledge and aesthetics. Now, it seems, the group has secured that triumph. Perhaps we shall live long enough to see all the other members of the group convinced of the uselessness of even that light intellectual ballast which they have so far managed to obtain, throwing it overboard and turning into slavish imitators of Musorgsky.

There is a saying that knowledge is power. To a much greater extent is it true that talent is power. The performance on 5 February convinced me that this power in the extreme left wing of our musical world is far more substantial than one might have supposed from their published works. At the same time, of course, I had to assure myself that all the ailments, all the vices of this group are far more infectious than I considered them hitherto. In union with bold and original talent our musical radicals' party can go a long way without stumbling. It is hard to foresee the countervailing forces acquiring a strong influence; it is only the public who can protest successfully against this wrong direction; but it is this very public – at least in the Mariinsky Theatre and the orchestral concert halls – which is most fascinated by this tendency. Therefore our immediate future will in all probability come to fruition on the basis of the catechism propounded in the music columns of the *St Petersburg Bulletin*.[17] Our composers will concur in despising Bach, Handel, Gluck, Haydn, Mozart and Mendelssohn.[18] It may very well be that even Glinka will join the list of repudiated authorities, for our radicals appear to be cooling towards him.[19] Constant use of harsh dissonances and distant modulations, constant pedals in the bass, the collapse of form, rhapsodical incoherence, fantastic arbitrariness in instrumental music, rejection of the quartet and chamber music in general, and in opera constant recitative with here and there a folksong, – all this, seasoned by escapades of dense and motley instrumentation – this is what lies ahead of us in the immediate future. Whether this period will be a prolonged one, and what will arise to replace it, it is still too early to guess. In any case

17 Laroche alludes here to Cui.
18 Rimsky-Korsakov was responsible later for the inclusion in Russian Musical Society programmes in 1875–6 of compositions by Bach, Handel, Haydn, Palestrina and Allegri. While Laroche's picture is somewhat exaggerated, Rimsky-Korsakov's outlook did evolve towards greater breadth of interest.
19 The evidence which prompted this statement is unknown.

there is no doubt that circumstances are at present extremely favourable to the strengthening of our musical radicals and therefore one must watch their temporary triumph in submission to fate in the conviction that truth will eventually, although with a delay, triumph.

(d) Ts. A. Cui: Three scenes from Musorgsky's opera *Boris Godunov* rejected by the Vaudeville Committee. The future of Russian opera. *St Petersburg Bulletin*, 9 February 1873, no. 40. Cui, pp. 225–35

What Cui christened the 'Vaudeville Committee' was the team charged with assessing the suitability of operas submitted to them for production in the imperial opera house. Cui wished to express the view that the composition of the committee rendered it unable to perform its task since too many of them had no qualifications or experience to judge works in an up-to-date idiom, musical and otherwise. How could three conductors principally of vaudeville, an Italian instrumentalist from the Italian opera company and a retired German conductor, how could these people, whose grasp of the Russian language was suspect, hope to arrive at a just appreciation of an opera on a Russian subject by a Russian composer in the forefront of musical modernism? Among such a committee, only Napravnik had any chance of reaching the desired verdict.

Cui's view of *Boris Godunov* as a whole is expressed in Chapter 8, item (e).

The benefit for Kondrat'yev,[20] the principal producer of the Russian opera, was made up of the first scene of Act II of *Der Freischütz*, the second act of *Lohengrin* and three scenes from Musorgsky's *Boris Godunov*. As I have conversed with my readers more than once on the subject of *Der Freischütz* and *Lohengrin*, I shall concern myself in the present note with the scenes from *Boris Godunov* only. But before I say anything at all about them, I shall call the reader's particular attention to the fact that it is not a question of the whole opera *Boris Godunov* but only of three excerpts from it; *Boris*, as a whole, will perhaps prove to be still more remarkable than these excerpts, or perhaps it will prove weaker; to satisfy oneself about this one must await either a production of the complete opera on the stage, or at the least its appearance in print, but in the meantime all my judgments must be taken to apply only to the three scenes from *Boris* which were performed at Kondrat'yev's benefit.

Musorgsky, like Korsakov too, is one of the most talented representatives of the New Russian Operatic School; they are diametrically opposite to one another in their natures and their kind of talent. Korsakov is primarily a symphonist, while Musorgsky is primarily a vocal composer;

20 G. P. Kondrat'yev (1834–1905), bass-baritone and producer. He made his Mariinsky début in 1864, and created the roles of the First Pilgrim in *Rogneda* and Pyotr in *The Power of the Fiend*. He was the theatre's principal producer from 1872 until 1900.

Korsakov submits judiciously to the demands of contemporary opera, while Musorgsky gives himself up to them wholeheartedly and tries to implement them with the greatest possible completeness; Korsakov is a musician to such an extent that for the sake of creating a well-rounded form, for the sake of the musical development of a phrase, he is at times capable of not paying due attention to the demands of the stage, to dramatic truth, whereas Musorgsky is a dramatic composer to such an extent that, resting content with truthful expression of the words, with irreproachable word-setting, with accurately communicating the stage situation, he is at times capable of not paying due attention to the quality of his music.

The scene in the inn of the Lithuanian border is put together in accordance with Pushkin, with only the most insignificant changes, [of which Cui gives some particulars]. This entire scene is astoundingly fine musically; it is written in the style of *The Stone Guest* and is worthy of *The Stone Guest*. We find in it the truest understanding of the stage, the most excellent, talented declamation, living, typical musical images, a wealth of original humour and inspiration, and a wealth of first-class music. We start off from the fact that the themes of all three songs are outstanding: the rollicking song of the hard-drinking peasant-woman about the grey drake, the powerful, energetic song 'Kak vo gorode bïlo vo Kazani' ('As it was in the town of Kazan''), and the drunken song typical in its uniformity, 'Kak ekhal yon' ('As he travelled'). In his elaborating of the accompaniment of these songs one cannot admire sufficiently Musorgsky's inexhaustible fantasy, the unheard-of diversity of these accompaniments and their vivid imagery.

Besides these three rounded songs, what melodic richness, what power of inspiration we find in nearly every phrase in this scene! Let us recall just 'Vip'yem charochku za shinkarochku' ('Let's drink a glass to the publican'), 'Ino delo p'yanstvo, ino delo chvanstvo' ('drunkenness is one thing, arrogance is another'), 'startsï smirennïye, inoki chestnïye' ('meek elders, upright monks'), 'Khristiane skupï stali' ('Christians have become miserly'), etc. In all these phrases the music has merged with the text to such an extent that when you have heard them once it is not possible to separate text from music; in all these phrases there is a wealth of typicality, a wealth of rhythmic and, finally – I shall repeat it yet again, of melodic richness.[21]

21 *Author's note:* Even now, many slaves to routine recognize as melodies only crude Italian eight-bar cantilenas, while phrases of recitative do not represent melody to them. A melody is a musical idea, and, for expressing an idea, any form is good. Not to recognize melody in phrases of recitative is the same thing as not recognizing the presence of an idea in ordinary, brief conversational speech and supposing that an idea is confined only to Karamzinian periods [for Karamzin, see Chapter 2, note 24]. It is, meanwhile, understood that a short speech which is concise, rich in content and ideas makes a stronger impression than if the same ideas were expressed in diffuse periods with a flavouring of many superfluous words for the sake of rounded form and a smooth flow of speech.

Besides, this entire scene has been constructed by the experienced hand of a dramatic composer, the proprietress's lively exchanges with Grigory about the route to Lithuania in Varlaam's second song 'Kak edet yon' ('As he travels') are very deftly carried out; there is much genuine comedy in Varlaam's halting reading; this whole scene is full of movement, truth, life, and its music is in spirit Russian folk (*narodnaya*) music. Everyone knows how good the Inn scene is in Pushkin, in how lively a fashion it comes across on the stage. With Musorgsky's music it creates a still stronger impression. There is enough of this perfection for the complete rightness of the present-day trend in opera and the power of Musorgsky's talent to be recognized fully. Such an extended, large-scale, varied and superb comic scene exists in no other opera at all. There is only one trifle in this entire scene which I do not like: the police officers' knocking on the door coincides with the words of Varlaam's song: 'i v dver' tuk-tuk' ('and knock-knock on the door'); I see in this coinciding a certain mischief with a hint of farce, which is not compatible with the artistic comedy of this scene. But one has only to replace this text with another one and this scarcely notice-able blemish will vanish straight away; it would not have been necessary even to mention it if I were not sticking obstinately to my usual principle in assessing good works – and *Boris*, judging from these scenes, is a super-lative work – of seeking out and indicating in the most painstaking fashion even the slightest defects.

In the scenes at Mniszek's Musorgsky has deviated from Pushkin; both scenes – the one in Marina's room and the one beside the fountain – are treated in a completely different way. In Pushkin these scenes are too much governed by reason, which is not much good for music, and in the first of them a character Ruzya appears, which would further increase the opera's cast and the difficulty of staging it.

In Musorgsky this act opens with a short women's chorus in which Marina is compared with a flower. Then Marina falls to daydreaming ambitiously about the throne in Moscow. A Jesuit comes in and begins to instruct her in how to entice and captivate the Pretender and propagate Catholicism in Moscow, saying moreover that for the Church one must sacrifice everything, even one's honour. At this point Marina interrupts him with the words 'Stoy, derzkiy lzhets!' ('Stop, insolent liar!'). Then the Jesuit, strong in spiritual authority, upbraids Marina, and the faithful daughter of the Church gives in to his threatening speeches. The second scene takes place in the garden beside a fountain. The Pretender is waiting for Marina. The Jesuit appears like an ambassador for Marina, and working on the Pretender through her love tries to make him entirely subject to himself. Some guests, who have left Mniszek's palace to take a stroll in the garden to the sounds of the polonaise, compel the Pretender to withdraw for a time. After returning and awaiting Marina, he, utterly absorbed in her, speaks of his love; she interrupts him with mockery to stir up ambition in him, and seeing that it has no effect throws the word *kholop* ('serf') in his face. In a fury the Pretender pushes Marina aside and predicts that she will grovel at his, the Tsar of Muscovy's, feet, and he will command everyone to laugh at the 'jester-woman from the Polish gentry'. At this point Marina, all meek and mild, begs his forgiveness and the act closes with a love scene while the Jesuit appears in the distance laughing loudly.

One can see from this that in comparison with the Inn scene this act is weaker and cruder in conception. It may seem paradoxical to many people that scenes with drunken monks should be more subtle than scenes set in the house of a noble magnate. But after all the most elegant subjects may be portrayed in a coarse manner, and the other way about. A certain relative crudeness of conception in this act lies in the inadequately motivated polonaise: Mniszek's guests come on to the stage and leave it again precisely and only so that Musorgsky may have the opportunity to let the public hear his brilliant polonaise, and the Pretender comes on and goes off so as not to impede this. The Jesuit's personality and his appearance at the very end of the act are also rather stilted and melodramatic in character.

The music of this act has great virtues, but as a whole it is not so far beyond reproach as in the Inn scene. Its character varies: here there is a chorus, here there are surges of lyricism, as a result of which the melodies become more rounded and achieve a certain development. The first short women's chorus is sweet but of low musical value; its Polish character proclaims itself both in harmonic features and in the abrupt syncopated rhythm throughout, like the rhythm of the *krakowiak* [a Polish folk dance in duple time]. The note F sharp gets on one's nerves in this short chorus through frequent repetition. The mazurka is of the same character as this short chorus but musically stronger: it is also sweet, it shares the same Polish character, and a single note (D sharp) is likewise repeated excessively; but apart from these things, it has an animation, a cheerfulness, and in the middle a charming episode 'Panne Mniszek slishkom skuchnï' ('Outpourings of tender passion are too tedious for Miss Mniszek'). Both these numbers are written very evenly. The same evenness distinguishes the music of the superb polonaise too, which is adroit, brilliant and original with a very beautiful, captivating trio. This polonaise as an entity is musically the best number in this act.

The remaining scenes – Marina with the Jesuit, and the Pretender with the Jesuit and Marina – are not written altogether evenly; they contain astounding, inspired episodes, but there are also phrases which are weak, with insufficiently defined melodic quality, and even sounds which are tame crop up in two or three places. In Marina's scene with the Jesuit his ingratiating, picture-like, rather pompous eloquence is outlined at once in a masterly fashion; it is difficult to resist the power to fascinate of phrases such as 'rech'yu lyubovnoyu, laskovoy, nezhnoyu' ('by loving, affectionate words'), but meanwhile even in this charming, animated music the Jesuit's dissembling and clever calculating show through. The music of the Pretender's monologue by the fountain is striking in its beauty, poetic atmosphere and magical orchestral timbre; the Pretender's actual speech, while fervent and truthful, could have been more inspired. The Pretender's scene with the Jesuit is weaker than the Jesuit's scene with Marina. It is true that it contains one wonderful phrase of the Pretender's which seethes with passion: 'ya broshus' k nogam eyo' ('I shall throw myself at her feet'), which is then repeated three times, but its impact is spoiled by other phrases which are dull ('ya za Marinu grud'yu stanu' ('I shall stand up for Marina')) or merely decorative ('o strashnom dne' ('of the dread day')), which perhaps match the Jesuit's character but are in any event disagreeable for the musician. I shall point out one technical blunder in this scene and also in the Jesuit's scene with Marina: the Jesuit has too many words and as a result it is difficult to hear them, and their rapid articulation has a bad effect on the power of the sound of the voice. (It is essential to listen to *Boris* with a libretto in one's hand.) In the ensuing short speech of the Pretender the audacious, self-confident phrase is very good: 'umchat'sya v glave druzhinï' ('to fly away at the head of the troops'), constructed on his principal theme. (This theme, with various modifications, accompanies the Pretender nearly all the way through; it was present in the Inn when he appeared, and in the first scene beside the fountain in this scene). In the scene with Marina her gibes are uncommonly successful ('nochey ne spish'' ('you will not sleep at night'), 'mï i v khizhine ubogoy' ('we, even in a squalid shack')): they are biting, and musical, and rich in expressiveness as well; unfortunately, some of the Pretender's replies are feebler and lessen the strength of impact, and I regard his sally 'v pukhovikakh valyat'sya' ('to loll about in feather-beds') as tasteless. But this dissatisfaction vanishes when you listen to 'tï ranish' serdtse mne' ('You wound my heart') or the very end of the duet from Marina's submissive words 'o tsarevich, umolyayu' ('oh Tsarevich, I implore you'). These inspired, heart-felt sounds, astounding in their beauty, passion, animation and rare musicality, disturb the listener profoundly and leave an ineradicable impression. I shall point out once more the Jesuit's scale repeated several times in this act, which is full of character and harmonized in masterly fashion.

From all that has been said one can reach the following conclusion: the Inn scene fully satisfies the contemporary operatic ideal in both conception and execution; at the present time it is hard to imagine anything more perfect in all respects than this scene. As far as the Polish act is concerned, it contains, despite its excellent general tendency, some trifling defects in conception (the poorly-motivated polonaise), and in technique (the superfluity of words), and in the music as well, since in some – admittedly, very few – places greater musical substance would have been desirable, a more beautiful melodic quality, a more rounded singing quality in the lyrical places.

Boris is orchestrated with great talent. If in places a certain lack of technical experience is perceptible in the instrumentation, manifesting itself primarily in the perpetual density of the colours, the massive quality which is sometimes disadvantageous to the soloists' voices, and the excessively frequent use of the effect of pizzicato, it nonetheless contains a good deal of originality, creativity and completely new effects. The use of the brass, even the trumpets, in *Boris* is especially new and noteworthy, in soft places where it lends the timbre a particular roundness and beauty. The instrumentation of *Boris* is purely operatic – colourful throughout and making an impact throughout; the characters' personalities and the circumstances on stage are set off by it miraculously.

Boris is performed, in spite of all the difficulty and innovativeness of the music, with astonishing perfection. A performance like this requires, besides the performers' talent, an ardent love for the work being performed and a profound understanding of it. [Here Cui goes into detail about the performers.]

Boris's success was colossal and complete. After the Inn scene and at the end the whole theatre from top to bottom stood and applauded unanimously. I cannot remember such a great success, such a great ovation, on the Mariinsky stage. The public has hitherto hailed only its favourite performers thus – Lavrovskaya,[22] Nilsson,[23] Patti.[24] A significant portion of this success of *Boris* is indeed due to the performance; but the same artists perform in other operas as well, and Lavrovskaya herself sang in Afanas'yev's *Amallat-Bek*,[25] though the result came out rather different. A talented performance is not enough: what is performed must also show talent.

When Musorgsky presented his opera to the Vaudeville Committee, many of the artists were present too. The Committee flew into a frenzy of well-bred indignation at the music of *Boris* and rejected the opera; the

22 Ye. A. Lavrovskaya (1845–1919). A contralto who made her Mariinsky debut in 1867, she remained there until 1872 and returned in 1879–80; in 1890–1 she sang at the Bol'shoy Theatre. She suggested the subject of *Eugene Onegin* to Tchaikovsky.

23 Christine Nilsson (1843–1921), Swedish soprano of European renown. Her tours included several visits to St Petersburg and Moscow between 1872 and 1875.

24 Adelina Patti (1843–1919). Legendary Italian soprano who sang in St Petersburg and Moscow in the winter of 1868–9.

25 This opera was first staged in St Petersburg in 1870. N. Ya. Afanas'yev (1820–98) did better in other genres, especially chamber music.

artists went into raptures over it and decided to acquaint the public with at least a few excerpts from it. Kondrat'yev chose three excerpts from *Boris* for his benefit performance, the artists learned their parts at home without interrupting the routine official rehearsals in the theatre, and *in one week*, thanks to Napravnik's energy and skill, they were presented on the stage. All honour to Napravnik and our artists in this matter, all honour for their love of art, for doing what they can to propagate good music, for helping a beginning composer of opera, for their profound sympathy with a fresh current in contemporary music; all honour for their understanding, for their striving to move forward. This gratifying fact will be remembered forever in the history of our opera. And on this occasion, as regards *Boris*, the artists, seemingly, made no mistake, but the Vaudeville Committee did. But perhaps, however, this is all nonsense. Perhaps the artists' enthusiasm for *Boris* is the fruit of their lack of understanding, the public's delight the fruit of their gross ignorance, and my opinions the product of delirium; perhaps all of us form an enormous, organized clique acting in concert for personal and self-interested ends; perhaps only the musical and non-musical columnists are right, the Vaudeville Committee is right – those enlightened, infallible, incorruptible judges, those steadfast guardians of pure, sacred and lofty art! Is that what readers think? Fortunately, one can reply to this question only with Homeric laughter.

And so, the New Russian Operatic School has been enriched by another remarkable work. It was not long ago that it sprang up, and it can already produce such operas as *The Stone Guest, The Maid of Pskov* and *Boris Godunov*. The most perfect of them is *The Stone Guest*, but *The Stone Guest* embodies only one type of contemporary opera – the domestic drama, individual passions, without the mass of the people. *The Maid of Pskov* contains first-rate music throughout, marvellous choruses, a most fundamental folk-scene, but the opera is somewhat uniform, there are unsatisfactory recitatives and theatrical blunders. *Boris* is fervent, impassioned and theatrically effective, though it has some purely musical defects (is there a single perfect opera in the world even from the most conventional point of view?) Nonetheless these are three extremely remarkable works which can stand comparison triumphantly with any of the best western operas. This rapid and brilliant emergence of the New Russian Operatic School (it began to emerge in theory about eight years ago,[26] and to become reality only some four years ago), the ardently favourable disposition towards it of many artists and of the public (*The Stone Guest* at the hardest time in the season, in autumn, never brought in less than three quarters of

26 Cui traces the intellectual origins back to about 1865, and thus to near the start of his own critical activities.

full box-office takings, and *The Maid of Pskov* brought in seven full-house returns), its success and the interest which it aroused, gave rise to a profound hatred for it too on the part of many people, and the hatred primarily of the writing fraternity. And indeed how could they do other than hate it? A new trend emerges, unbeknown to them, in spite of them, without their support or advice, without their protection, seizes public attention, and these gentlemen, with all the organs of the press but one at their disposal, cannot stifle it, they remain in the rear with their obtuse, immovable concepts, one cannot tell them anything, there is no one for them to listen to. How could they not hate it? Young Russian composers rise to the surface who do not submit to their judgements but try to take their own independent path. How could they not push them into the water: 'wherever you make your way to, you will choke, and then it's straight to the bottom!' [Cui cites examples.] The representatives of the New Russian Operatic School are people with great gifts, their works are remarkable, one cannot counterpose to them a single talented composer of the old tendency or a single talented opera written in the old forms. Their most vicious and most talented enemy was Serov, and even he joined them in his final work (*The Power of the Fiend*, an opera which though shocking in many details of its realization belongs undoubtedly to the New Russian Operatic School in the tendency which it represents).

The new trend is reproached for its allegedly destructive aspirations. This reproach is entirely unfounded: the new trend does not destroy, but is trying to extend the sphere of music, to lay down new paths, to add new ideas, new forms, new sources of musical pleasure, to those already in existence. What did Dargomïzhsky destroy in *The Stone Guest* when he created inspired recitative which merges with Pushkin's text and elevates the meaning of the text? What did Serov destroy when he selected for *The Power of the Fiend* the most matchless, the exemplary subject? What did Korsakov destroy, he who is utterly devoted to musical beauty, when he created the best of existing folk scenes in his *veche*? What did Musorgsky destroy when he created the largest-scale comic scene in existence with the seething life and inimitable truth of his Inn scene? The old exists as before, but something new has been added to it. And if in the eyes of the public the old fades and moves aside into the background, is it the fault of the new trend that it is more intelligent, profound and truthful than the old? I console the writing fraternity with the fact that next year the Italians will have six subscription series, and in three years' time eight, and with this in mind the theatre administration has already embarked on dealings with the necessary party to have the weeks renamed from seven-day ones to eight-day ones.

With the production of the scenes from *Boris* one may consider the activities of the Russian opera for the 1872–3 season finished. Had not *The Maid of Pskov* and *Boris* been produced at the very end of it, there would have been no reason for mentioning it. [Cui laments the departure of key singers, chaotic administration and the neglect of Russian works. Used intelligently, the existing personnel supplemented by a few solo and some chorus singers could do much better, especially since the Russian repertory is already considerable and expanding.]

(e) G. A. Laroche: A new Russian opera. *The Voice*, 1874, no. 29. Laroche 3, pp. 134–6

When he attended the première of *Boris Godunov* on 27 January 1874 Laroche reverted to his basic view of Musorgsky's compositional activities, retreating from the more sympathetic response shown in Chapter 7, item (c).

Our Russian opera company has the peculiarity that its most gifted, sympathetic, musically educated and stage-conscious artists have voices which are either naturally small or have fallen victim to time. For composers devoting their skills to the Mariinsky Theatre it is more tempting to imagine *these* artists as their performers than to anticipate that their compositions will be performed albeit by strong voices, but unmusically and undramatically. Our composers are therefore placed in a special position with regard to the vocal part of their operas: they can count more readily on well characterized, bold, poetic and pathos-filled declamation than on the charms of broad cantilena whose sustained notes require the physical resources for a beautiful and powerful timbre (to say nothing of vocalises which are accessible to only a few people on the Russian stage). On the other hand the remarkable perfection of our national opera's orchestra stimulates composers to seek compensation in the sphere of instrumental richness and brilliance. In consequence we are seeing a tendency in musical drama which (as a result of circumstances similar to ours but much less sharply marked) was formed in Germany about twenty years ago – musical declamation on the stage, recitatives and choruses with a rich symphonic accompaniment.

Musorgsky, the composer of the opera *Boris Godunov* which we heard yesterday, is wholly committed to these aspirations in theory, but does not possess all the resources to carry them out in practice. While gifted with a talent for recitative and for characterization, he is a very feeble musician and is unable to accompany his melodies in the way that the great masters of writing for orchestra can do; the actual composition of his opera has an air of clumsiness and amateurishness, although it reveals a natural gift in powerful flashes. Musorgsky is, more than the other members of the group to which he belongs, a follower of Dargomïzhsky, and unmistakeable traces of *The Stone Guest* and Dargomïzhsky's last romances can be found in many places (especially comic ones) in his score; but by a strange combination of circumstances which proved stronger than the composer, in places of a massive or colossal character he often lapses into Serov: thus the chords with which the bells in the first scene (or the second scene according to the libretto)[27] begin recall the introduction to Act I of *Rogneda*; also, the songs of a fast, dance character which one encounters in *Boris* are reminiscent in the way they are treated of the songs in the second and third acts of *Rogneda* and the corresponding acts of *Vrazh'ya sila* ('The power of the fiend'). I hasten to add that the [folk] song element which plays such a large role generally in the new opera gave Musorgsky grounds for one of the most successful numbers in his composition, namely, for the song of the pilgrim Varlaam *Kak vo gorode bïlo vo Kazani* ('As happened in the city of Kazan'') which is varied (in couplet form), if not with new devices then with most effective ones without the crudely decorative writing for which Serov was often reproached, but which Musorgsky falls into almost more often and more deeply.

The national and historical interest of the subject, the fascination of Pushkin's poetry (the text of *Boris*, however, is retained only partially in the new libretto), a scenario constructed in a highly adroit and lively manner,[28] and the superb acting of our artists make more of a contribution to the work's success than the pen of the composer: the tavern scene and the scene of Boris's death made a strong impression for just these reasons, as did in part the scene by the fountain, in which, however, one was too aware of the absence of melodic plasticity; several other scenes, for instance that between the Jesuit and Marina, hold no appeal whatsoever, although as usually happens at first performances a small handful of enthusiasts went into noisy raptures every time the curtain was lowered.

The composer was called fairly often; a laurel wreath in silver and a great many flowers were presented to the artist whose benefit performance it was (Platonova).[29] [. . . In general the performance was remarkably fine. . . .] Maybe the choruses went very well, but the abundance of dissonances and the inexpert use of the voices in the new opera reach a point where we cannot always vouch for the composer's intentions and tell his wrong notes apart from the performers' wrong notes, of which there were perhaps none

27 The scene in the Chudov monastery was not performed because of a prohibition on the stage presentation of priests. Elsewhere, characters affected by the ban were described differently.
28 The scenario and libretto were the work of Musorgsky himself.
29 For Platonova, see Chapter 6, note 14.

at all; I make the same remark about the orchestra. The costumes, sets and the whole production in general were superlative.

(f) G. A. Laroche: *The Oprichnik*, opera in four acts. *The Voice*, 17 April 1874, no. 105, p. 1. Laroche 2, pp. 55–61

This opera based on Lazhechnikov's tragedy of the same name was composed between 1870 and 1872. It marked Tchaikovsky's first operatic success when first staged at the Mariinsky Theatre on 12 April 1874.

'Before sitting down to write an opera I try to forget that I am a musician', Gluck once said, and these words, which are such an apparently poor recommendation for his operas, appealed so much to Richard Wagner and his disciples that they inscribed them on their banner. Shortly before his death the late Serov, by the way, placed a special article in *Muzïkal'nïy sezon* ('The musical season') entitled 'Velikoye slovo velikogo muzïkanta' ('A great word from a great musician')[30] which is a commentary on the utterance of Gluck cited above and is at the same time directed against the so-called 'New Russian School' which, in Serov's opinion, has followed Gluck's example insufficiently. I think that the author of 'A great word' would have softened his anger at the Mighty Handful significantly had he managed to live to see the production of *Boris Godunov*: in the person of Mr Musorgsky Serov would have found a composer who not only carried out but even significantly exceeded Gluck's demand. The creator of *Alceste* and *Iphigénie* never dreamed to what limits obliviousness of music could be taken by an opera composer; he never dreamed that a hundred years after him a generation would arise which would be able to give his careless word a literal and savage meaning probably remote from his own intentions. It would be inexact to say that progress in our time is confined to *obliviousness* of music: obliviousness presupposes prior acquaintance, a prior storing in the memory. Meanwhile, in our days such gentlemen are starting to work in the field of musical drama as remind one of Napoleon I's dictum about the Bourbons: 'They have learned nothing and forgotten nothing.' It is these gentlemen who seem to have the strongest vocation for the job of banishing music from opera. Earlier on Wagnerism had at its disposal people with a sound knowledge of art but who went counter to its laws as a result of a preconceived intention; the matter is far simpler now: to the aid of the spirit of party and fanaticism comes ignorance, and this alliance has already gained such victories that not only composers but also the public itself have begun to forget about music.

30 The article was in fact entitled 'Velikoye slovo velikogo khudozhnika' ('A great word from a great artist'); it appeared in no. 5 for 1869.

Composers of opera have organized a contest among themselves: each one tries to outdo his colleagues in rejecting music; it is difficult to predict what scale this persecution will assume and when it will stop, but it is entirely probable that seeing on our lyric stage works pervaded by the spirit which has recently won supremacy lies in store for us. Mr Tchaikovsky's opera does not possess the character of this desperate progress. I do not know whether it will harm him or do him any good, but the composer of *The Oprichnik* has a wealth of musical ideas, musical taste and musical knowledge. The graceful, gifted and experienced hand familiar to us from his instrumental compositions is easily recognized in his opera as well; an abundance of first-rate melodies, frequently of a completely independent individual stamp, is combined with the unabated interest of the harmonic treatment and with brilliant orchestral colouring. These are the qualities which we should not have been able to enjoy in *The Oprichnik* had the composer been able to 'forget that he is a musician' prior to writing his score. The wealth of musical treasures in the new opera is so significant that it will in any event occupy an important position both among Mr Tchaikovsky's works and among specimens of Russian dramatic music. To this is added a remarkably happy choice of subject. Lazhechnikov's[31] drama is the most mature and the strongest of his works; it was written at the time when his talent was at the culminating point of its development; it is not only pictorial and effective but also full of inner life and genuine, ardent feeling at the same time. It has no psychological subtleties, which were in general alien to Lazhechnikov; the psychological motives in it are simple and elementary, and this makes it rewarding for musical reproduction in the highest degree. At the same time, it abounds in stage movement and pathos-laden situations. But transferring a literary drama, even one of the most musical spirit, to the lyric stage wholesale, stretching out its conversations into recitatives, arias and ensembles is an impossible business; a slippery and ticklish need to discard one thing, move something else and insert a third item. The results of this reshaping are familiar to those who have made a comparison of well-known classics of dramatic literature with the operatic libretti taken from them. Literary merit, in so far as it depends on subtlety of thought, beauty of language and verse, is always sacrificed to considerations of musical attributes, which one can scarcely complain about since music, once it has thrown off the philosophical and analytical element alien to it, rewards the listener with extensive development of the lyrical element and, besides, wins him over with the sensual charm of sound. But there is another aspect which operatic adaptation of dramas ought to

31 I. I. Lazhechnikov (1792–1869), a pioneer of the Russian historical novel, and author of three historical dramas in verse, including *The Oprichnik*.

respect – that is the logical construction of the action and the development of the plot. Everyone knows, however, that in reality this requirement is little observed: year in, year out the Italian stage witnesses strange, dramatic rhapsodies in which the spectators have long since lost the habit of looking for logical sense but which bear the titles of well-known plays by Shakespeare and Schiller, and which of course would greatly surprise both Schiller and Shakespeare if the poets had occasion to see them. There are exceptions, but they are rarities, and unfortunately the libretto of *The Oprichnik*[32] is not among them. [Laroche cites examples to justify his charge of 'lack of connections and causality' in the libretto.] On the other hand, one must do justice to the librettist for the fact that in the scene of the curse he has introduced a dramatic motive into the opera which is not in Lazhechnikov and which, although not new, is highly effective. The abundance of material from everyday life in Act I consists of songs transferred by the composer from his earlier opera *The Voyevoda*. I think that these songs were more appropriate in *The Voyevoda*, and that the time spent on them in the new opera would have been better devoted to a more thorough development of Andrey's character and to the motivation for his desperate action which is at the root of *The Oprichnik*'s drama.

Mr Tchaikovsky is an artist of the kind one must approach with the strictest and highest demands. Otherwise one could perhaps have said that the libretto of *The Oprichnik* is no worse than the libretti of the majority of Russian operas, and be reconciled to its faults as the consequences of a custom which has become ingrained among us. As a musical work *The Oprichnik* is a comforting flowering oasis after the desert of dramatic declamation in which Russian composers have allowed us to languish in recent years. One cannot fail to welcome the freedom with which Mr Tchaikovsky makes use of the words; one cannot fail to welcome his striving for ensembles, that most precious property of dramatic music, and for coherent melodic cantilena in which a character's personality or the mood of the moment is outlined; one cannot fail to admire the rich talent which our composer manifests in both arias and ensembles.

In places, however, this freedom goes too far. Appearing before the *oprichniki* to take the oath, Morozov says to Vyazminsky: 'Kak pered Bogom, tak pered toboyu dushi ne postïzhu grekhom obmana. Nevoleyu idu, no ta nevolya vo mne, kak dukh nechistïy, poselilas'' ('As before God, so before you I shall not sully my soul with the sin of deception. I do it against my will, but this necessity has come to reside within me like the Evil spirit') and so on. This is how a man speaks at a moment of supreme emotion, at a moment when a desperate resolve has just surged through

32 An *oprichnik*, is a member of the *oprichnina*, for which see note 4 above.

him, ready (as we see here and later on) to ebb away again just as quickly. Words like these ought to be pronounced in impetuous recitative; Mr Tchaikovsky has set them to a broad extended melody in a slow tempo of an amoroso character. One could also reproach the composer with repeated errors in word-setting; but I am not going to dwell on a subject with which present-day critics busy themselves so zealously that they can more readily be accused of paying it excessive than insufficient attention.

I have said so much about the dramatic mistakes in the new opera that it is a pleasure to indicate a moment of high drama in it: this is the scene of the oath, when Morozov joins the *oprichniki*. With the exception of the arioso just mentioned, which I consider inappropriate, this entire scene is excellently arranged: based on an original, compact, rhythmically robust motive, worked out splendidly, it makes a tremendous impact by means of the short exclamations of the chorus which interrupt Morozov's and Vyazminsky's speech. The motive I am speaking about is taken from the melody of the chorus of *oprichniki* with which the scene ends. 'Slaven, slaven, kak solntse v krasnïy den', nash otets i tsar', gospodin Rusi velikoy' ('Glorious, glorious, like the sun on a fine day, is our father the Tsar, Lord of Great Rus''). Besides this scene, the motive referred to often appears in the orchestral accompaniment of other parts of the opera – everywhere where the idea of the *oprichnina* arises.

As I have started to speak about thematic development, I shall point out here the first-rate ballet in the last act, the music of which is based on three Russian songs: 'Vinnïy nash kolodez'' ('Our well of wine'), 'Na Ivanushke chapan' ('Ivanushka's wearing a long kaftan'), and 'Katen'ka vesyolaya' ('Cheerful little Katya') (all three from Mr Balakirev's collection[33]). This music is remarkable for the beautiful treatment of the motives: the melody 'Cheerful little Katya' which appears unexpectedly and with great force is harmonized particularly well. The melody in A flat major which forms one of the sections of these dances is also extremely beautiful and is the composer's own work. But if in the ballet in *The Oprichnik* we can fully recognize the master of instrumental writing which we have grown used to considering Mr Tchaikovsky, then the same cannot be said of the overture or, as the composer called it, the introduction. This introduction made up mosaic-like from motley bits and pieces picked up from various parts of the opera has the lack of coherence of a potpourri which is incomprehensible and enigmatic even in its individual moments.

So as not to revert any more later to the folksongs of which the composer, following the example of his contemporaries, has made use for his opera, I shall indicate two series of variations written with love and great

33 They are nos. 5, 17 and 22 respectively in the collection.

artistry. The first of these series is the song 'Solovushko v dubravushke' ('The nightingale in the leafy grove') which Natal'ya sings (four couplets, each with a new accompaniment); unfortunately, the composer has found it necessary to add to the original melody of this song an ending of his own invention (eight bars in the first couplet at the words 'Skuchno, skuchno mne, devitse, v teremochke; uteshay menya, solovushko, v kruchine' ('It's tedious, tedious for me, a girl, in this tower; console me, nightingale, in my woe'). This ending is of a sentimental character and not in the spirit of a folk melody. The same reproach cannot be levelled at the splendid variations which bring Act I to an end. The song 'Za dvorom luzhok' ('There is a little meadow beyond the courtyard') served as the theme; it is performed in unison by a combined chorus of sopranos and altos who repeat it six times against a changing accompaniment.

The most striking melodies in the opera, of course, are not those which the author has taken from folksongs and which of necessity serve only as illustrations of the character of everyday things, but those which were composed by himself and which are invested with a dramatic character. Among these is Natal'ya's short arioso (G flat major) in Act I. In spite of its very insignificant size, it is an exceptionally noble and effective number, which won all hearts last year when it was performed more than once at concerts. Also among them is Morozova's phrase 'Snega beley, solntsa svetley' ('Whiter than snow, brighter than the sun') as well as Morozov's phrase following it 'Matushka rodnaya, smoyu krovavuyu obidu' ('My dear mother, I shall wash away a bloody offence') in their duet. I shall point too to the graceful orchestral motive (D minor) which in Act III accompanies Natal'ya's words as she asks her cruel father 'Kaznit' eyo, no vïslushat' snachala' ('to execute her, but to hear her out first'), and also to the lyrical phrase which the composer has put on her lips after that ('Ne ya ego, sam Bog soyedinil' ('It was not I who joined him, but God himself')). Natal'ya's phrase 'Net, to ne son; rodnaya mat' rodnogo sïna proklinayet' ('No, it is not a dream; a mother is cursing her own son') in the big finale ensemble of Act III is conspicuous for its deeply felt grief and heartfelt pain, expressed not without originality. One must also note that the impact of this phrase is skilfully prepared by the extended and exceptionally rich pedal on a bass D (thirty-two bars); with regard to harmony this pedal is one of the most remarkable details in the new score. Later on, in the last act, the duet between Andrey and Natal'ya stands out particularly for the beauty of its melody (the phrase in $\frac{3}{4}$, A flat major: 'Akh! skorey bï konets pirovan'yu' ('Ah, let there quickly be an end of the feasting') and the phrase in $\frac{4}{4}$, D flat major: 'Tï mne zhizn' i svet' ('You are life and the world to me'), and also, in the quartet with chorus which follows this number, Vyazminsky's phrase

'Groza idyot iz tuchi' ('A thunder-storm comes from a cloud'). Speaking generally, the composer's constant concern for the vocal part of the opera and his gift, rare in our day and age, for melody, have the consequence that *The Oprichnik* sets the voice and skill of each singer tasks which are far more rewarding than any [other] Russian opera of recent times. If one adds to this the nobility of the harmonic style which is excellent and free, the often bold part-writing, the purely Russian art of finding chromatic harmonies in a diatonic melody, the rich pedals which the composer, however, uses too often, the ability to create rounded scenes and combine them into large musical wholes, and finally the inexhaustibly rich, euphonious and elegant instrumentation, then in the result we obtain a score which while possessing many of the virtues of our present-day operatic music is free of the greater part of its defects. This important musical significance must not close the eyes of either the critic or the composer himself to the theatrical shortcomings of the new opera. The friends of Mr Tchaikovsky's talent can gratify themselves with the hope that when he takes a stricter attitude to the dramatic plan of an opera, he will come to hold the same high position on the Russian lyrical stage as he already holds now on the platform for symphonic concerts.

(g) G. A. Laroche: Tchaikovsky's *Eugene Onegin* in the Conservatoire's production. *Moscow Bulletin*, 22 March 1879, no. 72. Laroche 2, pp. 106–9

The performance took place on 17 March 1879 in the Maly Theatre.

Composing an opera on a subject by Pushkin – what an inviting idea, what a temptation that is for a Russian musician. It ensnared Glinka, that Pushkin of music, and Dargomïzhsky, Pushkin's polar opposite as a composer, alike. To this idea we are indebted for the unfading beauties of *Ruslan* and the clever experiments of *The Stone Guest*, to say nothing of a number of more or less successful ventures by second-rate talents. The sound of our poetic genius's verses contains such pure, clear harmony that even the ear of the most ordinary reader yields to its charm; how much more naturally does it enflame a composer's fantasy. But in this temptation there lurks a considerable peril. The more the poet's work has become the meat and drink of the reading public, the more his verses are known by heart, the more difficult it becomes for the public to be reconciled to the unaccustomed operatic garb in which it encounters its precious subject-matter. The accent in a recitative, the orchestra's surges, the costumes' motley hues, the gas lighting – all these things represent the intrusion of a new, inimical element into what had been a sacred object of long standing. Such were the provisos surrounding the composer of *Eugene Onegin*; such were the unavoidable difficulties which he was summoned to overcome. The other perhaps even sadder difficulty is the need to lump together with verses whose irreproachable beauty has made them eternally classical verses of the ordinary librettist's kind – verses which might pass muster in other company but cannot do so alongside the jewels of Pushkin's art. To these embarrassments our gifted composer has added a further one on his own initiative. He has introduced a fundamental alteration to Pushkin in the last scene of his opera; he has made Tatyana show a weakness in her meeting with Onegin for which we would look in vain in the original poem. Unshakeable in the strict fulfilment of her duty but tormented deep down by a gnawing passion, Tatyana in the last chapter of Pushkin's *Onegin* is a truly tragic figure whose noble purity does not deprive her of a touching element of tenderness. Perhaps the composer thought that the latter element would be stronger if he lowered Tatyana a little from the pedestal on which we are used to seeing her and made her practically disprove her famous line 'I am pledged to another and will be true to him forever' by five minutes of kisses and embraces. Maybe this radical change brings greater operatic effectiveness; but Tatyana's character as created by the poet and reverently preserved by the composer throughout the opera until this scene is destroyed and replaced by another one.[34]

In my opinion, those are the not insignificant aesthetic objections which can be raised to the new opera. To a certain degree one detects in it an act of violence against the poetic work, and it takes all the talent and all the inspiration of P. I. Tchaikovsky to reconcile us to this act of violence or, rather, to make us forget it. As often happens in the chronicles of art, practical success does not bear out the theoretical assumptions, and the contradictions inherent in the nature of the task and caused by the personal interference of the librettist have not prevented the composer from writing an opera which is one of the most outstanding scores ever to have come from his pen. In few previous works has P. I. Tchaikovsky been to such an extent himself as in *Eugene Onegin*. The distinctive combination of a purely Russian landowner environment with the negative Byronic atmosphere which forms the aroma of Pushkin's poem, is just the material, it seems, which Mr Tchaikovsky's inspiration was searching for, waiting for. A rich stream of melody spouts from every page of the score; superlative cantilenas (especially for Tatyana, Lensky and Gremin) make us forget that we are living in the final third of the nineteenth century when, the general verdict has it, the vein of melody has run completely dry. Every aspect of the style is pervaded by unity and distinctiveness; but Mr Tchaikovsky's originality is not that sharply-angled originality which puzzles one more than it enchants

34 The composer subsequently regretted this change and removed it.

and which appeals to the listener's curiosity rather than his feeling. A kind of special autumnal softness, a special evening light evoking an elegiac mood, spreads over the whole work, but without impeding the plastic character-ization of individual roles and moments. The air of humour and unfeigned cheerfulness derives from the old-fashioned dances of a provincial ball; the severe romance sung in the opening scene subtly parodies the manner of Genishta or Gurilyov of blessed memory without ceasing to be excellent music. Of the individual characters the most successful in my opinion are – until the last scene – Tatyana (especially as she appears in the letter scene) and Lensky; Onegin is rather less significant, but in his case the task of portraying him was essentially antimusical. The atmosphere created by Gremin in his aria in the penultimate scene is not peculiar to him per-sonally, and cannot be described as his characterization; there is nothing more general than an outpouring of love, but the aria itself belongs among the pearls of Mr Tchaikovsky's entire score. The ensembles are fine musically, especially the two quartets in the action; I cannot say, however, that they changed the notion which I formed a long time ago of Mr Tchaikovsky's particular forte. Not only in *Onegin* but also in *The Oprichnik*, *Vakula the Smith*[35] and even in *The Voyevoda*[36] there are fine musical numbers, but the highlights of the score have always been lyrical in character, not dramatic, and in the present opera the most dramatic moment in the action is, I think, the weakest musically. I have in mind the great noise made by the guests on seeing the quarrel between Onegin and Lensky at the ball. It is one of those moments when the fantasy of the Mozarts and Meyerbeers feels a new surge of power, a new freedom, but where the fantasy of the Schumanns and Tchaikovskys, on the other hand, declines and grows poorer. One must observe that the subject of *Onegin* makes few such demands, and that in the work as a whole that *chiaroscuro* of elegiac sorrow and day-dreaming which Mr Tchaikovsky knows how to convey so elegantly and nobly is pre-dominant. The crowning glory of the opera in this respect, I think, is Tatyana's long letter scene. It is hard to imagine a more chaste gracefulness, a more winning sincerity; the beauty of the musical conception never for a moment infringes poetic truth, and service to the truth never for a moment fetters the free flight of musical inspiration.

The public's sympathies, which were altogether very warm and unani-mous, were shared between the composer, who was favoured with many curtain-calls, and the performers. At times it was possible to forget that these were conservatoire students and to accept the singers and the

---

35 *Vakula the Smith* was composed in 1874, staged in 1876, revised in 1885 and staged as *Cherevichki* ('Les caprices d'Oksane') in 1887.
36 For *The Voyevoda*, see Chapter 5, item (d).

orchestra as fully-formed artists. Worthy of special praise is the ensemble as a whole, that concerted animation and often amazing precision with which the young performers sang and played. It goes without saying that the strong hand of Mr Nikolay Rubinstein made itself felt in the conducting at every turn. [Laroche considers the singers, the designs and the production.]

(h) Cui: Notes on music – *Eugene Onegin*. Week, 4 November 1884, no. 45, cols. 1539–44

Cui saw a performance of the first Mariinsky production of the opera, the run beginning on 19 October 1884. Since its première, described in item (g) above, the opera had been staged in Moscow at the Bol'shoy, in St Petersburg by amateur forces, in Khar'kov, Odessa and Kiev before it reached the country's premier house. Perhaps the work's rapid progress had something to do with provoking Cui's querulousness, but one would have to observe that this is not a unique example of it in his later writings.

No Russian poet has inspired out composers so often as Pushkin. His short poems have served as texts for innumerable romances, and his large-scale works as the subjects for operas, beginning with Glinka. These works are evidence for what I have said: *Ruslan and Lyudmila*, *Rusalka*, *Torzhestvo Vakkha* ('The triumph of Bacchus'),[37] *The Stone Guest*, *Kavkazskiy plennik* ('The prisoner of the Caucasus'),[38] *Boris Godunov*, three *Mazepas* (by Messrs Shel',[39] Tchaikovsky and Davïdov;[40] the composer abandoned the last opera unfinished), *Eugene Onegin*, *Graf Nulin* ('Count Nulin'), *Tsïgane* ('The gipsies') (both operas by Mr Lishin)[41] and also, unless I am mistaken, *Domik v Kolomne* ('The little house at Kolomna') (by Mr Solov'yov).[42] In total, eleven operas. These remain untouched: *Bakhchisarayskiy fontan* ('The fountain of Bakhchisaray'), *Andzhelo* ('Angelo') (actually on a subject of Shakespeare's),[43] *Pir vo vremya chumï* ('A feast in time of plague'),[44] the

---

37 *The Triumph of Bacchus* is by Dargomïzhsky.
38 *The Prisoner of the Caucasus* was set by Cui himself in 1857–8 and 1881–2 and staged in 1883.
39 For Baron Fitingof-Shel', see Chapter 2, note 43.
40 This composer was K. Yu. Davïdov (1838–89), better known as an outstanding cellist. He began *Mazepa* in 1875, but broke off work in 1876 and sent the libretto to Tchaikovsky in 1881.
41 G. A. Lishin (1854–88), composer, pianist, music and theatre critic. He was best known for the composition of romances and melodeclamations.
42 N. F. Solov'yov (1846–1916) was a composer, music critic and teacher. He contributed to the completion of *The Power of the Fiend* after Serov's death.
43 Cui's *Andzhelo*, staged in 1876, is based on a play by Victor Hugo.
44 Cui composed 'dramatic scenes' in one act on this subject in 1895–7, and they were staged in 1901.

Stories of Belkin, especially *Kapitanskaya dochka* ('The captain's daughter')[45] with its magnificent scenes from the Pugachov revolt.

The reason for Pushkin's popularity among our composers lies not only in the quality of his genius but also in the forms in which this genius manifested itself: in the unfailing clarity and precision of his ideas, in the remarkable conciseness of his expression (particularly important for music, which always prolongs the spoken word) and lastly in the relaxed lightness and music of his peerless verse.

Of the works of Pushkin mentioned, the least suitable for opera is *Eugene Onegin*. It has no plot (*fabula*), no developing action, no stage movement, and the personality of the hero – coldly rational and sceptically indifferent – is completely unmusical. But *Onegin* contains so many charming lines, the images of Lensky and Tatyana are so congenial, that one must on no account reprove Mr Tchaikovsky for wishing to embody some scenes from Pushkin's novel in music, the more so as Mr Tchaikovsky has called his work not an opera but 'lyrical scenes'. The trouble is that with Mr Tchaikovsky the word has parted company here completely from the deed: he has called his *Onegin* 'lyrical scenes' and made every effort to make a formal opera out of it. Otherwise, why did he need the chorus of peasant-women in Act I? Why the formal finale of Act II with its formal two-part catastrophe (Andante and Allegro) and its formal arrangement of the characters in order of size along the footlights? Why were two balls needed, the second of which (as a repetition of the first) is not of the slightest interest (in Pushkin the two balls are outlined, but these are not 'lyrical scenes' – they are *operatic ballets*)? Why, finally, was the last scene necessary, where Onegin lays siege to Tatyana so energetically and her husband finds them almost *en flagrant délit*, a scene tasteless in itself and disgraceful in relation to Pushkin's work (in the stage production the husband's appearance is fortunately left out, but Mr Tchaikovsky meant it to happen because it is marked in the published vocal score of *Onegin* and, moreover, Tatyana's exit without Gremin appearing entirely fails to correspond with the final words of Tatyana, 'ya umirayu' ('I'm dying') and of Onegin, 'tï moya' ('you are mine'))? Surely all this was necessary so that, concealed behind the term 'lyrical scenes', charming maybe, but impracticable in the theatre, an opera could be written which was on an essentially impossible subject, but one taken from a work by Pushkin equal in popularity to Lermontov's *Demon*.[46]

Moving on to individual lines of the 'lyrical scenes', it is incomprehensible what sort of lyricism Mr Tchaikovsky found in such lines as 'glupoy lune na glupom nebosklone' ('to the foolish moon on the foolish horizon'),

45 Cui plugged this gap too with an opera composed in 1907–9 and staged in 1911.
46 See note 34 above.

or 'dyade samïkh chestnïkh pravil' ('to an uncle of the most upright rules')
etc. for their musical incarnation. One may indeed surmise that for future
'lyrical scenes' Mr Tchaikovsky will choose *Gore ot uma* ('Woe from wit')[47]
where Skalozub will sing an aria about 'distantsiya ogromnogo razmera' ('a
distance of enormous proportions').

All this demonstrates that Mr Tchaikovsky is far from being a refined
artist, that his taste is undiscriminating, and that he is unable to adopt a
critical attitude towards his task; and this in turn provides a natural explanation as to why his works are far beneath his talent, why such a gifted
composer has written so little that is good and so much that is weak,
especially in vocal music, for which he shows far less aptitude than for
symphonic music.

The principal and most characteristic feature of the music of *Onegin* lies
in its *melancholy uniformity*. This melancholy uniformity constitutes the
main essence of Mr Tchaikovsky's talent in which there is neither strength
nor breadth, neither wide span nor depth, neither cheerfulness nor dramatic
power: a mere quiet sorrow prevails, sentimentality and weak-nerved
tearfulness – very genuine, and sympathetic, but very uniform. Given a
talent of this character, Mr Tchaikovsky ought to have fought against this
tendency, chosen subjects which are brighter, not allowed himself more
than two pages of score in the minor out of every ten, and so on. But Mr
Tchaikovsky does not fight, he follows his bent without opposition, and
imposes hours of depression and boredom on his listeners. There are people
who are constantly bemoaning their fate and recounting their illnesses with
special enthusiasm. In his music Mr Tchaikovsky also bemoans his fate and
recounts his illnesses.

Furthermore, the uniform melancholy of the music of *Eugene Onegin*
gains particular intensity from the following causes also. It is *entirely* made
up of short phrases. Here is a strange thing: Mr Tchaikovsky is very often a
melodist in his symphonic and chamber music, i.e. where it is not so important, and ceases to be a melodist in operatic music and even in lyrical
scenes, where it is absolutely essential. In symphonic music short phrases
may serve as excellent themes in consequence of the large-scale polyphonic
working allowed there (e.g. the *Coriolan* overture, the first movement of
Beethoven's Fifth Symphony); in operatic music, on the other hand, which
permits polyphonic working only exceptionally, short phrases of melodic
recitative are essential for scenes which are dramatic; but for scenes which
are lyrical, with an unchanging mood, more extended cantilenas are essential. Among the short phrases which make up the music of *Onegin*, there
are some which are warm, beautiful, and sympathetic, but the majority of

47 A comedy written by A. S. Griboyedov (1795–1829).

them are utterly paltry, consisting of a few notes of the diatonic scale, and Mr Tchaikovsky tries in vain to hide their poverty by orchestral decoration, sequences, imitations and modulations which are on occasion even unnatural ones (Lensky's aria). These unchanging short phrases endow *Onegin* with an especial uniformity of form, which intensifies the uniformity of idea yet further.

There are many recitatives in *Onegin*. But they are not the recitatives of Dargomïzhsky or Musorgsky which reinforce the meaning of the most important phrases of the text and give them special power and expressiveness; they are not even Italian recitatives which serve as a framework for the opera's individual numbers and lend particular prominence to them; they are the same ariosos, with perfectly worthless phrases, thickly accompanied, with the text obscured and squeezed in, designed merely to heighten the cheerless uniformity of *Onegin*'s music.

In *Onegin* the *dramatis personae* have only two collective characteristics: the first serves for Larina and the nurse Filipp'yevna and comprises phrases with a folk colouring and a good-naturedly comic tint; the second serves for Tatyana, Onegin, Lensky and Prince Gremin and consists of continuous melancholy whining. Shuffle the music of these four characters as you will – exchanging Tatyana's for Gremin's, or Onegin's with Lensky's – and the degree of expressiveness and truth in Mr Tchaikovsky's opera will not be altered one bit. This lack of descriptiveness in the characters or, to be more accurate, its uniformity, renders the melancholy of *Onegin*'s music ultimately overwhelming. True, Mr Tchaikovsky has endeavoured to give Ol'ga gaiety and gracefulness, but as she has a certain part to play only in one scene, and that a brief one, she introduces a scarcely perceptible element of variety into the opera.

Moving from the general to the particular, I must chiefly point out the more or less successful musical phrases scattered through the opera.

As early as the very first bar of the introduction, the sobs begin which continue right to the end of the introduction, entirely based on a four-note phrase serving as the main element descriptive of Tatyana. The sobs go on further in the form of the two-part romance sung by the gentry ladies offstage. But this romance is not devoid of descriptiveness and represents a successful imitation of the romances of the pre-Glinka era. In the course of the second couplet Larina converses with the nurse. This is a very lifelike device. It would have come out superbly in the hands of Glinka (Susanin with Vanya and the Poles) or Musorgsky (the inn-keeper and the Pretender and Varlaam's 'Kak edet yon'). In the hands of Mr Tchaikovsky nothing has come of it; it has only rendered the romance completely unintelligible. The chorus of peasants, which vividly recalls the choruses in Act I of *Rusalka*, is not bad. In the following scenes, until the guests arrive, one encounters pretty little phrases in the parts of Ol'ga and Tatyana but primarily in the orchestra. Lensky's arrival with Onegin is preceded by a long, substantial and purely melodramatic crescendo – up to the diminished seventh inclusive, leading up to Larina's phrase 'prosi skorey' ('ask them quickly')(!). A melodramatic manner can in general be sensed in many places in Mr Tchaikovsky's 'lyrical scenes', especially in the orchestral preludes and entr'actes. Listening to these conventional horrors in sound, one might expect a bearded evildoer covered in blood to burst on to the stage brandishing a cardboard sword, but instead of him beardless heroes in tail-coats and frock-coats enter calmly, bringing with them a comical disappointment as a result of the failure to match the music to the situation on the stage. Later on, in the remaining scenes of Scene 1 of Act I, pretty little phrases with a strong smell of Gounod's *Faust* occur again; Lensky's arioso belongs among the finest pages of *Onegin*; it has sincerity, warmth and beauty, but in spite of all that this scene as a whole makes no impression whatsoever: it is all just as shallow, uniform, ungrateful vocally and untheatrical as would be, for instance, the gradual departure of all the characters from the stage.

In the second scene of Act I, which is almost entirely taken up by the Letter scene, one should take note of: the nurse's narrative with folk colouring, which is not bad; Tatyana's phrases 'akh nyanya, nyanya, ya stradayu' ('ah, nurse, nurse, I'm suffering') and 'tï v snovideniyakh' ('you, in your dreams') – both beautiful and not without passion and animation; the dawn (Gounod again) and Tatyana's conversation with her nurse at the end of the scene are beautifully handled. But these successful études afford the listener just momentary revival and do little to redeem the uniformity, emptiness (the orchestra's beautiful beating of the air while Tatyana is writing) and in places even the vulgarity ('puskay pogibnu' ('may I perish')) of the remainder, which is too protracted and wearisome.

The third scene of Act I – Onegin's reply to Tatyana – is of no musical significance, but it is beautifully edged around by the twice-repeated and very sweet little women's chorus.

Act II opens with a waltz, a successful imitation of the waltz in *Faust* (the first, main theme is a straight borrowing); there follow Triquet's French couplets, for which Mr Tchaikovsky has made use of the music of an ancient French song. The waltz is treated skilfully and written lightly, but it has little musical significance, whereas Triquet's couplets have none, except as a good evocation of the period; but the major key in these two numbers, the precision and clarity of their forms, combined with the superlative decorative and stage setting, have such a refreshing effect that the public awakens from its lethargic torpor and demands that the couplets be repeated. I shall make a short digression here. Triquet according to Mr Tchaikovsky pronounces the word *mademoiselle* on three notes, that is, five syllables are converted into three, and in the words *sourire* and *étoile* three syllables are converted into two. Earlier, Lensky had pronounced *mesdames* on two notes. One could reconcile oneself to the last example: Lensky might not know French very well (although in that case it would have been better to write *medam* in Russian). But for the Frenchman Triquet to make such gross errors in his native language is just too odd. One might say that this is a trifle not worth dwelling on. It is indeed a trifle, but a characteristic one, indicative of Mr Tchaikovsky's offhand attitude to his work and also explaining why (among other causes) this talented composer has written so few good works. The mazurka which follows Triquet's couplets is far weaker than the waltz. The Andante of the finale is a rather nice little romance, but one which cannot serve as the theme for a big ensemble in any circumstances. The Allegro of the finale is conventional and trite. But this scene is nonetheless the most vibrant in the whole opera.

In the second scene of this act Lensky's aria is far weaker than his arioso. But its sincerity cannot be denied, any more than that of all the music in *Onegin*. But sincerity on its own is not enough – good music is essential. And one cannot acknowledge the doleful diatonic moaning on a descending scale of which this aria consists almost exclusively as good music. Only in the middle ('*blesnyot zautra luch dennitsi*' ('on the morrow dawn's ray will shine')) and at the end do some refreshing short phrases occur. The duel scene creates a comical impression thanks to the unbearably stupid position in which Mr Tchaikovsky has placed his heroes. They stand at opposite ends of the stage and sing turn about, in canon, of themselves: 'vragi! davno-li drug ot druga' ('enemies! was it long ago that [thirst for blood put us apart] from one another'). At the end the question is asked 'ne razoytis' li polyubovno' ('shall we not part amicably'), and they answer in concert 'net! net! net! net!' ('no! no! no! no!'). In a little operetta this scene, if performed in a rather caricatured fashion, would provoke an irrepressible guffaw and be a huge success. The music is not bad at all, but even it is powerless to save this scene which is false to its very roots.

Act III opens with a polonaise at the ball, which, after the waltz in the previous ball just seen, produces only tedium. Tatyana's arrival is accompanied by very sweet, elegant music, Gremin's aria is banal – it is clear and well-defined at the beginning and the end but insufficiently shaped in its central section. Onegin's arioso is one of Mr Tchaikovsky's clichés, and one of the feeble ones. The beginning of the finale's duet (second scene) is not bad, but thereafter phrase repetitions, imitations, sequences, triplets, scales and other contrivances intended to conceal the poverty or vulgarity of the composer's ideas make their appearance and continue without interruption to the very end of the opera. This duet is also excessively long, like the Letter scene.

One must add to this that *Onegin* is written in a way which is ungrateful to the voices: they have no scope, no freedom, and frequently the chief musical interest (such as it is) is in the orchestra, not the singers' parts; that the declamation in *Onegin* is feeble and phrases are perpetually being interrupted by long inappropriate pauses which the orchestra makes vain attempts to cover up with its imitations; that tiresome three-bar phrasing predominates throughout the entire opera, and that the whole opera contains not a single musically outstanding moment, apart from the waltz and Triquet's couplets. The whole thing is uniformly facile, grey and melancholy (with what inimitable perfection Mr Tchaikovsky could depict St Petersburg's autumn weather!).

It follows from all that has been said that *Eugene Onegin* contributes nothing to our art. Its *music* has not a single new word to say; it all revolves around a narrow range of rather thin ideas which everyone knows, of short ideas repeated many times, though expressed euphoniously and perfectly decently. But as an *opera*, *Eugene Onegin* is still-born, unreservedly bankrupt and weak.

The opera is orchestrated superlatively.

[Cui next considers the singers.]

At the second performance, which I attended, the success was very moderate. The public apparently liked only the Letter scene, thanks to Mrs Pavlovskaya's[48] superlative performance, and the first ball scene, thanks to the 'Faustian' waltz and Triquet's couplets. It was only after these two scenes and, of course, after the end of the opera, that the composer was called out. It is also most curious that, out of Mr Tchaikovsky's entire opera, the only number to be repeated was the one whose music was not by Mr Tchaikovsky.

48 K. Pavlovskaya (1853–1935) was a lyric-dramatic soprano. She first appeared on the operatic stage in 1876, singing mainly at the Bol'shoy Theatre with an interlude (1884–88) at the Mariinsky.

CHAPTER EIGHT

The 1870s, opera apart

By the 1870s instrumental compositions of quality were emerging in a steady flow from the music-rooms of several composers. Symphonies written in this decade include the second, third and fourth of Tchaikovsky, Rimsky-Korsakov's third and Borodin's second. Tchaikovsky wrote his concertos for piano and violin, both first performed abroad (in Boston and Vienna respectively). Borodin heard his First String Quartet (and the Polovtsian Dances) performed for the first time. Musorgsky wrote *Pictures from an Exhibition* and added to his earlier songs *The Nursery* cycle, the *Songs and Dances of Death*, and the *Sunless* cycle. It has been impossible to find worthwhile contemporary responses to works which are now among his best known – such as the *Songs and Dances* and *Pictures* – so novel was his approach to music and so unsystematic his attitude towards arranging public performances. Tchaikovsky, on the other hand, had retrieved Russian ballet music from specialist composers of little flair, inaugurating with *Swan Lake* a line which led via the scores of Glazunov to the elevation of ballet to a far higher place in the hierarchy of the arts through the work of Diaghilev.

(a) G. A. Laroche: A new Russian symphony. *Moscow Bulletin*, 7 February 1873, no. 33, p. 3. Laroche 2, pp. 34–8

I cannot refrain from sharing my impressions with the reader after attending the recent concert given by the Russian Musical Society in Moscow on 26 January. The concert concluded with a performance of Pyotr Tchaikovsky's recently completed symphony[1], the second symphony by this master. I should like to say a few words about this event in Russian musical life, which to my mind has eclipsed all others in a long time.

We Russians do not possess a great wealth of instrumental music. Head and shoulders above everything else towers one solitary piece, Glinka's *Jota aragonesa*; the remaining orchestral pieces by this immortal composer are greatly inferior to it either in the strength of the composer's conception or

---

1 The symphony was composed during 1872. Laroche, of course, discusses its first version, whereas today we are more familiar with the revised version produced in 1879–80.

in the artistic skill with which it is realized. As far as works by other composers are concerned, even, for example, Dargomïzhsky's witty orchestral jokes,[2] they should not be taken on a par with Glinka's work. This then is the situation as far as the orchestra is concerned; we are even worse off for piano music, and chamber music is still very much in its infancy. (The whole tone of this somewhat negative appraisal would be completely different were I to consider the work of that genius Anton Rubinstein. But on account both of his artistic education and of many aspects of his work as a composer, the creator of the *Ocean* symphony belongs not so much to Russia as to Europe as a whole, and to Germany in particular.[3]) A situation such as this in the artistic world has a profound effect both on the public and on music criticism, and leads to a greater indulgence when evaluating new works. This indulgence is, for the most part, completely unconscious: we ourselves are not aware how little we demand of a Russian composer, and he in turn knows even less about what is asked of him; otherwise the applause and the praise of the press would be not so much a triumph of self-esteem as a source of the most exquisite suffering. But the symphony to which I listened on 26 January does not need the same lenient consideration. Indeed the most stringent yardstick can and in fact ought to be used to assess this work. It is a composition of European eminence, and I would add that this work is far removed from all the earlier compositional efforts of Mr Tchaikovsky, including the overture *Romeo and Juliet*.[4] A great many people are talking about this overture at the present time, especially in St Petersburg, and I willingly recognize that it contains pleasant melodic ideas, nobility in the harmonies, remarkably skilled instrumentation and poetic charm in many details. However, if we use again the same stringent European yardstick, we cannot fail to conclude that the resounding success of the music is due precisely to these details, and that it enchanted the audience and experts alike with the inspiration which bursts through in places. But these inspired parts prevented the majority of people from seeing the overture as a complete concept, a concept in which in my opinion there was a distinct lack of organic unity. This lack of wholeness, this method of composing big musical works from heterogeneous parts not in harmony with each other has until recently constituted the most serious and profound ailment in Mr Tchaikovsky's music. It appears that he was able to cope with all other technical difficulties, but mastery of form persistently eluded him. Mr Tchaikovsky seemingly recognized this shortcoming in

2 These are *Baba-yaga (S Volgi nach Riga)* ('Baba-yaga (From the Volga nach Riga)'), composed in 1862, *Kazachok*, completed in 1864, and the Finnish Fantasia, composed between 1863 and 1867.
3 Cf. Cui's comment in Chapter 6, note 5.
4 For further discussion of this work, see item (b) below.

himself and took active steps to combat it: at any rate one of his latest compositions – the [First] String Quartet – represents a significant advance in this particular respect.

I see Mr Tchaikovsky's Second Symphony as a new and indeed gigantic step forward. It is a long time since I encountered a work with so powerful a thematic development of ideas, such well motivated and artistically considered contrasts. I was struck by these very qualities in the first Allegro, with its pathetic and sorrowful character. In this Allegro three basic ideas – the main and secondary sections of the Allegro itself and the theme borrowed from the slow introduction – are grouped together, alternate, combine by means of counterpoint – firstly two ideas and finally all three ideas together – with a freedom and nobility, with perpetual harmony and with an inspired brimfulness of life such as show that the artist has reached a level of art rare in our day and age. Were I not afraid to take a sacred name in vain, I would say that in the strength and elegance with which Mr Tchaikovsky plays with his themes and makes them serve his own purposes there is something reminiscent of Mozart, something which brings to mind the Symphony in B flat minor[5] or the big Symphony in C major [K551, the 'Jupiter'] by the greatest of composers. Naturally, my comparison holds only for the mastery of counterpoint, a field in which Mozart shone. As far as content is concerned, there cannot fail to be a gulf between the harmonious reconciliation and the ideal objectivity which emanate from every page of Mozart, and the wretched disillusionment of the nineteenth century, an expression of which we find in Mr Tchaikovsky's Allegro, among other places. But in the works of our gifted compatriot disillusionment does not turn into antipathetic morbidity; for this he has a too sensitive and keen sympathy with the wholesome and majestic simplicity of our folksong.

Tchaikovsky has turned to Russian songs in many of his compositions, working on and varying them with a skilled touch. The Scherzo à la russe for piano,[6] the Andante of his String Quartet,[7] and many numbers from the opera *The Voyevoda*[8] contain good evidence not only of Mr Tchaikovsky's subtle and refined understanding of the spirit of these songs, but also of his talent for variation form. Both these qualities can be observed in the new symphony, but in a much higher state of evolution. The introduction to the symphony is based on a beautiful, peaceful and flowing melody in the style[9]

---

5 This is perhaps the G minor Symphony, no. 40.
6 The Scherzo à la russe for piano, op. 1 no. 1, of 1867.
7 The Andante of his string quartet: the slow movement of the composer's First String Quartet, op. 11.
8 For *The Voyevoda*, see Chapter 5, item (d).
9 The melody is not merely 'in the style of a folksong' but a Ukrainian variant of the Russian folksong 'Vniz po matushke po Volge' ('Down along mother Volga').

of our drawn-out (*protyazhnïye*) folksongs. The composer has borrowed a folksong directly[10] for the theme of the finale, this time one of an animated and lively nature. The theme of the introduction is developed by the composer in a series of magnificent variations, some of which are simply startling in the beauty of their orchestration; but far more remarkable and developed are the themes of the finale. As I have already pointed out, it leaves one with an impression of gaiety and even joviality. What is more, with its dance-like rhythm the theme belongs to the same category as *Kamarinskaya* and even the main themes of the finales of Beethoven's Seventh and Eighth Symphonies. The first phases of Mr Tchaikovsky's development of the theme do not destroy its light and unruly character, but in the middle section of the finale the theme suddenly takes on a new and grand meaning. Repeated in various keys in the upper registers of the string instruments, the theme is accompanied here by powerful exclamations from trumpets and trombones in alternation, coming in with long dissonances. No description could adequately convey the harmonic beauty and stupendous tragedy of this section. At this point it is not so much the skilled and unexpected harmonic combination, which in any case is remarkable, but rather the very contrast between the tragic strength and the carefree joy of the first pages of the finale which has such an effect on the listener. Thus sometimes in life brief Bacchic rejoicing gives way to the blows of a menacing, inexorable fate . . .

Despite the outstanding beauties of the remaining movements of the symphony, in my opinion the bold and stately finale decidedly outshines them all. This point is of particular interest since, in the majority of symphonies, the richest content is concentrated in the first movement (of course there are notable exceptions to this, such as Beethoven's Fifth and Eighth Symphonies and Mozart's big Symphony in C major), and the finale is weaker; thus, as a result, the progression normally considered necessary for artistic works is not present. The absence of this progression can be observed in highly celebrated compositions which are regarded, and rightly so, as models. This can be explained by the fact that we treat movements of symphonies as separate entities. It might also, perhaps, be partly due to the fact that after the powerful, stupendous impressions made by the first movement or movements of a symphony the listener needs some moral relaxation. However, I must confess that the continual growth of ideas and effects right up to the very end of the symphony seems to me more worthy of a monumental work. I am glad to see in Mr Tchaikovsky's piece the preponderance of the finale over the excellent first movement.

10 'Zhuravel'' ('The crane'), which is Ukrainian, like the folksong mentioned in the previous note.

I should now like to add a few words about the second movement of the symphony. This second movement is the usual Adagio with a flowing, more or less sensitive melody. The Adagio is headed Andantino marziale, yet might be more aptly named Allegretto. It is lively and somewhat humorous in character. Once more I am reminded of the comparison with Beethoven's Eighth Symphony which I made with reference to Mr Tchaikovsky's finale theme. Thanks to its light and humorous content, the second movement of Beethoven's symphony can give a partial insight into the manner chosen by Mr Tchaikovsky in place of the usual Adagio. I must point out straightaway that neither in its ideas nor in the way it is worked out does Mr Tchaikovsky's Andantino bring the slightest 'reminiscences' of the aforementioned piece by Beethoven. This Andantino is set apart by its great freshness and grace; in the modifications with which the main theme is repeated we can see again the skilled counterpoint and refined taste which we so enjoyed in the other movements. I should like to point also to the extraordinarily beautiful melodic passage (we cannot call it a fully rounded melody) which during the Andantino's evolution is picked up twice by the violins and cellos. This passage leaves an impassioned impression, one even of love, and in this way provides a stark contrast with the first theme of the Andantino.

As far as the scherzo of this new symphony is concerned, I must say frankly that I did not understand it. The scherzo appeared to represent an extremely interesting and witty game of harmonies and rhythms, but this brilliant game stirred no excitement in me and I failed to grasp the overall idea and essence of the piece. I have heard the symphony only once, and have not seen the score. This fact may mean that in conveying technical details I have been guilty of some inaccuracies. If this is the case, I apologize in advance to the composer. I know how unpleasant it is to find one's words misquoted; it must also be equally annoying to see one's symphony inaccurately described. However, as far as possible relying on my own memory, I have tried to be precise, and I hope that on the whole I have been successful. It is my wish that those readers who have not yet heard Mr Tchaikovsky's symphony will not confine their acquaintance with this work to my report. Indeed, I hope that they will have the opportunity in the very near future of hearing the symphony in a performance as excellent as the one I heard under the gifted and experienced baton of Nikolay Rubinstein.[11] It is my wish too that this symphony will soon be performed in St Petersburg where the name of Mr Tchaikovsky has noticeably grown in prestige and popularity in recent times. I wish also that people in the provinces, not only in the few towns which have a satisfactory orchestra, but even in places where there is nothing more than a piano, may be able to become acquainted

11 See Chapter 3, item (f).

with this music. Of course, in order for this to be achieved the Symphony must first be printed in a piano transcription.

At the present time when music publishers appear to have overcome their fear of Russian composers and, indeed, are very gladly printing their works, the publication of a capital work such as Mr Tchaikovsky's symphony should not be delayed.[12] I suggest that it be printed in addition as an orchestral score, since we can and must hope that when this work is performed in Germany it will be greeted with genuine sympathy from the audience, and will show the experts that in the sphere of musical composition contemporary Russia can, at least through this one figure, compete with contemporary Germany.

(b) G. A. Laroche: Russian musical composition in our day [: a general characterization of Tchaikovsky's work]. *The Voice*, 28 November 1873, no. 329, pp. 1–2. Laroche 2, pp. 38–50

With a few exceptions, the Russian composers who have embarked on a public career since the 1850s have all shown traces of Glinka's influence, although this influence has made itself felt in very different ways on the various natures. Glinka is the Russian Mozart; his genius has not only depth but also breadth – it was diverse, it embraced much. He showed equal capacity for song, symphony and opera alike, though to judge from external reasons he wrote symphonic pieces only exceptionally. His imitators, gifted with less wide-ranging abilities, have been able to dwell on some single aspect of Glinka, for instance, his recitative style, which is wholly distinctive and to a remarkable extent Russian (*natsional'nïy*); they have been able to copy some individual device of Glinka's technique, for example, his frequent use of double counterpoint in which one part has a descending chromatic scale – in a word, one may reduce imitation to the most one-sided style. But one can also, being to some extent under Glinka's influence, not be a simple imitator of him, and combine devices from his pen with others borrowed from some western model or other, or finally, with forms and technical ideas of one's own invention. All three of these elements (Glinka's influence, the influence of western masters and original substance) may be observed in the composer to whom I wish to devote this essay.

[Laroche lists the works so far composed by Tchaikovsky, of which 'the C minor Symphony is the highest point to which [his] work has risen yet'. In this article he will concentrate on those compositions which have been published.]

12 An arrangement of the Symphony for piano four hands was published late in 1873 (see Chapter 8, item (b)); the next publication, in 1880, was of the revised version.

The first of Mr Tchaikovsky's works to come from the press were some small piano pieces published by Mr Jürgenson[13] in Moscow. They enjoyed success there, apparently, at least to the extent that Moscow pianists very often performed them in their concerts. But this fame scarcely spread further, and one must observe that the internal substance of most of these little pieces offered no hope of great celebrity. It is not at all a matter of their being of small dimensions: there are things by Field,[14] Chopin and Schumann which are insignificant in scale but are full of ideas, animation and wealth of refinement. Boileau said that a well-written sonnet has the same value as a whole epic poem; if by that he meant to say that for a good sonnet one can give a bad epic poem, then he was comparing heterogeneous things which are therefore not subject to comparison; but if he meant simply that a work's aesthetic value does not depend on its size, then piano music abounds in examples which confirm his opinion brilliantly. The suites of Sebastian Bach are not performed complete, at least at concerts, yet some fugue of two short pages, or some tiny prelude or gavotte can electrify listeners all the same. The piano concertos of Mozart which are still able to enrapture inveterate lovers of his style have become antiquated to the public and set contemporary virtuosi no worthwhile tasks, but when Anton Rubinstein plays Mozart's little C minor Rondo[15] in front of thousands of listeners all the fantastic one-sidednesses, all the prejudices of the innovators fall silent in admiration, as if a vision filled with nobility and pure grace had floated in front of the listeners. Such is the power of genius in works restricted by the tightest framework.

But not all artistic natures are capable of being limited by such a framework: thus, for example, Berlioz earned his fame exclusively with compositions written on a large scale intended for a large mass of performers and designed for large halls. The one-sidedness which I see in Mr Tchaikovsky does not lie in the fact that following Berlioz's example he despises small forms; on the contrary – he resorts to them fairly often; but it is not hard to notice that his talent does not display itself in its full lustre in them, that Mr Tchaikovsky shows less inventiveness, less fire and less craftsmanship in small pieces than in large compositions. He needs the sumptuous, diverse colours of the most modern orchestra and the wide expanse of the symphonic form; it is only in these spacious and brilliant spheres that he feels at home, and where his palette becomes poorer he too becomes poorer with it.

I would not wish to apply this judgement to all of his small works in equal measure, however. There are among these works which are more or less successful: his romances, generally speaking, display more musical

13 For Jürgenson, see Chapter 6, note 46.   14 For Field, see Chapter 2, note 34.
15 K 511, Rondo in A minor, perhaps?

charm and animation than his piano pieces, perhaps because Mr Tchaikovsky too, like the majority of composers, comes at times under the influence of literary works and draws strength and a wealth of fantasy from them, and in a romance, which is always written to the text of a lyrical poem, the occasion for such a direct influence of poet upon musician is, of course, closer at hand than anywhere else.[16] It may very well be that the poems of Heine, Maykov,[17] Pleshcheyev[18] and others to which Mr Tchaikovsky has written his romances had that rousing and stirring effect on the composer which so often is the indirect reason for the coming into the world of fine musical thoughts; but similarly one may also suppose that the reason for the superiority of his romances over his piano compositions is a completely different one – simply that thinking about the timbre of the human voice inspires him more than thinking about the timbre of the piano. However it may be, there are among Mr Tchaikovsky's romances some very remarkable works, whereas the same cannot be said of his things for piano.

But if one judges them absolutely and not in relation to other, more substantial works by Mr Tchaikovsky, then one cannot fail to recognize

16 *Author's note*: The reader can see that I am carefully avoiding saying that Mr Tchaikovsky's romances portray musically the same thing which is portrayed poetically in the words to which they are written, or that the beauty of the music here derives from the beauty of the words whose meaning they express. There is nothing cruder than that prejudice, there is nothing more antimusical than that false love for music which is nourished by such unsuitable terms occasioning only misunderstandings and distorted interpretations. One cannot, of course, deny that fast and slow tempi, greater or lesser intensity of sound, the rising and heightening of melody, consonance and dissonance in harmony in their diverse combinations create pieces of varied character, and that the character of a piece may approach one range of ideas more closely than another; but only the general character or atmosphere of the ideas, and not their individual logical content may be discerned by the listener from the music itself; all the details, all the tangibly fixed features, contained through imagination in the music, the listener usually finds from the opera's libretto, the words of the romance or the verbal programme attached to certain instrumental pieces. Berlioz's Overture to Shakespeare's *Lear* (one of the French symphonist's most profound works) is without any doubt written in such a grandiose, titanic style and contains such gloomy, terrible pages that it corresponds to the character of Shakespeare's drama, but to the same extent it could be the overture to *Prometheus* and generally speaking to any poetic work whose principal motive is a proud, bold and desperate battle with surrounding forces. Its expressiveness, thus, is negative rather than positive; it is safe to designate operettas, farces, comedies and dramas for which Berlioz's *Lear* is unsuitable as an overture; but it is impossible without a verbal designation on the composer's part to name the author and the specific work by which he was inspired when composing his own music. This outlook does not deny the influence of poetry on the inspiration of musicians; but it does not recognize a clear and definite meaning for musical phrases. It does not follow that a symphony composed under the influence of reading *Eugene Onegin* will contain portraits of characters, situations and landscapes in Pushkin's long poem (*poema*). There was at one time a composer whose custom it was to find inspiration by reading the works of the Fathers of the Church. One could hardly expect, however, to find an aesthetician sufficiently daring to find a musical composition a complete exposition of theological doctrines.

17 A. N. Maykov (1821–97), lyric poet.
18 A. N. Pleshcheyev (1825–93), civic poet.

that they too possess some good qualities: they are all written with a great knowledge of the instrument, some even virtuosically, combining virtuoso interest with the solid technique and fine part-writing which never leave Mr Tchaikovsky; some are distinguished by agreeable and readily accessible melodiousness. To the group of works of predominantly virtuosic character belong the Scherzo à la russe and Impromptu (op. 1), dedicated to N. G. Rubinstein, the Valse-Caprice (op. 4) dedicated to Mr Door[19] and in part the Capriccio (op. 8) dedicated to K[arl] Klindworth.[20]

Of these works the Scherzo à la russe (B flat major) is of interest in comprising mainly a series of variations on the theme of a Ukrainian song which he copied out, if I am not mistaken, in the Kiev province.[21] The theme itself, in spite of its brevity and compression, stands out for its rare melodic charm; but its graceful and joyful character is not entirely kept to in Mr Tchaikovsky's treatment: some of the variations, executed in Glinka's manner, are interesting and euphonious, but a large part of them are based on such virtuoso devices (octaves, leaps with complete chords, martellato) as produce threatening peals of piano thunder which by no means suit the character of the song and so to speak kill it. The Russian Scherzo of which I am speaking here came before the public not in its original form: it is an adaptation of the first Allegro of a string quartet written by Mr Tchaikovsky in 1865 and performed at that time in the St Petersburg Conservatoire. The spirit of the song taken by Mr Tchaikovsky is far more closely akin to a string quartet than to a virtuoso piano étude, and having heard the song's original quartet treatment I can testify that it was more of a piece and more elegant than the later piano version which has had the good fortune to be published.

I mention this matter of adaptation because it occurs several times in Mr Tchaikovsky's artistic career. The matter itself cannot represent a reproach to an artist: adaptations occur in the works of the greatest geniuses, and with some, such as Handel, even with great frequency. It is necessary only that the latest version have a *raison d'être*, that it be justified by an unquestionable advantage over the earlier version. But Mr Tchaikovsky has rarely been lucky with his adaptations: his compositions are in the main better in their original form than in the altered one.

I am dwelling on Mr Tchaikovsky's Russian Scherzo in detail because it is particularly convenient to study the faults of his pen in this composition. In view of this, I shall indicate one more shortcoming of the same piece. It is written in a form to which Mr Tchaikovsky generally has willing recourse,

19 Anton Door (1833–1919). Austrian pianist who was a frequent visitor to Russia. He taught at the Moscow Conservatoire from 1866 to 1869.
20 Karl Klindworth (1830–1916). German pianist who taught at the Moscow Conservatoire from 1868 to 1881. He made many piano reductions of orchestral and operatic scores.
21 Laroche is not mistaken.

that of the short rondo, that is, it is made up of two sections, the first of which is repeated at the end, while the second differs from the first in key and mood. It is precisely this second section which represents the Achilles' heel of Mr Tchaikovsky's invention, for in melodic and harmonic interest it is incomparably lower than the first section and is joined on to it in an external, mechanical fashion. The shortcoming with which I am reproaching Mr Tchaikovsky here belongs in the realm of musical form, and I consider it my duty to remark here that in this very realm Mr Tchaikovsky has made great progress in the last two or three years. But it is precisely in the works of his earlier period (to which nearly all the piano pieces belong) that Mr Tchaikovsky often provides the spectacle of discord between form and idea, the spectacle of forms assimilated in a superficial manner and hurriedly filled up with musical ideas which are unserviceable for these forms and require a completely different grouping. The same lack of connection between the first and second sections of a rondo which I noticed in the Scherzo à la russe prevails, in my view, in the F minor Romance for piano, dedicated to Miss Artôt[22] (op. 5), in the little piece entitled *Ruines d'un château* (E minor, op. 2 no. 1), and in the Capriccio (op. 8). In all these pieces one senses that the first idea is the composer's cherished idea, occupying his imagination and developed by him with love, whereas the second is composed hastily, stimulated by recognition of the need to have some kind of second section and thus not only not showing any organic link with the first idea but being inferior to it taken on its own in musical merit. The task of a critic who points out these shortcomings of Mr Tchaikovsky's talent is the more pleasant in that they belong to the past, that the highly gifted composer, himself obviously recognizing them and feeling within himself the strength to occupy a far higher aesthetic plane, has been able to wage a struggle against them which has been not merely energetic but wholly successful. But let me return to Mr Tchaikovsky's piano pieces. Among those of them which I assign to the virtuoso category, the Impromptu (E flat minor, op. 1 no. 2) is more difficult than grateful on the ear, and sets the virtuoso an unrewarding task; the Capriccio (G flat major, op. 8), also of little aesthetic interest, except for a few beautiful harmonies, is remarkable in a technical respect in that (p. 4, bars 1–12 [bars 40–52]) it contains in embryo the idea on which the second part of the Scherzo of Mr Tchaikovsky's Second Symphony is based;[23] the most successful of them seems to me to be the Valse-Caprice, dedicated to Mr Door (D major, op. 4) in which the

22 Désirée Artôt (1835–1907). French mezzo-soprano, later soprano, whose performing career took her to Russia in 1868 where she made a deep impression on Tchaikovsky.

23 *Author's note:* The melody in the middle part with accents on the weak beats, accompanied by a motive in double notes, alternating in various registers, now high, now low, each struck twice [= bar 40 onwards].

mellifluous and likeable basic motives are combined with a splendidly brilliant piano texture. In melodic content, however, those little piano pieces by Mr Tchaikovsky which have no virtuoso pretensions are far more attractive than the pieces just enumerated; this is true in particular of the *Chant sans paroles* (F major, op. 2 no. 3) and the Romance (F minor, op. 5) mentioned above. This Romance is very uneven, and the middle section of it is out of keeping with the main one; but the melody of this main section is nonetheless lyrical, noble and elegant in the highest degree; Chopin's strain can be heard in it, so to speak, one can hear that graceful disillusion which is the basic mood of Chopin's nocturnes. I have already said that many of Mr Tchaikovsky's little piano pieces have been played in public in Moscow. It is highly desirable that the example of Moscow pianists should find rather more imitators not only because these pieces (especially those which are easier as regards playing technique) have many attractive aspects, but mainly because the public performance of Russian piano composers is capable of sparking off competition among them and directing their powers towards piano composition, the strengthening of which is far more desirable than that of symphonic composition, since our country has few orchestras but many pianos; a piano piece may consequently count on far wider dissemination than a symphony.

If one may level at Russian symphonic music the charge that it shows an abnormal predominance of supply over demand, that it is to a significant extent leading an artificial, hothouse life and therefore while vegetating in the cities is almost incapable of crossing into the provinces, the same cannot be said about our romances. Here the demand has really been great since long ago, and as far back as those times when no Schumanns were known in Russia, when our knowledge of music was at the very lowest stage, we had hordes of Varlamovs,[24] Alyab'yevs[25] and Gurilyovs.[26] The activities of the generation of that period in the field of the romance were perhaps more extensive than those of the present generation; one must not lose sight of the fact either, of course, that the public of that time was undemanding and gave encouragement to the mass of mediocrity which appeared on the sheet music market every year along with other things, while the present public, being familiar with Schubert and Schumann, is incomparably stricter and demands expressive word-setting, interesting harmony and a rich accompaniment from native composers.

Music-lovers who have cultivated their taste on the best German works of this kind will find their demands satisfied in the greater part of

24 For Varlamov, see Chapter 2, note 41.   25 For Alyab'yev, see Chapter 1, note 5.
26 A. L. Gurilyov (1803–58). Composer best known for romances and 'Russian songs' (i.e. songs close in idiom to urban folklore).

Mr Tchaikovsky's romances,[27] works which are elegant and rich, to which the critic can point with pleasure and pride. Standing at the summit of present-day harmonic technique, rich in chords and modulations, carefully polished in the piano accompaniment, these romances are free, however, from that one-sided predominance of the piano over the voice, of a stage prop over a member of the cast, which one so often notices in Russian and German romances of the last twenty years: with Mr Tchaikovsky one is not infrequently struck by the freshness and beauty of the melodic invention, and many of his romances may be recommended to singers for performance in concerts on account of their gratefulness to the voice. In this respect 'I bol'no i sladko' ('It is both painful and sweet') (words by Countess Rostopchina), and 'Net, tol'ko tot, kto znal' ('No, only he who has known', or 'None but the lonely heart') (words by Goethe in Mey's translation) stand out particularly among the songs in the first book; to these the romance from the same book 'Sleza drozhit v tvoyom revnivom vzore' ('A tear trembles in your jealous look') (words by Count A. Tolstoy) may also be added, where, however, the effectiveness of the vocal part is not accompanied as in the two preceding songs by charm of musical invention; of the romances in the second book the most effective and rewarding seems to me to be *Tak chto zhe?* ('So, what then?') (words by an anonymous author); also very beautiful in its uniform simplicity is 'Kolïbel'naya pesnya' ('Cradle song') (words by Maykov).

Of the compositions itemized here the most masterly in my opinion is 'None but the lonely heart'; it is one of those gems of inspiration and art enclosed within a tight framework of a few pages of which I spoke above and which, as I noted then, are in general not much characteristic of Mr Tchaikovsky's talent, which inclines towards the large scale and a complex orchestral apparatus. The passionate and expressive melody of this romance, harmonized with inimitable grace, is repeated three times, the jewel appearing each time in the setting of a new accompaniment, while the composer with rare inspiration has been able to find a harmonic gradation which makes a fascinating and at the same time stupendous impact.

Another category of romances by Mr Tchaikovsky, which captivate less by the sparkle of their melodies, draw attention to themselves by their poetic features and the refined charm of their harmonic details. To this category I assign 'Ne ver', moy drug' ('Do not believe, my friend') (words by Count Tolstoy), where the chromatic movement in the bass at the words 'uzh ya toskuyu, prezhney strasti polnïy' ('I pine, full of my previous

27 *Author's note:* Six Romances, op. 6. Moscow, from Jürgenson (words by Goethe, Heine, Pleshcheyev, Rostopchina, A. Tolstoy); Six Romances, op. 16. St Petersburg, from Bessel (words by Maykov, Grekov, Pleshcheyev).

passion'), later repeated with different words, is especially noteworthy; no less worthy of attention is the romance 'Ni slova, o drug moy' ('Neither words, oh my friend') (words by Pleshcheyev), particularly for its beautiful and pathos-filled sequence, which the composer has placed at the words 'I tol'ko sklonivshis', chitayut, kak ya v tvoyom serdtse ustalom' ('And only bending, they read, like me in your tired heart'). We find no less wealth of beautiful harmonies, combined with a poetic mood, in the romance 'Pogodi!' ('Wait!') (words by Grekov); the romance 'Poymi khot' raz' ('Catch just once') is distinguished by the energetic beauty and headlong power of its chords.

But for its technical function the last item in the second book, entitled 'Novogrecheskaya pesnya' ('Modern Greek song') is especially conspicuous; the words (by A. N. Maykov) are devoted to portraying the torments of sinners in hell. The notion of hell prompted the composer to take as a theme the famous medieval sequence *Dies irae est venturus*, of which, by the way, Liszt and Berlioz wrote remarkable symphonic workings. As a first-rate technician, equally remarkable for his innate talent for polyphonic writing and mature mastery acquired by schooling and toil, Mr Tchaikovsky was able to find aspects of the old Catholic theme which were ignored by Liszt and Berlioz; the third page of the romance is especially interesting to the specialist, where the theme is shifted from the strong beat to the weak one [bars 21 ff.], and likewise the fourth page, where the theme is combined with itself, so that one part performs it in long notes and another in short ones [bars 25 ff.]. But do not think, reader, that 'Modern Greek song' is nothing more than a dry contrapuntal exercise: no, for quite apart from all sorts of subtleties of part-writing it is a very good romance which conveys euphoniously and accurately the sombre mood with which the words are filled.

In finishing with Mr Tchaikovsky's individual romances, I shall remark that in general terms they disclose such a powerful gift and also such a sympathetic one that it would be highly desirable to see further new works of this kind in print as soon as possible. Besides good qualities which our composer shares with many of his contemporaries, he has one quality which one finds extremely rarely in our day – I mean the gift of melody. This gift has accounted for the success of two of his works to which I now intend to pass: the *Romeo* overture and the string quartet.

The older of them in chronological order is the overture. It has had the good fortune which does not often fall to the lot of orchestral works of being published not only in a piano arrangement but also in full score (the latter came out in Berlin, from Bote und Bock);[28] in addition Mr Klindworth himself, who is well known for his arrangements of the Wagner operas, has honoured it by making a two-piano version published by Mr Bessel. The

28 This full score (of the second version) was published in Berlin in 1871.

same Mr Bessel has also issued a four-hand arrangement for one piano from the experienced and adroit pen of Mrs Rimsky-Korsakov.[29] Generally speaking, this overture has been luckier than any of his works preceding it; especially in St Petersburg, the popularity of his name is based all but entirely on it, and one cannot but agree that in its inspired flight, the passionate pathos of its basic ideas combined with the sumptuous charm of its harmonies and instrumentation, this overture leaves the composer's previous works far behind. The second melody of the Allegro (D flat major) is one of those irresistibly bewitching tunes from whose effect the listener cannot free himself whatever the orientation of his taste or the mood of his soul; the accompaniment of this melody at its second appearance (a repeated second in the horn) is one of the most felicitous ideas ever to have dawned upon an expert harmonist. In just the same fashion, in the development of ideas the *Romeo and Juliet* overture abounds in interesting and elegant devices; I shall cite merely by way of example the combination of the theme of the introduction with the first theme of the Allegro (pp. 86ff. in the score; it is repeated on pp. 94ff.) or the same theme from the introduction over a dominant pedal with a counterpoint of a descending scale (pp. 90–2 in the score, with a repetition on pp. 99–100); all the harmonic material from which this spacious edifice of sound is built is noble, rich and precious. One cannot nevertheless acknowledge Mr Tchaikovsky's *Romeo and Juliet* as a classic or model work. There is a shortage of cement to bind together the many individual features, each more charming than the one before; the theme of the introduction, the first theme of the Allegro and the second theme of the Allegro are mutually alien to one another and seem as if they came from three different works; the overture form which is apparently kept to here serves as a screen behind which hides an incoherent rhapsody. Only the central section of the overture (from the end of the second theme to the return of the first one) is written in a concise and integral manner, because it all maintains the mood of the first theme of the Allegro, skilfully combining it with the motive of the introduction which does not infringe the unity here; but then the introduction itself is made up of two elements which are completely alien one to the other (the F sharp minor theme and the harmonic progression leading from G flat major to F minor). There is just as little connection between the two themes of the Allegro; the second relates to the first as in sonatas the Adagio relates to the first Allegro, and this relationship has nothing in common with that which should exist between the two themes of one and the same Allegro. Problems of musical form, unfortunately, cannot be solved by any sort of tangible proofs, and everything said about them relies only on the listener's musical feeling. I

29 See Chapter 6, note 40.

cannot nourish any certainty, of course, that the reader will feel exactly the same way that I do, but I think that I shall be quite close to the truth if I say that in its sympathetic talent, vividness of colouring, quest for the most powerful contrasts and complete absence of organic connection, Mr Tchaikovsky's *Romeo and Juliet* most closely resembles Litolff's *Die Girondisten* and *Robespierre*.[30] Only in his use of harmonic and contrapuntal resources the Russian composer reveals far more ability and care than the German.

Mr Tchaikovsky's string quartet, which is also fairly well known to the public, represents in many respects the antithesis of his overture. The quartet yields to it slightly as regards beauty and originality of melodic ideas; in formal skill it is far ahead of the overture. This is particularly true of the first Allegro, whose themes are at a decent average level but which is written so coherently and fluently that it makes a graceful impression such as could not have been made with more significant themes but less rounded form. In this respect Mr Tchaikovsky's quartet represents an extraordinarily important step forward, because none of his earlier works shows such skill in binding and grouping ideas one with another. In beauty of contents it is principally the second and third movements of the quartet which excel; the Andante in particular, which is based on two highly lyrical melodies, the first of which is a folksong and the second the work of the composer himself, is notable for its poetic character, the delicate charm of its harmony and the extremely skilful instrumentation. In this last respect it is curious to observe the quartet after the *Romeo and Juliet* overture, the strictest limitation of resources after unrestricted freedom: in both spheres Mr Tchaikovsky proves to be primarily a colourist and with equal inventiveness draws as beautiful and effective timbres from four instruments as from thirty. As regards the musical contents, the trio of the third movement of the quartet also deserves special attention; it is based in the main on a tonic pedal over which the motive of a descending chromatic scale, often encountered with Mr Tchaikovsky, is used. Finally, I shall also enter in my survey the very pungent, bold and, if I may put it this way, unceremonious harmony which occurs in the finale (p. 6 of the score, line 8, bars 1–8)[31] based on a series of unresolved auxiliary notes. This finale is written in a smart and humorous way; in general the string quartet with its radiant mood represents a rather rare exception among the works of Mr Tchaikovsky, in whose soul melancholy and disillusionment predominate, sometimes reaching a tone of sombre hopelessness.

30 Henry Litolff (1818–91), composer, pianist and music publisher. The overtures mentioned were composed in 1870 and 1856 respectively.

31 *Author's note:* The score and separate parts for the Quartet are published in Moscow by Mr Jürgenson.

The transition from such a tone to the most unclouded and enthusiastic celebration – that is the idea which lies at the root of Mr Tchaikovsky's large new symphony. Both in this idea and in the choice of keys (C minor and C major), it shows some similarity to the Fifth Symphony of Beethoven; it would be superfluous to add that this similarity does not extend to the style: there is nothing more opposed than the majestically simple frescoes of Beethoven and Mr Tchaikovsky's canvas which gleams with all the riches of the most modern style. Russian folksong,[32] to which the gifted composer has always been attracted, holds an important place in the themes of the new work: on its melodies are based the excellent introduction and the symphony's still more outstanding finale; alongside these borrowed melodies the motives which are the work of the composer himself shine by their beauty. The art of details, the ability to notice all those aspects and figures of a theme which are open to varied and beautiful harmonizations, the ability to invent themes capable of going together simultaneously – all these qualities of Mr Tchaikovsky, which were already displayed to a lesser extent in his works long ago, are here carried to the highest point of development. The symphony's rich, passionate and sensually beautiful first Allegro forms with its introduction (Andante sostenuto) an inseparable whole which is based on three themes, one slow one (a folksong) and two fast ones, both of them conceived as counterpoints to the slow theme so that they may be performed at the same time as it, something of which the composer has taken advantage for a lengthy series of the richest and wittiest combinations which are alike of interest to the analyst and agreeable to the ear. One must add to these three themes the staccato figure (four semiquavers and two quavers), which first occurs in the transitional section between the first and second themes of the Allegro and plays a very important role in the further development of the piece. Among the individual themes the second idea in the Allegro (which first appears in A flat major) stands out for its singing charm and passionate grace; the contrast between it and what precedes it is very strong, but it does not break the unity, whereas in *Romeo and Juliet* and others of his earlier works Mr Tchaikovsky, in seeking contrast, has come upon melodies which are intrinsically foreign to one another. This entire Allegro is equally first-rate whether judged on the basis of motives or harmonic devices or, finally, form. In relation to form the only comment which one might perhaps make is that the exceptional predominance in such an extensive piece of rich, quickly changing harmonies and complicated polyphonic style, forcing the listener's attention to be perpetually tensed, may to some extent tire it; but here too perhaps the composer has acted consciously and with artistic calculation, since after the

32 Strictly speaking, Ukrainian songs in two cases.

difficult and complex Allegro the light, almost playful Andantino marziale which forms the second movement of the symphony is doubly refreshing. This Andantino is in a style for which I have not previously met models in Mr Tchaikovsky's work and which in part approaches the French style; it is full of elegant humour, and in its second theme (G major) once more presents one of those examples of freely and rapturously flowing lyrical melody which are so characteristic of his rich creations. The refined harmonic combinations which our composer is so fond of and which have stretched in an unbroken thread through the whole of the first Allegro and its introduction have not altogether abandoned him in the Andantino either; but he uses them here with far greater moderation. The contrast between the first and second movements of the symphony is intensified further by the fact that the first movement is in the main thickly and loudly scored, whereas the second movement is played mainly piano and even pianissimo. The scherzo (third movement) returns us to the agitated mood in which we found ourselves when listening to the first movement, but combines it with the character of a certain special fantastic impetuosity, of an irrepressible run along the most unfamiliar, unexplored harmonic paths. Here too the motive of the descending chromatic scale prevails, a device of which I have already written that Mr Tchaikovsky uses it often (in which respect he is following Glinka's example); but the use of this motive, of interlocking double notes in various instruments and various registers accompanying it are here new, bold and original in the highest degree. As an expression of rapid, despairingly headlong and endless movement (one of the tasks most accessible to the art of music), this scherzo is a work of remarkable poetry. But the crown of the symphony I regard as the finale based on the Ukrainian theme 'Zhuravel'' (The crane'), the melody of which has a wild, almost reckless character; it offers an unprecedented model of the richest thematic exploitation in a long series of the most diverse variations. In his development of this theme Mr Tchaikovsky does not restrict himself to its initial character, but with the insight of inspiration discerns in it a side hidden from the ordinary eye – a capacity to assume a stately and even awesome character. This transition from light-hearted cheerfulness to the staggering, thunderous blows of powerful, weighty chords lends the symphony's finale a character of high poetry which obtains its conclusion in the final pages of the finale, which are full of unrestrained exultation. I cannot dwell here on the quite superlative technical details, in respect of which this finale is an inexhaustible wellspring, but I cannot pass over in silence the most fundamental of them – the alternating dissonant notes sforzando, intoned by one part of the orchestra at the same time as the other plays the theme. These mighty dissonances which force their way into the theme (pp. 86–93 of the four-hand edition [bars 325 ff.]) at first follow one another slowly, and then ever more quickly, and moreover the composer shows his amazing, legendary wealth of harmony and counterpoint.

But our assessment of Mr Tchaikovsky would be one-sided if we imagined him to be exclusively a contrapuntist who disposes huge masses of sound and shines in the most complicated tasks; Mr Tchaikovsky is devoid of one-sidedness and stiffness; as a true artist, he does not turn his back either on light, popular music, and there too he reveals the same masterly hand. This summer Mr Jürgenson published five numbers from his music for Ostrovsky's[33] *Snegurochka* ('The snowmaiden'). They include three songs of Lel' (mezzo-soprano): (1) 'Zemlyanichka yagodka' ('Wild strawberries, berries'), (2) 'Kak po lesu les shumit' ('As the forest resounds'), and (3) 'Tucha so gromom sgovarivalas'' ('The cloud came to an arrangement with the thunder'); Brusila's song (baritone) 'Kupalsya bobyor' ('The beaver bathed'); and one instrumental number 'Plyaska skomorokhov' ('Fast-dance of the Skomorokhs') (arranged for piano four hands). The music for *The Snowmaiden* is lively, light and artless; the absence of pretensions has a pleasant effect on it, the absence of that cosmetic matter without which some present-day Russian composers cannot approach the folk genre. Contrary to expectation, the orchestral *Fast-dance of the Skomorokhs*,[34] in which, it would have seemed, Mr Tchaikovsky's talent could have had the widest scope, has turned out to be weaker than the vocal numbers; and of these in their turn the most successful are those which adhered entirely to the form of a folksong: 'The cloud' and 'The beaver'. Judging by the numbers which have been published, *The Snowmaiden* is probably not one of the composer's principal services to our national art, but here too he has displayed his gifts and a purely artistic ability to understand his task and to rest content with it.

(c) G. A. Laroche: Musical observations and impressions (from Moscow). *The Voice*, 1878, no. 254. Laroche 5, pp. 75–80 and 2, pp. 97–100

The low sun pours streams of light and warmth upon Moscow; after endless rains, after terrible cloudbursts which have turned an arid city into a raging sea in places, summer has really arrived. Clouds of dust drift across Theatre Square; the streets are inundated with people, the ladies in summer dresses. Late, marvellous days have come along like an unexpected gift.

It seems as if a late and more or less unexpected summer has begun for the Russian opera in Moscow too. But the bad weather there had lasted not

33 For Ostrovsky, see Chapter 5, note 32.   34 For *skomorokhi*, see Chapter 5, note 25.

for months but for long years. Fifty years from now people will scarcely
believe the historian of Russian music when he begins his account of how in
the centre of Russia, in its ancient capital which has always been notable
for its patriotism but which has only just started to take an interest in our
nation's music; of how Russian opera was driven out of a government-
owned theatre to oblige a foreign speculator;[35] of how this expulsion struck
our nation's art at the precise moment of its blossoming a few years after
the foundation of two conservatoires and at the same time as new compositional talents were appearing. They will hardly believe him when he
recounts how the singers best loved by the public could not obtain any
engagements at all and had willy-nilly to seek a career either on the provincial stage or on the concert platform; how operatic scores which had
become illustrious in one capital and had long since been daily musical
bread there remained unknown to the public in the other capital for a
decade and more; how the population of a huge and wealthy city had
thrust upon it, despite its unambiguously expressed desire, a foreign opera
of doubtful quality [the Italian company], thrust upon it until such time as
the public finally stopped going to the opera and the Bol'shoy Theatre, one
of the most immense and most beautiful in the world, turned into a desert.

But . . . is it right at this very moment to speak in a tone of bitter
reproach about insults endured by the Moscow Russian opera at the very
moment when the Directorate, apparently honestly and openly, though not
entirely decisively, has taken a different path, and if they have not done
everything they should have for Moscow, have at least renounced the
previous system of victimization? [I. e., by placing the Bol'shoy Theatre at
the disposal of the Russian opera for several months of the season, by
engaging new singers and a new conductor and mounting new productions.]

[Laroche writes most entertainingly of mishaps in *A Life for the Tsar* on
30 August and *Faust* on 5 September.]

The day before *Faust* I watched, or to put it more accurately, 'listened' to
P. Tchaikovsky's ballet *Swan Lake* in the same theatre.[36] When he reads
that I 'listened' to a ballet, the reader will perhaps regard me as an exagger-
atedly conscientious reviewer, a specialist who is so afflicted by abnormal
honesty that even at the ballet he cannot for a second forget the job to
which he is appointed that he rigorously keeps up with every chord of the
seventh and shuts his eyes to everything else. Alas! The reader does me an
honour which I have not deserved. Were it not unbefitting for a serious
person to take an interest in ballet, then I should have to turn down with a

35 E. Merelli; see Chapter 4, item (c), and note 40 there.
36 The score was composed in 1875–6 and the ballet first performed with choreography by
    Reisinger in the Bol'shoy Theatre on 20 February 1877 .

grieving heart the title of 'serious person' and the rights and privileges attached to it. It will be different for others, but for me the 'soul-filled flight of the Russian Terpsichore'[37] holds an inexplicable fascination, and I have never ceased to regret that more talented musicians do not share my weakness and apply their compositional powers in this realm which, it seems, offers such splendid scope for a capricious imagination. With the smallest number of exceptions, serious, real composers keep aloof from ballet: I do not intend to decide whether some primness which compels them to look down on ballet as a 'low sort of music' or some other cause must take the blame for this. Whatever the truth may be, P. I. Tchaikovsky is free of this primness or, at least, for once in his life he was free of it. And many thanks to him for that: perhaps his example will find imitators in his circle, in the highest reaches of the composers' world. But for all that I love spectacles of this kind, at the performance of P. Tchaikovsky's ballet I listened far more than I watched. The musical aspect has a decisive predominance over the choreographic. As regards its music, *Swan Lake* is the best ballet I have ever heard – meaning, of course, a complete ballet and not the *divertissements* in such operas as *A Life for the Tsar* or *Ruslan and Lyudmila*. As regards its dances, *Swan Lake* is just about the most conventional, dull and poor ballet of all those performed in Russia.[38] It is true that the production is wretchedly poor. With different sets, in a different choreographic version which might perhaps require some additional or inserted numbers, the Moscow balletmaster's work, I am sure, will become interesting above and beyond the charming score with which the composer accompanied it. There remains, of course, the routine and extremely uncomplicated story: but who goes to the ballet for the sake of the story? That would be the same thing as going to the opera for the sake of the recitative. I think that in the altered and expanded version of which I am dreaming *Swan Lake* ought to be staged in St Petersburg, that it is sinful not to allow St Petersburg to hear the substantial and wonderful work of such a master as Tchaikovsky.

I shall not conceal that as I set out for the theatre I was a little apprehensive about the effectiveness and popularity of the music. I knew that I was going to hear music which was more noble, more rich in substance than ordinary ballet music; I knew that I was going to hear sonorous chords and beautiful modulations, that a rich orchestra armed with the whole apparatus of the art of the present day was going to spread out intricate patterns before me. But I was afraid that fear of the commonplace, which has often hurt Mr Tchaikovsky in his previous works, especially vocal ones, would make itself felt here too, that out of false shame he would write

37 Pushkin: *Eugene Onegin*, Chapter 1, stanza 19.
38 This was the general verdict on the first choreography for *Swan Lake*.

music which was too high-flown for ballet, too devoid of sensual charm and melodic accessibility. But I saw from the very first numbers that the composer had avoided this reef which my imagination had pushed him against. Melodies, each more plastic, lyrical and absorbing than the last, pour forth as from a horn of plenty; the rhythm of the waltz, which is predominant among the dance numbers, is embodied in such varied, graceful and winning contours that the gifted and versatile composer's melodic invention has never passed the test more brilliantly. The music of *Swan Lake* is entirely popular; what simple amateurs refer to as 'motives' occur in it by no means with less but rather with greater abundance than in any ballet by Pugni. With a lightness which no one would suspect in the learned composer of so many symphonies, quartets and overtures, Mr Tchaikovsky has noted the peculiarities of ballet style and, accommodating himself to them, has once more shown the resourcefulness which is one of the most precious properties of a creative talent. His music is wholly ballet music but at the same time is wholly good and interesting music for the serious musician. Often after a light dance motive harmonized transparently and serving as material for the first 'limb' of some dance, the symphonist in the composer awakens, and in the second 'limb' he illuminates us with a succession of deep, rich chords which remind you for a long time of the power of a non-balletic kind which he is keeping in check within himself. In the instrumentation the same abundance of resources holds sway, the same elegant taste, the same super-lative distribution of harmonic intervals through the mass of instruments which we were accustomed to meet in the creator of *Romeo* and *Francesca*,[39] but one can observe also the same shortcoming from which at least in my view the very best of his works suffer. This shortcoming is his excessive fondness for brass and particularly percussion instruments. I am aware that in ordinary run-of-the-mill ballet music percussion instruments are used still more unrestrainedly and coarsely than in *Swan Lake*, but that is no excuse for a subtle, thoughtful artist. Why do the trumpets, trombones and timpani thunder while a flock of swans swim across the depths of an empty stage? This moment demanded tender, quiet sounds. I noted several such moments in *Swan Lake* which in spite of the requirements of sensible characterization were accompanied by clamorous orchestration. I do not believe that the composer wished to make a concession to the tradition of ballet music in these cases: judging by others of his orchestral works which have nothing in common with ballet, I think rather that here too Tchaikovsky as in many previous instances was simply carried away by the weakness for noisy sonority which is characteristic of him. If I were to continue to refer to deficiencies in this charming score, I should remark that the character dances

39 *Francesca da Rimini* was composed in 1876.

in Act III are in my opinion much weaker than, so to say, cosmopolitan dances, and generally represent almost the weakest place in the score. [Laroche recommends that the ballet be taken up by the superior company in St Petersburg, and offers a lengthy list of recently completed compositions as refutation of Tchaikovsky's rumoured illness, among them *Eugene Onegin*.]

(d) Ts. A. Cui: The Popular Russian Symphony Concert (Borodin's Second Symphony . . . and Tchaikovsky's *The Tempest*). *Music Review*, 5 December 1885, no. 11. Cui, pp. 335–40

Although the concert took place after the period covered by this volume, the review is included so that Borodin's symphony in particular may be represented.

The Popular Russian Symphony Concert conducted by Dyutsh,[40] which took place on 23 November in the Hall of the Assembly of the Nobility, was of the utmost interest on account of its programme, made up exclusively of works by Russian composers, by virtue of the début of a new conductor and of the attempt to keep ticket prices as low as possible with a view to making the concert open to everyone.[41] The works performed were as follows: first, Borodin's Second Symphony.[42] [. . .] It is a capital work of staggering talent and thoroughly typical. Nowhere do the individuality and originality of Borodin reveal themselves in sharper relief than in this symphony; nowhere do his gifts appear with such versatility and diversity or his ideas so distinctively, powerfully and profoundly. In Borodin's Second Symphony it is power which predominates, power which is tough – in short, unconquerable, elemental power. The symphony is permeated by traits of Russian nationality (*simfoniya proniknuta narodnost'yu*), but the nationality of remote times; Rus' is perceptible in this symphony, but primitive pagan Rus'. This symphony might be known as a work concerned with the people's way of life. It is as much a picture of everyday life as the introduction to *Ruslan*, and much of *The Snowmaiden*, especially the scene with the *gusli*-players.[43] This unconquerable, elemental power makes itself felt most in the first Allegro and the finale. Right from the start, the first unison phrase startles the listener with its originality and strength. The latter quality increases and reaches its upper limit after the middle section,

40 G. O. Dyutsh (1857–91), conductor and folksong collector. Son of O. I. Dyutsh, for whom see Chapter 5, note 13.
41 'Open to everyone' is the literal meaning of the word *obshchedostupniy* ('popular') in the title. This event was the first official concert in a series which lasted over thirty years established by the wealthy patron M. P. Belyayev.
42 Borodin's Second Symphony was composed between 1869 and 1876 and first performed in 1877; it was known as the *bogatïr'* symphony after the mighty heroes of Russian folklore.
43 For players of the *gusli*, see Chapter 6, note 18.

at the return of the same phrase augmented twofold, halting on bleak, energy-filled chords. These two movements also contain gentle and beautiful contrasting episodes, but power predominates. This power is not clothed in the balanced, serene forms of western harmonization but manifests itself with rare and harsh originality both in the themes themselves and in their contrapuntal, harmonic and even orchestral treatment.

This harshness of thought and expression, which is quite unmitigated but at the same time is not deprived of colour by conventionally worked-out, custom-hallowed western forms, may prove shocking to many, but everyone must be struck by the force of its boldness and originality. Notwithstanding the resemblance in character between the symphony's first and fourth movements, there is a difference. In the first movement an atmosphere of grandeur is predominant, whereas humour prevails in the last movement. The first movement is like an everyday picture of some solemn ritual; the last movement is a vivid, motley, varied celebration of sparkling gaiety.

The character of the second movement (scherzo) and the third (Andante) changes markedly. The musical themes in these movements are full of fascinating passion (the syncopated theme in the scherzo), or full of appealing simplicity (the trio in the scherzo), or filled with charming poetry (the beginning and ending of the Andante). But the power of real life is not wholly absent from these two movements; it shows through in the angular playfulness of the opening of the scherzo and in the severe progressions in the middle of the Andante. To sum up, Borodin's Second Symphony is one of the most original, most highly talented works in the whole of symphonic music.

[Cui goes on to review the Piano Concerto of Rimsky-Korsakov and Glazunov's *Stenka Razin*, works which by their date of composition do not belong in this volume.]

Tchaikovsky's principal importance is not as a composer of operas or vocal music in general but as a composer of chamber and symphonic works. Among his symphonic compositions programmatic works are of special artistic significance: *Romeo and Juliet*, *The Tempest*,[44] *Francesca da Rimini* and, let us hope, the just completed *Manfred*.[45] Tchaikovsky's creative gifts operate most freely in this form; his appealing tunefulness, harmonic inventiveness, rhythmic ingenuity and his effective and colourful instrumentation are given free range. The musical elements of *The Tempest* are all successful. The opening, portraying the waves of the sea, is excellent both as sound and musically. The oscillation in the strings playing in various rhythms at the same time, the charming modulations, the wonderful sound of the horns as they play their theme – all these are highly poetic and make a strong

44 *The Tempest* was composed and first performed in 1873.
45 The *Manfred* Symphony was composed in 1885.

effect on the listener's imagination. Prospero's theme is not devoid of grandeur, though it was pointless for Tchaikovsky to endow him with such a specific religious quality, which does not quite match the personality of Prospero the magician. The love theme is a beautiful, lyrical, passionate cantilena which ends with delightful new successions of harmonies.

This melody is reminiscent in its shape of the melodies of Berlioz (particularly the long unison phrase in the strings). Ariel is nice, elegant, airy and full of beautiful harmonic details. Caliban is sharply characterized, artistically ugly and not without strength. As regards the use of this excellent material, it is not entirely above reproach. In a few places the seams at the transition to a new theme are very obvious, and the means employed for this are very elementary, such as, for instance, innumerable repetitions of the same chord (as in *Romeo and Juliet*). The development of themes is often replaced by mere repetition of them in a different key or with different orchestration (the love theme). In some places there are *longueurs* (the development of Caliban's theme). But despite these deficiencies which one encounters almost everywhere in Tchaikovsky as a result of his hasty and impatient style of work, *The Tempest* is an outstanding composition of Russian symphonic music in its level of talent, vivid colouring and poetry.

Finally, three excellent romances were performed at this concert: no. 8 of Rubinstein's *Persian Songs*,[46] which even yet remain his vocal masterpiece, full of beauty, colour, feeling and poetry (Rubinstein has always been successful with oriental music wherever it occurs); Korsakov's 'Na kholmakh Gruzii' ('In the hills of Georgia')[47] – a romance as musically fine as it is formally perfect (the first half descriptive and declamatory, the second lyrical and cantabile); Balakirev's 'Pesnya zolotoy rïbki' ('Song of the golden fish')[48] is equally remarkable in external appearance for its artistic fusion of the independent themes of the accompaniment and the voice as for its attractive and inspired inner content. Davïdov's romance 'I noch', i lyubov'' ('Both night and love')[49] was performed as an encore. [. . .]

After listening to works by many present-day Russian composers at one concert and comparing the present state of music here and in western Europe, it was not difficult to come to the following conclusion. There are no composer-geniuses (except for Liszt) at present; but in France, Germany and Russia there are groups including many gifted composers. Of these, the Russian group greatly surpasses the others in strength of talent, and the best proof of that is as follows. In the French group all the composers taken

46 Rubinstein's Persian Songs, op. 34, were composed in 1854.
47 *In the Hills of Georgia*, op. 3 no. 4, was composed in 1866.
48 This song was composed in 1860 and published in 1861; cf. Chapter 2, item (e).
49 Probably by K. Yu Davïdov, see Chapter 7, note 40.

separately are very similar to one another, and taken together they show a strong likeness to their forefather Gounod. There is an appreciable lack of originality in Germany too, and composers there are more or less of a reflection of Brahms. In Russia, despite the common aspirations by which perhaps only Tchaikovsky has not been completely gripped (Rubinstein stands apart), each of our composers (Balakirev, Korsakov, Tchaikovsky, Borodin, the late Musorgsky) possesses his own absolutely definite individuality, and originality is the highest manifestation of talentedness. This present situation is extremely gratifying. But no less gratifying is the future since coming to take the places of the composers I have mentioned, who are already of mature years, there have appeared such strong young talents as Lyadov,[50] Arensky,[51] Glazunov.[52] [. . .]

(e) Ts. A. Cui: M. P. Musorgsky (a critical study). *The Voice*, 8 April 1881, no. 98. Cui, pp. 286–96

Even in a study written shortly after Musorgsky's death, when his *œuvre* was complete, Cui's selection of works for comment may surprise us; cf. the introduction to this Chapter. Musorgsky's genius was appreciated fully only later.

There have been few composers with such a definite sense of particularity, such sharp individuality, as the late Musorgsky.[53] There have been few composers whose works have been notable for such high artistic qualities and such serious shortcomings as the works of Musorgsky. His nature, talented in the highest degree, generously endowed with the extravagant gifts essential to a creative artist in music, contained at the same time a certain antimusical leaven which often manifested itself disagreeably in his works. I do not presume to decide whether this strange mixture, this contradiction, is encountered in other realms of art, but the music of Musorgsky is not the only example of this incomprehensible, abnormal phenomenon. In many works of Berlioz one meets harmonizations which are gritty to the point of ugliness, melodies which are so unattractive and awkward as to be comical; one meets a crude ornamental quality and pomposity in his musical ideas. All these features are alien to the purposes of

50 A. K. Lyadov (1855–1914). This composer was briefly a pupil and then a Conservatoire colleague and collaborator of Rimsky-Korsakov.
51 A. S. Arensky (1861–1906). A composition pupil of Rimsky-Korsakov. By 1885 he had written one symphony and his Piano Concerto; he had been teaching at the Moscow Conservatoire since 1882.
52 A. K. Glazunov (1865–1936). This composer was a phenomenally gifted composition student of Rimsky-Korsakov. His *Stenka Razin*, op. 13, was composed in 1885 and first performed at this concert.
53 Musorgsky died on 16 March 1881.

music, obliged as it is, always and in everything, to preserve beauty and nobility in its sounds, and not to overstep certain boundaries in its quest for truthful depiction – otherwise it ceases to be music. Even such a colossal talent as Berlioz, however, was unable to guard against this, and only towards the end of his life did he succeed, and that not fully, in smoothing over those deficiencies innate in his musical constitution. In the same way, Dargomïzhsky too was often wanting in feeling for musical beauty and the capacity to reproduce it. I shall say nothing about Serov, who took his irrepressible striving for realism in many of the scenes in *The Power of the Fiend* to the length of sickening nakedness.

The following shortcomings in Musorgsky's musical constitution revealed themselves:

1 His lack of ability in symphonic music not accompanied by words; his lack of skill in controlling well-balanced symphonic forms, and in developing and working out musical ideas (the same shortcoming is met with in Weber and Dargomïzhsky). Recognizing his bankruptcy in this respect, Musorgsky devoted himself [almost] exclusively to vocal music; he has few instrumental compositions (the dances in the opera *Khovanshchina* ('The Khovansky business'),[54] the nice Children's Scherzo for piano, the Intermezzo,[55] a nature picture from the southern Crimea,[56] an orchestral Scherzo,[57] a Turkish March,[58] etc.), and they are of no particular importance. Sometimes Musorgsky himself would make good-humoured fun of symphonists and symphonic music.

2 His part-writing, harmonization and modulations, which are frequently careless, ugly, unnatural, occasionally even illogical, and in his later works – his poor harmonization, in only two parts, or harmonization based on a constant fifth in the bass.

3 Finally, his tendency to exaggerate, to carry accuracy in word-setting so far as to reproduce the accurate intonation of the voice, to take the pictorial quality of his portrayal to the length of imitation of sound and to carry musical truth as far as realism. This tendency caused him at times to pile up tiny details and separate episodes which were treated with talent and love, but were inappropriate and disturbed the integrity of the impression made, and which had subsequently to be omitted or discarded in spite of their musical virtues. (Thus, for example, it was

54 Musorgsky worked on this opera between 1872 and 1880, leaving it unfinished.
55 *Author's note*: Both these little pieces are in the album *Frühlingsblüthen* published by Rubets.
56 *Na yuzhnom beregu Krïma* ('On the southern shore of the Crimea'), composed for piano in 1867.
57 *Ivanova noch' na Lïsoy gore* ('St John's Eve on Bare Mountain'), 1880.
58 *Vzyatiye Karsa* ('The taking of Kars'), 1880.

necessary to cut the episode with the chimes and the musically utterly charming episode with the parrot in Act II of *Boris Godunov.*[59]

But in Musorgsky's musical nature it was *not the shortcomings I have pointed out which were predominant but the lofty creative qualities which form the property of the most significant artists.* He was rich in musical ideas which were fresh, original and diverse. One was struck now by their boldness, now by their gaiety and humour, now by their profundity and strength, now by their poetic beauty. Where there were no exaggerations in Musorgsky's harmonizations they were distinguished by their power, novelty and gracefulness. He possessed unusual rhythmic flexibility, as a result of which his musical phrases sat so naturally on the phrases of text and made with them a single inseparable whole. He was an inimitable setter of words to music, scarcely inferior in that line even to Dargomïzhsky. Over the whole course of his career as a composer he was always the most impassioned champion of the most advanced ideas, he despised routine ways, strove for what was new and not yet fully understood, and in this respect it fell to Musorgsky – a fate which comes to very few artists – to introduce fresh elements into music, to extend its boundaries, to enrich it with unprecedented contributions.

Musorgsky's work as a composer revealed itself with particular vividness in his opera *Boris Godunov* and his romances. It is not part of my task to give a detailed analysis of them, but I shall try to indicate their most remarkable aspects, to define their artistic importance and – the main thing – to point out what was new that Musorgsky managed to introduce into art.

As an operatic composer Musorgsky belonged to the group of musicians familiar under the mocking names 'the handful' (*kuchka*) and 'the gang' (*shayka*) – names which have now completely lost their caustic tone. This group's outlook on vocal music and especially operatic music was not established all at once. It resulted from many years of reflection and many years of toil, and led to the following beliefs.

Operatic music must be good music. However strange it may seem, operatic composers have always despised this principle with astounding audacity. One cannot find in any other sort of music so many commonplaces and trivialities (*poshlosti*), repetitions, copies and slavish imitations as in operatic music. That which could not be tolerated in symphonic music obtains full right to existence in operatic music. An opera with three or four successful scenes but which with those exceptions is filled to overflowing with trivial and empty noises enjoys fame and success. The New Russian Operatic School esteems the sanctity of art too highly to allow this; it seeks to make operatic music also 'musical' throughout. Fear of the commonplace

59 This refers to the event narrated by Feodor during the scene in the tsar's quarters.

and the trivial (*poshloye*) and the tame is just about the most characteristic feature of this school.

Vocal music must correspond strictly with the meaning of the text. Once again, an elementary rule broken by opera composers at every turn who have often forced their heroes to suffer and die to sounds of cheerfulness and dance music. The new school strives for the blending together of the two great arts of poetry and music; it is its wish that these two arts should complement one another, that the impression made by the poetry of a gifted writer should be intensified by the impression made by the music of a gifted composer, and that the musician in alliance with the poet should make an irresistible impact on the listener. As a consequence of this aspiration there arise the necessity of correct word-setting, the necessity for the successful choice of a subject suitable for music, and so on.

Operatic forms are the freest and most varied musical forms. They are not subject to routine rules and depend only upon the situation on the stage and upon the text, that is, on the general planning of the libretto and its details. This elementary truth has also been flouted unceremoniously by operatic composers at every step. Let us recall the chorus-members who sing loudly and zealously 'Corriam, corriam' but do not move from the spot. Let us recall the catastrophes interrupted by long ensembles with the cast arranged in order of size along the footlights, which resume only after the successful ending of the ensemble. Let us recall the arias, duets and trios cut out from old stencils which comprise the conventional two sections and which are preceded by conventional recitatives. All this is entirely false; only that which takes place on the stage should govern the composer. Where required, operatic numbers may be strictly rounded forms, even with a symphonic development (songs, prayers, overtures, marches, dances, entr'actes, etc.); where required, the rounded form with repetitions disappears, and the music flows in an unbroken stream (in dramatic, animated scenes). In just the same way the broadest cantilenas may serve as themes, but themes may also be narrowed down to the shortest phrases of melodic recitative. Our New School shuns neither ensembles nor choruses so long as the ensembles are intelligently motivated and do not hold up the progress of the drama, and so long as the choruses represent not the chorus-members but the people with its life and passions.

Add to this *the characterization of people, place and time*, and you have the main ideas whose most ardent, passionate and foremost champion was Musorgsky.

In realizing these ideals the New Russian School was not always able to keep within the proper limits. But these one-sided and, one must say, quite rare enthusiasms were such a natural and unavoidable result of the novelty of the matter, of the School's isolated position and of the brutal and not always honest struggle which it was obliged to wage with the universal coalition of our press in those days. Of all the composers of this circle, the greatest exaggerations are to be met in Musorgsky. But on the other hand, where they are absent he is the School's most brilliant, powerful and original representative (excluding, of course, Dargomïzhsky's *The Stone Guest*).

Boris Godunov was written by Pushkin to be read rather than for the stage.[60] On the stage, whether as a play or an opera, it displays major shortcomings which arise from the lack of co-ordination of the scenes which, it is true, have something to do with a well-known fact [Cui refers to the intervention of censors], but which are not linked organically one to another. In spite of that, the choice of *Boris Godunov* as the subject for his opera does Musorgsky great honour. It is far more honourable and tempting to be inspired by a great work by a great poet than to work on some run-of-the-mill libretto, though it might be more suitable in terms of the stage. What is more, many scenes in *Boris Godunov* set the composer tasks which are new and most rewarding (the scenes with the people, the inn scene, the death of Boris). What earn serious reproofs for Musorgsky in the libretto of *Boris Godunov* are the replacement without any real need of some superlative verses by Pushkin with his own highly questionable ones, and the Jesuit Rangoni – a new, unnecessary and crudely melodramatic character.

As regards the music of *Boris Godunov*, the vitality, comic quality, humour and the astounding truth inherent in many scenes of this opera are particularly splendid.

This *vitality* manifests itself especially clearly in the scenes with the people. Of these, the first scene, in which the people, made forcibly to kneel on the orders of the police officer, implore Boris to take the throne, is outstanding. The basic theme of this chorus is extraordinarily successful and in pure folk character, and it conveys this compulsion excellently, particularly on its repetition a semitone higher (which means more powerfully), with the insistent accompaniment of a single importunate phrase in the basses. The phrases which the people exchange among themselves ('i vzdokhnut' ne dast, proklyatïy' ('he won't even let us draw breath, damn him'), 'oy, likhon'ko, sovsem okhripla' ('oh, what a life, I'm completely hoarse') are also beyond reproach, well-aimed, characteristic, musical. Each one of them is the fruit of fresh and powerful inspiration. These individual exclamations, these exchanges among the people, have not been used by anyone else on such a scale and so successfully as by Musorgsky; they impart special animation and the tint of truth to his popular scenes.

60 This view was commonly held in the nineteenth century.

The choruses in the last act are still better (the stormy and multi-coloured scene at Kromy: vagabonds, mocking the tied-up *boyar* Khrushchov, the simpleton, Misail and Varlaam, the Jesuits, the Pretender). The mocking song of praise is amazingly good; it combines in the happiest manner beauty with cold, spiteful ridicule. All the recitatives are pervaded by the passion of a long-oppressed people, by a callous, inexorable thirst for vengeance, by irony, to which our people are so prone, and at the same time by music. The entrance of the simpleton chased by small boys is effective. His song is painful, simple, deeply felt. Varlaam and Misail, the Jesuits with their Latin tongue and Catholic church hymns – these are typical personalities taken alive from the real world. The general chorus *Gayda* is full of powerful energy. When in the midst of the turmoil people want to raise the Jesuits to the 'handsome tree', their strikingly successful cries 'Sanctissima Virgo, juva' ring out, and terror can be heard in those cries as well as submission to their wretched fate. The departure of the Pretender is brilliant, his speech is energetic, and the simpleton's song from the deserted stage with which the opera comes to an end so daringly, originally and artistically makes a strong, aching and cheerless impression ('Gore, gore Rusi! Plach', russkiy lyud, golodnïy lyud' ('Woe, woe is Rus'! Weep, Russian people, hungry people')). This entire scene reveals both first-rate talent and a remarkable knowledge of the stage in Musorgsky. Unfortunately, at the revival of *Boris* they have begun for some reason to leave out this fundamental scene of the opera.

Among the choruses in *Boris Godunov* I must also indicate the chorus of wandering minstrels (*kaliki perekhozhiye*) in Act I – a characteristic, beautiful and musically rounded chorus.

The *comic quality* may be felt most clearly in the scene at the Inn on the Lithuanian border. Along with the final scene which I have just described, this one is the best in the opera. In the Inn scene we find skilful understanding of the stage, talented declamation, typical images, much wit and much music. The themes of all three songs are outstanding: the rollicking song of the hard-drinking peasant-woman about the grey drake, Varlaam's energetic song 'Kak vo gorode bïlo vo Kazani' ('As it was in the city of Kazan'') and the drunken, sleepy song 'Kak edet yon' ('As he travels'), characteristic in its monotony. In the way he elaborates the accompaniment to them Musorgsky staggers us by his inexhaustible fantasy, the diversity, the brilliant imagery. The phrases of recitative in this scene contain a great wealth of melody and power of inspiration. The musical phrases 'Vïp'yem charochku za shinkarochku' ('Let's drink a glass to the publican'), 'Ino delo p'yanstvo, ino delo chvanstvo' ('Drunkenness is one thing, but arrogance is something else'), 'Startsï smirennïye, inoki chestnïye' ('Meek elders, upright monks'), 'Khristiane skupï stali' ('Christians have become miserly') and so on merge with the text to such an extent that when you have heard them once it is not possible to separate text from music. Moreover, how deftly Grishka's conversation with the proprietress about the way to Lithuania is constructed over the song 'Kak edet yon' in this scene, how much genuine comedy there is in Varlaam's halting reading! One may say without exaggeration that in this scene Musorgsky's music strengthens the impression made by Pushkin's immortal text. There is not another opera which includes such a large-scale, varied, truthful, superb comic scene treated in such a new and distinctive way.

Humour with tears through laughter, grieving and rending the heart, reveals itself on many pages of *Boris Godunov*, but it makes an especially strong effect on the listener in the painful song achieved through suffering of the simpleton, of which I have spoken already.

Truth in expression and stage truth also form the essence of *Boris Godunov*, but this truth manifests itself with special vividness in the fourth act in the scene of Boris's death, beginning with Pimen's narrative, which is marked by touching simplicity and tranquillity. The advice of the dying Boris to his son contains a great deal of beauty and warmth. The church bell which rings out over the stage after that, the ecclesiastical chant of the clerks in their black vestments with lighted candles in their hands, Boris's fragmentary phrases in the midst of this singing, his final shout 'Ya tsar' eshcho' ('I'm the Tsar still'), the *boyars'* silence, the superlative colouring in the orchestra – all this is permeated by such truth, is devised and executed with such mastery, that it produces a strong, ineffaceable impression.

I must add that *Boris Godunov* includes some further characters which are delineated in masterly fashion and well sustained (Pimen, Varlaam), and that the charming, poetic beauty of music is not alien to Musorgsky, as the parrot episode and the ending of Marina's duet with the Pretender ('O tsarevich, umolyayu' ('Oh tsarevich, I entreat you')) prove.

None of the composers of the New Russian Operatic School and none of their works have been subjected to such attacks and mockery as Musorgsky and his *Boris Godunov* ('musornaya muzïka' ('music for the dustbin') etc.), and yet *Boris Godunov* has enjoyed great, unceasing success. Its final performance, the twentieth as far as I remember, was completely full. And if this opera was withdrawn from the repertory, then that was just one of the many actions of our Theatre Directorate for which it is impossible to think of any logical reason from whichever point of view you look at it – artistic or commercial. Now that the composer is dead, when there is no need to pay him a fee for each performance, now *Boris Godunov* will probably reappear on the stage, and its success will increase and be consolidated.

Musorgsky has twenty-eight published romances, not counting the large vocal piece 'Rayok' ('The peepshow').[61] Musorgsky displays the same merits and shortcomings in his romances as in his opera. Unnatural, ugly, tough harmonizations occur in his romances too; barely artistic realism occurs as well, and superficial portrayal sometimes prevails over inner substance. But at the same time they contain an abundance of power, energy, expression, variety, humour, profundity and originality. Many of the texts the composer wrote himself, and he wrote them with talent. He often touched on topical subjects, the most burning questions of the day. Two of his romances, 'Seminarist' ('The seminarist')[62] (he learns his Latin by rote but is simultaneously thinking of his beloved) and 'Zabïtïy' ('The forgotten one'[63]) (the theme of Vereshchagin's[64] painting), were actually on this account withdrawn from sale, despite having the censor's authorization to publish. Thus it is in Russia that sagacity often reveals itself only after the event.

Musorgsky's comic talent receives special development in his romances. It is worth noting particularly that in them we encounter all sorts, all degrees of the comic, beginning with the light, naughty joke and ending with profound humour.

'Kozyol' ('The goat')[65] may serve as a sample of musical mischief (a girl is frightened of a goat, but is not frightened of an ugly, old though rich husband). The music of this romance has no serious merits, and does not lay claim to them; but it is undoubtedly witty and funny, and the onomatopoeia here is entirely appropriate.

'Po gribï' ('Gathering mushrooms')[66] – words by Mey – is notable for its playful, spry, cheerful music, in places with a hint of mockery ('a tebe, nemilomu' ('but to you, unloved one')), and with marvellously expressed, original harmonizations.

In 'Gopak'[67] – words by Mey from Shevchenko – this cheerfulness is carried to the length of general, sweeping, irrepressible revelry – perhaps rather vulgar but very powerful.

Finally, in 'Savishna'[68] and 'Ozornik' ('The ragamuffin'),[69] Musorgsky takes humour to the extent of startling, stupendous tragedy. In 'Savishna'

---

61 'The peepshow', text by Musorgsky, 1870.
62 'The seminarist', text by Musorgsky, 1866, showed the irreverence of a prospective clergyman.
63 'The forgotten one', text by Golenishchev-Kutuzov, 1874.
64 V. V. Vereshchagin (1842–1904) was a painter who specialized in war scenes. This picture showed the body of a soldier left on the battlefield by comrades now celebrating their victory.
65 'The goat: a society fairytale', text by Musorgsky, 1867.
66 'Gathering mushrooms', 1867.
67 'Gopak', text by Shevchenko translated by Mey, 1866.
68 'Savishna', 1866.   69 'The ragamuffin', 1867.

(the texts of both romances are by Musorgsky himself) a simpleton makes a declaration of love. He is deeply in love and at the same time confesses what a pitiable creature he is. The Ragamuffin teases a helpless old woman heartlessly, heaps ridicule on her, repeating mockingly 'vostronosaya, raskrasavushka, pucheglazaya, oy ne bey!' ('sharp-nosed, fair one, goggle-eyed, oh don't beat me!'). Both romances are first-rate in the profundity of their concept, they both despite their superficially comic quality provoke grave thoughts which cause the heart to sink. This is particularly true of 'The ragamuffin' – an excruciating scherzo full of power and novelty, musical from start to finish and distinguished by remarkable technical perfection, subtle and correct word-setting, to which the rhythm and the beat submit so simply and naturally.

To the same category of deeply tragic romances but without any admixture of the comic belongs 'Sirotka' ('The orphan').[70] [Here Cui repeats what he wrote in Chapter 6, item (g).] It is relevant here to mention some more ordinary romances by Musorgsky, such as 'Kolïbel'naya Eryomushki' ('Eryomushka's cradle-song'),[71] 'Strekotun'ya beloboka' ('The magpie')[72], 'Tsar' Saul'[73], 'Spi, usni, krest'yanskiy sïn' ('Sleep, fall asleep, peasants' son'),[74] and others which include many fine études and utterly original music.

Besides the four types of comic quality alluded to above, one encounters in Musorgsky a further one, in 'Klassik' ('The classicist')[75] and 'Rayok' ('The peepshow'), which is wholly new – parody and satire. [Here Cui repeats what he wrote about *The classicist* in Chapter 6, item (g).]

'The peepshow' has the same character, but it is incomparably superior to 'The classicist' in its dimensions, substance and serious musical qualities. 'The peepshow' is directed against four musical figures of that time (1871): Zaremba,[76] Rostislav,[77] Famintsïn[78] and Serov.

'The peepshow' is musical satire – graphic and talented, fine in details and powerful as a whole. Musorgsky adroitly notes his opponents' weak

70 'The orphan', text by Musorgsky, 1868.
71 'Eryomushka's cradle-song', text by Nekrasov, 1868.
72 'The magpie', text by Pushkin, 1867.
73 'Tsar Saul', text by Byron translated by P. Kozlov, 1863.
74 First version known as 'Kolïbel'naya pesnya', text by Ostrovsky from *Voyevoda*, both versions 1865.
75 'The classicist', text by Musorgsky, 1867.
76 N. I. Zaremba (1821–79). He taught at the St Petersburg branch of the Russian Musical Society and later for its Conservatoire, serving as its director from 1867 to 1871. He was a champion of strict counterpoint.
77 For Rostislav, see Chapter 2, item (d).
78 A. S. Famintsïn (1841–96). Professor of music history and aesthetics at the St Petersburg Conservatoire (1865–72). He edited *Muzïkal'nïy sezon* ('The musical season') from 1869 to 1871, and from 1870 to 1880 was secretary to the Directorate of the Russian Musical Society. See also Chapter 6, note 47.

sides, hits them with a good aim and mercilessly, and covers them in ridicule but does it in such a way as to preserve complete propriety and decency of tone at all times. Apart from power and pungency, 'The peepshow' seethes with life and gaiety and when well performed can provoke gales of irrepressible laughter. 'The peepshow' has lost its polemical significance at the present time, but it will retain its musical significance for a long time to come – so strongly does fresh, bright talent reveal itself in this infinitely original work, unique of its kind.

It is imperative to single out *Detskaya* ('The nursery')[79] – an album comprising five numbers [nos. 6–7 were then unpublished] from the whole mass of romances by Musorgsky, in consequence of its especial originality of purpose and realization. In each of them Musorgsky depicts some episode from a child's life, putting the words into a child's mouth. This task is carried out by him with unusual talent and success. It is impossible to convey in words the whole life-like truth of these sounds, now naive and now capricious, sometimes frightened, sometimes surprised, but always of splendid freshness and originality. In addition, the images in the accompaniment, the harmonic beauty, the perfection of the word-setting and the rich musical substance supplement the charm and make *The Nursery* the sole *chef d'œuvre* of its kind. True – Schumann too also wrote children's scenes, but they were written for piano, without a text, without a clearly defined programme and are pervaded by the personality of Schumann: it is he, Schumann, who is telling us about children. It is the other way round in Musorgsky: the programme is a most definite one, the children's personalities are outlined astoundingly, the author retires to the background, and the children themselves have their say. Moreover, perhaps nowhere else do the originality of melodic contours, the harmonizations and the truthfulness of expression of Musorgsky manifest themselves so clearly as in *The Nursery*.

Musorgsky left also a large opera, *Khovanshchina* ('The Khovansky business'), nearly finished though not orchestrated, and a comic opera *Sorochinskaya yarmarka* ('The fair at Sorochintsy'),[80] far from completed. *Khovanshchina* is in the hands of Korsakov to be put in order and – if it can be produced – orchestrated. The most talented of our young composers, Lyadov, wishes to complete *The Fair at Sorochintsy*. Although I have heard excerpts from *Khovanshchina*, and although three numbers from *The Fair at Sorochintsy* have been published, that is not sufficient to allow one to say anything positive about these two operas. I do not think, all the same, that

---

79 'The nursery', text by Musorgsky, 1868–70.
80 Musorgsky worked on this opera between 1874 and 1880. The subject is taken from Gogol.

that would add anything to the powerful, original and diverse sides of Musorgsky's talent which I have indicated in the present study.

To round out this musical description of Musorgsky, I must further say that he orchestrated with talent, in a colourful though rather motley way; that he was a powerful pianist, an outstanding vocal performer and a first-rate accompanist. He was a pupil of Gerke,[81] but when he became a composer he ceased completely to concern himself with playing the piano, though his technique was nonetheless remarkable, and his performances had brilliance and impact. There is no doubt that had he devoted himself to the development of pianistic virtuosity he could have stood alongside the greatest concert pianists. As a singer, Musorgsky possessed a small but agreeable baritone voice as a young man. His voice grew stronger later but lost its freshness and became hard and hoarse. But even with this voice – truly, a composer's one – he produced the most powerful impression – so much expressiveness, profundity and also simplicity in his performance. It was necessary to hear *The Nursery* or 'The peepshow' as he performed them in order to appreciate all the original charm of these works. As an accompanist he had no equals, and if he yielded to anyone at all then it was to Anton Rubinstein alone. He excelled by his especial sensitivity, he guessed all the singer's intentions in advance, as if they were joined by an electrical current; by his extraordinary accompaniment he gave encouragement and inspiration to the performer.

To sum up all that has been said, it is obvious that despite his early death Musorgsky did a great deal for art. He belonged among that limited number of the most gifted artists whose destiny it was to introduce into art much that was new and their own, whose destiny it was to extend the frontiers of art. In no one else's choruses is the people depicted more accurately and with such life-like truth as in Musorgsky's; no one else has such a broad comic and purely folk scene as the one in the Inn, no one else takes humour as far as such profound tragedy ('Savishna', 'The ragamuffin', the simpleton in *Boris Godunov*); Musorgsky created an infinitely talented and musical parody ('The peepshow'); it was he who created charming little genre pictures of unparalleled originality from the world of childhood. Musorgsky's services are great; of our composers who have died he follows Glinka and Dargomïzhsky and occupies an honoured place in the history of Russian music. It is true that Musorgsky's works contain major defects and shortcomings, but without these shortcomings Musorgsky would have been a genius.

---

81 A. A. Gerke (1812–70), Russian pianist whose eminent pupils included Musorgsky.

Index